# MBA MARKETING

# MBA MARKETING

Malcolm McDonald
*Emeritus Professor, Cranfield School of Management, UK*

Ailsa Kolsaker
*Marketing Consultant and Associate Faculty member of Portsmouth Business School, University of Portsmouth*

palgrave
macmillan

First published 2014 by
PALGRAVE MACMILLAN

Palgrave Macmillan in the UK is an imprint of Macmillan Publishers Limited, registered in England, company number 785998, of Houndmills, Basingstoke, Hampshire RG21 6XS.

Palgrave Macmillan in the US is a division of St Martin's Press LLC, 175 Fifth Avenue, New York, NY 10010.

Palgrave Macmillan is the global academic imprint of the above companies and has companies and representatives throughout the world.

Palgrave® and Macmillan® are registered trademarks in the United States, the United Kingdom, Europe and other countries.

ISBN 978–1–137–30029–4

This book is printed on paper suitable for recycling and made from fully managed and sustained forest sources. Logging, pulping and manufacturing processes are expected to conform to the environmental regulations of the country of origin.

A catalogue record for this book is available from the British Library.

A catalog record for this book is available from the Library of Congress.

Printed in China

*With thanks to all my colleagues for their wisdom.*
– Malcolm


*With thanks to my family for their unfailing support.*
– Ailsa

# CONTENTS

PART IV Monitoring Value

PART V Enhancing Value

# TABLES AND FIGURES

## Tables

## Figures

# ACKNOWLEDGEMENTS

The authors and publishers would like to thank the following for permission to reproduce copyright material:

PIMS Online for Figure 5.7

Malcolm McDonald and Ian Dunbar for Figure 5.11

Taylor & Francis for Figure 10.6, reprinted from L. De Chernatony and M. McDonald (2003) *Creating Powerful Brands 3e*, Butterworth-Heinemann, p. 411; and for Figure 15.3, reprinted from Christopher *et al.* (2002) *Relationship Marketing – Creating Stakeholder Value*, Butterworth-Heinemann, p. 48

John Wiley & Sons Ltd for Figure 10.7, reprinted from P. Doyle (2008), *Value-based Marketing – Marketing Strategies for Corporate Growth and Shareholder Value 2e*

*Marketing Week* for Case study 12.1

Pearson Education Ltd for Figure 12.1, reprinted from C. Fill (2009), *Marketing Communications 5e*, ©Prentice Hall Europe, 1994, 1999; ©Pearson Education Ltd, 2006, 2009

Elsevier for Figures 12.3, 12.5, 12.6, 17.1, 17.6, 17.7 and 24.1, reprinted from M. McDonald and H. Wilson (2002), *New Marketing*, and for Figures 13.3, 13.4, 13.5, 13.6 and 13.7, reprinted from M. McDonald, T. Millman, and B. Rogers (1996), *Key Account Management – Learning from Supplier and Customer Perspectives*, Cranfield University, UK

Anthony Millman and Kevin Wilson for Figure 13.1, reprinted from A. Millman and K. Wilson (1994), 'From key account selling to key account management', *Proceedings of the Tenth Annual Conference on Industrial Marketing and Purchasing*, University of Groningen, The Netherlands

Cranfield KAM Best Practice Club for Figure 13.2

Brand Finance plc for Figure 22.2.

# INTRODUCTION

IN THIS CHAPTER WE STUDY:

- define marketing
- develop a model of the marketing process
- expand on each of the component parts of the model
- emphasize the inherently cross-functional nature of the marketing process

This book is for MBA students with little or no prior knowledge of marketing. Unlike the plethora of textbooks on the market that follow the well-trodden path of one chapter/one topic, this book aims to provide a *value creation* approach to the essential principles of marketing. It is structured around a model of marketing that places centrally the creation of value for a range of stakeholders (customers, suppliers, distributors, collaborators, agents and society, to name but a few). Reading this textbook will not transform you into a skilled marketer overnight. It will, however, enable you to understand the core principles of marketing and, crucially, *know what questions to ask* the marketing team in your organization. Traditionally, marketing was thought to be only relevant to the private sector, however its relevance to the public and third sectors is being recognized increasingly. This book is appropriate for marketing in all types of organizations and contexts.

We define marketing as 'the creation of value by aligning organizational assets with consumer demands such that the latter is satisfied'. Value creation is a continuous activity, thus our conception of marketing is a *process* involving the analysis of the various options available and choosing those which promise optimal outcomes. Choices are constrained and informed by external conditions and the nature and strength of an organization's own asset value. By 'asset value' we mean both *tangible* assets, such as plant equipment, stock and financial holdings; and *intangible* assets, such as the skills and ingenuity of employees, brand equity, performance of managerial and operational systems; in other words, asset value extends beyond the balance sheet value to encompass all those qualities and abilities to which value may be attributed. We see asset value in action, for example, during corporate acquisitions, when companies are valued at sums that far exceed their tangible asset value. Because asset value is core to marketing, a thorough understanding is essential to chart organizational development and marketing success.

To start with, organizations must understand *who* they need to satisfy, *what* value is required and *how* best to deliver this value on a sustainable basis in line with overall corporate objectives. Marketing is thus a process for:

- Defining markets, and more specifically, target markets/segments;
- Identifying the value consumers seek by quantifying the needs of specific homogeneous groups or market segments;
- Creating value propositions to meet consumer needs, involving setting marketing objectives and strategies;
- Communicating these value propositions to everyone in the organization responsible for delivering them and securing their commitment and co-operation;

- Delivering these value propositions through products/services, supported by appropriate customer communications and customer service;
- Monitoring the value actually delivered against that required, utilizing information, knowledge and performance measures;
- Enhancing value by adjusting corporate ethos, ethics, culture and structure, if necessary, as a result of experiential learning and marketing research.

In an effort to assist organizations to gain a fuller understanding of the meaning and 'mechanics' of marketing, we have developed a map of the marketing process (Figure 0.1) which is intended to simplify some of the complexities of marketing and to provide a 'point of entry' to understand marketing. In simplifying complexities, it is not our intention to diminish the significance or scale of the many activities, principles and beliefs that constitute the marketing process.

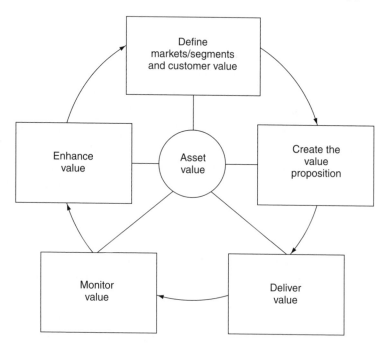

Figure 0.1 The marketing map

It should be noted that:

*The map is inherently cross-functional:* 'Deliver value', for example, involves every aspect of the organization. This is most important and is illustrated in Figure 0.2.

*The map represents best practice, not common practice:* Well-embedded processes in even the most sophisticated companies do not address explicitly many aspects of the map. Hence, it is crucial to identify best practice.

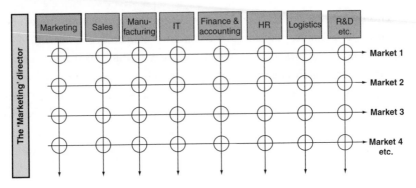

Figure 0.2 Cross-functional investment in delivering customer value

*The map is evolving:* The web and electronic customer relationship management (eCRM) require a radically different sales process; hence, exploiting new media requires a substantial shift in thinking which goes far beyond information systems and processes.

From the marketing map, it is clear that (i) the marketing process is cyclical, (ii) organizations need to understand the value stakeholders seek, (iii) continuous monitoring is required of value delivered and (iv) value is enhanced through continual capacity building. The cycle may be predominantly annual, but, equally, changes throughout the year may involve rapid iterations around the cycle to respond to particular opportunities or problems. The cycle contains five value-oriented sub-processes: define, create, deliver, monitor and enhance, all of which are integral elements of successful marketing.

The first two sub-processes, 'define markets/segments and customer value' and 'create the value proposition', are concerned with strategic marketing planning; that is, developing marketing strategies. The next two, 'deliver value' and 'monitor value', relate to actual delivery and outcome measurement. The fifth, 'enhance value', refers to learning derived from experience and the assimilation of this learning into the organization's operations to improve its marketing performance (and, by implication, asset value).

It is well known that not all of these marketing activities are under the control of the marketing department, whose role varies enormously. Typically, it would be in charge of defining markets/segments and customer value, and creating the value proposition. Responsibility for delivering value is shared by the whole organization, however, requiring cross-functional expertise and collaboration, for example, in the areas of product development, manufacturing, purchasing, sales promotion, distribution, sales and customer service. Similarly, the final sub-processes, monitoring and enhancing value, occur throughout the organization and involve every employee, function and unit.

The five arrows connecting the sub-processes comprise both inputs and outputs. For example, the output of 'defining markets/segments and customer value' is the target of prospective customers the organization wishes to reach and the associated value expectation. This then becomes the input to shape and drive the creation of the value proposition. In turn, the output of that sub-process is the marketing plan, which becomes the input to 'deliver value', and so on. The dual role played by these connectors highlights the seamless integration of the sub-processes that comprise the marketing process.

Let us consider briefly each sub-process in detail, focusing upon how they all work together to create and deliver customer value – and consequently, augment the organization's asset value.

# DEFINE MARKETS/SEGMENTS AND CUSTOMER VALUE

This is the starting point, whether the objective is to develop or review the marketing process. It involves defining the markets in which the organization operates, or wishes to operate, and mapping how these markets may be divided into segments of customers with similar needs. Choice of markets is influenced by the organization's corporate objectives and asset value. To identify markets and segments, the organization needs information about market characteristics, such as the market's size and growth, current profitability and estimated future potential.

Once each market or segment has been defined, it is necessary to understand what value the customers within the segment want or need; that is, the benefits sought through product ownership. This involves identifying customers' current requirements and making predictions about future needs. Knowledge about customers' purchase history, lifestyle and life stage can be helpful in developing patterns of likely buyer behaviour, which can then be used to pursue proactive as well reactive marketing strategies. It may emerge that subsets of the customers within a market have very different requirements, in which case the market may need to be segmented further.

The organization must also establish how well it and its competitors currently deliver the value the customers seek in order to understand competitor value positioning. From these market and competitive analyses, the relative attractiveness of the different markets or segments can be evaluated.

# CREATE THE VALUE PROPOSITION

This concerns selecting and prioritizing the range of markets and market segments in which the organization is to operate, and accordingly creating appropriate value propositions. These decisions will take into account both market/segment attractiveness and the organization's actual and potential ability to meet the needs of customers within those market/segments. They will also be shaped by corporate objectives. The setting of marketing objectives and strategies, and the production of marketing plans to articulate them, therefore dominate this sub-process.

Organizations normally start by defining the value they wish to receive from the market or segment in terms of market share, market volume, market value or profit contribution by segment. They must also define the value to be delivered to the customer in return, or the product/service benefits the customer cares about. These price/value propositions must then be set in a realistic context; that is, they must be accompanied by a definition of how the customer value is to be communicated and delivered.

Once these issues have been resolved, an estimate of the expected results of the marketing strategies can be made in terms of the costs to the organization and the impact of the price/value proposition on sales. This final step closes the loop from the earlier step of setting marketing objectives, as it may be that iteration is required if the strategies that have been defined are now considered insufficient to meet the financial objectives.

The output from the 'create the value proposition' sub-process is typically a strategic marketing plan, or plans, covering a period of at least three years. In some cases, specific plans are produced for each of the four 'P's, such as a pricing plan, a distribution plan, a customer service plan or a promotions plan. However, even when no marketing plans are produced, the organization takes decisions implicitly about what constitutes the offer to the customer and how this offer is to be communicated and delivered. The content of the marketing plans has to be communicated to, and agreed with, all departments or functions responsible for delivering the customer value articulated in the plans.

# DELIVER VALUE

This sub-process puts the plans into action. It focuses on the tactical, value-delivering activities of inbound logistics, operations, outbound logistics and service. Encapsulating these activities is the overall discipline of relationship management. The need to manage customer relationships effectively is driven by the fact that it is customers, not products, that generate profits, and there is a direct link between customer retention and profitability.

Value delivery thus concerns how the offer is communicated to the customer, and how a two-way dialogue is facilitated with the customer. Inherent within this are a number of decisions, including which media and channels to use, and whether or not (and how) they should be integrated; what level of service should be provided, given the need for individualization as well as cost-effectiveness; what is the requisite size and nature of the sales force; and how can business be developed through customer-retention programmes.

# MONITOR VALUE

The delivery of value through the implementation of the marketing plans results in performance, which then needs to be monitored closely for quality gaps and improvement opportunities. The organization must seek to establish whether the value identified as *required* by customers was indeed *delivered*, and whether the company *received* the expected return on investment. Value delivered can be monitored against the value proposition defined during 'create the value proposition'. As all aspects of value should be measured in terms of the customer's perspective, so customer feedback is important in order to understand the value *perceived* by customers as well as overall effectiveness of the marketing strategies by which the value was delivered.

By monitoring performance against internal indicators and industry standards, the organization will be able to ascertain the scope and level of its professionalism. To be 'future robust' in an increasingly challenging marketing environment requires substantial competence, skills, courage and conviction. Ensuring that such qualities and aptitudes exist in an organization is crucial for maintaining commercial viability as well as growing asset value.

# ENHANCE VALUE

This builds on current levels of professionalism in order to enhance value and thus raise the organization's market potential. It brings the marketing process full circle. While most organizations profess to learn from experience, surprisingly few demonstrate serious commitment to examine their performance and processes, and take the action required to redress weaknesses and reinforce strengths. Furthermore, the source of learning need not be confined to the organization itself. Other organizations in similar or disparate industries can also provide valuable lessons and guidance.

The key areas open to improvement include the structure and culture of the organization, and the ethos and ethics by which it operates. The way in which departments and functions are constructed, and the extent to which they collaborate and integrate, can have a marked impact on the organization's ability to enhance value. For example, the sharing of information, ideas and expertise across functions and processes is what enables augmented value to be realized. Careful management is needed to maximize the use of limited resources in achieving customer-based objectives. Strong leadership is required to overcome natural resistance to change and the barriers presented by outdated attitudes and practices. The maxim 'average products deserve average success' might also be applied to organizations.

# SUMMARY

Marketing is a dynamic *process* that requires constant input and monitoring. There are five component sub-processes (define/create/deliver/monitor/enhance), each of which makes a specific contribution to the marketing process, and this is explained clearly by breaking the sub-process down into manageable parts. The sub-processes interact and interrelate, giving the map a dynamic, iterative dimension. Attention must therefore be paid to *all* the sub-processes, for ultimate value emanates from their coalescence.

This map will be repeated at the beginning of each section in order to remind the reader how far they have progressed in the process of learning about marketing.

Before getting into the core of the book, however, there are a number of important issues concerning the different contexts in which marketing is practised, and each of these will be explained briefly in Chapter 1. Thereafter, the book deals mainly with core principles, tools and techniques of marketing from a value proposition perspective. The perspective is generalist, rather than specialist; it must be remembered that this is a book specially written for MBA students, general managers and other functional specialists who wish to gain understanding of the role of marketing in organizations.

# PART I
# DEFINING THE MARKET, TARGET AUDIENCES AND CUSTOMER VALUE

# CHAPTER 1
# TYPES OF MARKETING

IN THIS CHAPTER WE STUDY:

- consumer marketing
- services marketing
- industrial marketing
- capital goods marketing
- trade marketing

# INTRODUCTION

Marketing takes place in a variety of contexts. While the casual observer might think automatically of consumer marketing, there are numerous others. In this chapter, we introduce the most common forms of marketing; there are other, more specialist variants which are beyond the scope of this book.

# CONSUMER MARKETING

Consumer products are those which are sold to individuals and then consumed by them or someone to whom they are passed. Consumer marketing is probably the most accessible to those new to the study of marketing. Each of us is a consumer, so all of us have first-hand experience of consumer marketing. As consumers, we know that we want good quality products, at a reasonable price, that perform as we anticipate. In other words, we want products that have inherent value that will perform the task for which they were purchased, thereby satisfying our needs. The success or failure of any consumer product depends not only upon the organization that ultimately sells them, but also upon all the other companies involved in their production and distribution. Consumer products thus occupy a crucial position at the head of value chains that lead right back through retailers, distributors and manufacturers to the producers of the basic raw materials. Their success relies upon the whole value chain performing well, thus those managing consumer product marketing also determine the survival of that value chain. This sense of mutual dependency applies equally to consumer services.

The key marketing issue for anyone providing consumer goods or services is the large number of potential customers. Particularly now that the Internet enables global reach, the key task facing companies in consumer markets is how to make contact with customers when there are so many people who might be persuaded to buy their products in preference to a competitor's. This difficulty is compounded when those potential consumers are geographically dispersed or where they represent a small proportion of each community within a market. Over the years, this issue has been tackled in numerous ways and is an area of significant innovation, particularly in relation to retailing and branding. We shall explore this marketing fundamental in some depth throughout Parts I–III of this book.

This issue of who to target and how to reach them applies equally to companies supplying consumer durables such as refrigerators and fast-moving consumer goods (FMCGs) such as toiletries or food. The main differences between these two categories are frequency of purchase, absolute cost and degree of involvement in the purchase. For FMCGs, acceptance or rejection occurs in a relatively short space of time, which has implications for the way these products are marketed. Consumer durables, on the other hand, tend to be infrequent purchases but of some significance to a household, therefore the purchase tends to be a much more protracted and considered process, requiring a supplier to adapt their marketing accordingly. Whatever the category, consumer products have to be presented to the market; traditionally, this has happened in physical retail locations, but brands, manufacturers, retailers and – of course – consumers are turning to the Internet in droves.

## RETAIL OUTLETS

Consumer products are offered to the market by retailers. For manufacturers wishing to get their goods to market, it is crucial to select appropriate retailers in suitable locations (whether in the physical or virtual worlds) and to maintain good relations with them. Indeed, for some grocery products, simply being on the right shelf in the right part of the right chain of supermarkets is almost enough to guarantee success for a product line. The power of such retailers has given rise to a particular type of marketing referred to as trade marketing, as well as retailers' 'own label' product lines.

In recent years, the Internet has expanded retailing by enabling organizations to reach a much more geographically dispersed group of customers. Amazon needs no introduction as a leading example of a highly diversified online retailer with global reach. In terms of multi-channel retailing, Tesco is an example of a retailer exploiting innovative technologies alongside traditional channels to meet customer needs. Expanding into South Korea, whose consumers have a reputation for being hard-working and time-poor, Tesco harnessed mobile technologies to enable commuters to buy products from virtual Home Plus aisles at subway stations and bus stops. Using smartphones, shoppers can scan items (using QR – Quick Response – codes) and arrange home delivery. Tesco's Homeplus smartphone app is now the most popular shopping app in South Korea; Home Plus has grown rapidly to become the dominant online, and second most popular offline, grocery retailer. In this way, the Internet facilitates consumer marketing by making the right product available in the right (convenient and accessible) place at the right time.

## BRANDS

Consumer markets are crowded and competitive, so a strong brand is increasingly essential for grabbing attention and maintaining relationships with consumers without the need for personal contact. Strong brands are those that have a personality with which consumers can identify or that evoke a feeling that matches the buyer's personal values, aspirations and lifestyle. Some leading brands are so powerful that consumers not only associate strongly with the branded product (or service), but internalize the brand in such a way that they 'live and breathe it', rejecting all other options. Such people are easily recognizable. For example, someone possessing an iMac, Macbook Air, iPad, iPod and iPhone, or dressed head to toe in Nike sports apparel is doing more than simply using the branded products; they are demonstrating – very publicly – a close affiliation of personal and brand values.

Strong brands, therefore, wield significant power (see Chapter 10), and manufacturers and service suppliers who own them are able to exert considerable influence on retailers in terms of price, shelf location, competitor positioning, merchandizing, promotions policy, acceptance of new products and many other areas. Distinct retail brands are similarly able to influence lesser branded suppliers and to gain favourable locations and terms for their outlets. For these reasons, brand strategy is often at the heart of the marketing strategy of any company supplying consumer products.

# SERVICES MARKETING

Services can be conceputalized along a continuum, from 'pure play' at one extreme to an addition to tangible products which augment the core product. These characteristics, together with the deregulation of many professional and government services, have forced organizations to reconsider the traditional accepted philosophy of a product/service dichotomy. Is services marketing fundamentally different from product marketing, an extension of product marketing, or is the entire product marketing focus passé?

Services have become an increasingly significant sector of most advanced economies, so much so that during the last decade or so there has been a lot of academic interest in the application of a 'service-dominant logic' to the entire marketing discipline. Based upon the fundamental concepts of the centricity of the consumer, value creation and co-creation (the latter involving all parties in the production – consumption process), physical products are conceptualized as value-creating entities in the process of value co-creation rather than an end in themselves. It is certainly the case that the nature of many service-based products dictates greater emphasis upon certain elements of the marketing process. It is very important that organizations understand these elements and how they potentially affect the marketing tasks faced.

Defining a service for marketing purposes is not always straightforward as it will inevitably involve some degree of physicality or tangibility. Indeed, it is debatable whether intangibility can truly be demarcated and disassociated from tangible entities. The diversity of organizations involved in services and the tendency to highlight the service elements of an 'offer' for competitive purposes mean that they are sometimes hard to classify. One important element that merits consideration is the degree of tangibility involved in any service offering. Table 1.1 identifies four categories, varying from a 'pure' tangible product to a 'pure' service.

| A pure tangible product | A tangible offer, such as sugar, coal or tea. No services are bought with the product |
| --- | --- |
| A tangible product with accompanying services such as commissioning, training and maintenance | The offer has built-in services to enhance its customer appeal, e.g. computers, machine tools |
| An intangible product with accompanying minor goods | The offer is basically a service, but has a physical element, e.g. property surveyors, whose expert inspection is encapsulated in a report. Similarly, airlines offer in-flight meals or entertainment |
| A pure intangible product, where one buys expertise | The offer is a stand-alone service such as market research, psychoanalysis or ski-instruction |

Table 1.1 Variations in product tangibility

From this perspective, a continuum of tangible–intangible products emerges as illustrated in Figure 1.1. Point 'a' on the left-hand side of this figure illustrates an offer where there is no service element and the product is highly tangible. At the other end of the spectrum, point 'd' illustrates a product which is entirely a service and is therefore highly intangible. Points 'b' and 'c' show varying

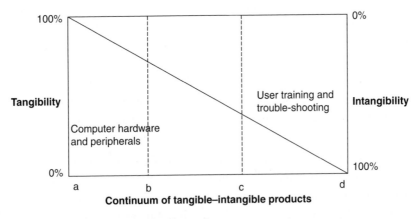

Figure 1.1 Continuum of tangible–intangible products

mixes. For example, point 'b' illustrates the mix of tangibility for a computer company.

Computer hardware and peripherals are highly tangible and can be regarded as commodities, whereas the service elements of user-training and troubleshooting are largely intangible.

The intangibility of a service leads to a number of other differences of significance for marketing, as follows:

- Services can easily be copied by competitors, since they cannot be patented and specified with drawings.

- Quality can be difficult to guarantee since services are not previously produced under controlled conditions. Instead, they are produced and delivered at the time of consumption.

- A service cannot be stored on a shelf or taken down and used at a later time. Services are therefore highly perishable.

- People are an intrinsic part of most services and are difficult to separate from the product.

- The true value of a service can only be assessed on consumption. Thus, the purchase of a service involves a high component of trust.

- Services are often very personal in their nature and can involve the customer in their delivery and consumption, as in the case of a golf lesson or making a purchase at IKEA.

The relationship between customer and supplier is therefore crucial to the success of services marketing. The close link between production and consumption, and the personal nature of many service products, emphasize this aspect. Where no personal relationship exists, the contrast between membership-type organizations and automated services is stark, leading any businesses to seek a means of marketing more concrete affiliations as a substitute. In looking at ways and means of marketing the specific features of service products, management of the relationship with the customer is, thus, always important. Additionally, since the nature of a service is difficult to convey to a customer prior to purchase or consumption, ongoing relationships become of paramount importance. Unlike a car, a service cannot be test-driven; it is hard for a potential customer to assess a bank before opening an account; and a stay in a hotel can only be judged during or after the event.

Product quality and integrity are also crucial to marketing services. As such, it is crucial, as far as possible, to provide tangible evidence of product quality. This highlights the need for careful attention to the 'product promise', such as the initial points of contact, descriptive literature and the peripherals that provide clues to product integrity. It is no coincidence that professional service businesses often have plush reception areas, holiday brochures are a master-piece of presentation and spa-based health clubs make a big show of testing the water. The problems associated with service evaluation can also be addressed by focusing on reputation, or by enhancing the value of a service through the provision of extra benefits such as free offers. Here, word of mouth or third-party endorsements become particularly influential, particularly in the online sphere. These can come from existing customers, referral markets and media institutions, all of whom can provide powerful testimony to the quality or value of an organization's offering.

Since many services rely heavily on a personal interaction between the service provider and customer, or depend on individuals exercising judge-ment when creating the service, considerable heterogeneity between purchases becomes possible, such that customer experiences can vary enormously. Thus, the performance of a waiter or shop assistant will have a great impact on cus-tomer experiences of the core benefits sought. Since so much of service quality delivery lies in the hands of those delivering the service, employees become a vital concern for effective services marketing. Obviously, recruitment policies are important as well as service modelling which identifies people-related 'fail points' in service delivery.

The process of service delivery requires careful specification, including identification of the skills necessary to reduce heterogeneity as a consequence of 'people problems'. It should also be noted that both the intangibility and heterogeneity of services mean that attention to detail becomes central to mar-keting effectiveness. It is often relatively minor factors that influence consumer perceptions and experiences of service quality. Details, however, are also that part of the process of delivering the service most influenced by individual employees, thereby giving further weight to the focus on process design and human resource management.

The fact that a service will require the customer's involvement in its creation and delivery enhances the need for efficient management of this customer–provider interaction. Unlike manufacturers, service providers cannot check quality prior to delivery. One solution has been to utilize technology to enhance consistency and improve accessibility, such as the introduction of e-tickets across a range of industries. Another approach entails staff empowerment, in which front-line staff are given decision-making authority. A further method involves creating holistic customer management (CRM) systems to ensure satisfactory service delivery.

For marketing managers, the perishability of a service places extra emphasis on understanding demand patterns and why such fluctuations exist. However, matching demand at all times is rarely possible or, indeed, cost-effective. In the end, the only alternatives are to try to change patterns of demand or to generate increased capacity at peak times. The techniques for managing demand revolve around incentives, such as offering better value and other sales promotion activities to encourage off-peak use, or using pricing mechanisms, such as premiums or discounts. Capacity can be enhanced by using part-time staff, subcontractors and shared facilities, or by carrying overheads in the form of staff, or assets, which are redundant at certain times. Managers, therefore, have to ensure careful coordination to balance the overall offer with the market's preferred pattern of utilization.

Services are sold into a whole range of markets, including industrial, consumer, government and not-for-profit. While each market creates its own unique marketing requirements, for services it is the distinct characteristics of the product which provide the major marketing challenges. In particular, it would seem to demand an expanded marketing mix beyond the four Ps of product, price, place and promotion, to include people, processes and customer service. These three additional elements significantly affect the success or otherwise of a service-based offering and will benefit from discrete programmes and action plans being developed for them. The features of service products also underline the importance of third-party markets such as recruitment, referral, influencer and internal markets, plus the overall concept of relationship marketing. Indeed, it has been argued that the recent interest in relationship marketing first grew from developments initiated within service businesses.

# MICRO MARKETING

Large numbers of potential consumers with similar needs lead many consumer marketing organizations to a mass marketing approach which tries to satisfy the majority of the market with an undiscriminating product, brand or approach as classically practised by Coca-Cola or McDonald's. Modern consumer marketers are, however, increasingly finding that markets are fragmenting as consumers become more sophisticated, individualistic and demanding. With the potential for varying the offer increasing as information technology becomes more sophisticated, micro marketing is increasing in significance. Micro marketing embraces mass customization, in which consumers configure their product or service from a series of modular offerings around a generic core. The relaunched Mini, designed and produced by BMW, is a good example of this. The base product is devoid of extras, which will add 50 per cent to the retail price once added, but allows purchasers to customize their car. The challenge for players in consumer markets is to find ways of keeping base costs low, while exploiting new, direct channels and satisfying consumer demand for customized products and services in innovative, customer-friendly ways.

# VALUE CHAIN MANAGEMENT

The competitive world of consumer marketing has led many suppliers and retailers to pay closer attention to the value chain at whose head they sit. These organizations have recognized that advantage can be gained by exerting influence across all those who affect their products and their ability to supply. These advantages include lower cost, higher quality, better availability, product innovation, speed to market and a host of other important competitive factors.

In industries such as automotive manufacture, management of aspects of the value chain is sometimes delegated to a small group of key suppliers who are expected to influence and coordinate other suppliers in the chain. In others, such as the computer supply industry, businesses like Dell are working directly with suppliers right down to the component level and beyond in seeking efficiency and innovation for competitive advantage.

# MARKETING INDUSTRIAL PRODUCTS

Whatever an organization is offering, whether commercial products, public services or charity, the fundamental principles of marketing always apply. Despite this, most organizations in industrial markets instinctively know that their markets are different and that marketing industrial products requires a different set of approaches to consumer marketing. To operate effectively in industrial markets, it is important to understand what these differences are since they highlight the areas upon which the organization must focus.

That stated, there is no simple or clear divide between industrial and consumer products and markets. On the product side, some products are sold in the same form to both industrial and consumer markets. Examples of this include bank accounts, motor cars, personal computers and parts for washing machines. In terms of markets, some consumer-goods manufacturers will only sell directly to other businesses, that is, trade sales. As a consequence, industrial marketing cannot be defined simply by the products involved or by the fact that it involves business-to-business selling.

The best way to conceptualize industrial marketing is to look at it as a continuum with obvious slow-moving industrial products at one end and fast-moving consumer products at the other. In the middle of the continuum are faster-moving industrial products and slower-moving consumer products, as illustrated in Figure 1.2.

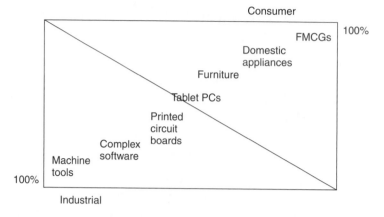

Figure 1.2 Continuum of industrial marketing

The existence of this continuum also illustrates the possibility of transferring marketing approaches between these different markets. While the context of their usage and the way in which they are applied may vary, no idea should be ignored because it is thought to be more appropriate to the realm of one market or product than another. Brands, for instance, are usually thought of as most appropriate for consumer product marketing. However, efforts by Intel and the success of Caterpillar provide contrary examples. Earth moving equipment is an unlikely candidate for branding, yet Caterpillar has established the stylish yellow-tabbed CAT logo as the symbol of the leading global manufacturer of off-road trucks, tractors and other multi-terrain vehicles. The power of the brand is demonstrated by its easy transfer to a range of high-priced heavy duty designer boots and associated apparel sold to the general public. The latter, though the smaller of the two businesses by far, trades off its sibling's well-established brand values of rugged, durable and dependable performance.

# ISSUES IN INDUSTRIAL MARKETING

The first issue concerns the way in which an industrial purchaser views a product it wishes to buy. Industrial products are often thought of as being more complex than the equivalent consumer products, which is obviously not always the case. What is different is the attention paid to the details of a product. Even a commodity product, such as sheet steel, cement or a simple component, will be considered in much greater detail by an industrial purchaser. This is because it will be used in more complex ways or that small variations will have potentially harmful consequences. As an example, the wrong grade of steel will not machine properly and may put cost up and quality down. Similarly, a personal computer with a slightly wrong specification may make previous software purchases obsolete or networking with existing machines impossible.

The implications of such detailed product evaluations are that industrial purchasers have greater information needs than consumer purchasers, both before and after a purchase is made. In turn, this implies larger numbers of people being involved in the purchase decision. Consequently, organizations marketing industrial products have to cope with a larger and more diverse decision-making unit and a greater degree of formalization in the procedures applied to a purchase. It also implies that a greater degree of personal contact between the supplier and buyer will be necessary, since this is the best way of providing complete information. Personal contact is necessary to isolate *who needs to know what* and *at what point in the decision-making process*, in order to improve the chances of a sale or continued sales.

Apart from costly and infrequently purchased capital goods, the volumes bought by an industrial purchaser are also likely to be higher than by individuals or families in a consumer market. This makes the loss of a supply agreement to both supplier and purchaser more significant. If a supplier fails to deliver the right quantity, the purchaser will find it difficult to continue their business. On the other hand, if a purchaser stops buying, this will have a significant impact on the supplier's income. In industrial markets, therefore, there is often a high degree of interdependence. Both supplier and purchaser will rely on each other for their continued existence. The loss of one purchaser in a consumer market is not nearly so significant. This situation is further complicated by the fact that it is difficult in the industrial context to find mass markets. Apart from there being smaller numbers of customers, one buying organization is likely to differ significantly from the next in their buying requirements. This means that segmentation in industrial markets has to be conducted on a different basis.

A further implication is that the degree of product variability required can also be greater. In some cases, a single customer can form an entire segment and can consequently demand a high degree of customization. In others, the consumer variables for segmentation such as demography, life-stage and lifestyle need to be replaced by alternatives such as size, applications and competitive positioning. Such heterogeneity is an important factor for the organization marketing industrial products.

In trying to understand, and give some structure to, the markets which industrial suppliers face, it must be recognized that their customers also have customers of their own, who may in turn have customers! Unless the customer is a country's Defence Ministry or some similar body, all industrial products will eventually translate into a consumer purchase. This means that the structure of the market in which an industrial organization operates can be complex, with a whole series of intermediaries or 'value adders' between them and the final consumer. Industrial suppliers are thus faced with a situation of derived demand for their goods and services. The way they perceive their market and the way in which opportunities are identified and defined can therefore become a very complicated process.

Paradoxically, these factors combine to make market research in industrial markets sometimes more problematic, and sometimes easier, than consumer market research. Because of their low numbers, potential customers are likely to be difficult to find, extract information from and generalize about. One cannot simply stand in shopping centres and stop passers-by or ring at random from the telephone directory. In addition, the influences on demand are likely to be more complex and remote from each organization, making them difficult to interpret. Where an organization has existing customers, however, market research is often easier since the people who hold valuable information and opinions should already be known and are usually quite willing to be approached.

# INDUSTRIAL MARKETING AND GENERAL MANAGEMENT

One of the consequences of the complexities which exist in the buyer–seller relationship in industrial markets is that many different functions within the selling organization are required to interact with various aspects of the customer organization. This can include service or maintenance sections, the design team, installation group, training, delivery and finance departments, as well as senior directors and the sales people. While many of these are also points of contact in consumer marketing, these contacts tend to be extensive and of greater significance in industrial markets.

Such complexity has also given rise to a need for Key Account Management (see Chapter 13). Supply relationships that are significant for both parties can easily falter if left on a simple transactional basis. Key Account Managers who take a relationship perspective on an organization-wide basis are more likely to ensure that potential problems are avoided.

The management of marketing in industrial organizations, therefore, tends towards a general management function with small decisions in one area having a greater impact on the customer and business success. This is not to say that such coordination is inappropriate for consumer markets, but that closer attention to building a marketing approach across the management functions has a higher profile.

In general, then, marketing industrial products is a diverse area which can utilize a number of the approaches developed by consumer marketing organizations. What is important is a recognition of the differences which exist in industrial markets and the implications these hold for the supplying organization. In particular, the way that the relationship between supplier and customer is managed takes on a different perspective, but one which must be well understood and nurtured over time for the achievement of continuing and successful business.

# MARKETING CAPITAL GOODS

The marketing of capital goods presents suppliers with some special concerns. These are generated by the nature of the products and the circumstances under which they are bought and sold. Capital goods can be pieces of plant and equipment, such as large machines, boilers or storage facilities or complete systems such as refineries, telecommunications networks or civil engineering projects. Customers will similarly be large organizations and may be either private or public sector. Whichever the case, the purchase will be a significant event for both the customer and the supplier in terms of the amounts of money involved and the benefits that the products will be required to deliver. Such high stakes mean that a systematic approach to marketing is required so that the risks involved are carefully managed.

By their nature, orders for capital goods tend to be few in number, even for the 'faster-moving' capital goods such as machine tools. In addition, their high cost also makes them very prone to economic fluctuations. Suppliers are thus often faced with a 'feast or famine' situation whereby they either have no orders and are standing around idle, or they are overwhelmed with enquiries and find it difficult to meet delivery or completion schedules. This is further exacerbated by the fact that each purchase is usually supplied against a different specification. It is unlikely that such large and complex products will be used in the same way, or serve exactly the same purpose, from one customer to another. Such a situation prohibits the creation of finished stock except at a very early stage in the manufacture or construction process.

The risk associated with the supply and purchase of capital goods also creates pressures which militate against the use of innovative technologies or approaches. On the supplier side, the consequence of product failure in terms of financial penalties or loss of reputation can be very high. Similarly, from the customer's point of view, a capital purchase will frequently have strategic, or at least operational, significance and buyers are likely to be anxious to reduce the chances of something going wrong by sticking to proven technologies or methodologies. Where innovation does occur, its adoption is therefore likely to be a slow process and the recovery of development costs a long-term activity.

The consequences of these factors for marketing cover a number of areas. High levels of customization plus the complexity of (particularly) larger products will mean that a product specification will take time to evolve and will typically be the result of much negotiation between supplier and customer. This will require suppliers to resource such negotiations and to maintain the ability to understand a customer's perspectives so that they can translate the benefits that customers seek into a product specification. Protracted negotiations and the absence of finished goods stock will create long order lead times, which will also require suppliers to maintain sales relationships over time. Without this, suppliers may risk losing an order through issues such as:

- changes in personnel;
- loss of interest;
- situational changes that will alter the product specification;
- the activities of competitors.

The size of an order may also require suppliers to join together, sometimes as international consortia, to be able to fulfil the requirements of a customer. Managing such relationships in a way which presents customers with a unified face is a distinct skill, but one which is important for the maintenance of relationships with customers. Such relationships, however, will also need to be continued after a sale has been made since capital goods usually involve lengthy construction and/or installation. Although repeat business is not as significant a feature of capital goods marketing as it is for other types of industrial products, client or customer referrals and references *are* an important aspect of selling and good relationships will be needed to ensure that these are forthcoming.

# DECISION-MAKING IN THE PURCHASE OF CAPITAL GOODS

The size and significance of a capital purchase will mean that large numbers of people are likely to combine to form the decision-making unit. Since relationships are an important factor in capital goods sales, personal contacts and the ability to keep and develop such relationships is a critical factor for success. Similarly, having the flexibility to maintain different types of relationships with different people is also important. The significance of capital purchases, however, can mean that governments will also have an interest in the product. Indeed, for some products, governments *are* the customer. Thus, there can be a political, as well as a commercial, influence in the decision to buy.

Thus, in some instances, such as a defence project, high levels of confidentiality may be required. In others, such as a large infrastructural civil engineering project, awareness of a country's development plans, the involvement of national suppliers or some 'tit-for-tat' investment by the supplier or the supplier's government may be a prerequisite for a successful sale. This political aspect, plus the complex nature of the 'buy-centre', may require a lot of 'politics' and building of credibility along a number of different dimensions for an organization to be a viable contender for a piece of business.

Marketing capital goods is, therefore, conducted in a complex market environment. Marketers are faced with long lead times and extended product life cycles, which make it difficult to innovate. In contrast, they are also faced with volatile demand and large variations between one purchase and the next. This is further complicated by the need to develop good relationships with customers, but with the likelihood that any relationship will only be temporary since any one customer is only likely to purchase once or, at best, infrequently. This demands that suppliers are able to be flexible in terms of relationships, capacity and the product they supply. It also demands that they take a long-term perspective on several counts including sales negotiations, product design and development, relationship management, profit planning and funding issues.

# TRADE MARKETING

In the marketing of consumer products and 'fast-moving' industrial goods, much effort is applied to 'pull' activities (i.e. creating demand among large numbers of users that will 'pull' products through the supply chain). This is the logic behind most branding strategies, sales calls and promotional activities such as couponing or distributing free samples through the door. An alternative or even complementary approach is to adopt a 'push' strategy focusing on intermediaries (the trade) and 'pushing' products through the supply chain to consumers. The power and influence of these trade intermediaries in developed economies has grown significantly over the last 30 years. Indeed, the ability to have your product on the shelves or in the catalogues of the more prominent intermediaries is often a key factor to gaining position and advantage in many end-use markets. Focusing marketing effort on these intermediaries is termed trade marketing. As its significance has increased, many organizations have had to develop new approaches to marketing and relationship management to be effective.

## THE RISE OF INTERMEDIARIES

Factors that have contributed to the increasing importance of trade intermediaries for suppliers of mass market goods and services are as follows:

### Retail power

As has already happened in North America and much of Western Europe, retailing and some aspects of industrial distribution have become dominated by a small number of large organizations such as Walmart in the United States, Tesco in the United Kingdom and Carrefour in France. Suppliers relying on these intermediaries for sales-to-end users can easily be denied access to such markets even if only one intermediary decides not to stock their products. Effective marketing to these intermediaries therefore takes on much greater significance. The strategy can no longer be a reliance on large sales forces placing their products in a wide range of different retailers or distributors in a 'hit or miss' fashion, but one which sustains effective presence in these outlets.

### Brand differentiation

In some markets, consumers are finding it increasingly difficult to differentiate between leading brands or suppliers. This is particularly true in markets for banking, mobile telephony or personal computing, but it is also observable in traditional fast-moving consumer areas such as washing powders or tinned foods. The result of this growing brand parity is that consumers more frequently purchase on the basis of availability and price within their chosen 'retail set'.

### Market fragmentation

As markets become more competitive and customers grow in sophistication, demands for individualized supply similarly increase. Demand consequently fragments making it less effective to adopt mass marketing techniques. While this has encouraged organizations such as Heinz, Amazon and wine importers to experiment with more direct and individualized marketing methods, it has also emphasized the value of reaching out to customers at the point of purchase. This requires trade promotions to encourage preferential stocking and point-of-sale support.

### E-commerce

Advances in information technology have meant that suppliers can be in direct contact with an intermediary on a real-time basis. This has enabled retailers and other intermediaries to reduce cost and increase efficiency by effectively delegating inventory responsibilities to a small number of key suppliers. Establishing oneself as one of these key suppliers in the eyes of intermediaries therefore becomes a priority for many manufacturers.

### Brand management deficiencies

Brand managers in many organizations are often young and ambitious people trying to leave their mark on a brand's performance. The most effective way of achieving short-term position is often through trade promotions since brand value enhancement in the eyes of the consumer is more difficult and inevitably a longer-term proposition. Trade marketing therefore becomes more valuable to a brand manager's career than brand development.

# TRADE MARKETING STRATEGIES

Traditionally, tactics for trade marketing have centred on the marketing mix elements of promotion and price. Table 1.2 provides an overview of the most commonly employed tactics in trade marketing.

As intermediaries have become an increasing focus for suppliers, tactical approaches have given way to more strategic marketing approaches. At the heart of this is an understanding of how both supplier and intermediary can mutually benefit from a well-managed long-term relationship.

One manifestation of this is the product profitability studies that analyse in great detail the way that cost attaches itself to a product during manufacture, distribution and handling within the retail environment. Thus, packaging that allows items to be transported around a retail outlet and deposited straight onto the shelves without the need to unpack and stack will save time, effort and, therefore, cost for the retailer. Another is the development of category management whereby a single supplier takes responsibility for a product category such as hair care or chocolate bar confectionery within a retailer's store. They will check the display effectiveness, restock routines and

| Promotion | Price |
| --- | --- |
| Point of sale material | Additional discounts |
| Merchandizing support | Supplying to retailer price points |
| Cooperative advertising | Supporting buyer margin targets |
| Joint trade fair representation | Price promotions |
| | Incentives to staff of intermediaries |

Table 1.2 Tactics for trade marketing

generally ensure they and the retailer are making the most from stocking the product.

Where category management has become widespread, as in the case of the United States, Germany and the United Kingdom, suppliers vie with each other to become 'category leaders', which has caused a need to adjust significantly the structure of many suppliers' brand portfolios.

The strategic importance of trade marketing has also led to heavy investment in information technology by many suppliers to enable logistics and communications to proceed as smoothly as possible. Other aspects of the relationship will be enshrined in joint product development plans, the sharing of 'best-practice' information and a long-term view of category development such as the introduction of new products, range extensions, brand development, supply arrangements, managing seasonal variations and so on. A typical example might be a decision to introduce more organic produce, different labelling information or recyclable packaging.

The factors that have led to the expansion of trade marketing have also stimulated many suppliers to reassess their relationship with end users. While some suppliers have concentrated on better marketing relationships with intermediaries, others have sought to strengthen their brand franchise so that retail or product categories will be weakened without the inclusion of their brand. This is quite apparent in a number of areas such as fashionable sports wear, pet foods and some aspects of the soft drinks market. It is also a major part of Intel's long-term strategy with their global 'Intel Inside' campaign.

At the same time, there has been an upsurge of 'direct' provision in many areas, particularly in the financial services arena. The advent of the Internet is dramatically fuelling this trend. While some retailers have added this to the range of services they offer, the possibility of direct provision for manufacturers is an attractive proposition. Not only does it imply higher margins but it also reduces their reliance on retailers who may not always approach supply relationships in a true 'spirit of partnership'.

The increase in global retailing and the emergence of 'category killers' are also good and bad news for suppliers. The global expansion of stores such as Toys-R-Us, Walmart and Carrefour means access to expanded markets and growth in line with the retailers. However, such stores are usually situated out of town and offer focused category goods at heavily discounted prices. Their predatory nature often decimates local retail competition, reducing suppliers' routes to a market, and puts them in a stronger position to demand lower prices from suppliers. At the time of writing, there is a big debate about the viability of traditional High Street retailing.

Managing the conflicting demands of these powerful intermediaries, including the need for independence and long-term profitability on the part of a supplier and the continuing possibility for creating a consumer or brand franchise, will be an important determinant of the way trade marketing develops in the future.

# SUMMARY

There exist many types of marketing, all of which have their own special characteristics and associated issues. Marketers need to be cognizant of the scope and features of the market they are in, trends affecting their particular industry, sector or marketplace, competitors' actions, as well as consumer wants and demands in order to develop appropriate strategies and tactics. The basic approach, however, remains more or less constant throughout; an organization has to perform market research, identify a target market, develop appropriate products, adopt a suitable pricing policy, promote sales and so on. While the principles are the same, the context is different and adopting a similar mindset for consumer marketing and, say, trade marketing can create problems. What emerges, then, is the significance of the *differences* rather than the *similarities* involved in the various forms of marketing.

# FURTHER READING

*Journal of Consumer Marketing* (2011) Vol. 28 (7). Special issue: The first decade: Emerging issues of the twenty-first century in consumer marketing.

*Journal of Services Marketing* (2010) Vol. 24 (2). Special issue: The Anatomy of Services Branding.

*Journal of Industrial and Business Marketing* (2012) Vol. 27 (7). Special issue: Business-to-Business Marketing Strategy.

*Industrial Marketing Management* (2013) Vol. 42 (3). Special issue: Theoretical Perspectives in Industrial Marketing Management.

# CHAPTER 2
# CONSUMER BEHAVIOUR

IN THIS CHAPTER WE STUDY:

- factors influencing consumer behaviour
- types of consumer behaviour
- perceptions, attitudes and learning
- the purchase decision-making process
- cognitivist and behaviourist perspectives

# DETERMINANTS OF CONSUMER CHOICE

In this chapter we explore the basics of consumer behaviour within the context of B2C (business to consumer) marketing. In contrast to organizational buying behaviour (B2B), B2C markets typically comprise numerous buyers whose characteristics and buying processes vary markedly in all sorts of ways. In order to offer 'the right consumers the right products at the right time in the right place' more effectively than competitors, providers of products and services need to understand consumer motivations, preferences, prejudices and priorities of consumers in their target market(s). They need to appreciate that every purchase decision is a *choice* based upon a wide variety of factors, taken not in the abstract, but in context.

Consumers have numerous alternatives; true monopolies are relatively rare. They choose between providers using a combination of rational judgement, based on facts and previous experience and subjective feelings that determine likes and dislikes. For simplicity at this introductory stage, this chapter assumes that consumers are both buyers and end users of the product or service being purchased, though in practice this may not always be the case.

In trying to comprehend why people buy what they buy, marketers have to make judgements about the importance they ascribe to consumers' expressed beliefs about certain products and services. People form attachments to different products and services which are not always entirely rational or easy to predict. For marketers, the challenge lies in trying to identify and make sense of the multiple factors that can influence a purchase decision. For example, the purchase of a tablet PC may be based upon evaluations by a prospective buyer of ease of use and how reliable it is likely to be. These evaluations are based upon a number of factors, such as experience, recommendations from friends and family or price. The Internet can be highly influential too, particularly electronic word of mouth (eWOM) on customer review sites. There is evidence that eWOM is more influential than traditional advocacy for several reasons: firstly, consumers visiting review sites actively seek opinions from strangers, no longer simply relying upon acquaintances (Senecal and Nantel, 2004). Secondly, eWOM reaches a very large audience (Litvin et al., 2008). Thirdly, it can remain online permanently and be accessed sometimes long after the review is published (Sun et al., 2006) and, finally, anonymity encourages people to publish reviews (Phelps et al., 2004) – this is particularly salient when eWOM is negative.

Alternatively, or additionally, personal evaluations of the product's physical attributes, such as weight, functionality, signal coverage, download speed, colour, size, 'look and feel' may be important considerations. Other, some-what more intangible factors, such a 'cool' brand, reputation for performance excellence, outstanding technical support, hassle-free after-sales service and upgrades and so on may also weigh heavily.

Some buyers may be heavily influenced by the extent to which the pur-chase augments their self-concept, or image and standing with their peer group. Self-image congruence, in which consumers buy products that they perceive as similar to their own self-image, is an important factor in under-standing consumer behaviour. Simply put, consumers who consider themselves modern, trendy and cool are attracted to modern, trendy, cool brands. Anton et al. (2013) find self-image congruence, along with perceived usefulness and enjoyment to be key drivers of consumer attitudes towards e-book read-ers. Congruence between the brand image and deeply held beliefs about self-concept can be powerful drivers, and marketers ignore subliminal mean-ings of consumption at their peril. Gerald Ratner's infamous 1991 denigra-tion of the jewellery sold in his UK High Street stores effectively killed off the company; consumers deserted in droves, £500 million was wiped off the value of the company; shortly afterwards it had to be sold and renamed.

Determinants of individual purchase decisions are complex and difficult for marketers to unravel. Marketers cannot possibly *know* exactly which fac-tor exerts the most powerful influence upon the final purchase decision, or which combination of factors are most powerful; they have to make judge-ments based upon in-depth knowledge of their target audience(s). In the past, this would be based primarily upon observing purchase behaviour, or by bespoke market research; nowadays it is relatively simple for marketers to gain consumer insights by logging on to the Internet. Intelligence can be gathered from a variety of sources, such as consumer-to-consumer (C2C) social networking sites, discussion forums, consumer-generated con-tent and customer review sites, all of which give consumers opportunities to share their thoughts, preferences, concerns and evaluations of products and services.

It is an accepted fact that consumers buy certain brands for sometimes irrational, emotionally based, yet valid reasons; compare the sales figures for Apple's iPhone and Samsung's Galaxy smartphone which offer simi-lar functionality and the same 'look and feel'. It is the job of the mar-keter to assess which of the attributes weigh most heavily in the purchase decision and to exploit this knowledge intelligently. The key to success-ful marketing is understanding consumer behaviour enough to make *sound* judgements, rather than second-guessing from the morass of information available.

# PERCEPTIONS, ATTITUDES AND CONDITIONING

Perception is defined in the *Oxford English Dictionary* as 'the mental action of knowing external things through the medium of sense presentations; insight or discernment'. In marketing, consumer perception is more important than reality. What makes Apple 'cool', Scotchguard trustworthy, Burberry luxurious? Not simply tangible product features, but the composite elements of the brand and the means by which brand attributes, characteristics, personality, values and benefits are communicated to, *and deciphered by*, consumers. In Chapter 12 we explore communication theory and practice; the key point here being that consumer perceptions concern the selection, organization and interpretation of a series of sensory stimulations to create meaning and relevance. It is crucial that marketers understand how to influence consumer perceptions. This will enable them to predict how brand communications might be received, decoded and interpreted to optimal effect. Perceptions are instantaneous and, over time, through exposure to a number of sensory stimulations around a brand, aggregate to form brand attitude. Marketers may seek to influence consumer perceptions directly using rather unsubtle techniques such as the Scotchgard's repetition of the strapline, 'The Brand You Can Trust', through actions that stand for key brand attributes, such as the entrepreneurial, innovative Virgin group of brands, to more subtle tactics, such as James Bond wearing an Omega watch.

An attitude is defined as a 'behavioural tendency that is expressed by evaluating a particular entity with some degree of favour or disfavour'. In contrast to perceptions, attitudes are relatively fixed and durable, and therefore difficult to change. Positive experiences of a product, service or brand, positive cultural frames of reference, or the recommendations of families and friends tend to contribute to the formation of a favourable attitude, while the converse is also true; negative experiences tend to lead to unfavourable attitudes which are difficult to change. To build positive attitudes, brands need to provide congruent experiences that lift the spirit, enhance the mood, or reinforce the positive perceptions. Although some marketers advocate attitude change strategies, in practice attitudes are relatively entrenched; the optimal route is to influence perceptions via a series of sensory stimulations, over a period of time.

The most effective brands have meanings that go far beyond the actual product or service. How do the megabrands create meaning for consumers? It is generally held that meaning is created through learning, and that through learning consumers are conditioned to respond in particular ways. Behavioural learning theory is based upon an input–output, stimulus–response model in which the individual responds in a predictable way to an input, or stimulus. In classical conditioning, an established relationship between a stimulus and a response, repeated over time, eventually promotes learning, for example, adverts for the Lynx range of men's grooming products, featuring young men who have used the products becoming irresistibly attractive to young females. Conditioned learning can be extremely effective as a means of short-circuiting decision-making; in this case young adults in the target audience respond well to the subliminal message being conveyed.

In contrast, operant conditioning works on the basis of reinforcement – reward. Whereas in classical conditioning, liking precedes trial, operant conditioning provides a reward, such as a free sample, from which reinforcement and learning occur. Operant conditioning underpins the rationale for sales promotions, for example, supermarket 'buy one, get one free' (BOGOF) offers, free samples of face creams or new perfumes in women's magazines and so on. Strategies based upon operant condition is particularly effective in low-cost, low-risk purchases, such as fast-moving consumer goods (FMCGs) or fast food, though care must be taken to understand thoroughly local market conditions. In 2010 KFC offered online discount coupons through its official website to Chinese consumers, only to find them circulating freely on other sites, downloaded and copied in unanticipated volumes. Inundated, KFC refused to accept coupons from 'non-official' sites, resulting in customer unrest and, eventually, police intervention.

## CASE STUDY 2.1  APPLE

Loyal customers of Apple greet each new product with an enthusiasm that non-loyals find incomprehensible. Yet, their behaviour is easily explained by classical conditioning theory. Consumers are conditioned to believe that buying *the latest* Apple product makes them trendy, edgy and cool. This is achieved by sophisticated technology and modern, sleek designs with a price tag to match. How does this conditioning occur? Apple releases are preceded by high levels of buzz marketing, in which opinion leaders play a central role via media articles and blogs. High profile pre-launch events, provision of demonstration models, pre-orders and turning the actual launch into an *event* all underline the simple message that Apple is *selling a lifestyle* which embodies 'sleek and cool'. Subliminal message = *We have made this especially for you; just think how you would feel using it, and what others would think of you when they saw you using it.* This makes each new product a 'must have' in which the launch triggers an automatic purchase response.

**CASE STUDY QUESTIONS:**

1. Outline how, exactly, the classical conditioning outlined in the case promotes associationist learning.
2. Discuss how Apple could further augment the conditioned response outlined in the case.
3. What other factors might affect a loyal Apple customer's purchase decision? To what extent can Apple influence these factors?

# MODEL OF CONSUMER BUYER BEHAVIOUR

Consumer behaviour has to be understood before marketing strategies can be developed. However, constructing a standard model of consumer buyer behaviour can be somewhat problematic. While the inputs and the outputs of decision-making can readily be identified and, to a greater or lesser degree, measured, intangible elements involving buyer characteristics and choice determinants is often more elusive. Kotler and Armstrong (2012) describe it as a 'black box', in other words, opaque. Predicting consumer buyer behaviour may be an imprecise science, but some simple models have been created to enable marketers to develop deeper understanding of consumers in order to acquire and retain their custom.

Figure 2.1 illustrates a classic input–output, stimulus–response model. There are two categories of input: internal stimuli over which the marketer has control (the expanded marketing mix: product, price, place, promotion, people, process and physical evidence, customer service) and external stimuli over which they have little or no control (political, economic, social, technological factors). Purchase decisions are framed indirectly by external stimuli and market conditions, and directly in response to the stimuli employed by the seller. Clearly, the more fully a company understands the stimuli that elicit greatest effect, the more likely it is to achieve a competitive advantage. Outputs refer to buyer responses. Outputs can be identified and assessed in various ways, such as time of purchase, the place of purchase, choice of brand, quantity purchased, the terms and conditions of purchase.

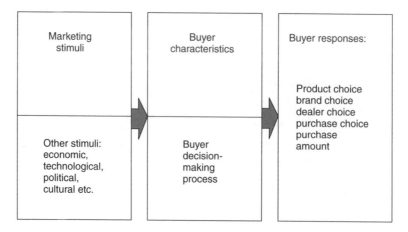

Figure 2.1 Black Box Model of consumer buyer behaviour

Analysis of inputs and outputs raises questions about who buys and how they buy, leading researchers to examine closely buyer characteristics in an attempt to identify the critical drivers in the purchase decision-making process.

# INFLUENCING FACTORS

An important element of the process of analysing and understanding purchase behaviour involves an analysis of the context within which purchase decisions occur. Pervasive social influences can be viewed on two levels: macro and micro level. Macro influences include culture, subculture and social class, while micro influences include the more immediate social environment of reference groups and the family. Let us consider each level in turn, as portrayed in Figure 2.2.

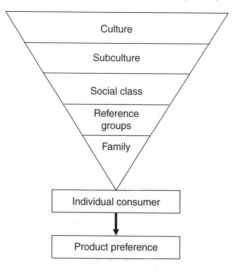

Figure 2.2 Social influences on consumer buyer behaviour

Macro social factors play a role in shaping the values, beliefs, attitudes and behaviours of individual consumers and provide useful bases upon which to segment markets. They have direct implications for designing effective relationship marketing strategies, especially where management of the marketing mix spans national boundaries.

# CULTURE

Culture can be defined broadly as 'a complex of learned meanings, values and behavioural patterns' (Peter and Olson, 2010) that are shared by a society. The relationship between the consumer and the product, often described as the 'product/self relationship', is culturally specific and thus of great interest to marketers seeking to identify the factors that influence purchasing and consumption.

Despite globalization, some idiosyncratic differences still exist between people from different regions of the world. When Euro Disney first opened on the outskirts of Paris in 1992, long queues formed at catering outlets. Research revealed that while Americans prefer 'grazing' (or snacking) all day as they tour a theme park, Europeans prefer a full meal between 12 noon and 2 p.m. Euro Disney had to create more suitable eating opportunities for visitors and the daily parades of Disney characters had to be rescheduled for 11.30 a.m. and 4 p.m. to avoid a clash with the lunch period. More recently, a cross-cultural study of IKEA's marketing strategy in the United Kingdom, Sweden and China exposes differences in consumer cultures which impact upon customer-facing elements of the retail experience as well as differences in back-office processes (Burt et al., 2001). Similarly, a cross-cultural study of online behaviour finds US consumers more trusting of company websites than Koreans against three attributes: competence, benevolence and integrity (Park et al., 2012). Cultural influences also play an important role in domestic markets, however because marketers operating within their home countries tend to be very familiar with the prevailing culture, they may not recognize the significant cultural factors that influence domestic consumer behaviour.

# SUBCULTURE

A subculture is a cultural group within a larger culture that has beliefs or interests that are at variance with those of the larger culture. Many types of distinction are used to classify subcultures, including ethnicity, religious or political affiliation, age and so on. Taking age as an example, marketers often distinguish categories of consumers in terms of their age group. People within certain age ranges frequently behave similarly, but in ways which set them apart from other consumers. The youth market, for example, exhibits many unique traits and behaviours, such as a strong need for peer acceptance, preoccupation with celebrities, strong interest in music, great interest in sex, high dependence on electronic gadgets, intensive engagement with peers via online social networks, short attention spans, preference for texting and instant messaging over longer, more intricate forms of communication, receptive to viral marketing and co-created content. Interestingly, youth subculture is not restricted to any particular nationality or location, being manifested in countries around the globe. These easily identifiable, enthusiastic and apparently insatiable consumers are every marketer's dream!

# SOCIAL CLASS

The concept of social class is drawn from sociology, where a social group is organized according to a recognized hierarchy based on the individual's status within the group. While the impact that social class has on consumer behaviour is a topic of considerable debate, marketers favour social class as a form of shorthand to describe their typical consumers. In the United Kingdom, for example, consumers are classified into six social classes, mainly determined by the occupation of the head of the household, as given in Table 2.1. This method of classification has remained in use for a number of years, despite unease at its decreasing relevance to modern society.

| Class name | Social status | Occupation of head of household |
|---|---|---|
| A | Upper middle | Higher managerial, administrative, professional |
| B | Middle | Intermediate managerial, administrative or professional |
| C1 | Lower middle | Supervisors or clerical, junior managerial, administrative or professional |
| C2 | Skilled working | Skilled manual workers |
| D | Working | Semi-skilled and unskilled manual workers |
| E | Subsistence level | Pensioners or widows, casual or lower-grade workers |

Table 2.1 UK socio-economic classification scheme

These systems of consumer classification tend to be culturally bound, having been developed on a parochial basis. They do not lend themselves to international comparison. Within Europe, there have been attempts to use a harmonized set of demographics, which focus on the terminal education age of the main income earner in the household, their professional status and the average net monthly level of household income. However, collecting this kind of data from across European markets can prove problematic in countries such as the United Kingdom, where it is common practice for survey respondents to think in terms of their gross annual salary, rather than the net monthly income of their household. These issues surrounding the difficulties of marketing research are discussed further in Chapter 4.

## MICRO SOCIAL INFLUENCES

Purchasing decisions are also influenced at the micro level by the people closest to the consumer, namely family, friends, relatives and peers. These people feature significantly in the consumer's immediate social environment and can be grouped into two types of influencer: reference groups and family. Their effect on consumers' attitudes and purchasing behaviour can be considerable.

# REFERENCE GROUPS

Reference groups are made up of people who belong to the same social circle and who are personally relevant to the individual making the purchase decision. They influence thought processes, feelings and, ultimately, buying behaviour. Influence may be overt, where a buyer seeks the advice of a friend before choosing between options, or covert where one is influenced subliminally via subconscious observation of the products, services and brands used by others in the reference group.

Some companies use reference groups explicitly in their marketing activities. For example, the well-known UK chef, Jamie Oliver launched the 'Jamie at Home' party plan business in 2009 based upon in-home selling techniques which actively encourage reference groups to exercise their aggregate power in the purchasing decision. Reference group endorsement is a widely used, powerful marketing tool. The UK satellite broadcaster, Sky TV partners with Marks and Spencer to offer M&S gift vouchers to Sky customers recruiting new subscribers; both the existing and new customer gain a reward. In this case, reference group endorsement is used to market Sky's services.

# FAMILY

Market research traditionally uses the individual consumer as the unit of analysis, but there are types of purchasing decision where the family becomes the decision-making unit. Studies of this phenomenon attempt to describe the various roles played by family members and the complexity of interactions that take place in reaching a collective decision. In focusing on the family as decision-maker, marketers first face the challenge of defining 'the family'. Demographic trends and relativist positions have invalidated the concept of the 'traditional nuclear family', requiring marketers to cope with multifarious, fluid models of family life.

Where households comprise adults and children, in certain circumstances both parties may be equally responsible for decisions, such as selecting a holiday destination or restaurant choice. Children may exert a strong influence, for example, in relation to the latter they may be strongly motivated not by the quality of food but availability of play facilities or 'freebies'; McDonald's is one of the largest toy retailers in the world through giving away promotional Disney toys when new films are released. 'Pester power' should not be underestimated; in fact, it is so influential and pervasive that in December 2011 the British government warned retailers that they would face new regulations to curb 'the commercialisation of childhood' including a ban on the use of children under 16 as brand ambassadors or in viral peer-to-peer marketing campaigns.

Present trends indicate that families will continue to be smaller, more affluent and more geographically mobile. At the time of writing, children enjoy the highest ever level of material goods, and this is set to continue, presenting tremendous scope for youth-orientated brands. Additionally, opportunities are opening up as people become increasingly willing to pay for services that maximize their use of time: for example, the home delivery of groceries, after-school clubs for children and so on.

A popular tool for analysing family purchasing behaviour is the family life cycle, which describes the typical changes that take place in families over a period of time. Traditionally, the family life cycle has concentrated on life-stage events such as marriage and the arrival of children, and schooling and the departure of children (often referred to as the 'full nest' and 'empty nest' life stages). However, given the evident changes in demographics, the family life cycle is no longer a straightforward linear model but something resembling a complex network of life patterns that may involve non-traditional relationship types or repeated life-stages. It is crucial that marketers map these stages so they can plan the positioning of existing, and opportunities for new products and services.

# PERSONAL CHARACTERISTICS

Influencing factors that have a more direct impact on consumer behaviour are those concerned with the individuals themselves. They include personal attributes, such as age, lifestage occupation, economic circumstances and lifestyle. Personal psychology also plays a role, influencing beliefs, attitudes and motivations. It is not uncommon for the same individual to display distinctly different buyer behaviour when purchasing a bottle of wine for home consumption and a gift for a dinner party. Equally, different motivations and preferences may become apparent when faced with a 'distress purchase', such as buying petrol when the petrol gauge in the car hits zero, compared to simply topping up a half-full tank.

Market research data on consumer buyer characteristics are usually presented in the form of a typology of consumer profiles for a particular set of products or services. The categories, with their memorable labels such as 'sporting thirties' and 'young survivors', can be assimilated quickly into marketing strategies, offering an abbreviated method of expressing a complex set of consumer characteristics and typical buying behaviours.

# TYPES OF CONSUMER PURCHASE DECISION

Understanding the purchase decision-making process as a fundamental part of creating a relationship with consumers requires an examination of the role and interaction of two important dimensions: involvement and degree of difference that consumers perceive to exist between competing brands.

'Involvement' is a term used to describe how personally meaningful the purchase is to the consumer. It implies that the act of purchasing is a conscious activity and that an element of effort will have been invested in making the final choice. The role of consumer 'involvement' refers to the factors listed in Figure 2.3.

- high degree of risk (performance, cost, psychology)
- high degree of brand differentiation
- hedonism and pursuit of pleasure
- lifestyle products
- special interest products (hobbies and leisure pursuits)

Figure 2.3 The role of consumer involvement

Purchases with high involvement are made by consumers who perceive there to be a high degree of risk. It is commonly assumed that 'risk' is financial, however this is too bounded a definition; in reality risk may also relate to performance (will it work?), financial cost of acquisition (is the price too high?), opportunity cost (what do I have to forego if I buy it?) or psychology (is it right for me?) (what will my friends think?). Generally, a high involvement situation is where the purchase is linked strongly to hedonism, such as a hobby or beauty/lifestyle product, an infrequent purchase, such as a car, or where the consequences of getting it wrong are significant, such as financial loss or denigration by peer group. Conversely, purchases with low involvement involve little financial or psychological risk and tend to be habitual, practical purchases of FMCGs.

# TYPES OF BUYING BEHAVIOUR

Essentially, there are four main types of buying behaviour, portrayed most commonly in the literature as a $2 \times 2$ matrix, as illustrated in Figure 2.4.

Figure 2.4 Typology of buying behaviour

### COMPLEX BUYER BEHAVIOUR

Often marked by consumer confusion, this behaviour is demonstrated when consumers are highly involved in a purchase and perceive significant differences among brands. For many people, the purchase of a laptop computer falls into this category. The rapid pace of technology is reflected in an overwhelming variety of features and applications, and to make an informed choice about which laptop is best requires a personal investment of time and energy. Marketers are presented with an opportunity to influence the purchase decision at the stage where consumers seek information about a product's attributes and differential value. Well-trained sales staff can also influence the purchase decision proactively by providing consumers with guidance and advice. If the purchase is managed well by the selling organization, the chances are that the consumer will return for future purchases, thus increasing the customer's lifetime value to the organization. The purchase decision-making process can therefore be seen to pass through the stages of 'awareness', 'trial' and 'repeat buying'.

## DISSONANCE-REDUCING BUYER BEHAVIOUR

'Dissonance' describes the after-sales feelings of the consumer who believes that there has been some sort of shortfall between expectations and performance. This is outcome of 'expectation-dissonance' modelling which measures the gap between what the customer was expecting prior to purchase and post-purchase, post-usage satisfaction. Dissonance-reducing behaviour is demonstrated where consumers are highly involved with the purchase, perhaps because it is something expensive which they would seldom buy, and where they perceive there to be few differences between brands. In order to address this type of behaviour, marketers need to concentrate their efforts on before- and after-sales communications to ensure that consumers feel confident about their choice of brand. This is essential to 'win over' consumers and move them up the loyalty ladder (see Chapter 15). Dissonance-reducing behaviour must be managed at all costs, to prevent consumers from generating negative publicity by word of mouth; in the Internet age, this can be particularly unmanageable and destructive.

## VARIETY-SEEKING BUYER BEHAVIOUR

This is characterized by low consumer involvement and perceptions of significant brand differences. In variety-seeking behaviour switching between brands occurs regularly. Such behaviour is driven not by dissatisfaction with the brand but by the desire to sample other brands. In order to be successful in such markets, marketers need to encourage habitual buying by ensuring that target brands or products dominate shelf space, that distribution strategies minimize stock-outs and that communications and promotional activities constantly provide reminders and reinforcement. Brand visibility and availability are key in building relationships with variety seekers.

## HABITUAL BUYER BEHAVIOUR

This occurs where consumer involvement is low and there are few perceived differences between brands. Habitual behaviour tends to be associated with low-cost, frequently purchased products, such as flour, milk or eggs. Consumers simply make their choice by reaching out for the same product time and again, more from habit than loyalty. Opportunities for relationship building may be perceived to be small, but the shrewd marketer will focus on promotions which serve to build a sense of brand familiarity and stimulate trial usage of the product. In these circumstances, it is crucial that the brand is always displayed prominently on the shelf, and that out-of-stock situations are avoided. Visibility and availability are the vital elements in managing habitual buyers.

# THE CONSUMER PURCHASE DECISION-MAKING PROCESS

While different types of buyer behaviour can be demonstrated, it is quite another matter to be unequivocal about why people buy what they buy. Most academic modelling defines decision-making as a linear process, as outlined in Figure 2.5.

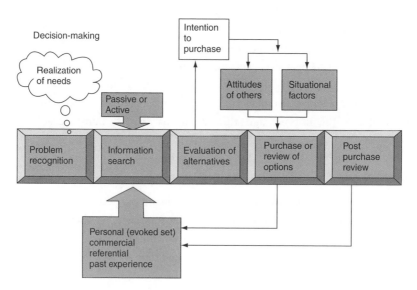

Figure 2.5 Linear decision-making process

The first step is the buyer realizing that (s)he has a need, or a problem requiring a solution. This realization can be triggered through internal stimuli, such as hunger pangs, or external stimuli, such as recalling a favourable review of a restaurant or noticing aromas emanating from a restaurant kitchen. This initial acknowledgement is usually followed by an information search: the consumer reads the menu displayed outside the restaurant and evaluates the offerings. If there are other eateries in the street, the consumer may wander along and look at what is available elsewhere. (S)he will then reach a conclusion and either enter the restaurant, move on down the road to a competitor, or possibly pick up a take-away on the way home. After eating, the consumer will demonstrate some form of post-purchase behaviour by making several assessments, such as whether the meal was satisfactory, better or worse than expected, was it value for money, whether it is worth coming again, and whether to recommend it to others. This post-purchase evaluation stage which includes an evaluation of what was provided compared to what was expected is known as 'expectation-disconfirmation' modelling (see Parasuraman et al., 1985, and subsequent articles); satisfaction occurs if expectations are exceeded; cognitive dissonance if expectations are not met.

Of course, it is often argued that decision-making is not necessarily linear; purchases can be made on a whim, stages can be missed altogether (such as evaluation of alternatives) or occur concurrently (need recognition, information search). A classic linear representation is also much criticized for denoting stages of similar duration; in reality, they can vary significantly, particularly on account of the feedback loops illustrated in Figure 2.5.

# APPROACHES TO CONSUMER BUYER BEHAVIOUR

Consumer behaviour can be studied from a cognitivist or behaviourist perspective employing different research 'lenses'; the former elevating the importance of psychology; the latter, behaviour. For the cognitivists, what goes on in consumers' minds is of far greater interest and relevance than what they *do*; behaviour may or may not be rational or predictable. For behaviourists, observed behaviour is paramount, being both rational and predictable. What goes on in consumers' minds may be of interest, but is far too complex, unstable, unpredictable and irrational to be of lasting importance. Adherents of the cognitivist approach deem the behaviourist approach over-simplistic; behaviourists consider cognitivists overly complex.

It is crucial that marketing managers are fully conversant with the two approaches as the design and focus of marketing and promotional activities will be heavily influenced by whichever predominates within the team. At a simplistic level, marketers of a cognitivist persuasion tend to favour image-based advertising and promotions, which appeal to consumers' values. They will offer brand benefits in ways that play on consumers' thoughts, feelings, attitudes and beliefs. Behaviourists, on the other hand, tend to use conditioning behaviour, where the marketing message is reinforced through skilful advertising. For example, the association between the Marlboro man and the Marlboro cigarette is now so strong that in some cases the company no longer includes the brand name in its advertisements. This is because the brand has succeeded in transferring the meaning of an unconditioned stimulus to a conditioned stimulus.

Historically, advertisers have adopted the behaviourist philosophy (probably for reasons of simplicity and measurability). However, more recently there has been a shift of emphasis towards creating moods and eliciting emotions which sit more firmly in the cognitivist domain. The rapid growth of e-retailing, e- and m-marketing and social networking provides multiple opportunities for consumer engagement, enabling marketers to connect with target audiences at the emotional as well as cognitive level.

# SUMMARY

An understanding of the consumer behaviour is a prerequisite for successful marketing. This requires that marketers understand the factors affecting buyer behaviour and how purchase decisions are made. Models of consumer buyer behaviour can, at best, help to promote this understanding, providing a framework for analysing how consumption decisions occur and how consumers may be persuaded to buy one product rather than an alternative. The development of models involves 'de-layering' the social influences and personal characteristics, motivations and perceptions.

The interaction of two key dimensions – consumer 'involvement' and consumer perception of differences between brands – produces four distinct types of buyer behaviour: complex, dissonance-reducing, variety-seeking and habitual. Understanding how best to manage buyers of these persuasions enables marketers to develop long-term, profitable relationships with consumers.

Typical stages in the consumer purchase decision-making process can be identified, although these will not always represent conscious actions in the minds of consumers. It is the task of marketing research (see Chapter 4) to make these steps explicit in order that they may be better addressed and exploited.

Marketers must decide whether they favour a cognitivist or a behaviourist approach to understanding consumer buyer behaviour if they are to give clear direction to marketing activities which support consumer relationships, such as market research, market segmentation, branding and marketing communications.

# FURTHER READING

Solomon, M. (2013) *Consumer Behaviour: Buying, Having and Being*, Harlow, Pearson.
A comprehensive, yet practical guide to understanding consumer behaviour.

# REFERENCES

Anton, C., Camarero, C. and Rodriguez, J. (2013) Usefulness, Enjoyment and Self-Image Congruence: The Adoption of e-Book Readers, *Psychology and Marketing*, Vol. 30 (4): 372–384.

Burt, S., Johansson, U. and Thelander, Å. (2011) Standardized Marketing Strategies in Retailing? IKEA's Marketing Strategies in Sweden, the UK and China, *Journal of Retailing and Consumer Services*, Vol. 18 (3): 183–193.

Kotler, P. and Armstrong, G. (2012) *Principles of Marketing*, Harlow, Prentice-Hall.

Litvin, S. W., Goldsmith, R. E. and Pan, B. (2008) Electronic Word-of-Mouth in Hospitality and Tourism Management, *Tourism Management*, Vol. 29 (3): 458–468.

Parasuraman, A., Zeithaml, V. and Berry, L. L. (1985) A Conceptual Model of Services Quality and its Implication for Future Research, *Journal of Marketing*, Vol. 49 (4): 41–50.

Park, J. K., Gunn, F. and Han, S. L. (2012) Multidimensional Trust Building in e-Retailing: Cross-Cultural Differences in Trust Formation and Implications for Perceived Risk, *Journal of Retailing and Consumer Services*, Vol. 19 (3): 304–312.

Peter, J. and Olson, J. (2010) *Consumer Behavior and Marketing Strategy*, New York, McGraw-Hill.

Phelps, J. E., Lewis, R., Mobilio, L., Perry, D. and Raman, N. (2004) Viral Marketing or Electronic Word-of-Mouth Advertising: Examining Consumer Responses and Motivations to Pass Along Email, *Journal of Advertising Research*, Vol. 44 (4): 333–348.

Senecal, S. and Nantel, J. (2004) The Influence of Online Product Recommendations on Consumers' Online Choices, *Journal of Retailing*, Vol. 80 (2): 159–169.

Sun, T., Youn, S., Wu, G. and Kuntaraporn, M. (2006) Online Word-of-Mouth (or Mouse): An Exploration of its Antecedents and Consequences, *Journal of Computer-Mediated Communication*, Vol. 11 (4): 1104–1127. 6101.2006.00310.

# CHAPTER 3
# ORGANIZATIONAL BUYING BEHAVIOUR

IN THIS CHAPTER WE STUDY:

- B2B contrasted with B2C buying behaviour
- drivers of change
- the decision-making unit and the decision-making process
- three types of buying situations
- the buyer–behaviour matrix
- strategic alliances
- key trends in organizational buyer behaviour

# COMPARISON OF B2B AND B2C BUYING BEHAVIOUR

Business buying behaviour is typically more formalized and structured than B2C. In contrast to B2C marketing, in B2B the number of buyers is relatively small and purchases tend to be relatively large. Marketers in B2B situations thus require specialist knowledge and understanding of context, trends, market structure and conditions, consumer demand, competitors and B2B decision-making processes.

As a rule, organizational buying decisions are born from necessity. A purchase invariably starts from within the buyer's organization as some kind of problem or need. The remaining 'buy stages' gradually unfold, sometimes over a period of weeks or even months. Although, due to the varying nature of business contexts, it is bold to generalize, as a rule, buying decisions can be relatively complex and protracted. As a comparator to B2C, Figure 3.1 indicates the stages of a 'typical' organizational buying decision.

Figure 3.1 Typical organizational buying process

# DRIVERS OF CHANGE

The business environment is increasingly global, dynamic and transparent, forcing companies to engage in a perpetual quest for greater efficiency, productivity and cost-effectiveness alongside ever-higher quality and customer-responsiveness. Simultaneous pursuit of these essentially dichotomous routes can be problematic, so it is important to map and understand the key drivers of change in order to develop appropriate strategies.

## CUSTOMER EXPERTISE, SOPHISTICATION AND POWER

Customers are becoming more and more demanding in their expectations of quality, reliability and compatibility. They increasingly demand customized solutions, fuelled by technological developments (Information and Communications Technology (ICT) and the Internet, in particular) and the concentration of buying power in fewer hands. The web enables business buyers to access and share information quickly and easily, making it simple to compare suppliers and partner with other companies to increase buyer power. B2B aggregator and consolidator sites continue to accelerate this trend across various industrial sectors.

## MARKET CONDITIONS

Some mature markets, such as North America and Europe, have reached a state of saturation, characterized by over-capacity, increased competition and eroding margins. Under these conditions, power is shifting increasingly towards consumers, particularly in the B2B market where the prospect of large orders encourages suppliers to look constantly for innovative ways to add value. Business customers are becoming more demanding, rationalizing portfolios of preferred suppliers and calling for increased value for money. Additionally, established companies in mature markets are finding themselves in intense competition with smaller, leaner businesses from emerging and growth-leading economics (EAGLEs). Banytė et al. (2008) observe that the development of ICT has been extremely active in recent decades, with the Internet spreading rapidly in organizational activities. Of note is that use of the Internet allows buyers and sellers to consolidate their positions and barter for better terms.

## PROCESS ORIENTATION

ICT and the web in particular have fuelled a switch from a single product approach to a systems orientation. According to Hunter et al. (2004), the benefits of ICT depend on different types of buying situations where diverse uses of the Internet are employed. For example, buyer organizations mostly use the Internet in the stage of search for potential suppliers and less in other stages of the buying. Where the purchase is relatively simple and low risk, the relative benefits of the web are reasonably limited. In contrast, where purchases are relatively high cost/high risk, bearing in mind the shift from marketing ready-made, tangible products to marketing by reputation, the web can play a significant role at each stage of organizational buying.

With the emphasis upon capabilities, resources, reputation and just-in-time (JIT) delivery against exact client specifications, companies have increasingly had to reconsider (and in many cases, reorganize) how to meet their customers' purchasing requirements. For some time now, companies have been increasingly likely to employ a web-enabled (either an off-the-shelf, or bespoke) procurement package as part of their ERP (Enterprise Resource Planning) system. This has the potential to reduce, quite radically, purchasing and inventory management costs, producing savings that can either be retained/reinvested in the company or, alternatively, passed on in part to clients thereby making the firm more price-competitive.

Pre-Internet, ERP systems would most commonly be bespoke and closed, with relatively limited external links. With the Internet, the emphasis has shifted to creating partnerships by employing web-enabled EDI (Electronic Data Interchange) to link partners along the supply chain, increasingly using XML as the standard, enabling markup language. Advantages can be measured in terms of reduced lead time, fewer errors, faster processing, lower costs, improved authentication and non-repudiation. SMEs are also increasingly investing in off-the-shelf solutions, as these continue to fall in price.

## TIME-BASED COMPETITION

Time horizons continue to become more compressed while the pace of change accelerates. The development of business systems, such as flexible manufacturing and JIT delivery, has encouraged companies to compete on speed-to-market. There is continuous pressure to innovate and as innovation cycles shorten, pressure to innovate increases, trapping companies in ever-tightening concentric circles. At this point, enhanced knowledge of, and involvement with, customer purchasing processes can lead to significant market share gains (designated 'customer relationship strategy' in Figure 3.2). Further, close relationships and greater understanding of specific requirements can promote significant innovations that meet customer requirements and are difficult for competitors to emulate.

The fundamental approach to 'outside-in' marketing, that is, responding to customers' needs better than competitors, is similar in B2B and B2C domains. There are some significant differences, however, in terms of *how* the business purchase is made and *who* is involved in the decision. Table 3.1 serves to illustrate this point.

Let us now take a closer look at four key aspects of organizational buyer behaviour: the decision-making unit (DMU); the decision-making process (DMP); behavioural segmentation of customers; and managing buyer–supplier relationships.

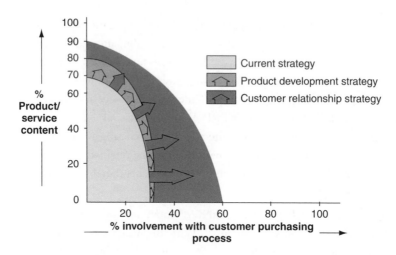

Figure 3.2 Product content versus involvement in the customer purchasing process

| | Business products | Consumer products |
|---|---|---|
| *Customer base* | Few, with concentrated buying power | Numerous, widely dispersed, relatively limited buying power |
| *Decision-making unit* | Group decisions; various buying influences | Individual and family involvement |
| *Decision-making process* | Rigid purchasing procedures | Impulse, planned or experiential |
| *Buyer–supplier relationships* | Close relationships over time; pre-sales consultancy and problem-solving | Short duration with very little close contact |
| *Product* | Technical complexity; detailed specification; standard or customized | Standard or customized (high end) |
| *Price* | High unit price; standard items from list; negotiated bidding | Low unit price from list; limited negotiation |
| *Promotion* | Emphasis on personal selling | Predominantly advertising and promotion |
| *Distribution/ logistics* | Mainly direct for make-to-order customized items; standard items often available from stock through distributors | Stock items through a network of wholesalers and retail distributors |

Table 3.1 Key differences in B2B and B2C purchases

# THE DECISION-MAKING UNIT

B2B buying behaviour is more complex than B2C as there is rarely just one person involved in the decision. Even relatively low-risk purchases, such as straightforward replenishment of office supplies, can involve numerous people in various organizational roles. The inclusion of several people is easier to understand and justify with regard to high-risk purchases (not always be high financial risk, but might also encompass either technological, safety, quality or reputational risk). It should be recognized, also, that regional and/or organizational culture can have a strong bearing on the buying process; for example, in Scandinavian companies purchase authority tends to be situated lower than in UK companies, meaning that decisions may be less protracted.

The size and composition of the DMU, being the management team involved in the purchasing process, varies according to the size of the order and the strategic nature of the decision. Despite widespread use of web-based procurement, which offers standardization and automation, the number of people involved in purchase decision can still be significant, as illustrated in Table 3.2.

| Number of employees | Number of DMU members | Average contacts made by supplier sales force during purchase process |
|---|---|---|
| 0–200 | 3.40 | 1.72 |
| 201–400 | 4.85 | 1.75 |
| 401–1000 | 5.81 | 1.90 |
| 1000+ | 6.50 | 1.85 |

Table 3.2 Involvement in purchase process

In certain situations involving the first-time purchase of large-scale capital goods and services, as many as 40 people from across the company may become involved at different stages of the decision-making process. The structure of the DMU can also be examined in terms of the different functions that are represented. These *roles* can be placed broadly into seven categories: policymakers, purchasers, users, technologists, influences, gatekeepers and deciders. Figure 3.3 illustrates the complexity of organizational buying decisions.

## POLICYMAKERS

Policymakers are individuals within the company who have the authority and responsibility for drawing up general policies that directly affect purchasing behaviour. The central purchasing of strategic items across a number of

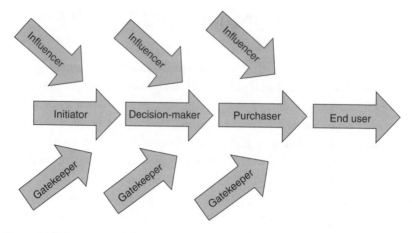

Figure 3.3 Roles in purchase process

business units, such as media buying in Unilever, is one example of a company policy. The outsourcing of IT is often directed by similar policy decisions.

## PURCHASERS

Purchasers are the actual buyers who are formally authorized to order products or services from suppliers. The purchaser's role can range from filling in purchase requisition forms to being the purchasing team leader responsible for making the final recommendation to senior management or the main board. Any assessment of the importance of the purchasing agent must consider the organization's attitude towards the purchase function, together with the level of risk associated with the purchase.

## USERS

Users are the people who ultimately use the product or service. It is likely that they will be concerned primarily with product performance and ease of use. If installation or application is technically demanding for the customer, then the provision of post-sales consultancy and support will become crucial, to the point of overriding commercial considerations such as price and delivery times.

## TECHNOLOGISTS

Technologists are the engineers or specialists, such as actuaries, and those with specialist knowledge who appraise the technical aspects of competitive offers and advise on key performance indicators (KPIs). It is the KPIs which enable the DMU to differentiate and judge suppliers against the company's own specifications – standards which the technologist is likely to have defined.

## INFLUENCERS

Influencers are the people who influence the DMP, either directly or indirectly, by providing information and criteria for the evaluation of alternative buying actions. Influencers can work inside the company or act as external advisers. For example, companies will quite often employ a systems integrator as a consultant in a major IT purchase to guide the DMU from the earliest stages of the purchasing process. Sometimes the DMU may visit a company that has made a similar purchase to discuss their experiences of using the product and the supplier against KPIs.

## GATEKEEPERS

Gatekeepers are people who control the flow of information to others within the company and the DMU. For example, buyers may have the authority to prevent salespeople from seeing users and deciders. Other gatekeepers include technical personnel and even personal secretaries.

## DECIDERS

Deciders are those with the authority to approve purchases. The decider is likely to be a senior manager where a complex purchase or company policy is involved. Otherwise, in more routine purchases, the buyer is usually the decider.

From a supplier's perspective, the composition of the DMU is critical, but it is not always constant and often subject to fluctuation. Garrido-Samaniego et al. (2010) find that the size and composition of the buying centre varies at the different stages of the procurement process and that the use of the Internet appears to have led to an increase in the number of functional areas that intervene in the buying centre. This can increase the complexity of the buying process as the individual priorities and interests of the constituent members will be represented as well as overall group dynamics. In other words, in meeting the collective concerns of the DMU, trade-offs may well have to be made during the purchasing process that could alter the perceptions of the key technical, problem-solving and relational benefits required from suppliers.

This need to deliver against key benefits is illustrated by an example, shown in Table 3.3, of the marketing of oil lubricants to a cement company. Even though the purchase is relatively straightforward, the DMU consists of six people, who display six distinct roles.

| DMU role | DMU job title | Benefits sought |
|---|---|---|
| Specifier/user | Engineer | No technical problems |
| User/influencer | Storeman | JIT deliveries, palleted barrels |
| Decider | Buyer | Lowest price |
| Gatekeeper | Finance Manager | System uses a purchase order number and pays according to usage |
| Influencer | Cement Sales Manager | Quid pro quo for new cement business |
| Gatekeeper | General Manager | An innovative supplier that contributes to a lean supply chain |

Table 3.3 Marketing oil lubricants to a cement company

# ORGANIZATIONAL AND PRODUCT INFLUENCES ON THE DMU

Various organizational 'demographics', such as a firm's size, purchasing policy or use of electronic data processing (EDP) and communications such as the intra- and extranet, can change the composition of the DMU and *how* and *what* it buys. Product factors that influence buyers' decisions include frequency of purchase, the strategic nature of the product or service being considered and loyalty to suppliers. Generally, there are three types of buying situations that have an impact on the way that the DMU is organized and how products and suppliers are selected: straight re-buy, modified re-buy and new-task purchase.

## STRAIGHT RE-BUY

The buyer reorders without requesting any product or service modifications. The buyer simply chooses a supplier from an approved list based on past buying satisfaction. Because it is a routine reordering situation, the supplier may propose an automatic reordering system both to save purchasing time and to reduce the risk of losing profitable, regular purchases.

## MODIFIED RE-BUY

Although the company has prior experience of the product, the particular purchase situation demands some degree of customization, such as changes in the product specification, price, terms or supplier. Approved suppliers, including those currently under contract to the customer, may use the purchasing opportunity to make a better offer to the customer in order to win new business.

## NEW-TASK PURCHASE

A company buying a product or service for the first time may have no experience of supplier capabilities or performance evaluation. Consequently, the greater the cost or risk, the larger the DMU and its informational requirements. The new-task situation represents the marketer's greatest opportunity and challenge: the aim is to reach as many key buying influencers as possible, and to provide help and information.

# THE DECISION-MAKING PROCESS (DMP)

Buyers who face a new-task buying situation are likely to adopt a formal decision-making process (DMP), which may involve up to eight separate stages. Purchases that are modified or are straight re-buys may skip some of these stages. Referring to Table 3.4, let us now look at the DMP for the typical new-task purchase.

Although the DMP is shown to be a linear sequence of progressive stages, in practice the stages are rarely neatly sequential or discrete. Sometimes the stages may occur out of sequence or simultaneously, or not at all if it is a fairly straightforward re-buy. Nonetheless, the DMP does provide a helpful guide to the distinguishing features of each of the typical buying stages.

Clearly, there is a relationship between the composition of the DMU and the DMP. Generally, as the *risk* associated with the organizational purchase *increases*:

- The DMU becomes more complex, with participants having more authority.
- DMP members will have greater levels of experience and heightened motivations.
- Suppliers with strong reputations and proven product solutions will be favoured.
- Information searches and sources, particularly personal and non-commercial communications, will be used increasingly to guide and support decisions.
- DMU role stress and conflict will increase, with bargaining negotiations taking place among members.
- Buyer–supplier relationships and communication networks become critical to fostering an atmosphere of co-operation and reducing perceived risk.

| Buying stage | Characteristics |
| --- | --- |
| Problem recognition | Changing business needs<br>Supplier review<br>Current product/service dissatisfaction |
| General need | Innovation<br>Cost savings<br>Improved performance |
| Specification | Buyer–supplier dialogue<br>Qualifying criteria<br>Differentiating criteria |
| Supplier search | Risk profile of purchase<br>Information gathering<br>Consideration set |
| Proposals submission | Qualification of suppliers<br>Set of alternatives<br>Proposal solicitation<br>Consideration set |
| Supplier selection | Proposals reviewed<br>Negotiation<br>Selection and ratification |
| Order specification | Blanket contract/order<br>Order fulfilment procedures<br>Relationship development |
| Performance review | Benchmark supplier performance<br>Evaluation performance<br>Endorse, modify or discontinue |

Table 3.4 Eight stages of the DMP

As business marketers become more involved with organizational buying procedures and customer practices in general, market segmentation can be improved, enabling the marketing mix to be tailored more specifically to the needs of distinctive customer groups. This requirement for customization is a characteristic of competitive, mature markets. The product life cycle, or PLC, contends that prices drop with customer familiarity and an unwillingness to pay for consultation services from suppliers. In addition, heightened competition results in the availability of equivalent products at similar or lower prices. Steadily, as the market becomes more of a commodity, customer differentiation is needed to target offers more effectively. In highly competitive markets, segmentation based on buyer behaviour characteristics can be used to help strengthen buyer–supplier relationships and reach the right levels of customization. Although we shall be dealing with market segmentation in more detail in Chapter 5, it is appropriate here to explore an organizational buyer behaviour approach.

# SEGMENTING BUSINESS CUSTOMERS IN MATURE MARKETS

Mature industrial markets have traditionally been assumed to be somewhat static and stable; however, recent research shows maturity to be a complex and diverse environment (Klepper, 1997; Malerba, 2006). Customers of varying sizes and ways of doing business may be entering or exiting the market, innovation may be high, alliances are being formed and merged, and there is a general interest in instigating distinct policies in outsourcing and managing supplier networks. In such an environment, the relationship between buyer and seller may represent a significant stabilizing force (Malerba, 2006).

Geiger and Finch (2011) reveal significant and often unacknowledged levels of uncertainty in mature markets, demanding a careful balance of relational and transactional selling strategies. There is evidence that business customers are motivated both by price and relationships. Cova and Salle (2008: 270) note that salespeople play a key role in the 'customer network value proposition', but besides good relationships (acting as a proxy for trust), price remains an important consideration. Pillai and Sharma (2003) argue that when the quality of supplier alternatives increases, as is often the case in mature markets, buyers may move away from a relational to a more transactional stance. This suggests that price should not be underestimated as a key decision criteria.

Against this background, it is useful to map customers along two dimensions: price and cost-to-serve, according to their purchasing characteristics (see Figure 3.4). Customers who demand a low price can be offered a 'no frills' product with minimal service, while those who value a customized offer will be prepared to pay a higher price for tailor-made adaptations. Price differentials founded on product quality differences alone tend to be small because competitors are able to offer more or less equivalent products.

In keeping with this rationale, suppliers operating in mature markets may expect their customers' buyer behaviours to follow the path of the *value line* in Figure 3.4. Zone C of this line represents the unbundled offer or core product, while zone B denotes a customized offer based on a range of value-added services. In both cases, the value-for-money of the offer is equitable to the buyer and the seller.

From the buyer's perspective, an alternative strategy exists which is linked to the *market power line* in Figure 3.4. Customers see only the price dimension of the matrix, because they are price-driven and do not know or consider the supplier's cost-to-serve. Customers are likely to shop around for the best price,

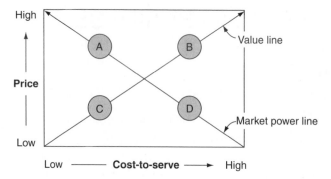

Figure 3.4 Price/cost to service matrix
*Source:* Adapted from Ranga et al (1992).

given that products themselves are largely undifferentiated, and to offer the bait of guaranteed purchase volume and large order sizes in order to drive prices down even further. Scrutinizing customers such as these choose to operate in zones D or C, depending on their knowledge of competitive offerings and their own market power.

In terms of supplier performance, operating in zone A implies that the supplier retains market power. This may be because of their having a truly superior product offering which competitors are unable to match for reasons of technological excellence or patent protection. In such circumstances, the supplier is able to support a high price. Remember, customers in zones A and B seek value through the superiority of the products or services that the supplier provides.

All locations *above the value line* indicate that the supplier meets the value requirements of the customer segments it serves and generates superior profits. In the areas *below the value line*, customer segments will be less profitable for the supplier, and possibly loss making.

The matrix serves to illustrate the possibilities of unearthing profitable customer segments using diagnostics closely associated with their patterns of buyer behaviour. Equally, as unprofitable customer segments are exposed, marketing and sales management will need to develop their marketing strategies, mindful of the costs of serving such price-conscious customers. Marketing planning may well involve the rationalization of customers who display blatant switching behaviours and who regard supplier relationships as purely transactional.

With increased turbulence in the marketplace, it is clear that firms are generally moving away from transaction-orientated marketing strategies and towards relationship-orientated marketing as a means of enhancing commercial performance and customer value. There is mounting evidence that competitive advantage will result increasingly from the types, and strength, of relationships that firms develop with other players in their value network.

# STRATEGIC ALLIANCES

Strategic alliances, or collaborative arrangements between firms, have become increasingly popular as a means of achieving strategic goals. They range from informal, collaborative arrangements to formalized joint ventures, or one partner taking an equity stake in the other. By sharing resources and capabilities, alliances enable economies of scale and effort and provide access to more highly developed resources and capabilities than a firm could achieve on its own. Strategic alliances come in many forms, for example, with suppliers, competitors, distributors or retailers. Close, collaborative relationships can help to build competitive advantage in a number of ways:

1. *Product/market development* – Organizations can work together to develop new products for new markets. For example, the Freemove alliance brought together four mobile telecommunications companies, Orange, Telecom Italia, Deutsche Telecom and TeliaSonera to develop a wireless mobile network across Europe. This was achieved at a significantly lower cost than the rival network created by Vodafone in significantly less time.

2. *Greater buying/bargaining power* – The B2B giant hub, Covisint, launched in 2000 as a strategic alliance in the automotive industry between General Motors, Ford and DaimlerChrysler. The object was to enhance buying power, enabling the 'big three' to drive a hard bargain with the multitude of suppliers serving the industry. By establishing a collaborative electronic portal, Covisint basically forced supplier to adopt EDI, squeezing out small suppliers and augmenting the alliances' bargaining and buying power.

3. *Increased effectiveness through innovation* – As supplier relationships solidify, the customer may ask key suppliers to invest in technology that will allow the supplier access to the collaborative platform. Suppliers are naturally more willing to innovate by investing in such assets and services when they enjoy a strong relationship with the customer. In the Covisint case, lack of trust, limited participation at the inception stage and perceived weakening of their relative position resulted in suppliers launching their own portal, SupplyOne to counterbalance the growing power of the automotive manufacturers.

4. *Systems cost reduction* – Closer relationships achieved through multiple linkages between preferred suppliers and organizations enable performance improvements, such as JIT deliveries, reduced inventories and shorter order cycle times. As trust increases and sales volatility decreases, the resulting cost savings can be shared by all parties.

5. *Enabling technologies* – Web-enabled collaborative platforms enable cost-effective procurement, delivery, payment, communication, collaborative

working and relationship building. The ability to track activities electronically has proved to be a major advantage. Enabling technologies can bring suppliers close to their key customers and are proven to drive down costs. From the suppliers' perspective web-enabled EDI allows them to better determine which customers are cost effective to serve (see Figure 3.4), while from the buyers' perspective, suppliers can be organized into tiers (tier 1 being preferred), and tendering/procurement/payment rendered both more transparent and cost effective.

## CASE STUDY 3.1  EXOSTAR

Exostar is an example of numerous strategic alliances across the aerospace and defence industries. Established in 2000 as an industry-owned online exchange to support the complex trading needs of the aerospace industry, it brings together all the major industry players. Exostar offers industry standard process flows for various transactional processes including purchase order, change order, forecasting and scheduling, commitment, advance ship notification, goods receipt. According to Exostar, 'organizations can achieve the necessary level of process integration to eliminate potential shortages, reduce obsolete inventory, track deliveries, proactively evaluate exceptions and automatically trigger replenishment cycles'. Key benefits accrue to both buyers and sellers in the areas of sourcing, procurement and supply chain visibility. Offering a wide network of buyers and sellers, working transparently and collaboratively, Exostar has grown rapidly to become *the* leading hub for the aerospace and defence industries. The strategic alliances that established and maintain the Exostar exchange have resulted in greater transparency, closer B2B relations and lower processing and collaboration costs.

### CASE STUDY QUESTIONS:

1. What are the key advantages of an industry-owned, aggregated trading hub?
2. Could the benefits outlined in the case study be attained without Exostar?
3. How do you think Exostar might develop further in future?

# OTHER KEY TRENDS

## QUALIFIERS AND DIFFERENTIATORS

The product- and service-related aspects of the supplier's offer have become hygiene factors, as they no longer serve to differentiate. Differentiation now flows from the problem-solving and relational capabilities suppliers are able to demonstrate over a period of time. Increasing levels of customization mean more cooperation and collaboration.

## CUSTOMER VALUE, NOT RISK REDUCTION

As customers have grown more sophisticated in their purchasing processes, they have become less averse to risk. Unfettered by the need to manage downside risk, suppliers have come to be seen as a resource to enhance the end-customer's perceptions of value. In some markets, such as laptop computers and PCs, this has led to the co-branding of products and related services.

## CONFLICT, WHAT CONFLICT?

The shift to flat structures and team-based working in organizations is altering perceptions of the buyer's role. The function of the DMU in purchasing decision is changing also; conflict, role stress and trade-offs among DMU members become less evident as collaborative solutions replace traditional divides. The buyer's role is changing from conflict management to the facilitation of a cross-functional team (see Figure 3.5).

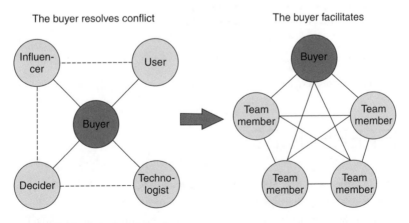

Figure 3.5 The buyer's changing role

# SUMMARY

With ever more rapid, radical changes to the business environment, it has become imperative that business marketers understand their customers' needs fully. Knowing how people buy makes it easier to sell to them, and possibly to anticipate future market demands. In mature markets customers are looking for positive added value from their suppliers in order to be able to discriminate between alternative products and services.

The move towards collaborative platforms, lean supply models and increasing customization is heralding an era of co-operation between buyers, suppliers, competitors and other stakeholders. Whether the supplier is tendering for a new-task purchase or a modified re-buy, knowledge of the DMU and DMP will be critical in influencing the purchase outcome successfully. This trend towards customization requires a higher level of customer selectivity and skills in market segmentation practices among suppliers. A buyer behaviour approach to market segmentation can help suppliers to choose between customers as both parties seek to develop profitable long-term relationships.

Looking to the future, as buying organizations move towards flat structures and team-based ways of working among DMU members, the nature of the DMP will simplify. There will be fewer suppliers considered at the search stage and more emphasis placed on the selection stage so that suppliers can demonstrate their capabilities in problem-solving and building relationships with the DMU.

For an in-depth discussion of managing key supplier–buyer relationships, see Chapter 14.

# FURTHER READING

Biemans, W. G. (2010) *Business to Business Marketing*, Maidenhead: McGraw-Hill.

A useful introductory text, including a number of recent mini-cases and insights.

# REFERENCES

Banytė, J., Vitkauskaitė, E. & Milašius, L. (2008) Impact of ICT on the Buying Behaviour of Lithuanian Construction Companies, *Economics and Management*, Vol. 13: 239–246.

Cova, B. & Salle, R. (2008) Marketing Solutions in Accordance with the S-D Logic: Co-Creating Value with Customer Network Actors, *Industrial Marketing Management*, Vol. 37 (3): 270–277.

Garrido-Samaniego, J., Gutiérrez-Arranz, M. & San José-Cabezudo, R. (2010) Assessing the Impact of e-Procurement on the Structure of the Buying Centre, *International Journal of Information Management*, Vol. 30 (2): 135–143.

Geiger and Finch (2011) Buyer-Seller Interactions in Mature Industrial Markets, *Journal of Personal Selling and Sales Management*, Vol. 31 (3): 255–268.

Hunter, L. M., Kasouf, C. J., Celush, K. G. & Curry, K. A. (2004) A Classification of Business to Business Buying Decisions: Risk Importance and Probability as a Framework for E-Business Benefits, *Industrial Marketing Management*, Vol. 33: 145–154.

Klepper, S. (1997) Industry Life Cycles, *Industrial and Corporate Change*, Vol. 6 (1): 145–182.

Malerba, F. (2006) Innovation and the Evolution of Industries, *Journal of Evolutionary Economics*, Vol. 16 (1): 3–23.

Pillai, K. G. & Sharma, A. (2003) Mature Relationships: Why Does Relational Orientation Turn into Transactional Orientation? *Industrial Marketing Management*, Vol. 32 (8): 643–651.

Ranga, V. K., Mariarty, R. T. and Swartz, G. S. (1992) Segmenting Customers in Mature Industrial Markets, *Journal of Marketing*, Vol. 56 (4) 72–82.

# CHAPTER 4
# MARKETING RESEARCH

IN THIS CHAPTER WE STUDY:

- what marketing research is
- the marketing research process
- the marketing information system
- types of marketing research
- the need for a cost–benefit appraisal of marketing research
- the contents of a marketing research brief

# WHAT IS MARKETING RESEARCH?

Marketing research is often conceptualized as a stand-alone activity that supports the marketing process. In fact, one might contend that research is absolutely crucial to successful marketing. It is the process that provides data, intelligence and insights, and without accurate, reliable and valid information, marketing cannot be successful.

While most managers never have to carry out market survey work themselves, they do need to know how the marketing research process functions in order to exploit its value fully. In particular, organizations adopting a multiple markets approach need to understand how the research process can assist in building long-term and profitable relationships in principal markets.

The output of the marketing research process should be twofold: first, an analysis that identifies key customer groups; and second, an understanding of what constitutes customer value among each of these groups, and how that value can be created, delivered and leveraged in a way that is perceived to be superior to competitive offerings. It is especially important that appropriate research methods are used in order that the data generated are relevant to the strategic decisions that are to be made.

So, what is marketing research? It is the systematic gathering, recording and analysis of data related to the marketing of goods and services, used to identify opportunities and obstacles, generate marketing actions and monitor marketing performance. As such, it is crucial to understanding the processes of relationship marketing and customer relationship management. It:

- Directs and supports decision-making;
- Reduces uncertainty and risk;
- Ensures that the business is able to identify changes in the marketing environment and plan to respond accordingly;
- Creates competitive advantage by mapping and improving understanding of competitors and enhancing marketing planning.

Before turning to types of marketing research, let us place marketing research more firmly in the marketing context.

# THE MARKETING ENVIRONMENT

We have defined marketing as the concept and process of matching the abilities of the supplying organization with the needs of the customer to the mutual benefit of both parties. The limitations that militate against this matching process working well are likely to be weaknesses within the company and external factors. However, on the positive side, companies also possess strengths, and the business environment is rarely completely hostile. As one commercial opportunity dies, another will appear. The successful company plays on its strengths and works to reduce its weaknesses. At the same time, it identifies and concentrates on the available opportunities, while consciously negotiating a way through the threats.

There are likely to be several important factors that can affect the extent to which it is possible for an organization to balance its resources and efforts with customer needs. The milieu in which the organization is operating is a critical factor. Known as the *marketing environment*, it consists of the following components:

- Customers;
- Competitors;
- Social and cultural trends;
- Political, fiscal, economic and legal policies;
- Technology; and
- Institutional patterns.

The two most obvious components of the marketing environment – customers and competitors – are examined in much more depth in Chapters 2, 3 and 6 of this book. The ability to know who our actual and potential customers are, and to understand in what ways different groups of customers have different needs is obviously central to any organization's success. Equally, since what competitors do will always affect a business, it is necessary to find ways of monitoring their activities and of building that information into decision-making.

A prime management concern in marketing is the *conversion of uncertainty into risk*. Uncertainty implies an inability to state the likelihood of any possible outcome occurring. By implication, all outcomes must be treated as being equally likely. Under *uncertainty* the manager must consider, say, the chance of failure in a new product launch to equal the chance of success. *Risk*, on the other hand, suggests that the likelihood of outcomes might be assessed more precisely. The marketing manager might feel that a particular new service launch has only five per cent chance of failure. Our ability to make successful decisions is enhanced if we are operating under conditions of known risk rather than uncertainty. If this conversion of uncertainty into risk is the prime marketing management task, the second is surely the reduction, or at least the minimization, of that risk.

To achieve either of these goals, the manager requires information. Good information is a facilitator of successful marketing action. Seen in this way, marketing management becomes essentially an information-processing activity.

Marketing research is therefore concerned with much more than simply telling us something about the marketplace. Rather, it is a systematic and objective search for, and an analysis of, information relevant to the identification and solution of marketing problems. Clearly, currency is crucial; like all other facets of marketing, research and intelligence-gathering need to keep apace with technological developments. Writing in *Marketing News* in 2005, Schultz contends that the marketing research remains rooted in refuted behaviourist concepts and over-simplistic stimulus-response models. Contending that today's consumers are too smart, busy, blasé or uncooperative for traditional research methodologies, Schulz advocated new approaches, including the embrace of new technologies. Technology has advanced apace in recent years, facilitating access to research populations, sampling methodologies, consumer trend monitoring, data collection and storage. At the heart of technology-enabled marketing research is the marketing information system (MIS), which we introduce in the following section and explore in greater detail in Chapter 21.

# MARKETING INFORMATION SYSTEM

The data gathered in marketing research need to be sorted and stored systematically. This is done in the Marketing Information System (MIS). Nowadays, this is most commonly an electronic database containing formally structured records of marketing research data used either only internally by employees of one organization or, in horizontal alliances, by collaborating partners. Typically, the MIS will contain data associated with other marketing processes, for example, customer support, product/brand management, advertising, sales and transactions.

As with all technology, the MIS is never (or, more accurately, *should never be*) and end in itself. Its usefulness depends upon the data adhering to a number of critical factors:

- Data currency (when and where collected)
- Relevance (capturing the right data)
- Reliability (consistency)
- Validity (measuring what it claims to measure)

As such, there should be procedures to determine what data to be captured, when and how to capture it and for what purpose(s) the data should be used. Additionally, it is important to note that *data* are *not* information; modern information systems (IS) make it relatively simple to store large amounts of data in an easily accessible form, however data are converted into information through the critical processes of analysis and interpretation. It is necessary to view marketing information as an invaluable resource. Currency, accuracy and validity are key, meaning that managers must be concerned with the problems of producing, storing, accessing and distributing it. Information must also be available at a sufficiently detailed level to be of direct use at the micro-level, and it must be kept up to date. Marketing information has a limited shelf life – it is perishable. Like other resources, information has a value in use. The less the manager knows about a marketing problem, the greater the risk attached to a wrong decision, the more valuable the information becomes.

The success of marketing research is dependent, therefore, upon ensuring that objectives are unambiguous, the research problem is framed clearly, data collection methods are fit for purpose, data are kept current and stored, sorted and applied purposively, and analysis and interpretation are undertaken competently and intelligently. The type of marketing research utilized must be relevant to the context, product or service being investigated.

# TYPES OF MARKETING RESEARCH

Marketing research can be *ad hoc* or ongoing. *Ad hoc* marketing research refers to situations where the identification of a research problem leads to a specific information requirement. So, when a French manufacturer of proprietary pharmaceuticals found that sales of its long-established cough remedy were failing, it decided to conduct a study of consumer attitudes and beliefs about cough remedies, and used the information gained to relaunch the brand.

*Ongoing* marketing research, as the name implies, provides more of a monitoring function, resulting in a flow of information about the marketplace and the company's performance in it. The importance of this is recognized by the Confederation of British Industry (CBI), which maintains a regular monitor, based on surveys, of business confidence and investment intentions in the United Kingdom.

There are many forms of marketing research to consider, which break down into four basic types:

- Internal – analysis of sales records, advertising levels, price versus volume and so on.
- External – use of sources outside the organization to complement internal research.
- Reactive – structured interviews and focus groups, and experiments.

- Non-reactive – interpretation of observed phenomena, for example, filming customers in-store, customer panels, retail audit, desk research.

As there are pros and cons for each type, a mix can be useful. For example, sales records can provide valuable insights, but are not good predictors of future performance as they are restricted to historic performance. Telephone interviews are quick and relatively inexpensive, but limited in the amount of technical information that can be obtained. Figure 4.1 provides a summary and useful framework for discussing the types of marketing research activity that are encountered most frequently.

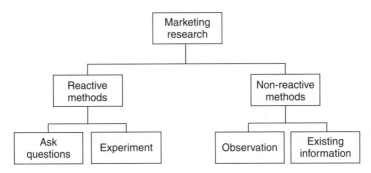

Figure 4.1 A framework for marketing research

## INTERNAL MARKETING RESEARCH

This is based on an analysis of company data gained from information such as sales trends, changes in the elements of marketing – price, for example – and advertising levels. Advances in database management (see Chapter 21) have greatly enhanced the speed and accuracy with which complex data analyses can be produced, enabling marketers to develop strategies that are more timely and customer specific.

## EXTERNAL MARKETING RESEARCH

This is conducted within the market and the wider competitive environment in which the company operates. Compared to internal marketing research, it generally accounts for the majority of total market research expenditure. External information gathering should always be seen as a complement to internal information and not as an alternative.

## REACTIVE MARKETING RESEARCH

As the term implies, this is information about the marketplace and the customers who inhabit it. It can involve the asking of questions, such as in a survey or during an interview, or it can involve experiments. Figure 4.2 summarizes the main forms of reactive marketing research.

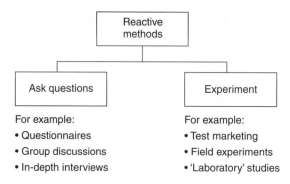

Figure 4.2 Forms of reactive marketing research

## QUESTIONNAIRES

Questionnaires are the favoured means of data gathering. They are a flexible instrument and can be administered by an interviewer or by the interviewees themselves. As we know only too well from the experience of being stopped in the street, approached via the fax or telephone, faced with postal surveys or confronted with questionnaires when visiting websites/using the Internet, this process can take place in various situations. However, before embarking on this method of marketing research, it is useful to be aware of the pitfalls that can result from the use of a questionnaire that has not been preplanned and checked carefully.

Loaded questions can have a distorting effect, as can ambiguous phrases. Even the order of the questions may upset the final result. The errors in the final population estimates from a questionnaire administered to a sample are called *bias* or *systematic error* of the estimates. In other words, the true characteristics of the population – for example, relative preferences between several types of industrial compressor – may be different from the estimate produced by the sample survey. This bias may result from the way in which the sample was chosen or from the means by which the survey data were collected.

Such pitfalls can be reduced by designing the questionnaire carefully and then *pilot testing* it. In other words, give the survey a trial run on a subgroup of the intended sample to isolate any problems, ambiguities or omissions that may arise in responses.

## GROUP DISCUSSIONS

Group discussions may be a more appropriate way to gather market information, as they attempt to draw insights for marketing action from smaller-scale, more detailed studies. Such studies are intended to provide qualitative cues, rather than quantitative conclusions.

In such circumstances a group discussion is a loosely structured format where the leader – often a trained psychologist – attempts to draw from the group their feelings about the subject under discussion. The group is chosen to be representative of the population in which the researcher is interested, although, naturally, any conclusions emerging from the discussions can only form the basis of qualitative generalizations about that population. Such interviews need not be conducted in groups. They can be equally effective in pairs or alone with the interviewer.

## SINGLE INTERVIEWS

Single interviews are an alternative way of deriving information. Sometimes they are extended or in-depth interviews, and have the advantage that both the interviewer and interviewee can explore certain lines of discussion more rigorously if this is perceived to be of mutual benefit, whereas a group discussion must always maintain a degree of structure if it is to be meaningful. Such a form of single in-depth interview will be used more often when information regarding specialized markets is required in industrial marketing research.

## EXPERIMENTS

Experiments are another type of reactive marketing research. Earlier in this book we assessed the benefits of test-marketing new products. Marketing experiments can also help us to gain a better understanding of how marketing processes work.

For example, a manufacturer of confectionery wanted to know if the effect on sales of a sales promotion was greater than spending a similar sum on in-store merchandizing improvements. The information needed to answer the question could only be obtained from the experiment, whereby a number of stores were selected in different areas of the country and used as the testing ground for these alternative promotional approaches. The stores chosen for the experiment were as alike as possible in terms of turnover on the brand in question and served similar types of customers.

One-third of the stores ran the 'money-off' promotion, one-third used the improved in-store merchandizing, and the remaining third carried on selling the product without any changes. After a period of two months, the manufacturer felt able to draw conclusions about the relative effectiveness of the two promotional methods by comparing store results with those stores where no changes were made.

Market experimentation need not necessarily involve the setting up of large-scale experimental designs such as the one just discussed. Sometimes, laboratory-type situations can be used to test marketing stimuli. Often, advertisements will be pre-tested in such laboratory conditions. Samples of the target audience for an advertisement will be exposed to the advertisement and their reactions to the sample sought. Eye cameras, polygraphs and tachistoscopes are just some of the devices that have been used successfully to record physical reactions to marketing stimuli.

While the theory of experimentation in the marketing context is sound enough, there are a number of drawbacks to its operation in practice. It is very often difficult to set up experimental situations that are microcosms of the total market. There is always the problem of controlling all the variables in the experiment – such as, for example, the actions of competitors – and, of course, the cost of setting up and maintaining market experiments can be prohibitive.

## NON-REACTIVE MARKETING RESEARCH

These methods are based on interpretation of *observed phenomena* or extant data. By definition, they do not rely upon data derived directly from respondents. Figure 4.3 summarizes the main forms of non-reactive marketing research.

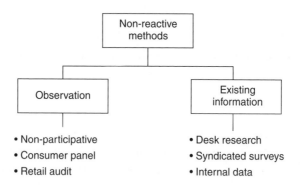

Figure 4.3 Forms of non-reactive marketing research

## DESK RESEARCH

Desk research should, in fact, be the starting point of any marketing research programme. Desk research involves the use of existing information to determine the extent of prior knowledge about the subject being studied. There is often a wealth of material to be obtained from published and unpublished sources, which can reduce the need to 'reinvent the wheel'. Official statistics, such as those published by governments, the OECD, the European Union (EU) and the UN, can provide detailed data on markets and patterns within those markets. Other sources, such as newspapers, technical journals, trade association publications and published market studies will provide a 'fill-in' to any later fieldwork that might be needed. Internal data derived from sales figures and sales reports can also be a guide to the direction that later studies might need to take.

## OBSERVATION

Observation can be a very effective marketing research technique. How people behave in the real world and how they react to stimuli can often be discovered best of all through watching and interpreting their reactions. Some observational methods, such as a camera in a supermarket, do not involve the direct participation of the researcher, and this can be a limiting factor. Often, the areas of activity in which we are most interested may only occur infrequently and the observation must be sustained over a period in order to capture a single activity.

## PARTICIPANT OBSERVATION

Participant observation, a phrase borrowed from anthropology, involves the observer attempting to become a part of the activity that is under observation. This form of marketing research is very limited in its scope, although one British research organization, Mass Observation, did some early pioneering work in this area in a number of studies, a famous example being a major study of consumer behaviour in public houses.

## RETAIL AUDIT

Retail audit is used widely as a secondary source of observation data. This has been developed and perfected as a technique over a period of time and, properly controlled, it can be a very accurate source of marketing information on brand shares, market size, distribution coverage and sales trends. The audits conducted by A. C. Nielsen Ltd are perhaps the most widely known, and work on a simple basis. Within a particular product field, a representative sample of stockists is chosen and their co-operation obtained. The investigator visits the stockists at regular intervals and notes two things: the current levels of stock of the product group being audited and the invoices or delivery notes for any goods in that group delivered since the previous visit. With the information on stock levels obtained on the *last* visit, it is a simple matter to determine the sales of each item being audited during the period between visits – that is, opening stock + deliveries between visits − closing stock = sales.

## THE CONSUMER PANEL

The consumer panel is another similar source of data. This is a sample group of consumers in a particular product field who record their purchases and consumption behaviour over a period of time. This technique has been used in industrial as well as consumer markets and can provide continuous data on patterns of usage as well as other data such as media habits. In recent years, online consumer panels have become popular, offering advantages in terms of time, accessibility, trackability and cost. With careful segmentation and targeting, data generated by such panels can offer valuable insights on consumer perceptions, attitudes and behaviours. Care must be taken to avoid the major pitfalls of online panels, namely attrition bias, panel selection bias and conditioning effects. Dynamic panels (in which new panel members are recruited on a regular basis) can reduce bias and conditioning effects.

## CASE STUDY 4.1 JOHN LEWIS CONSUMER INSIGHTS

The John Lewis partnership relies heavily upon its consumer insights research to understand and respond to consumer needs, wants and preferences, making it one of the most successful retailers in the United Kingdom. On its website the company states, 'Getting feedback can help to inform the business on a wide range of issues and can play a vital role in providing answers: if a particular area of the business is doing well and we want to understand the reasons so we can grow further; if there is a problem but the cause is uncertain; or if a number of options are on the table and we need to narrow them down.'

For John Lewis it is important to maintain an ongoing dialogue with their customers through research. The company employs formal methods of research and feedback, such as customer surveys, panels, focus groups, online feedback forms and regular mystery shopping. It also holds exit surveys at its stores. Longitudinal tracking surveys are used to monitor changes in customer perceptions to advertising, products, ranges, stores and customer service. Finally, one-off studies are used to investigate customer views on specific issues.

John Lewis prides itself on listening carefully to its customers. In response to customer feedback it developed online shopping, Waitrose Entertaining, and Quick Check, its scan-as-you shop service.

Source: www.johnlewispartnership.co.uk, 2013

# PRIMARY AND SECONDARY RESEARCH

It is also important to understand the difference between *primary* and *secondary* research. Collecting information directly from individual respondents for a specific purpose is known as primary research. Primary research may be either quantitative, investigating who, what or how many, or qualitative, investigating why, or a combination of both.

In contrast, secondary, or desk, research involves scanning available information sources to see what has already been published. Because secondary data are often out of date, insufficiently detailed or not analysed from a perspective relevant to specific research question being investigated, it should never be used in isolation.

# INTEGRATING MARKETING RESEARCH WITH MARKETING ACTION

It is important to undertake a cost–benefit appraisal of all sources of marketing information. There is no point in investing more in such information than the return on it would justify. Naturally, it is easier to determine the costs than benefits, particularly as the benefits can be difficult to pinpoint. They can be expressed in terms of additional sales or profits that might be achieved through the avoidance of marketing failures which could otherwise result if there is a lack of information. As Case study 4.2 demonstrates, a cost–benefit approach can be a valuable means of quantifying the value of marketing research in a managerial context.

## CASE STUDY 4.2 A COST–BENEFIT APPRAISAL OF USING MARKETING RESEARCH

A German company planned to launch a new product to the market. Estimated product development and marketing costs totaled two million Euros and risk of failure was calculated as 20 per cent. From this it was inferred that the maximum *loss expectation* was 400 000 Euros (that is, 20 per cent of two million). On balance, it was concluded that it would be worth paying up to this sum to acquire information that would help the company avoid such a loss.

Such a cost–benefit calculation implies that the information acquired would be totally reliable. But, because such *perfect information* is rare, and in this case could not be obtained, 100 000 Euros was budgeted for marketing research, which effectively discounted the probable inaccuracy of the information.

The use of marketing research by European companies has grown considerably over recent decades. Not confined to manufacturers selling into consumer markets, some of the most interesting work conducted in recent years has been on behalf of industrial marketing organizations, service companies such as banks and social organizations such as voluntary and government agencies. With this growth of marketing research has come increasing sophistication in the use of the techniques available to the researcher, now a professional whose advice is looked for increasingly in marketing decision-making. Similarly, the growth of companies that provide specialist marketing research services has multiplied, so it is now a major industry in its own right. This means that managers have the facility to monitor the effectiveness of marketing performance and to gain a better feel for what opportunities exist in the marketplace.

As Hardey (2011) observes, in recent years attention has turned to replicating established market research analytics into the ever-emerging facets of social media. Marketing, consumer behaviour and research converge to occupy an information-led and transparent world in which products, services and organizations are made visible as they are rated, tagged and followed. Bertrand (2013) contends that there is no better place than social media conversations for brands to research what drives consumers' recommendations and what ultimately builds trust. The challenge is to embrace this new, very public social media for marketing research purposes in such a way that methodological robustness, validity and reliability are protected. Regardless of which technologies and methodologies are used, anyone commissioning marketing research should ensure that a number of key principles are followed, as outlined in the next section.

### Preparing the marketing research brief

*Do we need a research brief?*

Regardless of who carries out the work, it is important that a clear brief should be produced against which the subsequent work will be undertaken and judged. The research brief – which should be produced in both written and verbal forms – is a key document and the starting point. In its preparation, the following two questions are important:

- What do we want to know? and

- What will we do with the information when we get it?

In this way, clearly defined objectives will be set and adhered to.


## WHAT SHOULD IT CONTAIN?

First, the commissioning company should think very carefully about what and how much it wishes to disclose in the brief. Ideally, the brief should be open, precise and factual – but there may be particular points that are best omitted; for example, the precise budget.

A good briefing document, preferably accompanied by product/service literature, may cover between one and five pages. Its elaboration/discussion at a briefing meeting should clarify points, confirm contents and remove any written ambiguities. At the end of the meeting, if a quotation is to be submitted, the consultant/agency should both see and show a firm commitment to the project.

A good research brief should contain the following:

- Background information on the market, the company, its products/services, market standing and so on.

- Research objectives – perhaps both primary and secondary. In this section it may be useful to define precise question areas to be covered by the research.

- Desired time scale – overall project completion date, together with any interim report times or key decision dates (for example, product development stages or interfaces with other departments).

- Report format/presentation requirements (if desired). This is a good opportunity, if the commissioning company wishes, to indicate preferences.

- Company liaison/contact; information to be made available in support of the research.
- Marketplace confidentiality or openness required from the research.

It is not suggested that the briefing document be seen as a 'straightjacket', but rather as a series of well-thought-out guidelines. As such, the expertise of the agency/consultancy should be sought in the briefing meeting, both with regard to the information and requirements of the brief, as well as in discussion of the best methods of achieving the brief's objectives.

## WHAT ELSE MIGHT WE DO?

While it is not necessary for the brief to define everything in detail – for example, research methodology or precise budget allocation – it could be helpful if some verbal discussion on these points were to take place during the briefing meeting. Given the expected expertise of the agency/consultancy, it is a very fair approach to provide a comprehensive briefing and ask for a written proposal offering the best solutions, including recommended methodologies, expected time frames and cost involved.

While guidelines as to the probable research budget are very helpful, indications of precise budget allocations frequently tend to be met by proposal documents/terms of reference just under or exactly equal to the figures given!

Some commissioning organizations set a proposal deadline or tender submission date. At the briefing stage, it may be best to indicate the competitive quoting levels involved, without necessarily defining or naming these precisely.

This stage should be seen as a further opportunity to confirm importance and commitment. Remember, the client retains the prerogative to reject all proposals, or require modifications to them. Normally, the costs involved in the briefing meeting and preparation of the research proposal are seen by the consultants/agencies as part of their prospecting/business development costs and involve no client charges (whether the proposal is accepted or not), unless specifically previously agreed.

# PREPARING THE RESEARCH PROPOSAL

## WHAT IS THE RESEARCH PROPOSAL?

Basically, the research proposal – a written document and personal presentation – is a best response to the marketing research brief. As such, it represents an ability to communicate, and this should be a selection factor – remember that the organization subsequently commissioned to carry out the research is providing an indication or preview of its listening, communication and presentation skills. This assessment opportunity for the client should not be overlooked!

The research proposal should provide a specification of what the research organization will do, how it will carry out the work and what it will cost. It is important that it conveys its understanding of what is expected and its competence to provide the work most efficiently. This understanding and competence should be in both written and verbal forms if presented personally.

## WHAT SHOULD IT CONTAIN?

A good research proposal should include:

- *Background information*: to convey a clear understanding of the project and the issues involved.
- *Objectives*: these should be clearly listed and defined very precisely against the needs of the problem.
- *Work programme and methodology*: these should cover how the objectives will be achieved and the way the work programme will be completed; they should detail sample size, research stages and questionnaire methods.
- *Fees/payment terms and time scales*: these should be clearly stated and broken down to show expenses and the work schedule.
- *Company details and research personnel involved*: to include research company competence and brief biographies of personnel, plus, if relevant, any business terms.
- *Summary of research project benefits* and the agency's confidence in its competence to 'deliver' what is required.

## HOW SHOULD THE SPONSORING ORGANIZATION RESPOND?

Acceptance of the proposal should be in writing. It should authorize the work and confirm the points of agreement and costs involved. This should provide a binding agreement as to what is to be done and at what cost, thus, it is hoped, eliminating any subsequent disagreement between the two parties.

# SUMMARY

From this brief summary of research principles and methods it can be seen that the scope of marketing research can be considerable. Yet, at the same time, we must recognize that even the most carefully designed and conducted studies can at best only provide *imperfect information* of market phenomena.

That stated, marketing research remains the link between the identification of market opportunities and their successful exploitation by organizations, whatever their specialism or function. It is the principal means of monitoring the environment in which the matching process takes place.

The gathering of data is only the first step in marketing research. Data must be given direction before they can become relevant information, and information is only relevant if the company has some purpose in mind and some marketing problem to solve. Information allied to purpose becomes *intelligence*: information that is consumable and usable by management in converting uncertainty into measurable risk. Conversion of uncertainty into risk, and the minimization of risk, is perhaps marketing management's most important task – and marketing research is vital in this process.

Whatever research method(s) is/are adopted, the research should be carried out with accuracy, thoroughness and professionalism. High research standards will ensure that the findings are valuable and usable. It is important to remember that the aim of marketing research is to help direct business strategy, which seeks to build and improve relationships with customers by leveraging product and service quality to have maximum impact on consumer satisfaction levels.

# FURTHER READING

Malhotra, N., Birks, D. and Wills, P. (2012) *Marketing Research: An Applied Approach*, Harlow: Pearson.

A comprehensive, user-friendly textbook providing sound guidance on marketing research strategies, methods and tactics.

Bertrand, G. (2013) Social media research: developing a trust metric in the social age, *International Journal of Marketing Research*, Vol. 55 (3): 333–335.

Hardey, M. (2011) To spin straw into gold? New lessons from consumer-generated content, *International Journal of Market Research*, Vol. 53 (1): 13–15.

Schultz, D. (2005) MR deserves blame for marketing's decline, *Marketing News*, Vol. 39 (3): 7.

# CHAPTER 5
# MARKET SEGMENTATION

IN THIS CHAPTER WE STUDY:

- market definition
- what causes markets to segment
- the difference between customers and consumers
- the meaning of market share
- the market segmentation process

# INTRODUCTION

Segmentation is crucial to successful marketing, yet commonly misunderstood. The objectives of segmentation are as follows:

1. To help determine marketing direction through the analysis and understanding of trends and buyer behaviour.

2. To aid the process of setting realistic and obtainable marketing and sales objectives.

3. To improve decision-making by forcing managers to consider in depth the options ahead.

Many companies pride themselves on their market segmentation even though these so-called segments are in fact *sectors*. Everyone with a marketing qualification knows that a segment is a group of customers with the same or similar needs and that there are many different purchase combinations within and across sectors. However, a common mistake is *a priori* segmentation. Most books state that there are several bases for segmentation, such as socio-economics, demographics, geo-demographics and the like. But this misses the point totally. For example, Robbie Williams and the Archbishop of Canterbury are both As, but they don't behave the same! Nor do all 18–24-year-old women (demographics); or everyone that lives in your street (geo-demographics).

Successful segmentation begins with consideration of *the market*. As already stated, all goods and services are made, distributed and used and the purchase combinations that result make up an *actual* market, so the task is to understand market structure, how the market works and what these different purchase combinations (segments) are. All schemes such as socio-economics, demographics, geo-demographics and psychographics are clearly very useful at a very high level of marketing. For example, young married couples represent a large group who need furniture, kitchens, carpets and so on, but within this substantial group there will clearly be several different need sets. This is what we mean by *segments*.

# WHAT CAUSES MARKETS TO SEGMENT?

In Western Europe and other advanced economies, most consumers have television, washing machines, cars and the like, so if Ford, for example, wants to grow sales, they can no longer rely on the kind of market growth enjoyed since the Second World War. Today they have to take sales from a competitor, which means paying very close attention to consumer needs. This is where market segmentation comes into its own, as will be explained later.

Clearly, in the early days, markets will tend to be homogeneous. But, as demand grows rapidly with the entry of the early majority, it is common for new entrants to offer variations on the early models and consumers now have a choice. In order to explain this more clearly, let us illustrate the approximate shape of markets. If we were to plot the car market in terms of speed and price, we would see very small, inexpensive cars in the bottom left-hand corner (see Figure 5.1). In the top right, we would see very fast, expensive cars. Most cars, however, would cluster in the middle, what we might call: 'The Mr. and Mrs. average market.'

Figure 5.1 Scatterplot – car market

As illustrated, the lawn mower market would look similar (see Figure 5.2). With lawn size on the vertical axis and price on the horizontal axis, at the bottom left would be small, inexpensive, hand-pushed mowers, with expensive sit-on machines for large estates in the right-hand corner. That leaves the mass of the market with average-size lawns and average-sized lawn mowers, which is where the mass market is.

We can now redraw this to represent the shape of any market, particularly at the early growth stage (the shape on the left in Figure 5.3). But when rapid growth begins, new entrants join the market and offer variations on standard products in order to attract sales, and it is at this stage that markets begin to break into smaller groups, while still growing overall (this is represented by the shape in the middle). Eventually, when markets mature, and there is more supply than demand, any market growth tends to come in the lower price end of the market, while the top end of the market tends to be immune (this is

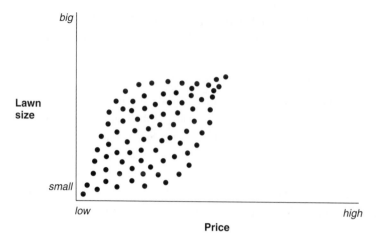

Figure 5.2 Scatterplot – lawn mower market

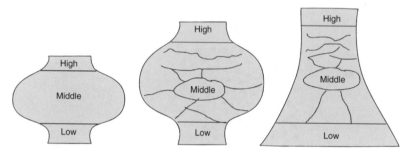

Figure 5.3 Market shape and maturity

represented by the shape on the right). It is usually the middle market that suffers at this stage, with many competitors vying with each other on price. This, however, is the whole point of market segmentation, for competing only on price is to assume that this is the main requirement of customers, whereas the truth is that this is rarely the case. It is just that a general lack of understanding about market segmentation on the part of suppliers about the real needs of customers in mature markets forces them to trade on price, so encouraging the market to become a commodity market.

The starting point in market segmentation is correct market definition which is crucial for measuring market size, growth and share, identifying relevant competitors and formulating strategies to deliver differential advantage. Few companies give sufficient attention to correct market definition and few can draw an accurate market map and therefore have little chance of doing anything remotely resembling correct market segmentation at the key influence points or junctions on the map. This process will be expanded on later in this chapter, but before this, let us clarify the terminology about customers and consumers.

# THE DIFFERENCE BETWEEN CUSTOMERS AND CONSUMERS

Let us start with the difference between customers and consumers. The term 'consumer' is interpreted by most to mean the final consumer, who is not necessarily the customer. Take the example of a mother or father who is buying breakfast cereals. The chances are that they are intermediate customers, acting as agents on behalf of the eventual consumers (their family) and, in order to market cereals effectively, it is clearly necessary to understand the needs of the eventual consumer down the buying chain.

Consider the case of the industrial purchasing officer buying raw materials such as wool tops for conversion into semi-finished cloths, which are then sold to other companies for incorporation into the final product, say a suit, or a dress, for sale in consumer markets. Here, we can see that the requirements of those various intermediaries and the end-user are eventually translated into the specifications of the purchasing officer to the raw materials manufacturer. Consequently, the market needs that this manufacturing company is attempting to satisfy must in the last analysis be defined in terms of the requirements of the ultimate users – the consumer – even though the direct customer is quite clearly the purchasing officer.

Given that we can appreciate the distinction between customers and consumers and the need constantly to be alert to any changes in the ultimate consumption patterns of the products to which our own contributes, the next question to be faced is who are our customers?

Direct customers are those people or organizations who actually buy directly from us. They could, therefore, be distributors, retailers and the like. However, as intimated in the previous paragraph, there is a tendency for organizations to confine their interest, hence their marketing, only to those who actually place orders. This can be a major mistake, as can be seen from the following case history.

A fertilizer company that had grown and prospered because of the superior nature of its products reached its farmer consumers via merchants (wholesalers). However, as other companies copied the technology, the merchants began to stock competitive products and drove prices and margins down. Had the fertilizer company paid more attention to the needs of its different farmer groups and developed products especially for them, based on farmer segmentation, it would have continued to create demand pull-through differentiation. The company carried out a segmentation exercise that revealed several distinct types of farmer, each with a different set of needs. Firstly, there was a segment they labelled 'Arthur'; he bought on price alone but represented only 10 per cent of the market, not the 100 per cent assumed by everyone in the industry, especially the sales force. Another type of farmer was labelled 'Oliver'; he would drive around his fields on a tractor with an aerial linked to a satellite and an on-board computer. He did this in order to analyse the soil type and would then mix P, N and K, which are the principal ingredients of fertilizer, solely to get the maximum yield out of his farm. In other words, Oliver was a scientific farmer, but the supply industry believed he was buying on price because he bought his own ingredients as cheaply as possible. He did this, however, only because none of the suppliers bothered to understand his needs.

Another type of farmer was called 'David'; a show-off farmer who liked his crops to look nice and healthy. He also liked his cows to have nice, healthy skins. Clearly, if a sales representative had talked in a technical way to David, he would quickly switch off. Equally, to talk about the appearance of crops and livestock would have switched Oliver off, but this is the whole point. Every single supplier in the industry totally ignored the real needs of these farmers, and the only thing anyone ever talked about was price. The result: a market driven by price discounts, accompanied by substantial losses to the suppliers. The company, however, armed with this new found information, launched new products and new promotional approaches aimed at these distinctive segments, and got immediate results, becoming the most profitable subsidiary of its owners and the only profitable fertilizer company in the country.

Let us now return to market dynamics and what happens to markets at the rapid growth stage. At this stage, new entrants come into the market, attracted by the high sales and high profits enjoyed by the industry. Let us illustrate this with another case history. Some time ago, a photocopier company had 80 per cent market share and massive profit margins. This is represented by the big circle in the middle of Figure 5.4. A small Japanese company entered

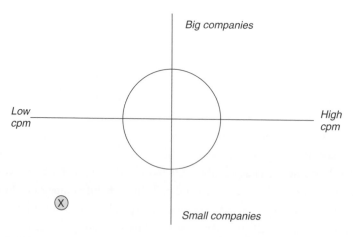

Figure 5.4 New entrant positioning

the market, eliciting no response from the market leader. The Japanese product was a success and the company stole market share, forcing the market leader to reduce prices. Within three years, the leader's market share was down to 10 per cent. This resulted from failure to recognise that the market was segmented, and trying to compete in all segments with their main product. The main point about this case history is that companies as a general rule should not attempt to compete in all segments with the same product, but should recognize that different segments or need groups develop as the market grows, and that they should develop appropriate products and services and position and brand them accordingly.

Let us summarize all of this by showing a product life cycle representation with some generalizations about how marketing strategies change over time (Figure 5.5). From this, you will see at least four major changes that occur over the life cycle. At the top of the far right-hand column is the word 'commodity', but this is by no means inevitable and only occurs in markets where the suppliers do not understand the power of market segmentation, as illustrated in the fertilizer case history. There are other options, including the option to get out of mature markets. Another is to move the goal posts, somewhat in the manner of First Direct, Direct Line, Virgin, Amazon.com and countless others. The strategy we want to concentrate on here, however, is market segmentation, which should be the very first consideration as markets begin to mature.

| Key characteristics | Unique | Product differentiation | Service differentiation | 'Commodity' |
|---|---|---|---|---|
| Marketing message | Explain | Competitive | Brand values | Corporate |
| Sales | Pioneering | Relative benefits distribution support | Relationship based | Availability based |
| Distribution | Direct selling | Exclusive distribution | Mass distribution | 80 : 20 |
| Price | Very high | High | Medium | Low (Consumer controlled) |
| Competitive intensity | None | Few | Many | Fewer, bigger international |
| Cost | Very high | Medium | Medium/low | Very low |
| Profit | Medium/high | High | Medium/high | Medium/low |
| Management style | Visionary | Strategic | Operational | Cost management |

Figure 5.5 Product/marketing lifecycle and market characteristics

An excellent example of good practice is Procter & Gamble in the United States supplying Walmart, the giant food retailer. P&G has a vast portfolio of brands, the majority of which are in mature, highly competitive categories. Multiple brands enable P&G to capture market share within individual product categories. Collaboration with Walmart (renowned for serving the mass market)

Figure 5.6 Demand pull

enables P&G to target specific segments within the Walmart customer base. As well as responding to end customer needs, P&G also serves the needs of its direct customer, Walmart. Integrated EDI enables just-in-time (JIT) stock replenishment and invoicing, based upon the demand-pull model illustrated in Figure 5.6. Though the market is mature, the partnership remains mutually beneficial and profitable.

Closely related to the question of the difference between customers and consumers is the question of what is meant by the term 'market share'.

# MARKET SHARE

Most business people already understand that there is a direct relationship between relatively high share of any market and high returns on investment, as shown in Figure 5.7. Quality and market share both drive profitability.

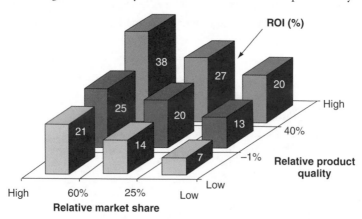

Figure 5.7 Relationship between market share and return on investment
Source: Pims Online

That stated, it is important to take great care in defining a 'market' (e.g. BMW is not in the same market as Ford). Correct market definition is crucial for measuring market share and market growth; the specification of target customers; recognition of relevant competitors; and, most importantly of all, the formulation of marketing strategy, for it is this, above all else, that delivers differential advantage.

The general rule is that a 'market' should be described in terms of a customer need in a way which covers the aggregation of all the products or services which customers regard as being capable of satisfying the same need. For example, we would regard the in-company caterer as only one option when it came to satisfying lunch-time hunger. This particular need could also be satisfied at external restaurants, public houses, fast food specialists and sandwich bars. The emphasis in the definition, therefore, is clearly on the word 'need'.

To summarize so far, correct market definition is crucial for the purpose of:

- Share measurement;
- Growth measurement;
- The specification of target customers;
- The recognition of relevant competitors;
- The formulation of marketing objectives and strategies.

# MARKET SEGMENTATION

We can now begin to concentrate on a methodology for market segmentation, this being the means by which any company seeks to gain a differential advantage over its competitors. Markets usually fall into natural groups, or segments, containing customers with a similar level of interest in the same broad requirements. Segments form separate markets in themselves and can often be of considerable size. Taken to its extreme, each individual consumer is a unique market segment, for all people are different in their requirements. While CRM systems have made it possible to engage in one-to-one communications, this is not viable in most organizations unless the appropriate organizational economies of scale have been obtained at a higher level of aggregation such as at segment level. Consequently, products are made to appeal to groups of customers who share approximately the same needs. It is not surprising, then, to hear that there are certain universally accepted criteria concerning what constitutes a viable market segment:

1. Segments should be of an adequate size to provide the company with the desired return for its effort.

2. Members of each segment should have a high degree of similarity in their requirements, yet be distinct from the rest of the market.

3. Criteria for describing segments must enable the company to communicate effectively with them.

While many of these criteria are obvious when we consider them, in practice market segmentation is one of the most difficult of marketing concepts to turn into a reality. Yet we must succeed, otherwise we become just another company selling what are called 'me too' products. In other words, what we offer the potential customer is very much the same as what any other company offers and, in such circumstances, it is likely to be the lowest priced product that is bought. This can be ruinous to profits, unless we happen to have lower costs, hence higher margins, than our competitors.

There are basically three major stages to market segmentation. The first establishes the scope of the project by specifying the geographic area to be covered and defining the market to be segmented, including analysis of how the market operates and where decisions are made about the competing products or services. Successful segmentation is based on a detailed understanding of decision-makers and their requirements. The second is essentially a manifestation of the way customers actually behave in the marketplace and consists of answering the question 'Who is specifying what?' The third stage considers reasons behind the behaviour of customers in the marketplace and answers the question 'Why?' and then searches for market segments based on this analysis of needs. The following sections provide an overview of the steps required to complete these three stages and is presented in a format for conducting a segmentation project using internal resources.

# DEFINING THE MARKET

The first step in market segmentation establishes the scope of the segmentation project by specifying the geographic area covered by the project and by clearly understanding from a customer's perspective the 'market' in which your products or services are competing with those of your competitors. Where necessary, the scope is modified to take into account the realistic capabilities of your organization. A clear geographic boundary enables you to size the market, to identify the localities in which the dynamics of the market have to be understood and, once the segments have been identified, to develop the appropriate marketing objectives and strategies for those localities.

Keeping the project within the borders of a single country is a manageable starting point because the stage of market development, the available routes to market and the pattern of marketing activity will probably be the same throughout the country. Even this, however, may be too broad for some companies, simply because their geographic reach is limited by physical and/or economic considerations, or even because their appeal has a strong local sentiment attached to it.

For companies trading in numerous countries around the world, there is clearly an enormous attraction in finding a single global segmentation model that can be applied to every country. However, the experience of globalization has highlighted for many of these companies that they have to 'act local' in order to succeed in their market. This does not mean that every country is completely unique in respect of the segments found within it. For the international company, a useful guide to predetermining which countries can be included in a single segmentation project is to ensure that in each of these countries the stage of market development, the available routes to market and the pattern of marketing activity are the same, or at least very similar.

# MARKET MAPPING

A useful way of identifying where decisions are made about competing products and services and, therefore, those who then proceed to the next stages of segmentation, is to start by drawing a 'market map'. This defines the distribution and value added chain between final users and suppliers of the products or services included within the scope of your segmentation project. It should take into account the various buying mechanisms found in your market, including the part played by 'influencers'. An example of a generic market map is given in Figure 5.8.

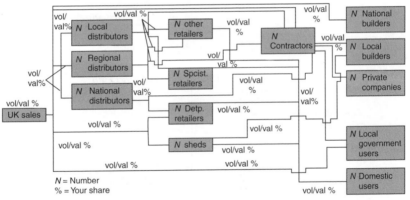

Figure 5.8 Market mapping

It is useful to start a market map by plotting the various stages that occur along the distribution and value added chain between the final users and all the suppliers of products or services competing with each other in the defined market. At the same time, indicate the particular routes to market the products are sourced through, as not all of them will necessarily involve all of these stages. Note at each junction on the map, if applicable, all the different types of companies/customers found there, as illustrated in Figure 5.9.

It is useful at this point to split the volume or value quantity dealt with by each junction between the junction types, as illustrated in Figure 5.10. The

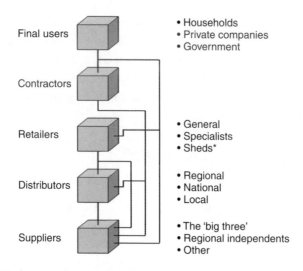

Figure 5.9 Market map showing the different junction types

*Note:* * 'Sheds' is the name sometimes used to refer to hardware superstores.

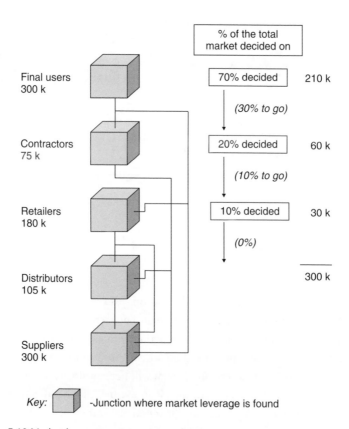

Figure 5.10 Market leverage points on a market map

easiest junction at which to start this page of market mapping is at the final users' junction, noting at each junction with leverage the volume/value (or percentage of the total market) that is decided there. Guesstimate these figures if they are not known and note this as a requirement for any follow-up work generated by this first pass at segmenting your market. This is also illustrated in Figure 5.10 which shows a market in which 30 per cent of annual sales are decided at junctions other than the final user junction.

So far, we have built a market map by tracking the distribution and value added chain found between final users and suppliers and shown the various routes that are taken through the map to link the two together. We then quantified the map. This was followed by expanding the detail to show the different types of companies/customers found at each junction on the map and these were also quantified.

# WHO SPECIFIES WHAT, WHERE, WHEN AND HOW

In this step we are developing a representative sample of different decision-makers which identifies the characteristics and properties of a purchase on which decisions are made along with the customer attributes that will be used to describe the decision-makers. Each constituent of this sample is called a micro-segment. The uniqueness of a micro-segment is that when determining which of the alternative offers to be bought, the decision-makers it represents demonstrate a similar level of interest in a specific set of features, with the features being the characteristics and properties of 'what' is bought, 'where' it is bought, 'when' it is bought and 'how' it is bought as appropriate to the micro-segment (see Figure 5.11). To this is added the descriptors which describe who

| Micro-segment | 1 | 2 | 3 | 4 | 5 | 6 | 7 | 8 | 9 | 10 |
|---|---|---|---|---|---|---|---|---|---|---|
| What is bought | | | | | | | | | | |
| Where | | | | | | | | | | |
| When | | | | | | | | | | |
| And how | | | | | | | | | | |
| Who | | | | | | | | | | |
| Why (benefits sought) | | | | | | | | | | |

Figure 5.11 Micro-segments

the micro-segment represents along with an estimate of the volume or value they account for in the defined market.

The principle behind this step is that by observing the purchase behaviour of decision-makers and understanding the key constituents of this behaviour, we have a platform for developing a detailed understanding of their motivations. It is, therefore, a critical link with the next step of the segmentation process, which looks at why decision-makers select the particular products and services they specify. This, in turn, becomes the basis on which the segments are formed.

The following process chart in Figure 5.12 describes a number of steps that will now be described. From this, you will see that the process begins with market mapping, which corresponds to a deep understanding of the market. This has already been discussed above.

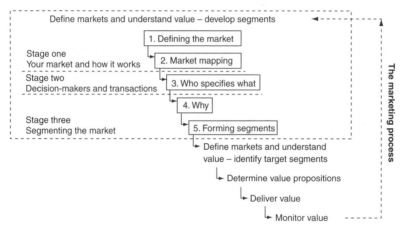

© Professor Malcolm McDonald and Ian Dunbar

Figure 5.12 First five steps of segmentation process

We can now turn to the process again, and move to steps 2, 3, 4 and 5, although it must be pointed out that segmentation can and should be carried out at all major junctions on the market map. Essentially, these time-consuming steps involve listing all purchase combinations that take place in the market, including different applications for the product or service, principal forms such as size, colour, brand, timing (monthly, weekly, etc.), principal channels and payment types such as cash or credit. Next it is important to describe who behaves in each particular way using relevant descriptors. For industrial purchases this might be standard industrial classifications, for example, size of firm, whereas for consumer purchases this might be socio-economic group, life cycle, age, sex, location, lifestyle or psychographics. Finally, and most difficult of all, each purchase combination needs a brief explanation of the reason for this particular type of behaviour. It is important to understanding the benefits sought, and it is often at this stage that an organization needs to pause and either commission market research or refer to its extant database of previous market research studies.

To summarize so far, it is clear that no market is totally homogeneous (Figure 5.13).

But one with many different purchase combinations

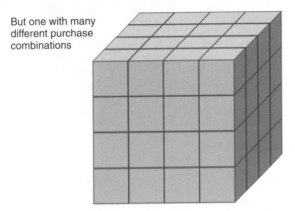

Figure 5.13 An undifferentiated market

In reality, markets consist of a large number of different purchase combinations, as illustrated in Figure 5.14.

Figure 5.14 Different needs in a market

However, as it is impracticable to deal with more than between seven or ten market segments, a process has to be found to bring together or cluster all those micro-segments that share similar or approximately similar needs (Figure 5.15).

Once the basic work has been done, any good statistical computer program can carry out cluster analysis to arrive at a smaller number of segments. The final step consists of checking whether the resulting segments are big enough to justify separate treatment, are indeed sufficiently different from other segments, whether they have been described sufficiently well to enable the customers in

Figure 5.15 Segments in a market

| Step 1 | Define the market to be segmented and size it (market scope) |
| --- | --- |
| Step 2 | Determine how the market works and identify who makes the decisions (market mapping) |
| Step 3 | Develop a representative sample of decision-makers based upon differences they see as key (including what, when and how) |
| Step 4 | Understand their real needs (why they buy; benefits sought) |
| Step 5 | Search for groups with similar needs |

Table 5.1 Market segmentation steps

them to be reached by means of the organization's communication methods, and finally, the company has to be prepared to make the necessary changes to meet the needs of the identified segments. Table 5.1 summarizes the key steps of market segmentation.

Market structure and market segmentation are the heart and soul of marketing. Unless an organization spends time on it, driven from the board downwards, it is virtually impossible for it to be market driven, and in any organization that isn't market driven, the marketing function will be ineffective, or at best, will spend its time trying to promote and sell product or services that are inappropriate for the market.

# SUMMARY

Market segmentation is fundamental to corporate strategy. Since market segmentation affects every single corporate activity, it should not be just an exercise that takes place within the marketing department and has to involve other functions. The most senior levels of management must lead this initiative if their organization is to be truly market or customer-need driven.

Once market segmentation has been carried out, positioning products and services to meet the different needs of the different segments is comparatively easy; the difficult part is segmenting markets. It is vital to focus on serving the needs of the identified segments, while it is dangerous to straddle different segments with the same offer. Not all customers in a broadly defined market have the same needs. Positioning is relatively straightforward, but segmentation is complex and challenging and, most commonly, positioning problems stem from poor segmentation. It is imperative to select a segment and serve it; avoid straggling segments.

# FURTHER READING

McDonald, M. and Dunbar, I. (2013) *Market segmentation: How to do it, how to profit from it*, Chichester: Wiley.

An in-depth examination of the principles, practice and application of market segmentation with a focus on bottom-line outcomes.

See also:

Christensen, C., Cook, S. and Hall, T. (2005) Marketing malpractice: The cause and the cure. *Harvard Business Review* Vol. 83 (12): 74–83.

Yankelovitch, D. (2006) Rediscovering market segmentation. *Harvard Business Review* Vol. 84 (6): 122–131.

# CHAPTER 6
# COMPETITIVE ANALYSIS

IN THIS CHAPTER WE STUDY:

- basic elements of competitive strategy
- implications of competing on cost and value bases
- sources of competitive advantage
- strategic issues surrounding market share
- forces driving industry competition
- the range of competitive information required
- use of competitive benchmarking

# DETERMINING COMPETITIVE STRATEGY

Marketing success depends not only upon identifying and responding to customer needs but also upon a company's ability to ensure that its response is judged by customers to be superior to that of its competitors. In other words, the development of marketing strategies must be based upon both customer satisfaction and competitive differentiation.

Just as we can remember the key components of the marketing mix by the shorthand of the 'four P's', so too can we focus on the basic elements of competitive strategy by reference to the three 'C's. The three 'C's in question are the Customer, Competition and Company. Figure 6.1 illustrates the triangular relationship that exists between the three 'C's.

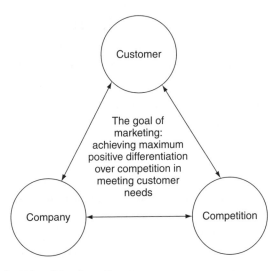

Figure 6.1 Marketing and the three Cs

Competitive strategy can therefore be seen as a search for differential advantage as perceived by customers. The key here is *perception*, since the ultimate test question is how does the customer evaluate our offer compared with competitive offers? This basic principle is the foundation for market *positioning*. A key component of the strategic process in marketing is the identification of an appropriate competitive 'position' in the marketplace. In essence, the position of a brand or offer is simply the customer's perception of the similarity or dissimilarity of a company's brand in relation to competitive offerings. As such it will be influenced by the particular marketing mix of product features, promotional appeals, price levels and place (distribution) factors that the company selects.

How do companies achieve this competitive advantage? Many commentators and academics have investigated this fundamental question and their findings tend to point in the same direction. Put very simply, successful companies have a cost advantage or a value advantage – or a combination of the two. The cost advantage means that the company can produce and distribute its products at a lower cost than the competition, while the value advantage means that the company's offer is perceived as providing differentiated benefits to customers – the product has greater 'added value'. Let us examine briefly these two fundamental sources of competitive advantage.

# COST ADVANTAGE

In many industries there will typically be one competitor who will be the low-cost producer and, more often than not, that competitor will have the greatest sales volume in the sector. There is substantial evidence to suggest that 'big is beautiful' when it comes to cost advantage. There are two main reasons for this: economies of scale, in which unit costs fall as production volumes increase (at least, up to the point where diseconomies set in); and 'the experience curve'.

The experience curve is a phenomenon that has its roots in the earlier notion of the 'learning curve'. Researchers discovered during the Second World War that it was possible to identify and predict improvements in the rate of output or cost effectiveness of workers as they became more skilled in the processes and tasks on which they were working. Subsequent work by Bruce Henderson, founder of The Boston Consulting Group, extended this concept by demonstrating that *all* costs, not just production costs, would decline at a given rate as volume increased. In fact, to be precise, the relationship that the experience curve describes is between *real* unit costs and *cumulative* volume. Further, it is generally recognized that this cost decline applies only to 'value added' – that is, costs other than bought-in supplies. The experience curve in its general form is shown in Figure 6.2.

There are many implications of this relationship for the development of marketing strategy, not least in the determination of pricing strategy. However, its importance in this current discussion is in the fact that if one company's relative market share is greater than that of its competitors then, other things being equal, it should be further down the experience curve. In other words, it will have a cost advantage. Such a cost advantage can either be used to lower prices, thus putting pressure on competitors, or to earn higher margins at the same price as competitors.

Later in this book, it will be suggested that it will generally be preferable to use such a cost advantage to reinvest in the product rather than to use it to

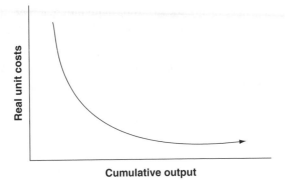

Figure 6.2 The experience curve

initiate price wars, and thus run the risk of reducing the product to the status of a 'commodity'.

# VALUE ADVANTAGE

We have already observed that 'customers don't buy products, they buy benefits'. Put another way, the product is purchased not for itself but for the promise of what it will deliver. These benefits may be intangible; that is, they relate not to specific product features but rather to such things as *image* or *reputation*. Alternatively, the delivered offering may be seen to outperform its rivals in some functional aspect.

Unless the product or service we offer can be distinguished in some way from its competitors, there is a strong likelihood that the marketplace will view it as a 'commodity', and so the sale will tend to go to the cheapest supplier. Thus, the importance of seeking to attach additional values to our offering to mark it out from the competition becomes more apparent.

What are the means by which such value differentiation may be gained? Essentially, the development of strategy based on additional values will normally require a more segmented approach to the market. As discussed in Chapter 5, when a company scrutinizes markets closely, it frequently finds that there are distinct 'value segments'. In other words, different groups of customers within the total market attach different importance to different benefits. Often, there are substantial opportunities for creating differentiated appeals for specific segments. Take the motor car as an example. A model such as the Ford Mondeo is positioned in the middle range of European cars; and within that broad category, specific versions are aimed at defined segments. Thus we find the basic, small-engine, two-door model at one end of the spectrum and the four-wheel-drive, high-performance version at the other. In between are many options, each of which seeks to satisfy the needs of quite different 'benefit segments'. Adding value through differentiation is a powerful means of achieving a defensible advantage in the market. In practice, what we find is that the successful companies will often seek to achieve a position based on *both* a cost advantage *and* a value advantage. A useful way of examining the available options is to present them as a simple matrix, as shown in Figure 6.3.

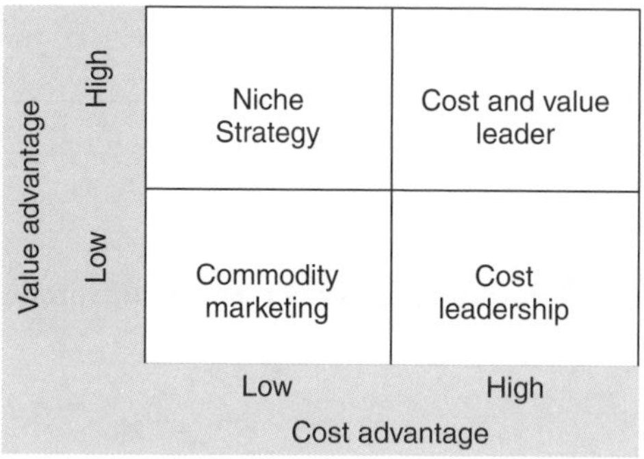

Figure 6.3 Sources of competitive advantage

Let us consider the options in turn. For companies who find themselves in the bottom left-hand quadrant of our matrix, the world is an uncomfortable place. These products are indistinguishable from their competitors' offerings and they have no cost advantage. These are typical 'commodity' market situations and the only ultimate strategy is to move to the right of the matrix (that is, to cost leadership) or upwards into a 'niche'. Often, the cost leadership route is simply not available. This will be the case particularly in a mature market where substantial market share gains are difficult to achieve. New technology may sometimes provide a window of opportunity for cost reduction, but it is often the case that the same technology is available to competitors.

Cost leadership, if it is to form the basis of a viable long-term marketing strategy, should essentially be gained early in the market life cycle. This is why market share is considered to be so important in many industries. The 'experience curve' concept, described briefly above, demonstrates the value of early market share gains – the higher the share relative to competitors, the lower the costs should be. This cost advantage can be used strategically to assume a position of price leader and, if appropriate, to make it impossible for higher-cost competitors to survive. Alternatively, price may be maintained, enabling above-average profit to be earned, which is potentially available to develop further the position of the product in the market.

The other way out of the 'commodity' quadrant of the matrix in Figure 6.3 is to seek a 'niche', or segment, where it is possible to meet the needs of customers through offering additional values. Sometimes, it may not be through tangible product features that this added value is generated, but through service.

For example, a steel stockholder who finds himself in the commodity quadrant may seek to move up to the niche quadrant by offering daily deliveries from stock, by providing additional 'finishing' services for his basic products, or by focusing on the provision of a range of special steel for specific segments.

What does not seem to be an established rule is that there is no middle ground between cost leadership and niche marketing. The relationship between size, differentiation and profitability is generally agreed to be as depicted in Figure 6.4. Being caught in the middle (that is, neither a cost leader nor a niche-based provider of added values) is generally bad news.

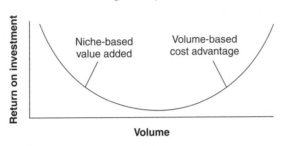

Figure 6.4 The dangers of the middle ground

Finally, perhaps the most defensible position in the matrix is the top right-hand corner. Companies occupying that position have products that are distinctive in the values they offer as well as being cost competitive. Clearly, it is a position of some strength, occupying 'high ground', that is extremely difficult for competitors to attack.

# MARKET SHARE STRATEGIES

In discussing the advantages and disadvantages of pursuing niches or volume, it is important that the issues surrounding 'market share' are fully understood. That there is a strong relationship between market share and return on investment has been confirmed by the analysis of data from thousands of companies participating in the PIMS study (Profit Impact of Marketing Strategy). This study, in searching for explanations of variations in profitability between firms, identified a strong correlation between market share and ROI.

However, a warning should be sounded. It may well be that profitable companies have high-market shares, but it does not follow that all high-market-share companies will be profitable. Quite simply, this is because market share can be bought – through increased marketing expenditure and effort, product development, or price reductions. All this can be good practice unless it is at the expense of long-term profit. Some companies have failed to recognize that investing in market share is really only viable early in a product/market life cycle. Similarly, other companies have been caught out when the product/market life cycle turns out to be much shorter than had been anticipated. In summary, market share strategies are long-term, and in volatile markets such strategies must be pursued with care.

A further issue surrounds the question, 'Share of *which* market?' In other words, of what is market share a measure? The answer is that it all depends on how we define the total market. A holiday tour operator specializing in the organization of cultural tours of sites of antiquity, accompanied by a professor of archaeology, is not operating in the same market as a tour operator offering ten days in Majorca for £300, yet they both offer holidays.

The definition problem is helped if we use the concept of the 'served' market. The served market is best described in terms of the specific needs that we seek to meet rather than some generic product category. Some have called market share in this context 'share of mind', meaning that when potential customers are contemplating a purchase to meet a specific need, they limit their choice to offerings they consider competitive. The marketing challenge may thus be seen as one of how to increase 'share of mind' among specific target groups.

# COMPETITIVE DRIVERS

As markets mature, as growth rates stabilize, or markets enter recession, the only way to grow a business faster than the growth of the market is at the expense of the competition. This implies a need to understand in the greatest possible detail the competitive context and the characteristics of specific competitors. Here the work of Michael Porter, a Harvard Business School professor, is particularly valuable in providing a framework for the systematic exploration of the competitive context.

## MARKET COMPETITION

Obviously, the more numerous or equally balanced the competitors, the more intense will be the rivalry within the market. If this is combined with a slow industry growth rate, and if fixed costs relative to variable costs are high, then the prognosis is for a high level of aggressive competition, probably accompanied by severe price-cutting. A further influencing factor will be the extent to which the competing products on offer are seen as substitutes by the marketplace, with few switching penalties for buyers. Kodak is often cited as a classic example of a company that failed to understand that *in the eye of the consumer* camera phones provided a perfectly acceptable alternative to the traditional camera. Further, innovative product development from its key competitors, Canon and Nikon, left it struggling to keep up.

Of key importance will be the relative cost structures of the major players in the market; these will be determined not just by market share but also by capacity utilization and production technology.

In certain circumstances, the fall of a giant in the industry, such as Enron, will cause reverberations across a number of associated companies and industries. Similarly, the dot.com revolution shook many competitors out of complacency and forced many of them into a fundamental reappraisal of their products and services.

## THREAT OF NEW ENTRANTS

In analysing markets, one of the factors to be appraised is the existence, or absence, of 'barriers to entry'. In other words, how easy is it for new entrants to enter the market? Typically, barriers might be provided by economies of scale, so that, without a minimum market share, unit costs will be uncompetitive. Similarly, heavy start-up costs – whether through the need for capital investment or high levels of marketing expenditure – can provide a barrier. Government regulation, as, for example, in the telecommunications industry, might also prove an effective barrier.

Conversely, markets may be easy for new competitors to enter where product differentiation is low, where there are no legacy systems to maintain or where technological innovation can quickly overcome cost barriers. The airline, music and publishing industries provide excellent examples of how new 'lean and mean' competitors can enter markets where existing players felt relatively safe and secure. For example, British Airways failed to perceive the extent of the threat caused by new, low-cost rivals; Barnes and Noble was completely wrong-footed by the emergence of Amazon, and the innumerable High Street retailers across all sectors failed to comprehend the impact of new online rivals. At the time of writing, two niche retailers, Jessops (cameras) and HMV (music) have just gone into receivership; neither recognized fully the threat caused by the proliferation of new online sellers offering wider choice at significantly lower prices.

## THREAT OF SUBSTITUTES

One factor that can alter the strategic balance in a marketplace considerably is the development of products that meet underlying customer needs more cost-effectively than existing products. The development of synthetic fibres had a major impact on the demand for natural fibres; video cameras virtually eliminated demand for home movie products. More recently, streaming video has had a significant impact on sales of DVDs, while streaming music has dramatically affected CD sales.

## BARGAINING POWER OF BUYERS

The competitive climate of a market will clearly be influenced by the extent to which customers wield power through purchasing strength. Thus a market that is dominated by a limited number of buyers, or where a buyer takes a larger proportion of the seller's output, will substantially limit the seller's opportunities for individual action or development. The UK grocery market illustrates the situation well, with a handful of major retail chains being able to exert considerable influence over manufacturing suppliers' marketing policies, and thus their profitability. Opportunities for backward integration up the value chain is another source of competitive threat from buyers.

## BARGAINING POWER OF SUPPLIERS

Many of the potential threats that exist from buyers can also come from the suppliers to an industry. If the supply of critical materials is controlled by a few suppliers, or if an individual company's purchases from a supplier constitute only a small part of that company's output, then freedom of manoeuvre may be limited. If opportunities exist for forward integration by suppliers, this constitutes a further source of potential competitive pressure. Alternatively, backward integration by retailers can reduce suppliers' bargaining power and increase retailer's power and influence. The international High Street fashion retailer, Zara, for example, with its vertically integrated business model and full control over design, production, shipping and retailing, has continued to flourish throughout the current economic downturn.

## CASE STUDY 6.1 HMV

The fall of HMV into the hands of the receivers in January 2013 demonstrates the imperative of engaging in continuous strategic competitive analysis and responding quickly and effectively to changing consumer tastes, habits and demands. In 2012, HMV had around 35 per cent of the UK CD market, however total market size was diminishing. Huge debts, incurred through an expansion strategy in the world of physical retailing, led to its downfall. According to Neil Saunders of Conlumino retail research agency, 'The brand certainly has some value, however, while someone could arguably turn a profit in running some of the stores for a period of time they would still be betting against the future. By our own figures, we forecast that by the end of 2015 some 90.4 per cent of music and film sales will be online. The bottom line is that there is no real future for physical retail in the music sector.'

According to Saunders, 'This outcome was always inevitable. While many failures of recent times have been, at least in part, driven by the economy, HMV's reported demise is a structural failure. In the digital era where 73.4 per cent of music and film are downloaded or bought online, HMV's business model has simply become increasingly irrelevant and unsustainable. HMV did not react early enough to the digital trend; it did not give shoppers a reason to keep buying from it. Admittedly, the company has tried to innovate through selling more electricals and gadgets but, unfortunately, these initiatives were never going to be enough to counteract the terminal decline in its core business.'

*Source: The Guardian (excerpts)*

**CASE STUDY QUESTIONS:**

1. Summarize the key reasons for HMV's decline, identifying the balance between predictable/non-predictable and controllable/non-controllable factors.
2. Framed by this analysis, discuss what actions HMV could have taken to avoid, or mitigate, the decline.

Since Porter conceived the Five Forces model, the world has changed quite dramatically. While, as illustrated, it still has validity as a useful framework for detailed analysis, numerous other macro-level factors also need to be taken into account when employing it as an analytical tool. Prasad (2011) identifies a number of external forces, or 'complementors', totally beyond the control of individual organizations that can shift consumer preferences and change the balance of forces, as well as history and culture as two key determinants of force intensity. Prasad counsels that in order to product a reasonably robust Five Forces analysis, the intellectual rigour inherent in the model must be combined with pragmatic understanding of the social, cultural and historical context.

# COMPETITIVE INFORMATION

Competitive analysis at this level requires access to a wide range of information, necessitating a continued monitoring of all sources of data. The range of competitive intelligence that should be gathered is listed below. Some of the issues listed appear to be obvious, and yet it is surprising how often we lack accurate information about them. Ideally, a 'data bank' on the competitive environment should be established; use should be made of annual reports, annual statutory returns, Dun & Bradstreet reports (or equivalent), trade press and financial reports and publications from trade associations, as well as company catalogues and advertisements, to discover:

- Who are the competition . . . and where are they?
- Who else might become a competitor?
- Their shares of market segments and trends.
- Their product line, performance, quality, service.
- Their management, its skill, philosophies.
- Size and development of their sales force and organization of sales effort.
- Their promotion strategy.
- Their pricing policy, terms, discounts.
- Their distribution and service strategies.
- Their technological capability.
- Their financial strength.
- Their objectives.

Information can often be gathered from customers and suppliers about competitors' actions or intentions. If personnel are recruited from competitors, they should be debriefed as far as professional ethics allow. In fact, it is often surprising to see just how much openly available competitive intelligence can be gathered by making use of publicly available databases.

There is a significant body of empirical evidence indicating that, generally speaking, managers are not particularly skilled at competitor analysis. They know it is important, but because of its intrinsic complexity many are simply not very good at it. Managers can sometimes take shortcuts, focusing on a few competitor attributes that they consider 'key' and therefore using a less extensive, less conscious categorization model. Cassidy and Buede (2009) reveal that experienced forecasters are usually no better than inexperienced and sometime worse. Practitioners and 'experts' are no better than novices; in fact, Lawrence et al. (2006) identify an 'inverse expertise effect' where novices outperform experts. This is somewhat worrying, given the imperative of competitor mapping and the fact that there is a mass of rich data in the public domain, much of it freely available online.

Table 6.1 gives some indication of the sources of competitor information, most of which is readily accessible. In Chapter 4 we highlight the imperative of an effective *marketing intelligence system* that collects, interprets and disseminates

| | Public | Trade/professionals | Government | Investors |
|---|---|---|---|---|
| What competitors say about themselves | • Advertising<br>• Promotional materials<br>• Press releases<br>• Speeches<br>• Books<br>• Articles<br>• Websites<br>• Blogs<br>• Social media sites<br>• Personnel changes<br>• Recruitment advertisement | • Manuals<br>• Technical papers<br>• Licences<br>• Patents<br>• Courses<br>• Seminars | • Company<br>• House reports<br>• Lawsuits<br>• Office of fair trading and monopolies commission | • Annual meetings<br>• Annual reports<br>• Prospectuses<br>• Stock/bond issues<br>• Speeches to security analysts |
| What others say about them | • Books<br>• Articles<br>• Websites<br>• Blogs<br>• Social media sites<br>• Case studies<br>• Consultants<br>• Newspaper reports<br>• Environmental groups<br>• Unions<br>• Ex-employees | • Suppliers/vendors<br>• Trade press<br>• Industry studies<br>• Customers<br>• Opinion leaders<br>• Blogs<br>• Social media sites<br>• Contractors/sub-contractors | • Lawsuits<br>• Government ministries<br>• National plans | • Security analysis<br>• Reports<br>• Industry studies<br>• Credit reports |

Table 6.1 Sources of competitor information

this information on a regular and systematic basis. Large companies in competitive developing countries, such as China and Brazil, operate world-wide monitoring systems, which, quite legally, screen and index all material, patents, licences and academic journals in their fields of interest. To be a viable basis for marketing strategy, competitive analysis must be organized and managed as an ongoing activity – not just an *ad hoc* response to a particular circumstance. The important topics of conducting a *marketing audit* and ensuring that the *marketing information system* is fit for purpose are addressed further in Chapter 21.

# COMPETITIVE BENCHMARKING

The ultimate test of the efficiency of any marketing strategy has to be sales – not just measured against volume targets, but rather in terms of profit. Those companies who strive for market share, but who measure market share in terms of volume sales, may be deluding themselves in that volume can be bought at the expense of profit. The only market share measure that counts in the long run is the *sterling share* of the market. In other words, what percentage of the total expenditure made by customers in this market ends up as sales revenue?

Because market share is an 'after the event' measure, we need to utilize continuing indicators of competitive performance; this will highlight areas where improvements in the marketing mix can be made.

In recent years, a number of companies have developed a technique for assessing relative marketplace performance, which has come to be known as 'competitive benchmarking'. Originally, the idea of competitive benchmarking was literally to take apart a competitor's product, component by component, and to compare its performance in a value engineering sense with the company's own product. This approach has often been attributed to the Japanese, but many Western companies have also found the value of such detailed comparisons.

However, the idea of benchmarking is capable of extension beyond this simple comparison of technology and cost-effectiveness. Because the battle in the marketplace for the 'share of mind' that we referred to earlier is essentially concerned with perceptions, it is perceptions that that we must measure.

Companies such as IBM have led the way in conducting regular surveys among customers, in which they seek to measure exactly how their customers see them as suppliers, not just of a product, but of a total service. Not only does IBM measure the perceptions of customers concerning the relative performance of their products compared with those of competitors – it also seeks to measure the image that customers have of it compared with other groups in the 'office automation' field, such as Xerox, Hewlett Packard and Digital.

The measures that are used in this type of benchmarking programme include delivery reliability, ease of ordering, after-sales service, the quality of sales representation and the accuracy of invoices and other documentation. These measures are not chosen at random but are selected because of their importance to the customer. Market research, often based on in-depth interviews, would typically be employed to identify these 'key success factors'. The elements that customers identify as being the most important then form the basis for the benchmark questionnaire. This questionnaire is administered to a sample of customers on a regular basis – for example, British Telecommunications carries out a daily telephone survey of a random sample of their domestic and business customers to measure customers' perceptions of service. For most companies, an annual survey could suffice; in other cases, perhaps quarterly, particularly if market conditions are dynamic. The output of these surveys might typically be presented in the form of a competitive profile as in the example in Figure 6.5.

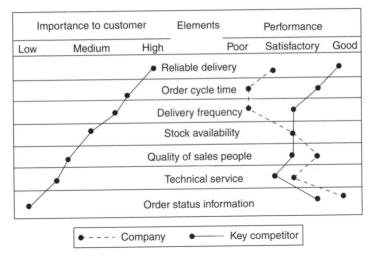

Figure 6.5 Competitive benchmarking

# SUMMARY

The ability to present customers with a total offer that is recognized as superior to competitive offerings has become the prime task of marketing. We have seen that it is possible to gain competitive advantage both through lower costs and through greater product and service differentiation. Knowledge of the competition and market conditions, as well as understanding of significant threats (such as new technology or changing consumer habits) are as important as knowledge of customers. Increasingly, leading companies are developing marketing information systems that enable continuous, systematic monitoring of competitive strategy and performance (see Chapters 21 and 22). In the current hypercompetitive climate, the phrase 'competitive advantage' has become the rallying cry in so many organizations. With everyone playing the same game, it has become even more crucial to build marketing strategies that take account *explicitly* of the increasingly dynamic competitive landscape.

# FURTHER READING

Hooley, G., Saunders, J. Piercy. N. & Nicoulaud, B. (2008) *Marketing Strategy and Competitive Positioning*, Harlow: Pearson.

An exploration of marketing strategy, competitive analysis, potential positioning strategies and strategy implementation.

See also:

Davis, J. A. (2010) *Competitive Success: How Branding Adds Value*, Chichester: Wiley.

# REFERENCES

Cassidy, M. F. & Buede, D. (2009) Does the accuracy of expert judgment comply with common sense: Caveat emptor. *Management Decision*, Vol. 47: 454–469.

Lawrence, M., Goodwin, P., O'Connor, M. & Onkal, D. (2006) Judgmental forecasting: A review of progress over the last 25 years. *International Journal of Forecasting*, Vol. 22: 493–518.

Porter, M. E. (1980) *Competitive Strategy*, New York: Free Press.

Prasad, A. (2011) The impact of non-market forces on competitive positioning. *Journal of Management Research*, Vol. 11 (3): 131–137.

# PART II
# CREATING THE VALUE PROPOSITION

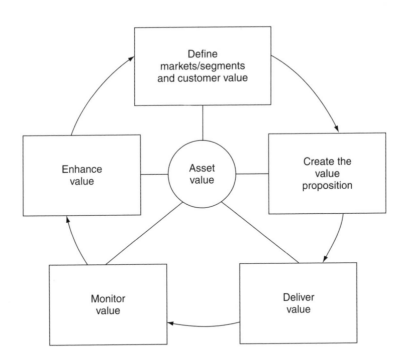

# CHAPTER 7
# MARKETING PLANNING

IN THIS CHAPTER WE STUDY:

- the purpose and focus of marketing planning
- the benefits and contents of a marketing plan
- the difference between strategic and tactical marketing planning
- the problems with a forecasting and budgeting approach
- the location of marketing planning within corporate planning
- the steps of the strategic marketing planning process
- the requirements of a marketing planning system

# WHAT IS MARKETING PLANNING?

The purpose of *marketing planning* and its principal focus are the identification and creation of competitive advantage. Marketing planning is the planned application of marketing resources to achieve marketing objectives. Given the increasing turbulence and complexity of the marketplace, and the rapid pace and impact of technological change, the need for a disciplined, systematic approach to the market has never been greater. Nor, it must be said, has the possibility of having one been so real.

The advent of computerized data collection and analysis, and the Internet with its time- and location-independent reach and interactive dialogue capability, has made previously remote marketing opportunities accessible. Our ability to share and act on information and ideas has also developed. Increasingly, we see functional silos replaced by cross-functional networks.

Marketing planning today is distinguished by the fact that all levels of management are involved, with the resulting intelligence coming from the market rather than from the heads of a remote group of planners with little or no operational involvement. The marketing axiom has taken an about-turn: nowadays 'you don't manage your customers, your customers manage you'. A recent article by Coumau et al. (2013) in McKinsey Quarterly advocates involving corporate boards in marketing. The basic premise of the argument is that social media and the proliferation of data are changing the nature of business – customer relations; in light of this, it can be beneficial to spread marketing strategy beyond the marketing department. Taking board members to visit innovators and peer companies has been found to increase marketing's share of budget, customer satisfaction and profitability. These findings reflect the shrinking distance between an organization and its market and the imperative of the entire organization taking some responsibility for strategic marketing planning.

By *strategic marketing planning* we mean the management process leading to a marketing plan. It is a logical sequence and a series of activities leading to the setting of marketing objectives and formulation of plans for achieving them. (The precise steps in the strategic marketing planning process and the contents of a marketing plan are discussed later in the chapter.) It involves deep understanding of the market, competitors, the organization itself and consumers. Accurate planning is crucial to marketing success. In small, undiversified companies this process is usually informal, whereas in larger, more diversified organizations, the process is often systematized. *Formalized marketing planning* by means of a planning system is, *per se*, little more than a structured way of identifying a range of options for the company, making them explicit in writing, formulating marketing objectives that are consistent with the company's overall objectives and scheduling and costing the specific activities most likely to bring about the achievement of the objectives. Marketing objectives must be realistic and achievable, based upon an honest evaluation of the marketing capabilities of the organization. According to Phillips et al. (2001), essential marketing capabilities should be determined by evaluating skills and competencies at the individual, group and organization level. If capability levels are low, then the organization needs to analyse whether it can afford to buy in specialist marketing expertise from an agency, which then becomes a broader resource issue. Whatever the outcome, there is little point in setting objectives without concurrent analysis of the organization's ability to achieve them.

Although simple to grasp intellectually, strategic marketing planning is notoriously the most difficult of all marketing tasks. There are several reasons for this: first, it demands a highly structured, logical, rational approach, unencumbered by personal preferences and organizational politics – but these are the realities of corporate life. Second, it requires access to valid, accurate, reliable data. Paradoxically, even in our information-rich world, this can be difficult to find. A recent article by Kotler and Kotler (2013) bemoans the lack of availability of micro-economic enterprise, consumption and demographic data to inform strategic decisions and marketing planning. They find plenty of macro-economic statistics at national level but a lack of willingness even among large corporates to devote resources to disaggregating data to a level relevant for marketing. Inadequate data is a major barrier to successful marketing planning. Third, it is imperative to pull together into one coherent, realistic plan all the diverse elements of marketing, and this 'coalescence' requires at least some degree of institutionalized procedures as well as an inevitable compromise between conflicting objectives. For example, consider these four typical business objectives: maximizing revenue, maximizing profits, maximizing return on investment and minimizing costs. Each has its own special appeal to different managers within the organization, depending on their particular function. To achieve a kind of 'optimum compromise' demands accurate and collaborative understanding of how these variables interact and steadfast rationality in decision-making.

Commercial success is, of course, influenced by many factors apart from just planning procedures. A myriad of contextual issues adds to the complexity of the marketing planning process. These include company size, degree of internationalization, management style, degree of business environmental turbulence and competitive hostility, marketing growth rate, market share, technological developments and so on. However, irrespective of the size or complexity of the organization, some kind of structured approach to situation analysis is necessary in order that meaningful and realistic marketing objectives can be set.

Issues to be considered in marketing planning are:
- When should it be done; how often; by whom; and how?

- Is it different in large and small companies?
- Is it different in diversified and undiversified companies?
- Is it different in international and domestic companies?
- What is the role of the chief executive?
- What is the role of the planning department?
- Should marketing planning be 'top down' or 'bottom up'?
- What is the relationship between operational (one year) and strategic (longer-term) planning?

## THE BENEFITS OF A MARKETING PLAN

Studies indicate that up to 90 per cent of industrial goods companies do not, by their own admission, produce anything approximating to an integrated, co-ordinated and internally consistent plan for their marketing activities. This includes a substantial number of companies with highly elaborate procedures for marketing planning. Certainly, few of these companies enjoy the advantages of formalized marketing planning and its output, an effective marketing plan.

The benefits to an organization of having a marketing plan are that it:

- achieves better co-ordination of activities;
- identifies expected developments;
- increases organizational preparedness to change;
- minimizes non-rational responses to the unexpected;
- reduces conflicts about where the organization should be going;
- improves communications;
- forces management to think ahead systematically;
- enhances the matching of available resources to selected opportunities;
- provides a framework for the continuing review of operations; and
- demands a systematic approach to strategy formulation, which leads to a higher return on investment.

# STRATEGIC AND TACTICAL MARKETING PLANNING

The crux of marketing planning lies in knowing the difference between strategy and tactics. All organizations need to a have longer-term (strategic) marketing view as well as a short-term (tactical) marketing operation. Much of the difficulty surrounding marketing planning derives predominantly from not understanding the real significance of a strategic marketing plan as opposed to a tactical, or operational, marketing plan. A strategic marketing plan is for a period that extends beyond the following fiscal year and usually covers three to five years. It is the backdrop against which operational decisions are taken, determining where the company is, where it wants to go and how it can get there. A tactical plan is for a shorter period, normally for one year or less. While similar in content, its level of detail is much greater as it contains the scheduling and costing out of the specific actions necessary for the achievement of the first year of the strategic plan.

The pragmatic, profit-related reasons for needing to develop a strategic marketing plan, and for doing so before deciding operational courses of action, are illustrated by the 'survival matrix' shown in Figure 7.1. The horizontal axis represents strategy as a continuum from ineffective to effective, while the vertical axis represents tactics on a continuum from inefficient to efficient. Those firms with an effective strategy and efficient tactics continue to thrive, while those with an effective strategy but inefficient tactics merely survive. Those firms to the left of the matrix are destined to die.

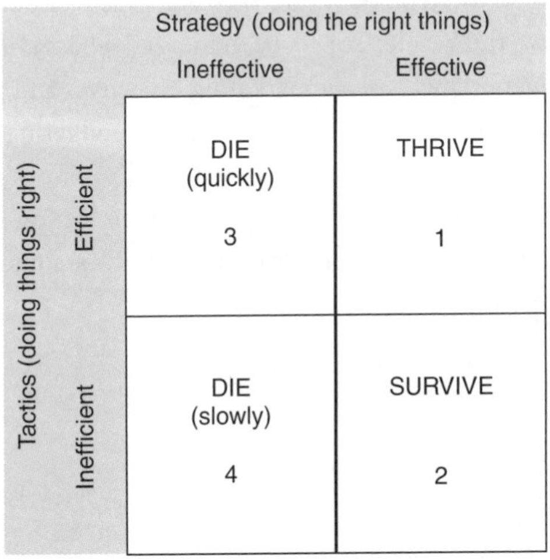

|  |  | Strategy (doing the right things) | |
|---|---|---|---|
|  |  | Ineffective | Effective |
| Tactics (doing things right) | Efficient | DIE (quickly)  3 | THRIVE  1 |
|  | Inefficient | DIE (slowly)  4 | SURVIVE  2 |

Figure 7.1 The survival matrix

Tactical marketing plans should *never* be completed before strategic marketing plans. Most managers prefer selling the products they find easiest to sell to the customers that offer the least line of resistance. However, those who prepare tactical plans first and then extrapolate them merely succeed in extrapolating their own shortcomings. Such preoccupation with short-term plans is a typical mistake of companies that confuse sales forecasting and budgeting with strategic marketing planning.

# PROBLEMS ASSOCIATED WITH MARKETING PLANNING IGNORANCE

Widespread ignorance about marketing planning, and confusion about the difference between strategic marketing planning, sales forecasting and budgeting, has curtailed or killed off many organizations with evident growth potential. Such agonizing outcomes can be avoided to a great extent by fully understanding what marketing planning is (and is not), and assimilating this understanding in practice.

A frequent complaint is marketing's preoccupation with short-term thinking, and an almost total lack of 'strategic thinking', or considering the longer-term implications of external and internal influences on the organization. Another complaint is that marketing plans consist largely of numbers, which bear little relationship to, and offer little insight into, current market position, key opportunities and threats, significant trends and issues, or indeed, how to meet sales targets. Financial objectives, while being essential measures of the desired performance of a company, are of scant practical help, since they say nothing about *how* the results are to be achieved. The same applies to sales forecasts and budgets, which are *not* marketing objectives and strategies. Basing company plans on a combination of forecasting and budgeting systems can only work if the future is going to be the same as the present or the past. As this is rarely the case, reliance on a forecasting and budgeting approach simply produces 'tunnel vision' and often leads to the following common problems:

- lost opportunities for profit;
- meaningless numbers in long-term plans;
- unrealistic objectives;
- lack of actionable market information;
- interfunctional strife;
- management frustration;
- proliferation of products and markets;
- wasted promotional expenditure;
- confusion over pricing;
- growing vulnerability to changes in the business environment; and
- loss of control over the business.

These problems are symptomatic of a much deeper problem emanating from a lack of marketing planning. Marketing planning is about marketing objectives (*what* you want to achieve *vis-à-vis* products and markets) and marketing strategies (*how* you plan to achieve your marketing objectives). Case study 7.1 highlights the danger of relying on forecasts and budgets in the absence of a marketing planning system.

## CASE STUDY 7.1 MARKETING PLANNING IGNORANCE

The headquarters of a major multinational company, with a sophisticated budgeting system, used to receive plans from all over the world and co-ordinate them in quantitative and cross-functional terms (such as number of employees, units of sale, items of plant and square feet of production area) together with the associated financial implications. The trouble was that this complicated edifice was built on initial sales forecasts, which were themselves little more than a time-consuming numbers game. The really key strategic issues relating to products and markets were lost in all the financial activity. Eventually, this resulted in serious operational and profitability problems for the firm.

### CASE STUDY QUESTIONS:

1. Discuss whether sales forecasts are indeed 'little more than a time-consuming numbers game'. Provide justification and evidence to support your argument.

2. What are the key strategic issues relating to (i) products and (ii) markets upon which the company should have focused?

# THE NEED FOR A MARKETING PLANNING SYSTEM

As companies are dynamically evolving entities operating within a dynamically evolving environment, some means of evaluation of the way in which the two interact has to be found to enable them to be better matched. As companies get larger, their operational problems become more complex. Written procedures are needed to make the marketing strategy explicit and the marketing concept understood. Thus, the bigger and more diversified the organization, the bigger the need for standardized and formalized procedures. Organizations without effective marketing planning systems, while it is possible that they are profitable over a number of years, especially in high-growth markets, will tend to be less profitable over time and experience problems that are the very opposite of the benefits referred to above. Furthermore, companies without effective marketing planning systems tend to suffer more serious commercial and organizational consequences when environmental and competitive conditions become hostile and unstable. Even companies with well-structured, well-informed, well-resourced marketing planning systems can suffer setbacks, presenting executives with tough decisions (see Case study 7.2).

## CASE STUDY 7.2 HONDA CIVIC

Based upon marketing intelligence, trend analysis and detailed research into consumer preferences, Honda has positioned itself as innovative and eco-friendly. In 2012 Honda launched the ninth generation Civic to the US market. The USP was a 19 per cent reduction in carbon dioxide compared with previous incarnations. However, pre-launch images attracted little praise for 'green' credentials; on the contrary, opinion leaders' comments focused upon the car's inadequate interior design. Honda's US Vice-President, Vick Poponi, admitted that the company had misjudged the market, 'We read the market wrong.' 'After the Lehman shock, we thought there would be different consumer behaviours. We knew that unemployment would last a long time and that there would be recessional trends. We thought consumers would be more sparse in their needs and be tightening their belts. The Civic was going to reflect that world.'

Honda executives had a major decision to make. Either let the Civic run for the traditional three model years of the five-year cycle before implementing mid-cycle improvements. This would involve heavy discounting and other incentives and could potentially harm brand image. Alternatively, they could publicly acknowledge the shortcomings and revamp the Civic sooner, requiring additional expenditure on machinery and tooling, straining Honda's R&D resources. Making big changes to the car before three model years would also signal to competitors that Honda was acknowledging it had made a mistake.

The US market accounts for almost 50 per cent of worldwide sales of the Civic, hence the decision was of some magnitude. It was decided to make numerous changes and launch a new model in

2013. The flat organizational structure and employee commitment allowed Honda to meet the deadline. Nonetheless, the company attracted criticism for approving the 2012 model in the first place. According to Jim Hall, research consultant at 2953 Analytics, 'It wasn't a bad product, but it wasn't good enough to be a Honda. They have to fix their processes or else this becomes the norm.'

Reference: Autonews.com January 2013

**CASE STUDY QUESTIONS:**

1. Explain how it is possible for a large, resource-rich company like Honda to 'read the market wrong'.
2. Do you think Honda executives made the right decision? Justify your view.
3. Had the executives opted to let the model run for three years before making the usual mid-cycle changes, what actions could they have taken to avoid damage to brand image?

# THE STRATEGIC MARKETING PLANNING PROCESS

As mentioned earlier, the strategic marketing planning process is a series of logical steps that have to be worked through in order to arrive at a logical 'common format' for the implementation of strategy or marketing plan. It is the systemization of this process that is distinctive and that lies at the heart of the theory of strategic marketing planning.

Figure 7.2 outlines the constituent ten steps, highlighting the difference between the *process* of marketing planning and its output, the actual written marketing *plan*. A more comprehensive description of the components and procedure for producing a strategic marketing plan is provided at the end of this chapter.

Experience has shown that a strategic marketing plan should contain a mission statement; financial summary; market overview; SWOT analyses; assumptions; marketing objectives and strategies appropriately prioritized; and a budget containing details of timing, responsibilities and costs, with forecasts and financial outcomes. To ensure that these elements appear in the marketing plan, it is necessary to complete each of the first nine planning steps in succession before producing the detailed one-year plan. However, the dotted lines in Figure 7.2 indicate the reality of the marketing planning process; that

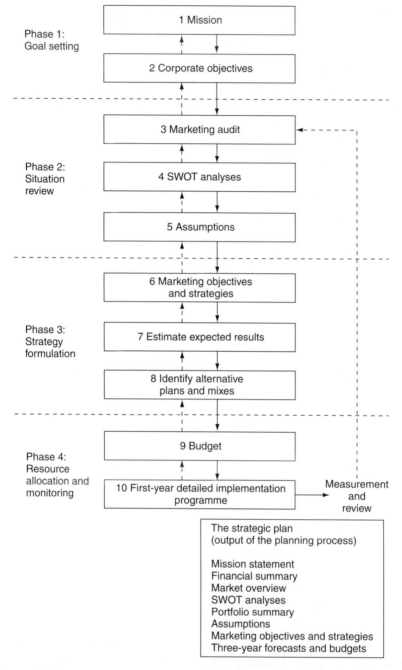

Figure 7.2 The strategic marketing planning process

is to say, it is likely that each of these steps will have to be gone through more than once before final marketing programmes can be written.

Although it is generally accepted that each of the marketing planning steps is applicable in most cases, the degree to which each of the separate steps in the diagram needs to be formalized depends to a large extent on the size and nature of the company. For example, an *undiversified* company generally uses less formalized procedures, since top management tends to have greater functional knowledge and expertise than subordinates, and because the lack of diversity of operations enables direct control to be exercised over most of the key determinants of success. Thus situation reviews or the setting of marketing objectives, for example, are not always made explicit in writing, although these steps still have to be considered.

In contrast, in a *diversified* company it is usually not possible for top management to have greater functional knowledge and expertise than subordinate management, hence the whole planning process tends to be formalized in order to provide a consistent discipline for those who have to make the decisions throughout the organization.

## MARKETING AUDIT

As the marketing audit referred to in Step 2 of Figure 7.2 is the primary mechanism for monitoring marketing performance in relation to the creation and delivery of customer value, it is dealt with in detail later in Part IV of the book. However, for the purposes of proceeding with the strategic marketing planning process, let us explain briefly what this first step entails.

A marketing audit is a systematic, critical and unbiased appraisal of the organization's market environment and of its operations. It amounts to the collection and analysis of information to answer the question: 'Where is the company now?' Both the external and internal variables that impinge on the company's marketing performance are examined. The marketing audit is essentially a database of all market-related issues of the organization, which forms part of the organization-wide management audit. The marketing audit is sometimes referred to as PEST analysis (Political, Economic, Sociological and Technical), although this alternative name does not include competitor analysis.

## SWOT ANALYSIS

To decide on marketing objectives and future strategy, it is necessary first to summarize the unit's *present* position in its market(s). The marketing audit must now be summarized in the form of a SWOT analysis. The acronym SWOT derives from the initial letters of the words *strengths, weaknesses, opportunities* and *threats*. In simple terms:

- What are the opportunities?
- What are the present and future threats to the unit's business in each of the segments that have been identified as being of importance?

- What are the unit's *differential* strengths and weaknesses *vis-à-vis* competitors? In other words, why should potential customers in the target markets prefer to deal with your company rather than with any of your competitors?

The SWOT should include reasons for good or poor performance. By identifying the critical success factors (CSFs) for the organization, and important outside influences and their implications, the key issues to be addressed will emerge.

It is important to be aware that SWOT analysis has been criticized as subjective, unsystematic, non-quantitative (in other words, lacking rigour) and therefore of little practical use and minimal predictive value. Agarwal et al. (2012) advocate moving away the classic SWOT, which takes an 'outside-in' approach to 'Meta-SWOT' which takes an 'inside-out' resource-based view starting with an analysis of the internal resources and capabilities of the organization. In reality, both approaches analyse the *strategic fit* between the organization and its environment. The key point is that as part of the planning process the organization needs to undertake detailed analysis of their current and desired positions, thereafter producing a detailed plan of how to move from the former to the latter. This inevitably begins with an audit.

# GUIDELINES FOR COMPLETING THE SWOT ANALYSIS

The marketing audit will have identified what are considered to be the key markets upon which the company should focus. For presentation purposes, it is helpful to prepare a SWOT for each of these key products. Each of these SWOTs should be brief and interesting to read.

Point 1 below indicates how the *opportunities* and *threats* section of the SWOT should be completed. Point 2 concerns *strengths* and *weaknesses*.

1. *Summary of outside influences and their implications.* This should include a brief statement about how important environmental influences, such as technology, government policies and regulations and the economy have affected this segment. There will obviously be some opportunities and some threats.

2. *Some important factors for success in this business.* How does a competitor wishing to provide products in the same segment succeed? Relatively few factors determine success: factors such as product performance, quality of software, breadth of services, speed of service and low costs are often the most important ones.

A brief statement should now be made about the company's strengths and weaknesses in relation to the most important factors for success that have been identified. To do this, it will probably be necessary to consider other specialist suppliers to the same segment in order to identify why your company can succeed, and what weaknesses must be addressed in the long-term plan.

A sample form for completing a SWOT analysis, leading to strategy formulation, is given in Figure 7.3. This form should be completed for each of the organization's market segments.

## PLANNING ASSUMPTIONS

Having completed our marketing and SWOT analysis, assumptions now have to be made and written down explicitly. There are certain key determinants of success in all companies about which assumptions have to be made before the planning process can proceed. For example, it would be no good receiving plans from two product managers, one of whom believed the economy was about going into decline by 2 per cent, while the other believed the economy was about to grow by 10 per cent.

Assumptions should be few in number, and if a plan is robust – that is, possible irrespective of any assumption made – then so much the better.

## MARKETING OBJECTIVES AND STRATEGIES

The next step in marketing planning is the writing of marketing objectives and strategies, the key step in the whole process:

- *Objectives* are what you want to achieve; and
- *Strategies* are how you plan to achieve your objectives.

There can be objectives and strategies at all levels in marketing. For example, there can be advertising objectives and strategies and pricing objectives and strategies. However, it is important to remember that marketing objectives are about *products and markets only*. Common sense will confirm that it is only by selling something to someone that the company's financial goals can be achieved, and that advertising, pricing and service levels are the means (or strategies) by which we might succeed in doing this. Thus pricing objectives, sales-promotion objectives and advertising objectives should not be confused with marketing objectives. In other words, we can say that marketing objectives are about one or more of the following:

- Existing products in existing markets;
- New products for existing markets;
- Existing products for new markets; and
- New products for new markets.

SWOT analysis

(Note: This form should be completed for each product/market segment under consideration)

1 SBU description
here, describe the market for which the SWOT is being done.

2 Critical success factors what are the few key things from the customer's point of view, that any competitor has to do right to succeed?

1
2
3
4
5

3 Weighting how important is each of these CSFs? Score out of 100.

Total 100

4 Strengths/weaknesses analysis score yourself and each of your main competitors out of 10 on each of the CSFs. Then multiply the score by the weight.

| Comp / CSF | You | Competitor A | Competitor B | Competitor C | Competitor D |
|---|---|---|---|---|---|
| 1 | | | | | |
| 2 | | | | | |
| 3 | | | | | |
| 4 | | | | | |
| 5 | | | | | |
| Total (score weight) | | | | | |

5 Opportunities/threats what are the few key things outside your direct control that have had, and will continue to have, an impact on your business?

Opportunities

1
2
3
4
5

Threats

6 Key issues that need to be addressed

7 Key assumption for the planning period

1
2
3
4
5
6
7

8 Key objectives

9 Key strategies

Financial consequences

Figure 7.3 Sample form for SWOT analysis

They should be capable of measurement, otherwise they are not objectives. Directional terms such as 'maximize', 'minimize', 'penetrate' and 'increase' are only acceptable if quantitative measurement can be attached to them over the planning period. Measurement should be in terms of sales volume, money value (pounds, euros or dollars, for example), market share and percentage penetration of outlets.

Marketing strategies are the means by which marketing objectives will be achieved and are generally concerned with the four 'P's – that is, product, pricing, place and promotion decisions. Figure 7.4 highlights the need to plan and integrate the marketing mix elements against defined marketing objectives. The important process of defining marketing objectives and strategies is considered in Chapter 8.

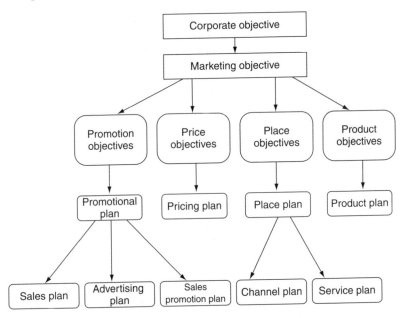

Figure 7.4 The marketing mix is defined against the marketing objectives

Having completed this major planning task, it is normal at this stage to employ judgement, experience and field tests to assess the feasibility of the objectives and strategies in terms of market share, sales, costs and profits.

## PROGRAMMES

The general marketing strategies are now deployed into specific 'sub-objectives', each supported by more detailed strategy and action statements, with timings and responsibilities clearly indicated.

## USE OF MARKETING PLANS

A written marketing plan is the background against which operational decisions are taken on an ongoing basis; consequently, too much detail should not be included. We should remember that its major function is to determine where the company is *now*, where it wants to *go* and *how* to get there. This is central to the company's revenue-generating activities, and from it flow all other corporate activities, such as the timing of the cash flow and the size and character of the labour force. Finally, the marketing plan should be distributed to those who need to know what is going on, since its purpose is an aid to effective management.

# INTERNATIONAL MARKETING PLANNING

The process of marketing planning outlined in this chapter is universally applicable, irrespective of company size and complexity. The only real difference concerns the degree of formality of the processes and procedures. In the case of a company operating internationally, a more formalized approach is advisable in order to gain the economies of scale and scope that give international organizations their competitive edge. For example, in order to create a truly international brand such as Perrier or Castrol GTX, the key elements of global branding must be planned centrally. These issues are outlined in Chapter 10, where the following definition of a global brand is also given:

> A global brand is a product that bears the same name and logo and presents the same or similar message all over the world. Usually, the product is aimed at the same target market and is promoted and presented in much the same way.

Consequently, it is clear that the brand's positioning must be planned and controlled centrally. This will embrace the channels used to reach the target market, the price position within the market and, of course, the way it is promoted. In many organizations, product planning needs to be controlled centrally in order to ensure a balanced global portfolio. This will entail an understanding of a product's position in its life cycle in a country and region of the world in order to ensure that appropriate objectives and strategies are set for it, together with the decision of when and how to allocate resources.

# DESIGN AND IMPLEMENTATION OF A MARKETING PLANNING SYSTEM

As a rule, formalized marketing planning procedures result in greater profitability and stability in the long term and help to reduce friction and operational difficulties within organizations. The really important issue in any system is the extent to which it enables control to be exercised over the key determinants of success and failure. Research has shown that certain conditions must be satisfied for a marketing planning system to work. There must be:

- *Openness* – any closed-loop planning system, especially if it is based only on forecasting and budgeting, will deaden any creative response and eventually lead to failure. Therefore there has to be some mechanism to prevent inertia setting in through the over-bureaucratization of the system.

- *Integration* – marketing planning that is not integrated with other functional areas of the business at general management level will largely be ineffective.

- *Coherence* – separation of operational and strategic marketing planning will lead to a divergence of the short-term thrust of a business at the operational level from the long-term objectives of the enterprise as a whole, with the short-term viewpoint winning because it achieves quick results.

- *Leadership* – unless the CEO understands and takes an active role in strategic marketing planning, it will never be an effective system.

- *Time* – it can take three years to introduce marketing planning successfully.

As we have seen, a successful marketing planning system follows requisite, key steps:

- There will have to be guidance provided by the corporate objectives;
- A marketing audit must take place;
- A gap analysis must be completed;
- SWOT analyses must be drawn up;
- Assumptions and contingencies must be considered;
- Marketing objectives and strategies must be set;
- Individual marketing programmes must be established; and
- There must be a period of measurement and review.

All this work will take time, and will certainly require discussions with other functional departments, either to get information or to ensure collaboration. Thus it is important to schedule the tasks and timing, and to present the plans in a clear manner – for example, diagrammatically, as shown in Figure 7.5.

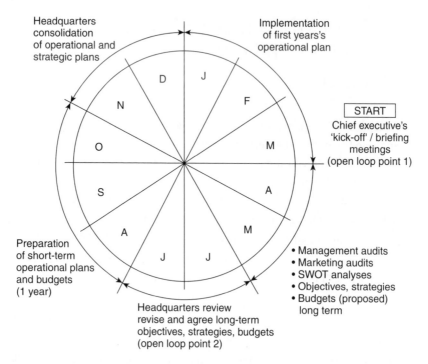

Figure 7.5 Strategic and operational planning – timing

The circle represents a calendar year and the time periods are given as examples to indicate the sequence of planning activities. As the company becomes more experienced in planning, the timetable can probably be tightened up and the whole planning period shortened. In the second planning year, months 11 and 12 could be used to evaluate the first year's plan and thereby prepare information for the next round of corporate planning. The planning process is an iterative one and a continual undercurrent throughout the year.

It is also clear from the planning cycle that key account planning must take place at the same time as, or even before, draft plans are prepared for a strategic business unit.

Significantly, there are two open loop points. These are the key times, or opportunities, in the planning process when a subordinate's views and findings should be subjected to the closest examination by a superior. By utilizing these 'oxygen valves', life can be breathed into marketing planning, transforming it into the critical and creative process it is supposed to be, rather than the dull, repetitive ritual it so often turns out to be.

There is a natural point of focus in the future beyond which it is pointless to plan for. Generally, small firms can use shorter horizons because they tend to be flexible in the way in which they can react to environmental turbulence in the short term. Larger firms need longer lead times in which to make changes in direction, and thus require longer planning horizons. While three and five years are commonly used, the planning horizon should reflect the nature of the markets in which the company operates, and the time needed to recover capital investment costs.

Remaining sensitive and responsive to the marketplace raises another question: Who should make marketing decisions? Top management who are remote from the scene, but, as indicated earlier, can play a valuable role in strategic marketing planning? Those at 'the sharp end' who have intimate knowledge of the markets but less corporate authority? Location of marketing planning within the company is an important aspect of successful marketing planning. Generally speaking, it should take place as close to the marketplace as possible in the first instance, but the plans should then be reviewed at a high level within the organization to pick up any issues that have been overlooked. One means of formulating an informed, overall strategic view is to conduct a hierarchy of audits and SWOTs at each main organizational level (that is, individual manager, group manager, profit centre, head office) and then to consolidate them.

Since, in anything but the smallest of undiversified companies, it is not possible for headquarters to set detailed objectives for operating units, it is suggested that at the situation-review stage of the planning process, strategic guidelines be issued outlining possible areas for which objectives and strategies will be set (for example, financial, operational, human, organizational, marketing), or the CEO give a personal briefing at kick-off meetings. Strategic and operational planning must be a top-down and bottom-up process. Understanding this total interdependence between upper and lower levels of management in respect of audits and objective and strategy setting is crucial to achieving the necessary balance between control and creativity.

The vital role that the chief executive and top management *must* play in marketing planning underlines a key point. That is, it is *people* who make systems work, system design and implementation have to take into account the 'personality' of both the organization and the people involved, and these are different in all organizations. The attitudes of executives vary, ranging from the extremes of the impersonal and autocratic to the highly personal and participative. There is some evidence to indicate that CEOs who fail, first, to understand the essential role of marketing in generating profitable revenue in a business; and, second, to understand how marketing can be integrated into other functional areas of the business through marketing planning procedures, are a key contributory factor in poor economic performance.

The most common design and implementation problems with marketing planning systems are:

- Weak support from the chief executive and top management;
- Lack of a plan for planning;

- Lack of line management support:
  - Hostility;
  - Lack of skills;
  - Lack of information;
  - Lack of resources; and
  - Inadequate organizational structure;
- Confusion over planning terms;
- Numbers in lieu of written objectives and strategies;
- Too much detail, too far ahead;
- Once-a-year ritual;
- Separation of operational planning from strategic planning;
- Failure to integrate marketing planning into total corporate planning system; and
- Delegation of planning to a planner.

When marketing planning fails, it is generally because companies place too much emphasis on the procedures and the resulting paperwork rather than on generating information useful to, and consumable by, management. Also, when companies relegate marketing planning to a 'planner' it invariably fails, for the simple reason that planning for line management cannot be delegated to a third party. The real role of the planner should be to help those responsible for implementation to plan. Equally, planning failures often result from companies trying too much too quickly and without training staff in the use of procedures or providing them with sufficient resources.

# CONTENTS OF A STRATEGIC MARKETING PLAN

A well-designed, systematic, robust strategic marketing plan should comprise the following:

## MISSION STATEMENT

- A declaration of the *raison d'être* of the organization, covering its role, business definition, distinctive competence and future indications.

## FINANCIAL SUMMARY

- A brief outline of the financial implications over the full planning period.

## SWOT ANALYSES

- Only the SWOTs (not the audit) go into a marketing plan.
- Summaries emanating from the marketing audit.
- A brief, interesting and concise commentary.
- Focus on *key* factors only.
- List *differential* strengths and weaknesses *vis-à-vis* competitors.
- List *key* external opportunities and threats.
- Identify and pin down the *real issues*; not a list of unrelated points.
- The reader should be able to grasp instantly the main thrust of the business; he or she should even be able to write down your marketing objectives.
- Follow the implied question, 'Which means that…?' to get the real implications.
- Do not over-abbreviate.
- Spend time on the SWOT. It is worth it.

## ASSUMPTIONS

- Critical to the planned marketing objectives and strategies.
- Must be few in number.
- If a plan can happen irrespective of the assumption, the assumption is unnecessary.

## MARKETING OBJECTIVES

- Goal statements about products/services and markets only.
- They articulate what the company is committing itself to and the corresponding resource implications.
- They flow from the SWOT and must be compatible.
- They should be quantifiable and measurable. Avoid directional terms such as 'increase', 'improve' and so on.
- There will be hierarchy of objectives throughout the organization.
- Set priorities for the chosen marketing objectives.
- Do not confuse objectives and strategies (objectives – what we want to achieve; strategies – how we plan to achieve objectives).

## MARKETING STRATEGIES

- Product, pricing, place and promotion policies.
- Marketing strategies must eventually be transformed into detailed marketing actions, which are articulated in the product, price, place (distribution) and promotion (communications) plans.

- Forecasts come last (not simple extrapolations); they are not objectives.

- Specific sub-objectives for products and segments, with detailed strategy and action statements (what, where, when, costs and so on).

- A consolidated budget for the full planning period, detailing annual costs and revenues.

- Budgets and forecasts *must* reflect marketing objectives. Objectives, strategies and programmes *must* reflect agreed budgets and sales forecasts.

Adherence to a well-designed and well-implemented marketing planning system can do much to prevent marketing plan failure.

# SUMMARY

Marketing planning is a managerial process leading to a marketing plan. Increasingly dynamic markets and the need for organizations to be close to consumers means that marketing planning is no longer confined to the marketing department. This is how it should be, as effective marketing planning underpins the successful creation and delivery of the value proposition which entails commitment at the highest levels. The roles of those involved in marketing planning need to be clearly specified and articulated in order to avoid conflict and ensure that there is shared understanding of marketing objectives, strategies and detailed tactical plans.

There is a process for marketing planning, the formalization of which is a function of size and product market complexity. Naturally, resources and competencies can be key influencers of marketing planning effectiveness, but much can be achieved even with limited resources provided there is a formal planning process, a clear sense of direction and acknowledgement that marketing success is a shared responsibility across the organization.

# FURTHER READING

McDonald, M. and Wilson, H. (2011) *Marketing plans: How to prepare them; how to use them,* Chichester: Wiley.

A practical, down to earth marketing planning book that explains and demonstrates how to prepare and use a marketing plan.

# REFERENCES

Agarwal, R., Grassi, W. and Pahl, J. (2012) Meta-SWOT: Introducing a new strategic tool, *Journal of Business Strategy*, Vol. 33 (2): 12–21.

Coumau, J-B., Fletcher, B. and French, T. (2013) Engaging boards on the future of marketing, *McKinsey Quarterly*, Vol. 1: 104–107.

Kotler, M. and Kotler, P. (2013) Breaking down: The challenge of acquiring global marketing data, *Marketing Research*, Vol. 25 (1): 12–13.

Phillips, P., Davies, F. and Moutinho, L. (2001) The interactive effects of strategic marketing planning and performance: A neural network analysis, *Journal of Marketing Management*, Vol. 17: 159–182.

# CHAPTER 8
# DEFINING MARKETING OBJECTIVES AND STRATEGIES

IN THIS CHAPTER WE STUDY:

- the relationship between marketing objectives, strategies and the value proposition
- the main components of marketing strategy
- different types of product/service benefits
- techniques of benefit analysis and gap analysis
- the Ansoff matrix
- differing degrees of product/market newness

# STRATEGIC MARKETING AND THE VALUE PROPOSITION

Marketing objectives and strategies play a central role in creating the value proposition. The link between strategic planning and business performance has long been recognized; however, it is relevant to ask whether formalized strategic planning has continued relevance in the twenty first century. Many strategic planning models were conceived in the mid-late-twentieth century and in turbulent times might it be better to act opportunistically? Recent research by Moon (2013), which takes into account the severe market and technological turbulence of recent years, detects a strong link between strategic thinking and marketing performance, underlying the imperative of sound strategic planning.

To remain competitive, organizations need to incorporate strategic flexibility into their planning model. Defined as the ability to anticipate and adapt to external and internal environmental imperatives (Nadkarni and Narayanan, 2007), this is imperative in turbulent times. Internally, this might include resource reallocation or investment in technology; externally, it might encompass adapting to rapidly changing market or industry conditions. Strategic flexibility can enhance organizations' risk management not only through an ability to respond more quickly to current events but also by reacting rapidly to potential future scenarios (Grewal and Tansuhaj, 2001). Such flexibility should be a prerequisite of any strategic marketing process.

Embedding strategic flexibility however does not mean abandoning robustness; on the contrary, the ability to respond rapidly to changing circumstances necessitates a high level of strategic planning. The first step is to define strategic objectives, from which detailed plans can be developed. The value proposition lies at the heart of marketing objectives. Put simply, we can ask, 'Why would either party want to engage with the other, and what would entice them to act to do so?' This deceptively simple question raises a multitude of issues that combine to shape the 'give and take' of commercial relationships. This is the core of the value proposition to the customer defined by the marketing objectives, or what the organization aims to achieve *vis-à-vis* its chosen market segments. The marketing objectives will then be delivered by marketing strategies.

Clearly, successful relationship development through strategic marketing depends on the construction of a manifestly strong and purposeful statement of value that respects the agendas of both parties. The creation of such a value proposition by the supplying organization depends first on choosing and prioritizing the markets and segments in which it wishes to operate. These decisions will be based on the analyses produced in the previous process (defining markets and customer value) and will take into account both the market's/segment's inherent attractiveness and the organization's actual and potential ability to meet those customers' needs and expectations. Target market selection will thus also be influenced by the corporate objectives. To understand how all these elements fit together, let us start by looking in some depth at the process of setting marketing objectives and developing marketing strategy.

# MARKETING OBJECTIVES AND STRATEGIES

## MARKETING OBJECTIVES

Marketing objectives concern both what the organization hopes to receive from each segment in terms of, for example, market share, volume, value or contribution and what it hopes to deliver to customers in return. This price/value proposition (what the supplier gives/gets and what the customer gives/gets) can be thought of as the four 'P's translating to four 'C's:

| | |
|---|---|
| Product: | Consumer wants and needs |
| Place: | Convenience (access, availability and distribution) |
| Price: | Cost |
| Promotion: | Communication |

For example, 'consumer wants and needs' will be met by the 'product', as they help to shape product design and development. The customer is concerned with 'convenience' of purchase, which influences how the supplying organization will 'place' the product in the marketplace. Similarly, the customer is interested in the total 'cost' of product purchase and ownership, not just the upfront 'price'. Through two-way 'communication' customers declare their requirements and learn about suppliers' offerings, while suppliers publicize their products and services and gain customer knowledge through 'promotion'.

The important point about marketing objectives is that they are concerned solely with *products and markets*, as it is only by selling something to someone that the organization's financial goals can be achieved. If profits and cash flows are to be maximized, the organization must consider carefully how its current customer needs are changing and how its products/services offered need to change accordingly. Further, they should be capable of measurement; otherwise they are not objectives. Marketing objectives are normally stated in standards of performance for a given operating period, or conditions to be achieved by a given date.

Marketing objectives are the nucleus of managerial action, providing direction to the marketing plans. An objective will ensure that a company knows what its strategies are expected to accomplish, and when a particular strategy has accomplished its purpose. Without objectives, strategy decisions and all that follows will take place in a vacuum.

All organizations serve a mix of different types of market, and marketing strategies enable them to select the customers, and hence the markets, with which they wish to deal. Marketing strategies are the routes by which an organization seeks to achieve its marketing objectives through the range of products/services it offers to its chosen markets. Marketing strategies are thus generally concerned with the four 'P's of the marketing mix:

- Product – the general policies for product deletions, modifications, additions, design, branding, positioning, packaging and so on;
- Price – the general pricing policies to be followed for product groups in market segments;
- Place – the general policies for channels and customer service levels; and
- Promotion – the general policies for communicating with customers under the relevant headings, such as advertising, sales force, sales promotion, public relations, exhibitions, direct mail, the Internet and so on.

The main components of marketing strategy are the company, customers and competitors. When setting marketing strategies, it is important to know your company's position in the market, as well as the positions of your competitors, so that ideally you can meet customer needs by doing something your rivals are not expecting, and will find difficult to emulate or supersede. The point to remember about differentiation as a strategy is that your company must still be cost effective.

Michael Porter's generic strategies matrix, shown in Figure 8.1, demonstrates that some markets are inherently more prone to lack of differentiation in products and services. In such cases, the attainment of low costs must be a corporate goal if adequate margins are to be obtained. The ultimate strategy for commodity market situations, where there is no differentiation or cost advantage, is to move to either a cost leadership or a niche strategy. A niche position is achieved through offering added value, whereas in a cost leadership position, the values offered are cost competitive.

Some of the marketing strategies available to managers include:

1. Change product design, performance, quality or features.
2. Change advertising or promotion.
3. Change unit price.
4. Change delivery or distribution.

5. Change service levels.

6. Improve marketing productivity (for example, improve sales mix).

7. Improve administrative productivity.

8. Consolidate product line.

9. Withdraw from markets.

10. Consolidate distribution.

11. Standardize design.

12. Acquire markets, products, facilities.

In order to determine marketing strategies, obviously the first step is to understand fully what constitutes a product or service, and what is the role of the product/service in the marketing mix. Thereafter one can analyse how to create value for prospects in selected target markets.

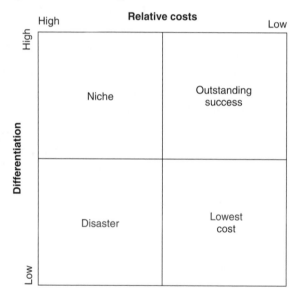

Figure 8.1 Porter's generic strategies matrix

## THE BENEFIT ANALYSIS WORKSHEET

The following process describes how to match product benefits to target markets. Taking a specific market segment, the process is relatively straightforward:

1. Produce a comprehensive list of benefits;

2. Identify the three major benefits for this customer segment;

3. Identify a further four benefits;

4. Identify all the other benefits on the list that are valued to a lesser extent by this key market segment;

5. List all products/services supplied to this segment.

Finally, combine the information just assembled by completing the benefit analysis worksheet (see Figure 8.2).

# NOTES ON COMPLETING THE WORKSHEET

1. Write down the products or services offered in the spaces provided at the left side of the worksheet. There are six spaces. If more are needed, extend the worksheet on to another sheet of paper.

2. Write down the benefits identified above so that the three major benefits are put as headings to columns 1, 2 and 3 of the worksheet. The next four benefits are entered as headings for columns 4 to 7 inclusive. All other benefits are written as headings to column 8 and onwards.

3. Consider the first product or service listed on the worksheet. Score it according to how well it supplies the benefit at the end of each column. It will be noted that the first three benefits can score a maximum of 12 points, the next four a maximum of 6 points and the remainder a maximum of 3 points.

4. Repeat this process for the products and services.

Figure 8.3 is an example, provided here purely for illustration.

# INTERPRETATION OF THE WORKSHEET

The 'total' score is an indicator of how many 'benefit points' each product is providing. In the example shown in Figure 8.3, Product A scores the most points and is ranked first, Products C and D come next to rank equal second, while Product B is ranked third. Not only does this technique enable products or services to be compared and measured against the benefits they supply, it also gives rise to some very pertinent questions. For example:

- Why are Products B, C and D not competitively priced?
- Can the performance of the products, especially A and D, be improved?
- Why are the safety scores of B and A so low?
- Why is packaging so uniformly poor?

**Benefit analysis worksheet**

| Products or services \ Customer benefits | Major benefits | | | Secondary benefits | | | | | Lesser benefits | | | | | | | Total | Ranking | Notes, comments, etc. |
|---|---|---|---|---|---|---|---|---|---|---|---|---|---|---|---|---|---|---|
| | 1 | 2 | 3 | 4 | 5 | 6 | 7 | 8 | 9 | 10 | 11 | 12 | 13 | 14 | 15 | | | |
| | Score max. 12 each | | | Score max. 6 each | | | | | Score max. 4 each | | | | | | | | | |
| | | | | | | | | | | | | | | | | | | |
| | | | | | | | | | | | | | | | | | | |
| | | | | | | | | | | | | | | | | | | |
| | | | | | | | | | | | | | | | | | | |

Figure 8.2 Benefit analysis worksheet

| Product | Price | Performance | Safety | Design | Packaging | Durability | Discount | Delivery | After-sales | Instructions | | | Total | Rank | Comments |
|---|---|---|---|---|---|---|---|---|---|---|---|---|---|---|---|
| A | 12 | 9 | 9 | 6 | 3 | 4 | 6 | 1 | 3 | 3 | | | 56 | 1 | |
| B | 6 | 10 | 7 | 4 | 3 | 6 | 6 | 1 | 1 | 2 | | | 46 | 3 | |
| C | 8 | 10 | 10 | 4 | 3 | 3 | 6 | 3 | 3 | 2 | | | 52 | 2 | |
| D | 4 | 8 | 12 | 6 | 3 | 6 | 6 | 3 | 1 | 3 | | | 52 | 2 | |

Figure 8.3 Benefit analysis worksheet results

- Can the design of B and C be improved?
- What are the immediate steps that might be taken to improve the benefits provided to customers?
- Taking into account the ranking of the individual products or services (that is, their total benefit scores), is the correct allocation of energy and resources being made to each? Might their relative importance be reappraised?

Such questions asked of any company can only lead to a search for improvement. This will be just as true for our products or services as it was in the illustration given here. Moreover, since all such improvements are based on providing greater customer benefits, they hold every prospect of bringing about important changes. This process can be repeated for other market segments of our business.

# THE PRODUCT/SERVICE LIFE CYCLE

The idea of benefit analysis that we have just explored is a very important one. It does have one drawback, however. It is like a 'snapshot' of the company's products or services at a given moment and cannot portray what is happening over a period of time. Historians of technology have observed that all technical functions grow exponentially until they come up against some natural limiting factor, which causes them to slow down and eventually to decline as one technology is replaced by another. The same phenomenon applies to products and is embodied in the product life cycle (PLC).

The PLC is a conceptual tool that provides a means of describing the sales patterns of products, be they goods or services, over their time in the market. If absolute sales of a product within a market or segment are plotted on a period-by-period basis (usually annually), the 'standard' life cycle approximates to an S-curve, as shown in Figure 8.4. Note that the

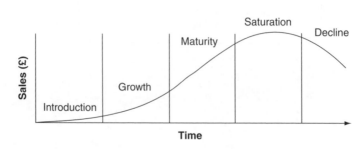

Figure 8.4 Product life cycle

PLC is a generic academic model; while the principles are sound, in reality, product life cycles adopt a number of different shapes and are never smooth, deviations from this norm being caused by the nature of the product, consumption patterns or actions taken by the company to prolong one or more stages.

From a management perspective, the PLC concept is helpful in that it focuses attention on the likely future sales pattern if no corrective action is taken. Understanding the concept and the determinants of its shape can thus be a powerful aid to the development of marketing strategies. It is important to note that an organization is only concerned with the life cycle trend of a total market or segment, and with the sales of its product within it.

Product life cycles usually experience a number of successive stages. As depicted in Figure 8.4, the early part of the sales curve denotes a struggle to get the product or service known; sales are hard to come by and a lot of time and energy goes into developing contacts in order to create awareness and acceptance of it. It is aptly called the *introduction phase*.

Assuming that the product or service is acceptable to its target market, there then comes a time when it 'takes off'; everybody seems to want to buy it. This is the *growth phase*. But no market is infinitely expandable, and eventually the rate of growth slows as the product or service moves into the *maturity stage*.

Eventually a point is reached where there are too many firms in the market; price wars break out and some firms drop out of the market. Sales level off or decline gradually as demand has largely been satisfied, if not by our company then by the many competitors who have been equally attracted by the growth potential of the market for this product/service. This is the *saturation phase*.

After a period of relative stability, interest in our product/service wanes and sales start to fall more quickly. This is the *decline phase*. Exactly how far sales are allowed to fall is largely a managerial decision, as we shall see.

## WHAT DOES THE PLC TELL US?

The PLC appears to hold true for all products and services. However, both its shape and duration can vary. The PLC can be prolonged through careful management and investment, or indeed hastened to an early demise by poor management, wasting resources and opportunities. For example, the life cycle for fashion items and fad products can be steep, but short-lived, whereas the life cycle of aircraft can run to many years, displaying a consistent sales pattern. There is a recognized propensity for life cycles to become shorter as the rate of technological innovation increases and customers' expectations heighten. The mechanical typewriter, for example, may have enjoyed a life cycle of decades while its latter-day equivalent, the word-processing program, may have a life cycle measured in years.

The level of sales plotted on the vertical axis is usually given in unit or revenue terms. For marketing purposes, it is often of more value to measure sales against the growth in the market as this gives a better indication of the product's competitive ability and attractiveness to the customer. Of course, absolute sales volumes are also important as they determine revenue and current profitability.

The PLC can be used in a number of ways:

1. As a *predictive* device, forecasting how products may behave in the future and allowing corrective action to be taken. It can help us to understand how products relate to markets and to appreciate where certain elements of the marketing mix may be more appropriate to particular PLC stages.

2. As a *comparative* device, warning of any significant deviations from the total market experience (see Figures 8.5 and 8.6) or enabling a strategic balance to be achieved among products within the same range.

3. As a *formative* device, assisting the design of future product/market strategies based on sales performance in combination with experience and additional analysis. It can provide clues about what are the most appropriate strategies to use at different stages of the life cycle to best support and invest in our product or service.

4. As a *manipulative* device, indicating when short-term strategies might be used to 'distort' the life cycle to our advantage. For example, suppose this curve represented one of our products or services, as in Figure 8.5.

Figure 8.6 tells us that we have just passed through the growth phase and appear to be entering the maturity phase. If we take no action, we could expect the sales curve to level out and eventually decline.

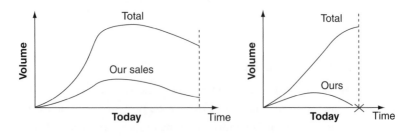

Diagram A

The life-cycle curve follows the movement of the market curve, but on a smaller scale.

Diagram B

The life-cycle curve peaked while the total market curve was still growing. Something must have been going very wrong for this to happen. What was it? Why are we in decline at this stage?

Figure 8.5 Product/market strategy and the product life cycle (1)

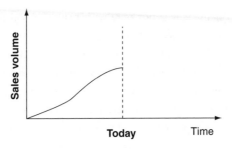

Figure 8.6 Product/market strategy and the product life cycle (2)

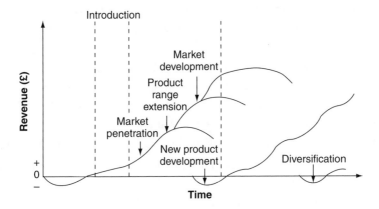

Figure 8.7 Product/market strategy and the product life cycle (3)

However, we could take steps to delay this process. We could, as Figure 8.7 shows, improve the product or extend the range and thereby stimulate more sales. When that initiative has run its course and sales start to level out again, we could extend the market or develop a new segment. Again, this stimulates the sales curve and extends the period of growth.

However, these actions all cost money and so they have to be weighed against the level of increased sales they would be expected to generate. Eventually, there comes a time when it becomes counter-productive to prop up an ailing product or service in this way. The section on portfolio management in Chapter 9 will help us in making the go/no-go decision about investing in particular products or services. But, for now, let us concentrate on understanding more about the life cycle.

# LIFE CYCLE – COSTS AND STRATEGIES

As the above example has shown, with respect to product management a company must be prepared to vary its strategies as the product or service moves through its life-cycle. But it is not only with respect to product management that alternative strategies should be considered. Pricing, distribution and promotional efforts also need to be reviewed regularly. For example, early promotional efforts will almost certainly have to concentrate on creating awareness of the product, especially if it is a completely new product or service concept. Later in the life of the product, when awareness levels are high, it is likely that a company will need to spend more effort on positioning and imagery in what often turn out to be crowded markets during the growth phase. Similarly, distribution channels are likely to change, as is pricing. Clearly, it may prove fatal to refuse to bow to price pressures as the market reaches maturity, because if hard-won market share is lost at this crucial stage it could well affect profits adversely.

So, market circumstances change over the life of a product or service, and a company's policies should also change accordingly. Table 8.1 illustrates a set of guidelines used by one company in the electrical components market to help it determine appropriate marketing strategies at different stages of the life cycle. In this case, the company combined the two stages of maturity and saturation.

Drawing a product life cycle can be extremely difficult, even given the availability of some form of time-series analysis. This is connected with the complex question of market share measurement.

As intimated, the firm needs to be concerned with its share (its proportion of volume or value) of an *actual* market. However, in order to measure an actual market, great care must be taken to ensure that a company is measuring the right things. Take the example of the company measuring the institutional markets for nylon carpet. It is clearly nonsense to include concrete in their measurement of the floor-covering market because concrete, although a floor covering, does not satisfy the needs that customers have for warmth and colour, and is therefore not part of their market. Neither, probably, should wool carpets or linoleum be included. To help with this, let us remind ourselves of key definitions:

- Product *class*: for example, carpets;
- Product *form*: for example, nylon rolls; and
- Product *brand*: for example, 'X'.

'X' as a brand, for the purpose of measuring market share, *is concerned only with the aggregate of all other brands that satisfy the same group of customer wants*. Nevertheless, the manufacturer of 'X' also needs to be aware of the sales trends of other kinds of carpets and floor covering in the institutional market, as well as of carpet sales overall.

Let us now broaden the discussion to a consideration of managing a range of products or services and the ways in which they satisfy market needs. The

| | Introduction | Growth | Maturity/saturation | Decline |
|---|---|---|---|---|
| Costs | Can be high, because of inexperience in supplying and the cost of promotion | Increasing due to increased volume and fighting off competition. High growth requires funding | Stabilizing/reducing as experience and reduced competition take effect | Can be high if not managed because of diseconomies of scale; for example, only small runs |
| Demand | Unpredictable. Forecasts can vary widely | Upper limits might be forecast but volatile situation sensitive to prices and competition | Fairly well defined | Known and limited |
| Competition | Largely unknown | Many new entrants jump on 'bandwagon'. Competition fierce | Marginal competitors leave. Remainder tend to specialize in particular segments | New entrants are unlikely. Competition declines |
| Customer loyalty | Trial usage, new relationship, little loyalty | Some loyalty, but to ensure supplies many customers might have more than one supplier | Well-established buying patterns with high customer loyalty | Extremely stable. Customers are not motivated to seek new suppliers |
| Ease of entry | Relatively easy because market leaders have not yet emerged. Customers feeling their way | More difficult as some suppliers begin to establish market share and benefit from economies of scale | Difficult because of established buying patterns. New business has to be won | Little incentive to enter |
| Price | Price to capitalize on newness (high) or to penetrate the market (low) | Price competitively | Price defensively | Price according to perceived product life; for example, high for milk |
| Promotion | Active and aggressive | Active and aggressive | Selective and specialized | Minimal, if at all |
| Product/service range | Limited and specialized to meet the needs of early customers | Rapid expansion in order to capitalize on new opportunities | Range expansion slows down or ceases | Range narrows as unproductive items are dropped |

Table 8.1 Life cycle stages – characteristics and responses

art of successful product management must be based on a clear view of just *how* the present and future product range will continue to meet the twin goals of customer and corporate objectives.

As a first stage in successful product management it is important to think of the 'product' as a variable in the marketing mix, in the same way that we consider price or promotion as a variable. The extent of freedom to manoeuvre on the product variable will depend largely on the internal resources of the firm and where its strengths are in relation to the competition as identified by a SWOT analysis. Answering the following questions can help us establish the appropriateness of current product strategy and provide a firm basis for developing future product/market strategy.

- What benefits do customers seek from this type of product?
- Does our product provide these benefits in a greater proportion than competitors' products?
- What competitive product advantages are causing us to lose market share?
- Does our product range still provide 'value-in-use' to the customers in relation to its cost to them?
- Does each product in our range still meet the corporate objectives set for it?

In managing a portfolio of products (see Chapter 9), an important strategic decision is knowing when and how to phase out declining products and phase in new. Innovation and new product development (NPD) have attracted increasing attention in recent years (both in the corporate and academic worlds) in response to increasingly competitive markets and increasingly demanding consumers. The need to adapt quickly and decisively is key; a recent study by Kandemir and Acur (2012) identifies a positive association between proactive strategic decision-making flexibility and NPD performance, thus underlining the link between strategy and outcomes.

# PRODUCT/MARKET STRATEGY

What is product/market strategy? Very simply, it is the totality of the decisions taken within the organization concerning its target markets and the products it offers to those markets. Strategy implies a chosen route to a defined goal and an element of long-term planning. Thus the product/market strategy of the firm represents its commitment to a particular direction in the future.

The effective company is one that plans for growth, and in terms of its product/market strategy seeks to plan its *product portfolio* well in advance – in terms required or determined by product policy. The company must plan for growth and both product policy and product/market strategy must be growth orientated, but clearly the growth must have a purposeful direction if future profits and cash flows are to be maximized. This direction is provided through appropriate growth policies, indicating the *vectors* (variable directions) along which the firm is intended to move.

## THE ANSOFF MATRIX

While the PLC is an effective aid to understanding how products behave in markets, it is not without drawbacks. The PLC model is not especially adept at examining a range or portfolio of products, as the life cycle may vary from one product to another. Also, the life cycle has little/limited value as a predictive tool. Once the product has run its course, the PLC does not enlighten strategy for new products in new markets; it is relevant only to existing products within existing markets.

A helpful device for considering product/market strategy is the Ansoff matrix (1965). Widely used, the Ansoff matrix, shown in Figure 8.8, is a useful planning aid as it describes the four possible combinations of products and markets, or the four categories of marketing objectives. Marketing objectives consider the two main dimensions of commercial growth: product development and market development.

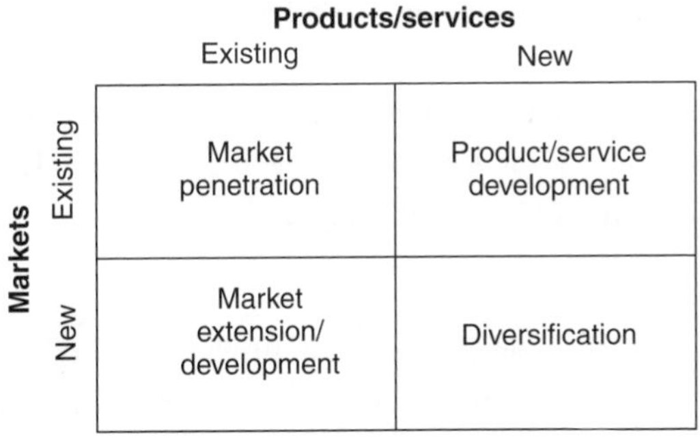

**Products/services**

|  | Existing | New |
|---|---|---|
| **Markets** Existing | Market penetration | Product/service development |
| **Markets** New | Market extension/ development | Diversification |

Figure 8.8 The 'Ansoff' matrix

The Ansoff matrix identifies the following strategic options:

1. Selling existing products to existing markets/segments (market penetration);
2. Extending existing products to new markets/segments (market extension);
3. Developing new products for existing markets/segments (product development); and
4. Developing new products for new markets/segments (diversification).

Like all models, the Ansoff matrix does not provide an 'answer' to any strategic decision; it simply provides a framework for analysis. The longevity of the model attests to its simple but practical approach to the product/market strategic analysis.

## Market penetration

This involves keeping existing customers and finding new ones in the same market, without changing the products/services offered. This implies that pricing and promotion will have to be very competitive, because other suppliers are not just going to sit back and let us take their business. However, there are fewer unknowns and therefore, in theory, fewer risks.

## Market extension/development

This strategy involves finding new users in new markets for the existing product/service. It might mean going further afield geographically (or even exporting), opening up new market segments or discovering new applications for the products/services. This strategy implies that the company has marketing strengths and the wherewithal to make inroads into new markets. Again, the element of dealing with the unknown makes this a slightly more risky strategy.

## Product/service development

This strategy involves the modification of existing products/services to improve their quality, style or whatever characteristics are valued by customers. The ultimate goal would be to increase sales or profits, or even reduce costs, by taking advantage of new technology. This strategy implies that the company possesses the technical resources and skills to make it a viable proposition. Given the failure rate of new products/services and the element of the unknown associated with this strategy, it must be considered as slightly risky.

## Diversification

This strategy involves developing new products/services for new markets/segments, and implies that new resources and skills will have to be developed. Since both products and markets will be new, it is a very high-risk strategy. Diversification is what has led many companies to become bankrupt, and why many of those that diversified through acquisition during periods of high economic growth have since divested themselves of businesses that were not basically compatible with their own distinctive competence.

There will be different marketing responses to each permutation in the matrix, and the formulation of marketing objectives for each quadrant will be different for different companies. Students encountering the Ansoff matrix for the first time have a tendency to apply it as though companies might select any of the strategies equally. In practice, however, as we have illustrated, *risk* and *resources* are critical determinants of the selected strategy. For example, if 'new products in existing market' is the preferred option, a degree of technical innovation is implied, which may entail risk and certainly demands resources. Similarly, 'new markets' assumes an element of unfamiliarity which also represents risk and requires investment in information acquisition and analysis, in addition to the actual costs incurred in serving new markets. The newness factor of the product/market combination corresponds to the level of risk that the company has to manage; thus, pursuing marketing objectives concerned with new products in new markets is the riskiest strategy of all because it takes the organization away from its known strengths and capabilities into the unknown.

It is also worth noting that the strategies in the Ansoff matrix are not always either/or choices; a company may begin by, for example, increasing market penetration; then augment the product portfolio by developing new products for the existing market; thereafter, at a later stage, enter a new market. The procedures described in Chapter 9 provide a means of determining the most appropriate product strategy to follow.

## GAP ANALYSIS

Corporate objectives and strategies are very important to the marketing planning process. Objectives and strategies set at the corporate level must be supported by marketing objectives and strategies. Gap analysis is a technique used to explore the shortfall between the corporate objectives and what can be achieved by various strategies. As described in Figure 8.9, what it says is that if the corporate sales and financial objectives are greater than the current long-range trends and forecasts, then there is a gap to be filled. The operations gap can be filled by reducing costs, improving the sales mix and/or increasing market share. The strategy gap can be filled by finding new user groups, entering new segments, geographical expansion, new product development and/or diversification. The marketing audit should ensure that the method chosen to fill the gap is consistent with the company's capabilities and builds on its strengths.

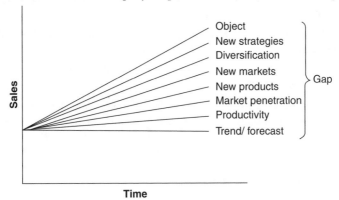

Figure 8.9 Gap analysis

# SUMMARY

Marketing objectives and strategies form the keystone of the value proposition. While objectives are concerned solely with products and markets, strategies enable operating decisions to bring the supplying organization into the right relationship with the emerging pattern of market opportunities which previous analysis has shown to offer the highest prospect of success.

In managing products or services, the marketer must pay due regard to the benefits that customers seek as well as to the position in the product life cycle. The appropriate marketing mix at the point of introduction will not be effective at the maturity stage, for example. The Ansoff matrix provides a useful framework for identifying the strategy options available to the organization as it seeks to develop its product/market base.

# FURTHER READING

McDonald, M. (2013) *Marketing Plans: How to Prepare Them – How to Use Them*, 5th edn, Butterworth-Heinemann, Oxford.

A practical, down to earth marketing planning book that explains and demonstrates how to prepare and use a marketing plan.

# REFERENCES

Ansoff, I. (1965) *Corporate Strategy*, McGraw-Hill, Maidenhead.

Grewal, R. & Tansuhaj, P. (2001). Building organizational capabilities for managing economic crisis: The role of market orientation and strategic flexibility, *Journal of Marketing*, Vol. 65 (2): 67–80.

Kandemir, D. & Acur, N. (2012) Examining proactive strategic decision-making flexibility in new product development, *Journal of Product Innovation Management*, Vol. 29 (4): 608–622.

Moon, B-J. (2013) Antecedents and outcomes of strategic thinking, *Journal of Business Research*, Vol. 66 (10): 1698–1708.

Nadkarni, S. & Narayanan, V.K. (2007) Strategy frames, strategic flexibility and organizational performance: The moderating role of industry velocity, *Strategic Management Journal*, Vol. 28 (3): 243–270.

# CHAPTER 9
# PRODUCT PORTFOLIO STRATEGY

IN THIS CHAPTER WE STUDY:

- product portfolio management
- the 'diffusion of innovation' curve
- the Boston matrix and the directional policy matrix
- the criteria that define market attractiveness
- the risk/reward continuum
- methods for screening and testing products pre-launch
- the difficulty of forecasting future sales

# PRODUCT PORTFOLIO MANAGEMENT

Product strategy is an integral component of marketing management; after all, without products there would be no need for any marketing at all. Recent years have witnessed a heightened interest in product portfolio management as it is recognized increasingly that the key to successful product strategy is a balanced portfolio of products that includes both established and new products. New products may result from pressures to customize or from advancements in technological expertise, while existing products must be managed to maximize return on investment during their entire life cycle. The overall objective of product portfolio management is to ensure that resources are allocated to maximize the value of the portfolio while balancing risk and return.

Every organization should take care to maintain a market rather than a product focus. It is important to remember that successful products are those that customers want to buy rather than those that companies want to sell. As sustainable customer value (achieving a mutually acceptable level of customer and shareholder/stakeholder satisfaction for a mutually acceptable level of customer and shareholder/stakeholder investment) requires a market-driven approach with commercially driven acumen, we must recognize not only the behaviour of products but also consumer behaviour.

## DIFFUSION OF INNOVATION

As we saw in Chapter 8, the Product Life Cycle (PLC) demonstrates that products, like everything else, follow a distinct life cycle. A useful concomitant is the diffusion of innovation (DoI) model (Figure 9.1), which refers to the cumulative percentage of potential adopters of a new product or service over time. Devised by Rogers in 1962, it remains valid to the present day.

Various studies indicate that rate of diffusion is a function of a product's:

- Relative advantage (over existing products)
- Compatibility (with lifestyles and values)
- Communicability (is it easy to communicate?)
- Complexity (is it complicated?)
- Divisibility (can it be tried out on a small scale before commitment?)

Diffusion is also a function of product newness which can be classified broadly under three headings:

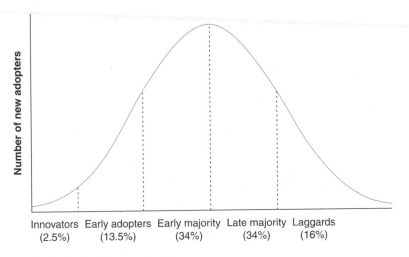

Figure 9.1 'Diffusion of innovation' curve

- Continuous innovation (for example, the new miracle ingredient)
- Dynamically continuous innovation (for example, disposable lighter)
- Discontinuous (for example, microwave oven)

Discovering a typology for those who are prepared to buy and try new products ('innovators' and 'early adopters') can help considerably in the promotion of new products. If we can target early advertising and sales effort at winning over the trendsetters and opinion leaders in the market, then we can proactively increase the chances of also convincing the more conservative customers to adopt the product.

At any point in time, a review of a company's various products would reveal different stages of growth, maturity and decline. If the objective is to grow in profitability over an extended period, then the product portfolio should reveal a situation in which new product introductions are timed to ensure continuous sales growth. The idea of a product portfolio is for an organization to meet its objectives by balancing sales growth, cash flow and risk. Ideally, a company should have a portfolio of products whose life cycles overlap, as Figure 9.2 demonstrates. This guarantees continuity of income and growth potential. It is therefore essential that the whole portfolio is reviewed regularly, and that an active policy towards new product development and divestment of old products is pursued.

A successful business would develop a portfolio more like that in Figure 9.2(b). In fact, over the years its growth could be attributed to a number of well-timed and profitable product/service launches like those shown in Figure 9.3. Therefore, in order to achieve a successful product/service portfolio,

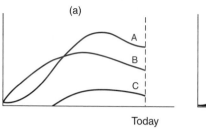
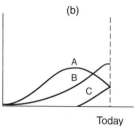

This is not a good pattern. All three products peaked some time ago and are now in decline. There is no new products to offer a promise for the future.

This is a good pattern. Product A, the earlier breadwinner, is in decline; but product B still holds a prospect of growth and product C is in its introduction stage, offering a bright future.

Figure 9.2 A portfolio of several product life cycles

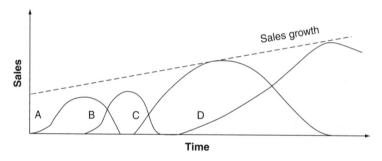

Figure 9.3 Ideal product introduction pattern over time

it will be necessary to manage output and bring it into line with longer-term objectives. It is generally accepted that in relation to the management of new product portfolios, strategic fit with overall business objectives is vitally important. However, a recent paper by McNally et al. (2013) urges caution as their findings suggest that this orientation may constrain innovation, the latter being an important driver of competitive advantage in turbulent contexts. A related consideration for managers to bear in mind is the requirement not only to generate profits but also sufficient funds to invest in new products and services.

In many respects, the idea of the product portfolio is similar to the investor's portfolio of stocks and shares. The investor, for example, may wish to achieve a balance between yield or income and capital growth; some shares might produce more of the latter and less of the former, and vice versa. Again, the investor might attempt to achieve a balance in terms of risk – some shares having a higher risk of capital loss attached, against which must be balanced the prospect of higher returns.

# CASH MANAGEMENT

All organizations have products that produce different levels of sales and profit margins. Profit occurs from the mix of products, ranging from low margin/high turnover to high margin/high turnover. The purpose of the marketing plan is to spell out at least three years in advance what the desired product combination is. RONA (return on net assets) can be portrayed as the business ratio:

$$\frac{Net\ profit}{Net\ assets} = RONA$$

Profits, however, are not always an appropriate indicator of portfolio performance, as they will often reflect changes in the liquid assets of the company, such as inventories, capital equipment, or receivables, and thus do not indicate the true scope for future development. Cash flow, on the other hand, is a key determinant of a company's ability to develop its product portfolio.

## THE BOSTON MATRIX

The Boston Consulting Group's simple matrix, given in Figure 9.4, is useful in product portfolio planning as it classifies a firm's products according to their cash usage and their cash generation along the two dimensions, relative market growth rate and market share. It shows graphically the positions of products in terms of their cash usage and cash generation, making it easier to see the relationship between multiple products. The Boston matrix is based on the principle that cash – not profits – drives a product from one quadrant to another. The relationship of market share to cash is as follows: the higher the market share, the higher the output. This is accompanied by lower unit costs (driven

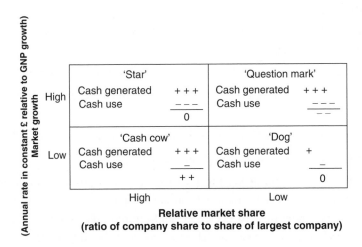

Figure 9.4 The Boston matrix – cash-flow implications

by economies of scale and the experience curve). Overall, this results in higher margins and revenue.

Note that the definitions of high and low market growth are defined according to prevailing circumstances in the industry.

The four quadrants in the Boston matrix are assigned the somewhat picturesque labels, 'Star', 'Question Mark', 'Cash Cow' and 'Dog'. The nomenclature is indicative of the relative prospects of the products in each quadrant.

- The *question mark* is a product that has not achieved a dominant market position and thus has a high cash flow; or perhaps it once had such a position and has slipped back. It will be a high user of cash because it is in a growth market. This is also sometimes referred to as a *wildcat*, or *problem child*.

- The *star* is typically a newish product that has achieved a high market share and is probably, on balance, more or less self-financing in cash terms.

- The *cash cows* are leaders in their markets where there is little additional growth, but a lot of stability. These are excellent generators of cash.

- *Dogs* have little future and are often a cash drain on the company. They are probably candidates for divestment, although such products often fall into a category aptly described by Peter Drucker as 'investments in managerial ego'.

Since the 'Cash cow' is the only quadrant that actually generates cash, some very clear messages come from the Boston matrix:

- To manage the product/service portfolio effectively the cash generated by the 'Cash cows' must be used to invest in 'Stars' and selected 'Question marks'.

- Investing in 'Question marks' with good prospects should lead to them developing into stars.

- Investing in 'Stars' should develop them into tomorrow's 'Cash cows'.

- The higher the relative market share of a 'Star' the better are its prospects as a 'Cash cow'.

- High investment in a 'Cash cow' should never be necessary.

- Investment in 'Dogs' is generally money wasted.

The Boston matrix can be used to forecast the market position of our products, say, five years from now if we continue to pursue our current policies. Figure 9.5 illustrates this process for a manufacturer of plastic valves. The area of each circle is proportional to each product's contribution to total company sales volume.

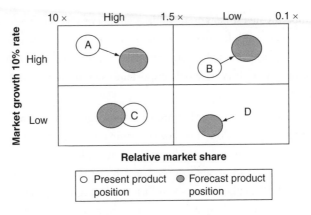

Figure 9.5 The product portfolio, current and projected

## THE DIRECTIONAL POLICY MATRIX

There are, however, factors other than market growth and market share that determine profitability, so many companies use an expanded version of the Boston matrix known as the directional policy matrix (DPM). In common with other product strategy models, the DPM has been around for some time, having been developed in the 1970s by Shell, General Electric, McKinsey and others as a multi-factor approach to portfolio management; nonetheless, it remains a useful planning tool. As shown in Figure 9.6, the axes become relative business strengths and market attractiveness, indicating the relative importance of each market to the business. The same purpose is served as in the Boston matrix;

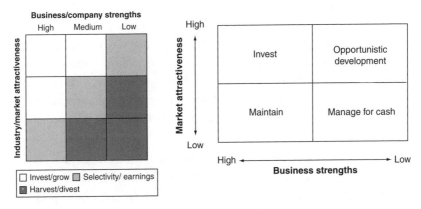

Figure 9.6 The directional policy matrix (DPM)

*Notes*: DPM prescriptive strategies – Invest for growth – businesses that are relatively high in business strengths and market attractiveness. Manage for sustained earnings – businesses with medium strengths in markets of medium-to-low attractiveness. Maintain strong position in moderately attractive markets, but do not invest to increase market share. Manage for cash – business with a relatively weak position in a relatively unattractive market. Harvest for current profitability or divest.
Opportunistic development – business with low business strength, but high market attractiveness.

that is, comparing investment opportunities among products or businesses. The difference is that multiple criteria are used. Although originally introduced as a $3 \times 3$ matrix rather than the conventional $2 \times 2$ matrix, the DPM is today used in either format. It is extremely important when using the DPM to define markets clearly.

The vertical axis of a DPM represents the degree to which a market is attractive to an organization. The key determinant of market attractiveness is its potential to yield growth in sales and profits. The horizontal axis of the DPM is a measure of an organization's strengths, or potential strengths, in the marketplace. Ideally, judgements about business strength or position should be validated by independent research, and certainly, product proficiencies should be based on known customer requirements. Programme guidelines for different positioning on the DPM are provided in Figure 9.7.

# DEVELOPING NEW PRODUCTS AND SERVICES

It should be apparent by now that a company's product portfolio is highly dynamic and needs to be managed proactively and kept under continuous review. According to Adner and Helfat (2003) and Eggers and Kaplan (2009) the ability to manage the portfolio effectively may be a dynamic managerial capability that affects heterogeneity in firm performance over time. New product development and product portfolio management are therefore crucial to company success. Experience tells us that a significant proportion of most organization's revenue comes from products that have been introduced in the recent past. In practice, most new products and services emerge gradually from modifications of existing ideas and technology – from putting together familiar things in a slightly different way. It is this interplay between existing products or services and the search for improvement and innovation that provides the dynamism for the growth-orientated company (Cooper et al., 2001).

However, the search for growth, prosperity and market opportunity is not without risk. New products are costly to develop or acquire, and are in grave danger of failure. As mentioned in Chapter 8, this danger is most poignant when new products are introduced into new markets. However, the chances of product failure can be reduced if marketing principles and personnel can be involved at every stage leading up to and including product launch.

It has been estimated that for every successful new product, between 50 and 70 new ideas have to be considered and that only one in four products that

| Main thrust | Invest for growth | Manage for sustained earnings | Manage for cash | Opportunistic development |
|---|---|---|---|---|
| Market share | Maintain or increase dominance | Maintain or slightly milk for earnings | Forgo share for profit | Invest selectively in share |
| Products | Differentiation – line expansion | Prune less successful Differentiate for key segments | Prune aggressively | Differentiation – line expansion |
| Price | Lead – aggressive pricing for share | Stabilize prices/raise | Raise | Aggressive – price for share |
| Promotion | Aggressive Marketing | Limit | Minimize | Aggressive Marketing |
| Distribution | Broaden distribution | Hold wide distribution pattern | Gradually withdraw distribution | Limited coverage |
| Cost control | Tight control – go for scale economies | Empahsize cost-reduction, viz. variable costs | Reduce aggressively both fixed and variable | Tight – but not at expense of entrepreneurship |
| Production | Expand, invest (organic acquisition, joint ventrue) | Maximize capacity and utilization | Free up capacity | Invest |
| R&D | Expand – invest | Focus on specific projects | None | Invest |
| Personnel | Upgrade management in key functional areas | Maintain, reward efficiency, tighten organization | Cut back organization | Invest |
| Investment | Fund growth | Limit fixed investment | Minimize and divest opportunistically | Fund growth |
| Working Capital | Reduce in process – extend credit | Tighten credit – reduce accounts receivable increase inventory trun | Reduce aggressively | Invest |

Figure 9.7 Programme guidelines

are test-marketed prove successful once launched nationally. Products that are successful tend to:

- deliver a significant differentiated benefit;
- possess a good technological fit with the supplying organization; or
- originate from businesses which 'have done their marketing well'.

These characteristics are more likely to be achieved where new product teams are created that comprise representatives from the organization's major management disciplines: operations, engineering, finance, human resources and marketing. Good marketing input is crucial; without it, new products become a game of Russian roulette.

The essentiality of marketing knowledge in the development of new products and services stems from the fact that customer value is created when an organization's offer is 'faster, better, cheaper' than the competition. Achieving these superior qualities means getting closer to customers. The organization must understand fully what turns customers 'on' or 'off', and most importantly, must heed this insight in daily practice. We are all familiar with the increasingly sophisticated customization programmes of companies' intent on boosting our 'wallet share' and their profit share through targeted communications, and aggressive cross-selling and up-selling techniques. But how many companies know (demonstrably) where to draw the line between helping customers and harassing them? The point is that sustainable growth is more about generating new solutions that offer value to customers than about introducing new products and services to the marketplace.

## STRATEGY OF MINIMAL RISK

The least risky way of dealing with the development of new products and services is to copy others. By taking this stance, the company avoids all the costs associated with developing new ideas and creating markets for them. Instead, it takes the ideas and modifies them according to its capacity. It then 'surfs' the wave in the marketplace created by the innovator. The key to success with this strategy is *timing*. Getting into the market too early, before the new idea becomes accepted, can put a company in the position of a trailblazer with all the attendant costs. But if a company arrives too late, the market for the idea may have been monopolized by others. Nevertheless, it does seem that a risk/reward 'rule' appears to operate along a continuum, as in Figure 9.8.

Figure 9.8 Risk/reward continuum

## CREATIVE IDEAS

The potential sources of new ideas for products and services are virtually boundless. They can range from the sudden insight, the 'eureka' kind of invention, through to some very analytical techniques, for example:

- Brainstorming – a technique that involves a group of people 'free thinking'.
- Talking and listening to customers or intermediaries.
- Monitoring technological developments.
- Monitoring new legislation (for example, that which has impact on safety, the environment or crime reduction).
- Running an ideas scheme among staff.
- Attribute listing – listing the attributes of a product or service and then modifying them in the search for an improved version.
- Carrying our market-gap analysis.
- Keeping in touch with what competitors are doing.
- Setting up a 'think tank' with staff and/or appropriate outsiders.
- Analysing past sales figures for significant trends.
- Making forced relationships – new ideas are listed and then worked at in pairs.
- Conducting specific market research.
- Monitoring customer queries or complaints.
- Lateral thinking – looking at familiar ideas and turning them back to front.
- Applying new ideas stemming from the availability or application of new materials. For example, new plastics materials are being developed that can make them ideal substitutes for more expensive metal products.
- Applying new ideas stemming from the availability or application of new technologies.

Irrespective of *how* we generate new ideas for products or services, there seem to be three universal 'laws' of which we should be aware:

- Successful innovators have a much better understanding of user needs than their less successful contemporaries.
- The odds against a new product or service being successful are very high, in the order of 30 to 1 against. Therefore, to have one good idea it is likely that we would need to have considered about 30; in other words, the quality ideas come from quantity.
- The key sources of new product/service ideas are likely to be based on research and development and market research. Attractive though they might seem, successful ideas generated by creative-thinking techniques have been fairly limited, because they are likely to be product- rather than market-focused.

Perhaps generating the new idea for a product or service is the most difficult part of the process of innovation, but there are clearly many other factors to take into account before we rush to the marketplace:

- Is there a need for the new product or service?
- What sort of demand will there be?
- Are the customers likely to be new or existing ones?
- Can I reach the new customers?
- Will the new product/service fit in with the existing range?
- Do we have the resources and expertise to provide the necessary service?
- What does the competition provide? How does it compare?
- What will be the costs of providing this new product/service?
- What will be the result if we don't provide it?
- Will it make money?
- Is it what we want to make, or like making?
- Is it consistent with the image of our company?
- What life could we expect from the new product/service?

# SCREENING PROCEDURE FOR IDEAS FOR NEW PRODUCTS OR SERVICES

All the considerations we have just raised make it essential that new ideas for products or services are screened rigorously to ensure they will be viable. The screening procedure should look something like that shown in Figure 9.9.

We have seen that new products are the lifeblood of a company in its attempt to survive in a dynamic and competitive marketing environment. The search for viable and profitable new products must be a continuing task of marketing management, but it is a task that is fraught with risk.

For the majority of companies, the introduction of a new product involves a great deal of investment, both in the development process and in the initial introductory stage when market acceptance has to be won if the product is to succeed. This investment can represent a considerable slice of a company's resources, not only financial but also physical and managerial, yet there can be no fail-safe guarantee that the investment will yield the sort of return that the company would consider acceptable. In some cases, a single new product failure

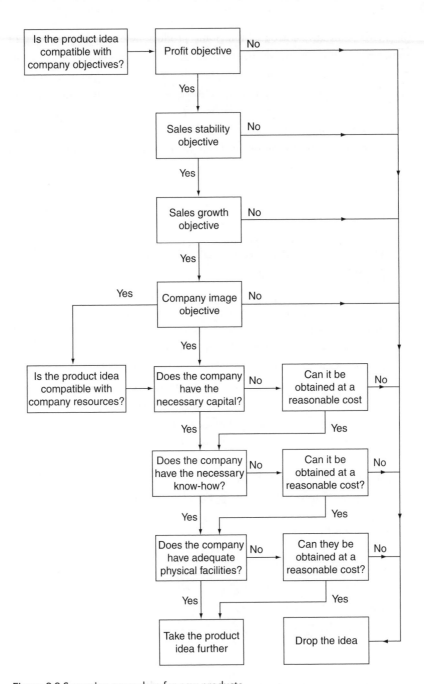

Figure 9.9 Screening procedure for new products

could bring disaster to a company, especially if it had pinned all its hopes on the new product only to find that the outcome fell far short of expectations.

There are examples in the consumer, industrial and service markets. Research indicates that, in some product areas, up to 80 per cent of all new products fail, in the sense that they do not meet marketing targets and are withdrawn soon after introduction. Some product fields, such as grocery or cosmetics, are more prone to early failure than others. This being the case, why are they introduced? In many cases, there is a perceived imperative to innovate. Hyper-competition creates a need 'to be seen to be doing something'. An increasing proportion of organizational resources are devoted to product innovation; product life cycles are shortening; the imperative to stay ahead of the competition through innovation becomes strong driving force. Sometimes, as Case study 9.1 illustrates, undue haste can have major consequences.

## CASE STUDY 9.1 BOEING 787 'DREAMLINER'

The Boeing 787 *Dreamliner* launched in October 2011. In January 2013 Japan Airlines and All Nippon Airways grounded their entire fleet. Of the 49 *Dreamliners* delivered to date, 24 were being operated by the two Japanese airlines. By January the planes had been plagued by a series of technical failures, including battery fires, oil and fuel leakages, cracked windscreen, brake problems and engine failure. While aircraft manufacturers expect teething problems, the series of potentially catastrophic mishaps led the Civil Aviation Authorities around the world to ground the aircraft and launch comprehensive reviews.

With an innovative carbon-fibre reinforced plastic (CFRP) fuselage and an all-electric control system replacing heavy hydraulic pumps, the *Dreamliner* outperforms traditional planes in terms of fuel economy and is therefore able to fly further than traditional medium-sized aircraft. For passengers, the *Dreamliner* offers greater comfort than normal, achieved by high ceilings, spacious cabins, large windows, carefully controlled cabin pressure and humidity.

The development and launch of the *Dreamliner* had not been without problems, however. Despite numerous design issues, production and delivery delays, somewhat unusually Boeing manufactured and delivered a relatively large number of 787s. More commonly, aircraft manufacturers deliver a small number initially so that teething problems can be rectified. However, the initial problems had caused delays, and perhaps in a bid to make up for lost time and feeling pressured by the imperative to innovate, Boeing had gone ahead and launched the aircraft, thereby risking the reputation of the *Dreamliner* at this crucial product launch stage.

Although assembled in the United States, the plane relies on parts from numerous suppliers, many of them Japanese. Any order cancellations would therefore affect Japanese industry as well as Boeing itself, and Japanese airlines were among the first customers. There was some speculation that Boeing's leadership, organizational structure and outsourcing decisions may have contributed to the problems with the *Dreamliner*. Others put the blame squarely on the product development process.

**CASE STUDY QUESTIONS:**

1. What went wrong with the product development process? Were some factors more critical than others?

2. What do you think is meant by 'Boeing's leadership ... may have contributed to the problem'? Discuss the extent to which successful product launch is the responsibility of senior management as opposed to the engineers who designed the aircraft.

3. Do you think the decision to launch and deal with teething problems as they arose was the right one?

4. What *should* Boeing have done to ensure that the *Dreamliner* launched without problems?

What, then, should marketing managers do to reduce the uncertainty that surrounds the new product launch? There are no crystal-ball revelations about prospects for success or failure in this area, but some procedures can be very helpful in quantifying the risks implicit in a new product launch. We shall now go on to explore some of these methods, but before we do so, we should first look more closely at some other factors involved in the new product-testing decision.

## TESTING PROCEDURES

Let us consider the means of testing available to a European manufacturer of sisal-based floor coverings who markets his products to the 'contract' market; that is, a market where an intermediary, often with an architect or a purchasing agent, buys the product for use in offices, hospitals and schools. This is a fairly complex market where various types of floor coverings are available. It is a highly competitive market and, frequently, the floor covering is specified on the basis of some total, overall scheme for interior decoration. On the advice of marketing consultants, this company was attempting to formalize its new product-testing procedures. Previously, they had tried to identify trends in

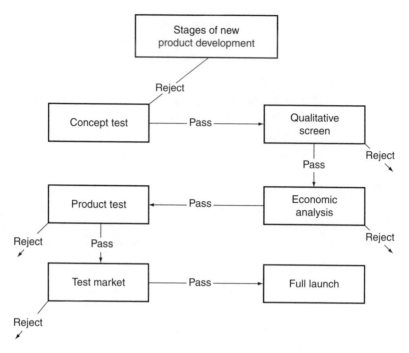

Figure 9.10 Stages of new product development

styles and colours on the basis of past sales. There had always been an attempt to perform a 'break-even' analysis on the basis of projected costs and prices. Beyond this, new product testing was more a matter of technical assessment or product quality.

The consultants suggested a process of testing that involved several stages. (This process, which we shall examine in detail shortly, indicates activities that should take place, in one form or another, in all new product testing.) Each stage in the analysis provided the opportunity to pause and make one of three decisions: launch the product now; collect further information; or abandon the product now. The three decisions were given the shorthand of Go (launch the product), Go On (carry on testing) and No Go (reject) (see Figure 9.10). In the case of the floor-covering manufacturer, the sequence started with a test designed to give a broad picture of how acceptable the product concept was to its potential market.

# CONCEPT TEST

This was administered by means of a dozen interviews conducted by trained interviewers, with architects and purchasing agents representative of the target market. The purpose of the test was to expose them to details of the technical specification, possible colour range and recommended uses of the product. Sometimes artists' impressions of designs and colours were shown. The results of this stage of the test sequence were entirely qualitative but they served to eliminate all those products that were complete non-starters. It was scarcely possible to make a decision to launch the product at this stage.

# QUALITATIVE SCREEN

This was the next stage, and formed a screening process that posed two basic questions:

First, *is the product concept compatible with company objectives?* Issues involved were, for example:

- Does the concept complement our existing market offering?
- Is it compatible with the image that we seek and the segment of the market with which we identify?

Second, *is the product concept compatible with company resources?* Issues involved here were:

- Does the company have the capital to get this product to market and to develop an initial level of sales?
- Does the company have the necessary know-how and adequate physical facilities to handle the product successfully?

# ECONOMIC ANALYSIS

If a product concept survived the screening process, it would proceed to the next stage of analysis. This entailed evaluating potential financial viability, employing various cost/revenue scenarios.

It was conducted at a fairly simple level as the company at that time had only a limited knowledge of how the market would react to products priced outside the narrow band with which the company was familiar. It was acknowledged that this stage of the testing sequence could be made considerably more sophisticated by applying methods of investment appraisal that were common in other companies.

Once this stage of the testing had been concluded successfully, the company might feel sufficiently confident of the viability of the concept to move ahead to a full-scale market launch. Such a decision would have to be based on some highly positive results from the initial stages of the test sequence, since the cost of setting up a promotional programme would be substantial. More often a decision would be taken to go on to the next, more expensive, stage of the analysis.

# PRODUCT TEST

In this case, the product test was designed to gain impressions from a relatively large number of potential customers of how they would react to the physical product when it was compared with competing products. The expense of product testing lies in the fact that considerable quantities of the physical product must be provided. The aim of the test is to identify a representative sample of the target market and to interpret the reactions relative to the competing products. Aspects of the product tested at this stage would be physical characteristics, the range available and the suggested usage, price and image connotations. This company recruited a panel of architects and purchasing agents who were invited to compare, according to a number of appropriate criteria, the proposed new products with selected competitive products. The analysis of these results enabled a picture to be built up of how the proposed new product compared with existing products in a number of key dimensions.

It was at this stage that the company normally made the final decision as to whether or not to launch the new product. Clearly there would still be some uncertainty about the new product's success, but the sequential testing had enabled this uncertainty to be reduced to an acceptable level. The company could have gone on, as many do, to the next test.

# TEST MARKET

This, as the name implies, is an attempt to reproduce the conditions of a full-scale launch but on a much smaller scale. Often, a town or geographical area is chosen as representing the ultimate market; the product is launched in that town or area alone and its progress observed. As a test of this kind is very much an 'experiment', it is necessary to ensure that conditions within the test market would be such that they could be reproduced on a national scale. For example, no extra promotional effort should be expended other than an amount proportional to the total to be spent in the proposed full-scale launch.

It should be noted, however, that test markets can never be completely reliable indicators of ultimate market performance. Quite apart from the problems of 'grossing up' small-scale test-market results to provide a global picture, there is always the possibility of unusual competitive activities that distort the results.

# PILOT PROJECTS

The use of pilot projects (small-scale versions of a larger undertaking taken in advance of a full-scale rollout) in testing products is becoming increasingly popular. Because such experiments are conducted in a real context, with every aspect of a true operation, they provide a realistic guide as to the potential outcome of a formal product launch. Valuable lessons can thus be learned at less cost, and with the opportunity for addressing inherent problems or revoking the product altogether, before the product is firmly introduced in the marketplace.

While we have portrayed these stages of testing as a sequence, it should be clear that some of the stages could be conducted concurrently, as with the qualitative screen and the economic analysis. Whatever the sequence, the purpose of new product testing remains the same: to reduce uncertainty surrounding the product to a level acceptable to the company while still enabling the launch to be made at the earliest possible time.

The methods of product testing might vary from marketing situation to marketing situation but, whether the product is a new airline service, a heavy-duty transformer or a vinyl wallpaper, the principles are universal and benefits considerable.

# FORECASTING FUTURE SALES

The problem of estimating the level of future sales of any product, new or old, is ever-present and may be solved only imperfectly. Knowing in advance what levels of sales could be achieved, given a particular marketing mix and a particular marketing programme, would reduce considerably the complexity of the marketing decision. However, few people can claim the ability to predict the future accurately and in detail, and the marketing decision-maker has to fall back on other, less precise methods.

Even some of the most carefully prepared forecasts of future sales can be disproved by events. The wider environment in which the forecast is set changes in ways that are not always foreseen, and thus are not incorporated into the forecast. Energy crises, crop failures, droughts, revolutions – these are just a few of the major events that can upset the sales forecast. It could be suggested that, if the world is so dynamic, what is the purpose of forecasting in any case? The answer is quite simply that any attempt to reduce the uncertainty that surrounds the future will, if used as a flexible input to the planning process, make us question the appropriateness of what we are currently doing. It must be recognized, however, that forecasts are useful only if they are indeed used in a flexible way. Sales forecasts can too easily become straitjackets that inhibit the organization's activities, as when they are seen as targets, endowed with all the sanctity that numbers tend to assume in a management context.

Forecasts deal with contingencies, not certainties. The Head of Planning in a large multinational chemical company is quoted as saying, 'We have to have alternative plans that can deal with either/or eventualities.' Establishing the nature of the 'either/or' is the task of the market forecaster. Parallel to the need for flexibility is the need to recognize that the output of the forecast should be expressed in terms of a *range* of possible outcomes. Sales estimates share the imprecision of most forecasting methods. Beyond this, however, it must be recognized that the process whereby any sales level is achieved is essentially *probabilistic*. In other words, chance has a central role in the outcome of any marketing process. Our forecasts can, and should, be made to incorporate the probabilities that are implicit in the marketing environment in which we operate.

The successful use of forecasting can be seen in the case of a manufacturer of household durables. Prior to the start of each fiscal year they worked out three different forecasts: 'optimistic', 'pessimistic' and 'most likely'. If taxation levels changed, competitive activity became particularly aggressive, or if some other phenomenon occurred to alter the market, the manufacturer could adopt an alternative plan without having to repeat the forecasting procedure. This approach enabled the company to react to market conditions with immediate flexibility.

But how do we start to grapple with the sales estimation problem?

## UNDERSTANDING MARKET POTENTIAL

The distinction between actual and potential customers is vital to successful sales estimation. Forecasters are concerned with establishing what proportion of the total market potential will be represented in their sales estimates. Market potential has been defined as the maximum possible sales opportunities for all sellers of a good or service. As such, it refers to the potential sales that could be achieved at a given time, in a given environment, by all the firms active in a specified product/market area or segment. Thus the concept of market potential extends our view of the market for our product, in that we see the product as competing against alternative means of satisfying the same need. Successful sales estimation will therefore depend on determining the proportion of the market that can be achieved, given a specific marketing mix and marketing programme. This situation is illustrated in Figure 9.11.

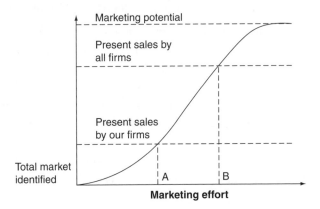

Figure 9.11 Market potential curve

A presentation of this kind, of course, gives a static picture of actual and potential sales at a given time and in a given environment; it could be influenced both by environmental changes and by changes in marketing effort by any of the firms (including ourselves) in that product/market area.

Looking at the sales-estimation problem in this light, we see how it can be possible for estimates to become self-fulfilling prophecies, in that the estimate and the marketing mix/programme are interdependent. It is not impossible to imagine that the actual success of any product might be influenced strongly by what managers' believe to be potentially achievable.

## THE FORECASTING HORIZON

Clearly, the time period we select for the forecasting exercise will influence our approach and our choice of estimation techniques. Most managers are accustomed to thinking in terms of short-, medium- and long-term forecasting, the actual length of these periods being determined by the organization's planning requirements. As an example, a manufacturer of wine bottles in Spain knows that its short-term forecasting requirements are based on its need to plan production schedules on a weekly basis. Its medium-term requirements are determined by the industry demand over the period of time it takes to install and make operational additional production capacity – in this case, a year. And the longer-term forecasting must take into account changing consumer requirements, such as easy-to-open bottles and changing technology in the bottling and packaging fields.

Precise definitions of what constitutes the short, medium and long term for any company will clearly vary, but should ultimately depend on the reaction time implicit in a company's activities and its organization. The reaction time for firms in ladies' fashion markets must necessarily be much shorter than for those companies engaged in the construction of hydroelectric power projects. Their definition of the forecasting horizon will vary considerably.

The firm's definition of that horizon will also be influenced by the variability of demand in their markets. For established products, that variability may not be pronounced, particularly if allowance is made for seasonal variations. Even though on a week-by-week basis sales may seem to fluctuate widely, there will often be an underlying steady-state or a recognizable upward or downward direction in sales. The forecasting task for manufacturers of beef stock cubes, a product in a steady state that has lasted for many years, is quite different from that facing the Swedish firm Uddeholm as they launch on a completely untried market a new grade of stainless steel for use in the processing of fertilizers.

# SUMMARY

The key to successful product strategy is a balanced portfolio of products that includes both established products and a steady flow of new products. The product portfolio can be analysed in terms of revenue-producing potential using the Boston matrix, and more comprehensively using the directional policy matrix (DPM).

The function of the Boston matrix is to aid forward planning by suggesting strategy for the future development of the product range: invest selectively in Question marks; invest in and grow Stars; maintain Cash cows; and examine Dogs critically and delete them as appropriate. 'Dog' products generate poor cash flow, and the costs of maintaining them can sometimes impede or destabilize overall business progress. While the axes of the Boston matrix consider *market growth rate* and *relative market share*, the axes of the DPM consider numerous variables under the headings *market attractiveness* and *business strengths*.

Because the chance of failure is high in new product launches, the use of formalized methods of appraisal is advocated, including market research as well as economic analysis. Forecasting is somewhat uncertain and therefore largely probabilistic and the task is influenced both by the forecasting horizon and market stability. Product portfolio management is therefore a proactive managerial activity, requiring a balance between risk and return, continuous portfolio review and the ability to plan strategically against a background of uncertainty.

# FURTHER READING

Baker, M. and Hart, S. (2007). *Product Strategy and Management*, Harlow: Pearson.

A specialized book focusing specifically on products. In-depth coverage of theoretical foundations, new product development and the various aspects of product management.

# REFERENCES

Adner, R. & Helfat, C.E. (2003). Corporate effects and dynamic managerial capabilities. *Strategic Management Journal*, October Special Issue 24: 1011–1025.

Cooper, R.G, Edgett, S.J. & Kleinschmidt, E.J. (2001). *Portfolio Management for New Products*, Cambridge, MA.: Perseus.

Eggers, J.P. & Kaplan, S. (2009). Cognition and renewal: Comparing CEO and organizational effects on incumbent adaptation to technical change. *Organization Science*, Vol. 20 (2): 461–477.

McNally, R., Durmuşoğlu, S. & Calantone, R. (2013). New product portfolio management decisions: Antecedents and consequences. *Journal of Product Innovation Management*, Vol. 30 (2): 245–261.

Rogers, E. (1962). *Diffusion of Innovations*, New York: Free Press.

# CHAPTER 10
# STRATEGIC BRAND MANAGEMENT

IN THIS CHAPTER WE STUDY:

- the concept of 'the augmented brand'
- the difference between a brand and a commodity
- qualities of successful brands
- the concept of brand management
- components of a brand
- positioning of corporate and global brands
- the brand as a marketable asset

# WHAT IS A BRAND?

A brand is a name, term or symbol (or combination of these) that identifies a company or product and differentiates it from competitors. It is also an important strategic asset in an increasingly competitive world. A successful brand identifies a company, product or service as having a sustainable competitive advantage. Company, rather than product, brands have come to dominate consumer mindsets, with Coca-Cola, Apple, IBM, Google, Microsoft, General Electric, McDonalds and Intel dominating the various 'Top Brands' league table; all have built up significant brand equity. Brands do not need to be global to be powerful however; in niche, local and regional markets, small to medium sized enterprises (SMEs) can also benefit greatly from having a distinctive, memorable, trusted brand.

According to Buil et al. (2013), the main drivers of brand equity are brand associations and brand loyalty, while in a study of chocolate eaters, Kuikka and Laukkanen (2012) find that brand loyalty is driven primarily by satisfaction with the brand, followed by brand value and brand equity. These, and similar, studies highlight the imperative of careful brand management and customer care.

The distinction between a brand and a product can be demonstrated by revisiting Figure 8.1 briefly (repeated here as Figure 10.1). The two outer circles comprise the services and intangibles that circumscribe the core product elements, and it is here that the concept of 'brand' is embodied. It is this wider, peripheral sphere that we examine in this chapter, with particular emphasis on brand name and value perceptions.

A brand name is not just a name on a product or service. It is an entity that offers customers (and other stakeholders) added values based on factors that extend beyond functional performance. These added values, or brand values, differentiate products and help to determine customer preference, affinity and loyalty, which in turn reinforces brand equity. Buil et al.'s (2013) findings underscore the relationship between brand equity and consumer responses, thus creating a benign circle.

While some might consider brand values to be 'intangible', for the purchaser or user, these additional attributes are very real. This is illustrated well in the widely known *blind test* (that is, where the brand identity is concealed) in which consumers compared Diet Pepsi and Diet Coke:

| | |
|---|---|
| • Prefer Pepsi: | 51 per cent |
| • Prefer Coke: | 44 per cent |
| • Equal/can't say: | 5 per cent |

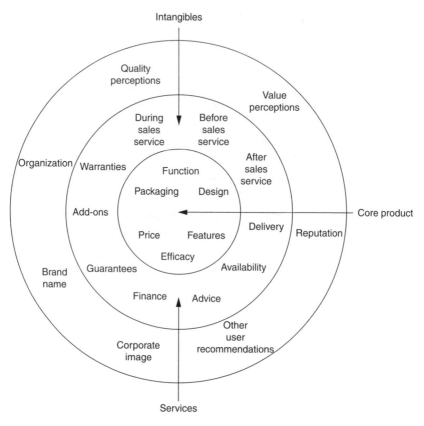

Figure 10.1 What is a product?

When the same two drinks were given to a matched sample in an open test (that is, the true identity of the brands was revealed), the following results were produced:

| | |
|---|---|
| • Prefer Pepsi: | 23 per cent |
| • Prefer Coke: | 65 per cent |
| • Equal/can't say: | 12 per cent |

How can this outcome be explained if not in terms of the added values that are aroused in the minds of consumers when they see the familiar Coke logo and pack? Here, the value is emotional and it has been consciously fostered over the years by successful advertising. While emotions may be intangible, the outcomes are easy to measure; high emotional value promotes brand loyalty, and Coke drinkers rank among the most loyal on the planet. So, brand value, brand loyalty and brand equity are all inter-related and mutually reinforcing.

It is not only in the area of emotional and psychological benefit that organizations create new forms of added value and differentiation for their brands.

The notion of 'the augmented brand', as shown in Figure 10.2, illustrates this fact. Many companies now view added services as a major element of their brand offer. For example, some airlines provide their valued customers with transport to and from the airport, offering an end-to-end service. Freight forwarders provide logistics support to help their customers to complete cost effectively. Industrial manufacturers offer engineering services so that their companies can be seen to supply more than parts alone.

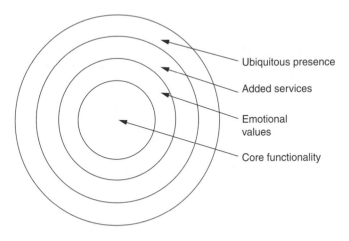

Figure 10.2 The augmented brand

Another means of adding value is to make it easier to buy the product or use the service. Telephone and online banking, for example, have increased ease of access to core product benefits via secure, 24-hour services. Boden's online and printed catalogue model offer a 'no hassle' returns service (with pre-paid envelope). RS Components supplies engineers and maintenance professionals with a worldwide e-purchasing 'same day dispatch, free delivery' solution. The ubiquity of e- and m-commerce creates 'anything, anytime, anywhere to anyone' connectivity. However, raising the stakes through added values also raises customers' expectations and, in turn, concomitant pressure on suppliers to deliver increasingly customized products and services.

The unveiling of these value perceptions and their power to influence customer choice has given new impetus to the marketer's task and the host of tools at his or her disposal. When making a purchase decision, a customer is swayed by a complex range of factors associated with the complete product offer. The marketer's ability to identify those factors of greatest importance to the customer and to ensure that they are prominent in the offer will increase the likelihood of closing the sale. More significantly (if sustained), it will increase the probability that the customer will develop a sense of bonding and trust with the supplying organization, leading to future purchases as a repeat and, ultimately, loyal customer. Despite its intangibility, a well-developed brand can exert influence on customers and competitors alike, and thus contribute to the way a product, service or company is positioned in the marketplace. It should be stressed that when we refer to the term 'brand' in this book we use it to encompass not only consumer products but a whole host of offerings, including consumer and industrial products and services, people, places, companies and so on. The issues of brand perception and position surrounding 'added values' serve to further clarify the definition of a brand as compared to a commodity.

# THE DIFFERENCE BETWEEN A BRAND AND A COMMODITY

Commodity markets are characterized typically by a lack of perceived differentiation by customers between competing offerings, and thus purchase decisions tend to be taken on the basis of price or availability and not on the brand or company name. In other words, one product offering in a particular category is much like another. While there may be quality differences, the suggestion is that, within a given specification, one carton of milk, for example, is similar to any other carton of milk.

In such situations, one finds that purchase decisions tend to be taken on the basis of price or availability, not brand or manufacturer's name. Thus one could argue that the purchase of petrol falls into the commodity category, and while the petrol companies do try to promote 'image', they inevitably end up relying on alliances and promotions to generate repeat purchase. For example, 2005 BP paired up with Marks and Spencer to offer M&S Simply Food at BP Connect forecourt sites. This enabled BP to leverage the M&S brand attribute of superior quality food, for the first time available at convenient, roadside, 'on the go' outlets. Regarding promotions, at the time of writing, BP's 'Today's Offers' include deals on Evian and Volvic water, Powerade soft drink, Tuborg lager, Wrigley's gum, Whiskas cat food, as well as a range of CDs, and free screen wash with every car wash. These are examples of how to convert a commodity into a brand, which then merits a price premium.

Conversely, one can also find examples of once-strong brands that have been allowed to decay and in effect become commodities. This process of decay is often brought about because the marketing asset value has been allowed to erode, perhaps through price cutting or through a lack of attention to product improvement in the face of competition. For example, the orange squash brands, Suncrush, Kia-Ora, Jaffa Juice were reduced to commodities through failure to promote brand values, excessive use of 'below the line' promotional activities and price cutting. As a result, at the time of writing, orange squash has been commoditized to the extent that the major brands are now retailers' own-label products. Figure 10.3 depicts the process of decay from brand to commodity as the distinctive values of the brand become less clear over time, and the brand's ability to command a premium price therefore diminishes.

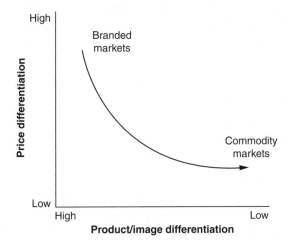

Figure 10.3 From brand to commodity

The price of a brand is clearly not what customers pay for it. Rather, the price of a brand is the sum total of everything the customer has to do to realize its value. This includes the cost of ownership as well as purchase. For example, customers spend time, energy and money searching for the right product and sales outlet. They may also make an investment in related travel, purchase, usage and eventual disposal of the product. Customers may also incur expenditure and perhaps inconvenience in the repair, replacement, relocation or upgrading of the product. Successful marketers have exploited this phenomenon and used brands as strategic marketing tools; witness the rise in customer communications that expressly convey to customers more about brand values than product/service benefits and that attempt to reach customers on every possible level: personal, financial, emotional, operational and relational.

# THE DIFFERENCE BETWEEN SUCCESSFUL AND UNSUCCESSFUL BRANDS

At the beginning of this chapter we said that a successful brand is one that identifies a product as having sustainable competitive advantage. The PIMS database (Profit Impact of Market Strategies), along with other databases, shows conclusively that strong, successful brands enable organizations to create stable, long-term demand, and to build and hold better margins than either commodity products or unsuccessful brands. Strong brands can also help new entrants establish a foothold, even where there is an established, dominant brand. Kim (2013) finds that second-mover, challenger brands can dilute the first-mover's superiority as customers turn to the product delivering the stronger value. Customers' beliefs are based on bounded rational trust and belief in a brand's equity can make the second-mover overcome the disadvantages of being the inexperienced competitor.

Successful brands contribute profitability by adding values that entice customers to buy (repeatedly) and encourage channel intermediaries, such as retailers, to stock them. They attract a high market share and a premium price. Typically, the brand leader obtains twice the market share of the number two brand, and the number two brand obtains twice the market share of the number three brand. The brand with the highest market share is always much more profitable, as a well-known PIMS study found that brands with a 40 per cent market share generate three times the ROI of those with a market share of only 10 per cent. Experience has also shown that the superior profitability generated by customer preferences can be self-perpetuating in terms of creating brand loyalty and customer referrals.

Successful brands also safeguard and strengthen their organizations. They provide a firm base for expansion into product improvements and variants, added services, new outlets and countries, and so on. In addition, they protect organizations against the threat posed by intermediaries, imitators and other competitors. And last, but not least, they help to transform organizations from being faceless bureaucracies to being dynamic businesses that are delightful to work for and deal with.

We must not, then, make the mistake of confusing successful and unsuccessful brands. The world is full of products and services that have brand names, but they are not successful brands. They fail to fulfil several important criteria:

- A successful brand has a name, symbol or design (or some combination of these) that identifies the 'product' of an organization as having a sustainable competitive advantage; for example, Coca-Cola, IBM, Tesco.
- A successful brand invariably results in superior profit and market performance.
- Brands are only assets if they have a sustainable competitive advantage.
- Like other assets, brands depreciate without further investment; for example, Hoover, Singer, MG and Rover.

Generally speaking, an organization that is successful at branding has a customer orientation and culture that puts customers first. Moreover, this commitment to customer satisfaction and service excellence is reflected in the customers' belief that that the product:

- will be reliable;
- is the best;
- is something that will suit them better than Product X; and
- is designed with them in mind.

These beliefs are based not only on perceptions of the brand itself relative to other brands but also on customers' perceptions of the supplying organization and opinions about its reputation and integrity. The key to prosperity is a 'win-win-win' strategy. Companies with successful brands study their customers and consumers and provide them consistently with a product of excellent value, for which they are prepared to pay a premium and create demand pull through the retail chain. For their part, retailers are delighted with the gross margin return they get from their inventory investment in leading brands. This recipe ensures that customer, retailer and supplier all get what they seek from co-operating. There are no losers.

## CASE STUDY 10.1 VIRGIN ATLANTIC

Virgin Atlantic is very clear about its core brand values and works hard to keep the brand meaningful and up to date. In 2008 the company commissioned a London-based agency, Circus, to review and refine the brand values. Circus identified the core brand values as 'making every day a happier day. Virgin Atlantic is a tonic for the soul, delivering great products and great experiences for customers all around the world'. Additionally, Virgin Atlantic was seen to be constantly challenging itself to see and do things differently, thereby demonstrating a spirit of adventure and exploration. The imagery on the fleet and the brand logo were revamped accordingly in order to reflect core brand values. The creative style and design were crafted specifically to enable flexible use across a variety of marketing materials.

Highlighting the imperative of conveying brand values, attributes and personality through creative design, the approach was summarized by Circle's Head of Design, 'It is essential that we set a firm, confident foundation for the future of the Virgin Atlantic brand, one which is relevant in the new commercial environment. It is critical that we portray and live our differentiating brand values.'

> The brand is hailed by opinion leaders and consumers alike as highly successful, the core values appealing to passengers in each of its target markets.

**CASE QUESTIONS:**

1. What are the key product/service features of Virgin Atlantic that define the brand values?
2. If you were Marketing Manager, how might you further enhance *specific* values that appeal to *specific* target markets?
3. Discuss the extent to which you agree that the Virgin Atlantic brand has a 'firm, confident foundation for the future'. What actions need to be taken to ensure that the brand remains relevant?

As the case study illustrates, the title 'successful brand' has to be earned. The organization has to manage the brand reputation carefully so that customers will associate it uniquely with superior value. This means investing in every aspect of the company's operation so that the product delivers the added values it promises, and meets the physical, emotional, psychological (and even potential) needs of customers. The organization must provide concrete and rational benefits that are sustained by a marketing mix which is compatible, believable and relevant.

# RISE OF RETAILERS' OWN BRANDS

Key Note's 'Own Brands Market Report 2012' noted continued growth of own-brands in UK retailing. The market has grown by nearly 52 per cent over a five-year period, to almost £119 billion. Growth is driven primarily by consumer demand for value for money in the face of the continuing recession. Supermarkets, in particular, have been quick to respond by developing own brands, new product development and diversification.

Evidence indicates that consumers are keen to hunt out a bargain, but are unwilling to sacrifice on quality. Consequently, as Key Note observes, some own brands have been subject to something of a makeover following increased investment, making them much more sophisticated and attractive to customers than previous incarnations. Premium own-brand product lines such as Sainsbury's Taste the Difference and Tesco's Finest ranges have launched successfully in recent years. At the same time, the low-priced ranges, such as

Tesco Basics and Waitrose Essentials, also continue to do well. Bergès et al. (2013) confirm that consumers now consider retailers' own brands to be reliable, quality brands in the own right. Further, Mayer and Vambery (2013) find a significant portion of consumers (from over 40 per cent to a high of 85 per cent) feel that the quality differences between branded and generic products have diminished and the price premiums charged by branded products are often no longer justifiable.

A parallel trend is the entry of supermarkets into non-food categories. Until relatively recently, own-brand lines, for example, electrical items, were unpopular with consumers, being perceived low quality and unreliable. As products have improved in quality, non-food lines such as clothing, homeware and small electrical goods have grown in popularity, driven by demand for low-cost items and the convenience of buying everything in one location. Both these trends demonstrate that even well-established brands are vulnerable to attack; consumers demand value for money pricing *and* quality products. According to Mayer and Vambery (2013), poor product performance combined with insufficient differentiation leads to the process of 'unbranding' in which brand value is lost. In order to maintain value, brands must be proactively and consistently managed.

# BRAND MANAGEMENT

The concept of brand management was created by Procter & Gamble (P&G), which in the 1930s encouraged two of its brands to compete and has since been reaping the rewards. P&G learned that a strong brand reassures the customer; it gives confidence in terms of the quality and satisfaction that can be anticipated from buying it. From all of this comes the possibility of long-term profits.

Many brands are now household names, but the fascination with managing brands has moved beyond the household goods categories to a more holistic approach. Take British Airways, for example. At one time the company was organized on the basis of a number of 'marketing centres', which were essentially geographical areas such as North America, Europe and Australia. With such an organization, it was very difficult to get a focus on customer service and to track down the real needs of customers. There is now an 'umbrella' or 'master brand', which is British Airways itself, promoted by the integrated marketing communications campaign 'To Fly, To Serve' via digital, TV, print and outdoor advertising. First launched on Facebook, the campaign is credited with reminding and reinforcing BA's core brand values in consumers' minds.

Often brands are managed as mini businesses with brand managers acting like mini-CEOs competing for the company's resources in order to uphold the brand's distinctive advantage and grow market share. This has the positive effect of acknowledging that the money and effort spent on developing the brand's position is in fact an investment in the generation of future benefits. Where category management is used as a basis for organizing consumer goods marketing, suppliers organize their brand portfolios to match their retail customers. They appoint category 'champions', whose focus is on maximizing profit from a category for the retailer rather than developing brand franchises. Regardless of what form brand management takes, its function is to optimize the brand's potential through managing its constituent parts carefully.

Managing a portfolio of brands, as Davis (2010) observes, is analogous to managing a financial portfolio with the objective of maximizing brand value and customer satisfaction. Portfolio strategy enables management to assess and develop the ideal brand structure, taking into account the company's needs and expectations along with the brand contribution. Companies such as P&G expertly manage brand portfolios by investing in those that perform well while eliminating unsuccessful brands. Each portfolio has a structure, or *brand architecture*, defining the relationship of the brands to each other. Mapping brand architecture enables a company to identify, organize and align resources to support each brand individually and the portfolio as a whole.

Managing the brand portfolio requires devoting care and attention to the three principle components of a brand:

- *brand strategy* (which stems from its position in the portfolio);
- *brand positioning* (what the brand actually does and with what it competes);
- *brand personality* (its sensual, rational and emotional appeal).

## BRAND STRATEGY

The first of these, *brand strategy*, stems from the position of the brand in the portfolio of the organization that owns the brand. Sometimes some poor brands are competing in high-growth markets, while others are competing in mature or declining markets. Thus the objectives for the brand could well call for different levels and types of investment (invest or harvest), innovation (re-launch, augment, cut costs), sales and distribution patterns (extension, reduction, broad, narrow), market share, usage aims (new, existing behaviour) and so on.

The first point to be made, then, is that an organization must be clear what the appropriate objectives are for a brand. As with product and marketing objectives generally, the brand objectives should reflect and reinforce the corporate objectives.

## BRAND POSITIONING

The second component, *brand positioning*, is concerned with what the brand actually does and with what it competes. In other words, brand positioning starts with the physical or functional aspects of the product (the central circle in Figure 10.1). For example, Canada Dry is positioned in the United Kingdom as a mixer for brandies and whiskies, rather than as a soft drink competing with Coca-Cola, Pepsi-Cola and 7-Up. Similarly, Tide is presented as a tough, general-purpose laundry detergent, rather than a cleansing agent for woollens and delicates; Tesco a high-quality superstore rather than a low-price supermarket; EasyJet.com purports to be the web's favourite airline, distancing itself from the higher-cost, long-standing carriers.

Positioning is usually performed against identifiable motivators in any market, only one or two of which are of real importance when developing a brand. These dimensions are best seen as bipolar scales along which brands can be positioned. Examples of these are provided in Table 10.1 and Figure 10.4.

| Expensive | ↔ | Inexpensive |
|-----------|---|-------------|
| Strong | ↔ | Mild |
| Big | ↔ | Small |
| Hot | ↔ | Cold |
| Fast | ↔ | Slow |
| Male | ↔ | Female |
| Local | ↔ | Global |

Table 10.1 Bipolar scales for brand positioning

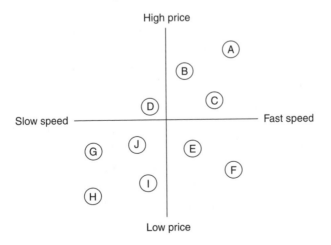

Key: ○ = competing brands

Figure 10.4 A brand position map

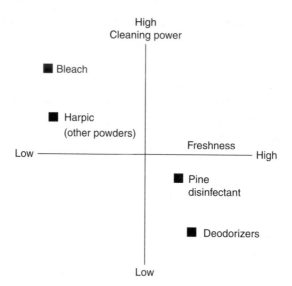

Figure 10.5 Bipolar map for detergents

Because these dimensions are so obvious, they are easy to research in order to establish which are those that people regard as the most fundamental basis for buying. It will be obvious that not all consumers look for the same functional performance, so market segmentation becomes important at this stage. A useful starting point in this kind of primary market interpretation is to draw a bipolar map, as shown in Figure 10.5. Figure 10.5 shows an actual bipolar map for detergents.

Clearly, the physical dimensions of any market will change over time, so this kind of basic research should be conducted on a regular basis to establish, first, what the main dimensions are, and second, whether the position of any competing product has changed. Competing products in commodity markets, because they are largely undifferentiated, are seen by the customer as occupying virtually identical positions, and thus to all intents and purposes are substitutable. The more distinctive a brand position, however, the less likelihood that a customer will accept a substitute.

In highly mature markets, brands are likely to be positioned close to one another. This indicates that the basic functional or physical characteristics are less likely to be the sole basis on which a product or service is selected.

This brings us to the final component, brand personality. While products can be copied, a successful brand is *unique* and, particularly in mature markets, a key discriminator in the marketplace.

## BRAND PERSONALITY

Brand personality is a useful descriptor for the total impression that consumers have of brands, and in many ways brands are like people in that they have their own physical, emotional and attitudinal characteristics. Thus they are a complex blend of different characteristics that together create a brand identity. In this way, two brands can be very similar in terms of their functions, yet have very different personalities. For example, the Ford Focus, Volkswagen Golf and Vauxhall Astra all perform similarly in terms of size, speed and price, yet each has a totally different personality, the result of a blend of three sorts of appeal: sensual, rational and emotional.

*Sensual appeal* refers to the way the product or service looks, feels, sounds, smells or tastes. It is easy to imagine how this appeal can differ in the case of, say, cigarettes, beer or cars. In the service sector, Virgin Airlines has been very successful on this dimension. *Rational appeal* concerns the way the product or service performs (what it contains, its relative costs and so on). *Emotional appeal* is perhaps the most important aspect of a brand, and has a lot to do with the psychological rewards it offers, the moods it conjures up, associations it evokes and so on. It is easy to see the overt appeal of certain products as being, for example, particularly masculine, feminine, chic, workmanlike or 'flashy'.

Brand personality is also the result of a whole gamut of influences, such as places where it is sold, price, other brands from the same manufacturer, how it is used, the kinds of people who buy and use it, after-sales service, the name of the brand, advertising, point-of-sale material, PR, sponsorship and many others. However, for any brand to be successful, all these elements have to be consistent, since they all affect the brand's personality, and it is this personality, above all else, that represents the brand's totality and which makes one brand more desirable than another. At its simplest, brand personality converts a commodity into something unique and enables a higher price to be charged for it.

One of the present authors, in a book entitled *Creating Powerful Brands* (de Chernatony and McDonald, 2003), combines brand functionality and personality in a matrix. This matrix is shown in Figure 10.6. The vertical axis refers to a brand's ability to satisfy utilitarian needs, such as quality, reliability, effectiveness and so on, where the consumer's need for such benefits is high. The horizontal axis represents the brand's ability to help consumers to express something about themselves – for example, their mood, their membership of a particular social group, their status and so on. Brands are chosen on the latter dimension because they have values that exist over and above their physical values. We call this dimension 'representationality'. For example, products such as Yves St Laurent neckties are effective brands for expressing particular personality types and roles, with functional attributes being secondary.

It is possible, by means of market research, to identify the degree to which consumers perceive a brand as reflecting functionality and representationality, and then to plot these on a matrix. Having done this, it is then possible for

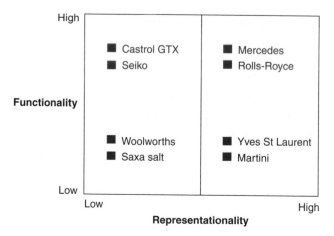

Figure 10.6 Brand functionality and personality
*Source:* de Chernatony and McDonald (2003).

the marketer to consider how best to use the resources available to support the brand.

For products and services in the top right-hand quadrant (that is, ones that both provide functional excellence and are good vehicles for non-verbal communication about themselves), a creative strategy that reinforces consumers' lifestyle requirements should be adopted, communicated through appropriate media channels. Additionally, the quality of the brand needs to be maintained through high standards of quality control and continuous product development. Also, strict control over channels of distribution should be exercised.

For products and services in the top left-hand quadrant (that is, ones bought by consumers because of a high utilitarian need rather than because of a need to say something about themselves), product superiority needs to be maintained continuously as 'me-tooism' is a continuous threat to such brands. Also, heavy promotional support is important in communicating the functional benefits of the brand.

For products and services in the bottom right-hand quadrant (that is, ones that are less important for their functional attributes, but which are high as symbolic devices), it is clearly important to reinforce continuously the cultural and lifestyle aspects of the brand, and a heavy advertising presence is almost certainly more important than product-development issues.

For products and services in the bottom left-hand quadrant (that is, those that are bought by consumers who are not particularly concerned about either functional differences or self-image), successful branding is more difficult, because it is likely that they need to have wide distribution and be very price competitive. Cost leadership then becomes important to the brand owner, which entails being an efficient producer. Brands in this sector are obviously vulnerable, and to succeed an attractive price proposition is usually necessary.

# THE COMPANY AS A BRAND

It will by now be obvious that it is frequently the case that a company's name is the brand used on different products or services, as opposed to an individual brand name for each product, as in the case of, say, Persil.

To present themselves in the most favourable way, firms develop a corporate identity programme, ensuring that all forms of external communication are co-ordinated and presented in the same way. Corporate identity can be a valuable asset, which, if effectively managed, can make a major contribution to brand success.

Classic examples of this include IBM, Virgin, Mercedes, Sony, Yamaha and countless others. It works well as a policy, given the prohibitive costs of building individual brands *ab initio*, provided the product or service in question is consistent with the corporate image. In this respect it is easy to see why Ford has been unable to compete effectively in the high-class car market, or Mars was able to enter the ice-cream market using the Mars corporate brand name, but uses the brand name 'Pedigree' in the animal foodstuffs market.

While there is a 'halo' effect of using a famous corporate name on a new product or service, there are also risks to the total portfolio, should any one new product prove to be disastrous. For example, Levi Strauss was known and respected for jeans. Their extension into Levi tailored classic suits failed because of wrong associations. And adding the name Pierre Cardin to bathroom tiles in Spain did little for the value of this core brand!

Peter Doyle has developed a useful matrix for considering what an appropriate strategy might be towards corporate, as opposed to individual, product branding. This is provided in Figure 10.7.

# GLOBAL/LOCAL BRANDS AND THE BENEFITS OF 'GLOCALIZATION'

As markets and brands become increasingly global, so the task of global brand management is becoming more mainstream and important. Strategically, when

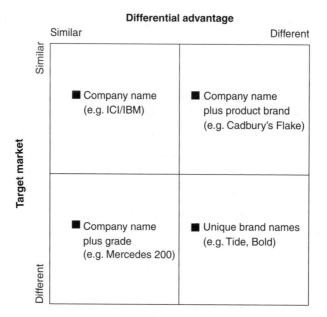

Figure 10.7 Corporate brand positioning
*Source*: Doyle (2008).

selling a product in various international markets, there are only two broad options: either, develop a global brand, such as American Express or Coca-Cola, or have a local brand in each country or region of operation.

Our definition of a global brand is 'a product that bears the same name and logo and presents the same or a similar message all over the world.' The product is usually aimed at a similar target market in the various locations, and is promoted and presented in much the same way. The decision to either develop a global or local brand is based upon a number of factors: customer type; cost of production, distribution, promotion, competitive market structure, channels, legal constraints, and operational structures. Global branding offers the potential of economies of scale, but the benefits have to be weighed very carefully against the difficulty of setting up a global brand, as the following matrix, Figure 10.8, demonstrates. Although three of the quadrants reduce to fairly obvious choices, the top right-hand quadrant is still something of a poser. Our own inclination is that, when faced with great difficulty, but high economies of scale, we would endeavour to establish global brands.

Of course, while the matrix only represents a concept, it is possible to develop concrete data for it in much the same way as the directional policy matrix, described in Chapter 9. For example, all the savings attributable to economies of scale could be calculated – manufacturing, R&D, purchasing, logistics, better management control and so on. Equally, local differences

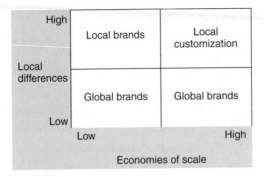

Figure 10.8 Global versus local brands

could be assessed, taking into account the infrastructure of markets, demand homogeneity, culture, political/legal framework, market structure, competition and the like.

By looking at international markets in this way, the odds come out very much higher in favour of global brands compared to local ones. Predictions about future trends only serve to reinforce this hypothesis:

- prices will tend to harmonize towards the lowest levels;

- purchasers will buy internationally to gain maximum price advantage; and

- major distributors (especially importers) will operate transnationally and take advantage of remaining price differentials and low-cost suppliers.

There is plenty of evidence confirming these predictions as accurate and, as markets become increasingly global, there is no reason to think this will change in the near future. The growth in global branding is a direct result of the explosion of media consumption, particularly among the young. In every country the data show that the younger consumers are significantly more aware of international brands, particularly in fields such as TV, music, films and sports.

The portents are clear. Already, large global retailing groups are appearing, and if an organization does not have a strategy, particularly in FMCG categories, it does not appear to have very good prospects. It is brand names that win customers, make profits and create customer loyalty. A good brand, at the end of the day, is the company's best marketing asset. For that reason it is short-sighted not to invest in the brand. To allow it to slip and become a 'me-too' commodity is tantamount to commercial vandalism.

Responding to 'the shrinking world' and increasing globalization, major international companies have developed strategies that combine a global, generic brand and local preferences. Typically, standard products are designed to be adapted to fulfil the needs of local markets. For example, the global mega-brand, McDonald's, collaborates with local suppliers in its various markets such that its products use local ingredients and appeal to local tastes. The golden arches appear, unchanged, in all locations, so the brand is easily identifiable, but all other aspects, such as the design and furnishing of its restaurants, as well as marketing and promotional advertising materials are adapted to the local context. For example, religious and cultural reasons mean that meals sold to the Indian market contain no beef or pork and there is a wide range of McSpicy and Big Spicy products that appeal to local tastes.

# BRAND VALUATION

The question of asset protection and development is, in a sense, what marketing is all about. As brands are arguably the most important of all marketing assets, it is vital to ensure that they are regarded and treated appropriately in terms of resource allocation, strategic priority and 'market value'. We touched on the first two of these issues earlier in the chapter, so let us now consider briefly the matter of brand value from the perspective of brand ownership.

Being an asset of definable proportions (summarized as the current and future potential to deliver and communicate benefit within the market context), it should be possible to measure and value a brand. Like any other item of property, be it a company, an item of equipment, or a piece of real estate, a brand has a worth in the marketplace. The decision to own or to acquire a brand therefore involves judgements about the role, robustness and 'rearability' of the brand. How does it factor in the company agenda? Will it be sustainable? Is it capable of being built up and cultivated?

Traditionally, brand value has been represented as the singular ability to generate profits. However, there is growing recognition that company brands can also work across multiple markets as a means of improving customer retention rates and long-term profits. This is evident in brand terminology. For example, we are increasingly concerned with 'brand awareness', 'brand association', 'brand image', 'brand equity', 'brand recognition', 'brand recall', 'brand loyalty', 'brand switching', 'brand extension', 'brand elasticity' and so on. As regards estimating a brand's financial, or sale, value ('brand valuation'), we use the criteria of brand 'width', 'length', 'depth', 'breadth' and 'weight'. Clearly, then, brands do possess a relative value determinable by those who own, operate and trade in them.

Buying a major brand nowadays often makes more sense to organizations than launching a new brand, with all the risk and uncertainty this entails. This is just one of the reasons why brand valuation has emerged as a major issue in recent times, and why brands are increasingly sought-after as assets. The trend towards acquisitions by brand-led businesses seeking to accelerate product ranges and pursue geographic expansion looks set to continue.

Some of the more spectacular examples of the value of brands as assets can be seen in acquisitions in which colossal premiums were paid above the balance sheet asset value. For example, in 2010 Kraft bought Cadbury's for £11.4 billion, while in 2013 Swatch acquired the Canadian watch and jewellery brand, Henry Winston for $750 million. The premium prices reflect, to a large degree, the brand equity and branding expertise of the acquired companies. The reason why brands may be valued at figures far in excess of their balance sheet value is in recognition that relationships with customers, not factories, generate profits, and it is company and brand names that secure these relationships. When brand names are neglected, their distinctive values are eroded and they can no longer command a premium price. Consequently, they offer no unique added values and decay into commodities.

Behind the brand name, of course, lies a world of other relationships, between, for example:

- *people* – employees, shareholders, suppliers, alliance partners, industry colleagues, legislators and so on;
- *resources* – information, 'intelligence', expertise, experience, finance, plant, equipment, materials, time and so on; and
- *events* – political upheavals, economic upturns and downturns, technological developments, social and cultural trends, ecological catastrophes/discoveries and so on.

The role of brand is thus not confined solely to delivering and communicating value but also extends to creating value. Consider the 'people' factor for a moment. It is an accepted rule in marketing that happy employees make for happy customers (and thus happy shareholders, suppliers, retailers and so on). It is also a known fact that dynamic and successful businesses tend to attract dynamic and successful people. By recruiting a highly skilled, enthusiastic and committed workforce, a company endows itself with value creators who will generate the present and future customer value in which customers want to invest. It also confers upon itself the qualities that support membership in lucrative value chains and networks. Having superior resources, and the flexibility to respond successfully to threats and opportunities, has a similar effect in ensuring the company continues to achieve customer value excellence.

Given the significance of brands to building customer relationships and corporate profitability and sustainability, understanding the implications of brand value is fundamental to good marketing planning.

# SUMMARY

The following quotation is from *Creating Powerful Brands* (de Chernatony and McDonald, 2011), 'A successful brand is an identifiable product, service, person or place augmented in such a way that the buyer or user perceives relevant, unique added values which match their needs most closely. Its success results from being able to sustain these added values against competitors.' Being able to do this on a global basis will bring great rewards, but it will not be easy.

Brands are key strategic weapons that need to be managed carefully and consistently. Often, a company has a portfolio of brands that must be managed in order to maximize return on investment as well as customer value. This entails paying close attention to the three key components of a brand: the brand strategy, the brand positioning and the brand personality. For a brand to succeed, it has to have sensual, rational and emotional appeal. The degree to which functionality and representationality are important to consumers will determine the brand strategy.

Global branding versus local branding as a strategy will depend ultimately upon the homogeneity of demand patterns in different countries and the concomitant economies of scale to be enjoyed from created global brands.

Brand success lies in its sustainability. By understanding how customer value is created, the offer can be branded and positioned to create customer preferences and continually enhance the value of the brand.

# FURTHER READING

de Chernatony, L., McDonald, M. & Wallace, E. (2011) *Creating Powerful Brands*, Oxford: Butterworth-Heinemann.

A grounded, simultaneously theoretical and pragmatic overview of how to create, manage and sustain strong brands across consumer, service and business markets.

# REFERENCES

Bergès, F., Hassan, D. & Monier-Dilhan, S. (2013) Are consumers more loyal to national brands than to private labels? *Bulletin of Economic Research*, Vol. 65: 1–16.

Buil, I., Martínez, E. & de Chernatory, L. (2013) The influence of brand equity on consumer responses, *Journal of Consumer Marekting*, Vol. 30 (1): 62–74.

Davis, J. (2010) *Competitive Success; How Branding Adds Value*, Chichester: Wiley.

de Chernatony, L. & McDonald, M. (2003) *Creating Powerful Brands*, 3rd edn, Oxford: Butterworth-Heinemann.

Doyle, P. (2008) *Value-Based Marketing – Marketing Strategies for Corporate Growth and Shareholder Value*, 2nd edn, Chichester: John Wiley & Sons Ltd.

Key Note 'Own Brands Market Report 2012', available at: www.keynote.co.uk

Kim, S. (2013) The viability of a second mover's market win with higher brand equity, *Journal of Strategic Marketing*, Vol. 21 (3): 201–216.

Kuikka, A. & Laukkanen, T. (2012) Brand loyalty and the role of hedonic value, *Journal of Product and Brand Management*, Vol. 21 (7): 529–537.

Mayer, P. & Vambery, R. G. (2013) Unbranding: threats to brands, opportunity for generics and store brands, *Journal of Consumer Marketing*, Vol. 30 (2): 140–149.

# CHAPTER 11
# PRICING STRATEGY

IN THIS CHAPTER WE STUDY:

- dangers of a cost-based approach to pricing
- components of price
- concepts of the demand curve, and the consumer and supplier surplus
- the trade-off approach to pricing
- pricing strategies suggested by the experience curve
- the relevance of relationship pricing
- the concept of dynamic pricing
- challenges for international pricing management

# THE PRICING DECISION

The pricing decision is one of the most important issues the marketing executive has to face. Its impact will usually be reflected in the quantity of the product sold, the contribution to profits that the product will make and, even more crucially, the strategic position of the product in the market place. In addition, in a multiproduct company it is frequently the case that a decision taken on the price of one product will have implications for other products in the range. It is not surprising, therefore, that much has been written and discussed on the subject of pricing, and that it has created considerable controversy as to how the price decision should be made.

Frequently, this controversy has centred around the role that costs should play in determining price. Traditionally, the price of a product is based on the identification of the costs associated with manufacturing, marketing and distributing the product with the subsequent addition of a mark-up to reflect the desired profitability. Such an approach has been criticized on a number of counts. First, it can prove to be extremely difficult in practice to identify the true costs that can only be allocated to a specific product on an arbitrary basis. Second, such a cost-plus approach to pricing ignores the demand sensitivity of the marketplace. It may be that a price determined on a cost-plus basis is higher than the market can bear. Attempts have been made to overcome these problems by using a *marginal cost* approach rather than a *full cost* approach, so that the pricing decision becomes one of attempting to maximize the contribution the product will make – that is, the difference between the *price* and the direct and attributable *costs*.

The basic problem with any cost-based approach to pricing is that it assumes implicitly that the customers are interested in *the company's* costs, whereas in reality customers are only concerned with *their own* costs. This can be expressed another way – customers seeks to acquire benefits and it is in order to acquire those benefits that they are prepared to pay a certain price. Seen from this perspective, the company making the price decision is faced with the need to identify the value – in the customers' eyes – of the benefits inherent in its product. The costs of that product thus become irrelevant to the pricing decision even though they are highly pertinent to the profitability of that decision. In other words, *costs determine profits*, not price.

# BENEFITS AND PRICE

Throughout this book we have suggested that in any purchase decision customers are seeking to acquire 'benefits'. A product must bring with it the promise of performing certain tasks, of solving identified problems, or even of providing specific gratifications. Thus the product is not bought for the particular components or materials that go into its manufacture *per se*, but rather it is bought for what, as an entity, it can do.

The implication of the benefit concept from a pricing point of view is that the company must first identify the benefits the customers perceive the product is offering, and then attempt to ascertain the value the customers place upon them. The key issue here is that it is customer *perception* that is important. It may be, for example, that two competing companies offer products that are, for all intents and purposes, technically identical, and yet one company can command a premium price. Why should this be so? It may be that additional benefits offered by one company in the way of technical advice or after-sales service are perceived to be superior to those offered by another. Erdem et al. (2010) indicate that consumer responses are influenced by the relative weight consumers assign to price in its positive versus negative role; consumers who perceive price in its positive role pay higher prices. It could also be that the image of the company is seen as superior. Whatever the reason, there are many cases of this type of 'differential advantage' that cannot be explained simply in technical or quality terms.

Strong brands have always been able to command a price premium. For example, an academic study of the price advantage IBM has traditionally had in computers, found that IBM machines are priced substantially higher than competing machines of equal performance; this price differential appears to be independent of machine size. Since a substantial percentage of users are still willing to buy IBM machines even though their relative price is high, the implication is that IBM offers customers something to induce them to pay a substantial premium for an IBM machine. The study identified that this price premium was achieved not through superior hardware or technology but rather through the image that IBM had for quality, reliability and customer support.

Another way to look at this price advantage is to think of the maximum price at which the product could be sold as being the sum of two elements. First, there is the 'commodity price' element; this is the base price for the generic product, which would be determined by supply and demand in the marketplace. On top of this should be added the 'premium price differential', which reflects the totality of the benefits that customers perceive will be acquired through purchase of that product. Figure 11.1 shows this concept diagrammatically.

The existence of this 'premium price differential' can only be explained in terms of perceived benefits. The task of the pricing decision-maker therefore becomes one of identifying these benefits and placing a customer value on them. It is really a 'bundle' of benefits, and so the first step in this suggested

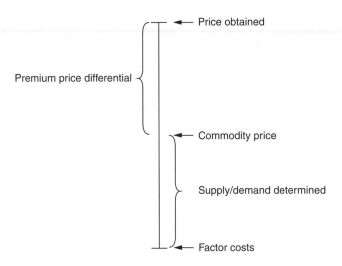

Figure 11.1 The components of price

approach to pricing is to 'unbundle' the product and identify the individual benefit components that together constitute the totality.

# PRICE AND VALUE

Every purchase by a customer is a trade-off. The trade-off is between the value the customer places on the acquisition of the product versus the costs that are involved in that acquisition, plus any subsequent costs that might be involved – for example, maintenance or upgrading costs. (These costs represent 'the total cost of ownership'.)

There is nothing new in this idea. Economists have long talked about the concept of 'utility'. While some of their ideas on the relationship between price and demand may seem naïve, there is nevertheless an important message for the pricing decision-maker in the recognition that price must be seen in terms of value.

The Victorian economist Alfred Marshall was the first to fully articulate the idea of price as a reflection of the value placed on a product or service by the consumer. He developed the concept of the *demand curve*, which simply stated that the higher the price charged for a product, the lower will be the demand for it as potential customers see the price exceed the product's perceived value to them. It is interesting to note that this concept suggests that the price charged for a product may be lower than the value placed on it by some customers. This is the notion of a 'consumer surplus'. In Figure 11.2, a demand curve for a particular product is represented and the price currently prevailing in the marketplace is $P_1$.

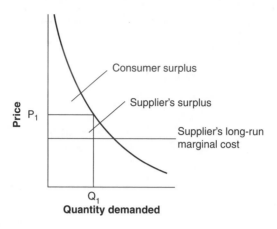

Figure 11.2 The demand curve

It can be seen from Figure 11.2 that there are some consumers, albeit fewer in number, who would in fact be prepared to pay a higher price. The number of such consumers obviously declines the higher the price that is charged. Consumers who fall into this category are in fact paying a price less than the value gained through purchasing the product. They are enjoying a consumer surplus. At the same time, it can also be seen that the price $P_1$ is in fact higher than the supplier's long-run marginal cost. In other words, in this case there is a 'surplus' accruing to the supplier as well. This analysis is an over-simplification of the real world, but it might be a useful focus for price decision-makers to think of their problem along the lines suggested by Figure 11.3.

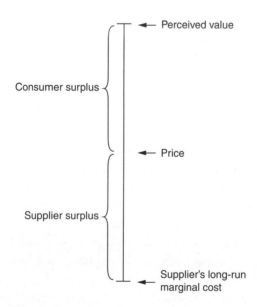

Figure 11.3 Consumer and supplier surplus

The pricing problem can be seen in this way as an attempt by the supplier to achieve the greatest possible 'surplus' over long-run marginal cost while still pricing no higher than the perceived value placed on the product by potential customers.

An alternative way of looking at this is to see the problem in terms of the need to identify what value the target market places on a product and then to convert that value into a market price. The first step towards solving this problem is to recognize that there will be different groupings of customers with different perceptions of a product's value. These groupings are in effect *market segments*. Thus we might identify a specific segment of the market that seeks certain benefits from a product and values them at a particular level. For example, Evian serves various segments using differentiated packaging for various users and use categories, including the sporty/active, new mums and consumers 'on the go', allowing the brand to employ a segmented pricing strategy.

However, it is not sufficient just to identify the perceived value of a product to the customers and then set a price equal to that value. Frequently, there will be costs other than price that customers face in acquiring the product. These additional costs over and above purchase price could include freight, installation, training, maintenance, service, spares support and other 'life cycle costs', as they are sometimes termed. In addition, there may be perceived costs in terms of risk of product failure or, particularly in the case of consumer products, social and psychological risk.

From the customers' point of view, therefore, it could be argued that the decision to purchase is a trade-off between all the costs involved on the one hand and the perceived benefits resulting from acquisition on the other. This relationship may be expressed as follows:

Highest price the customer will pay = perceived benefits − costs other than price

Thus it can be seen that in the pricing decision it is as important to understand the cost structure of our potential customers as it is to know our own! It is essential to the pricing decision to recognize the total cost impact on a customer of the acquisition of our product. Even though customers may not have evaluated fully the implication of the acquisition, the supplier will be better positioned to sell to the customer if these costs are known. The appropriate concept here is that of 'life cycle costs', which refers to all the customer costs that will be incurred by the customer from the acquisition of the product through to the end of its useful life. For example, in pricing a piece of numerical control equipment, the manufacturer should identify the effects that the equipment will have on the customer's manufacturing economics, its likely life, any maintenance and upgrading costs, and its disposal value, if any.

Given a full analysis of the life cycle cost implications of the product, the pricing decision-maker can now focus attention on the identification and quantification of the product's perceived benefits.

# BENEFIT EVALUATION

One of the first attempts to break loose from the constraints of cost-orientated pricing and to seek instead to incorporate some recognition of perceived value was the technique developed by the Glacier Metal Company, which it termed 'product-analysing pricing'. This attempted to build up a final price by identifying the physical features that go into the product, and then to value these features in customer terms. The method was based on a statistical analysis of previous prices obtained for similar products to provide quantified estimates of the relative contribution of each physical component to the final price. The analysis was limited as such to the physical attributes of the product and did not quantify non-physical benefits other than by talking loosely about the 'product surround'. Because of these limitations it did not provide the pricing decision-maker with the crucial information on customer evaluation of perceived product benefits – both physical and intangible. To do this we need to seek an alternative approach to benefit evaluation.

# TRADE-OFF ANALYSIS

In recent years a number of developments have taken place in the fields of mathematical psychology and psychometrics that have great value in quantifying the relative importance potential customers place on the various attributes of a product. These techniques are based on a type of trade-off analysis called 'conjoint measurement', a powerful device for quantifying the intangible as well as the physical benefits present in a product. The 'trade-off' approach to pricing follows a sequence of logical steps.

## STEP 1 IDENTIFICATION OF BENEFIT COMPONENTS

It is important to recognize that the potential customers for a product will have their own perceptions of the benefits contained within that product. To identify these perceived benefits it is necessary to conduct a limited, small-scale survey of potential and/or actual customers. The purpose of this study is to elicit the key features or benefits that are expected to be acquired as a result of using the product. Direct questioning can be used, such as, 'What is it that makes

Brand X different from Brand Y?' More sophisticated procedures for elicitation of benefits exist, but essentially they all have the same purpose: to draw from customers their own perceptions of product features rather than the manufacturers'. So, in a study of customers for a new chemical compound, the following attributes might emerge:

- quality;
- availability;
- impact on customers' production economies;
- storage conditions necessary; and
- technical assistance.
- The question is, then: 'What relative value is placed on each of these components?'

## STEP 2 QUANTIFYING BENEFIT VALUES

Because a product is, in effect, the totality of its component attributes, a way must be found of separating these and measuring their individual value to the customer. It is here that conjoint analysis becomes particularly useful. Using the attributes identified in Step 1, the researcher presents to the sample of customers a variety of hypothetical products that contain different configurations of the previously identified attributes, each configuration having a different price. Thus, for the example of a chemical compound, the hypothetical product configurations in Table 11.1 might be constructed.

| Attribute | Product 1 | Product 2 |
|---|---|---|
| Quality | Impurities less than one part per million | Impurities less than ten parts per million |
| Availability | Make to order | Available from stock |
| Impact on customer's production economies | No impact | Improves usable output by 10 per cent |
| Storage conditions | Stable product, long shelf life | Requires high level storage environment |
| Technical assistance | Manufacturer provides high-level technical advice | Weak |
| Price | £5 per pound | £5.50 per pound |

Table 11.1 Attribute levels

Clearly, there are many different combinations of attribute levels. Only two examples are given here but they will be sufficient to demonstrate the concept of a trade-off. The question put to the survey respondents is: 'Given that the two alternative products above are available, which would you prefer?' Both products have their advantages and their disadvantages, and the final choice will be based on the trade-off of the pluses and minuses. By extending the questioning to include other configurations of the same attributes it is possible, using conjoint analysis, to produce a numerical 'weight' for each attribute that reflects the relative importance attached to each of the attributes in question. More specifically, it enables the researcher to identify for each attribute the weight given to different *levels* of that attribute. Thus for 'quality' it will be possible to determine the extent by which 'impurities less than one part per million' is preferred over 'impurities less than ten parts per million' – or any level of impurity in the range under consideration.

However, the greatest advantage of using conjoint analysis in this context is that it also provides the researcher with *the relative utility of different price levels*. Thus we have a means of interpreting the price equivalence of differences in the perceived values of different combinations of product attributes. Step 3 describes this procedure.

## STEP 3 DETERMINING THE PRICE EQUIVALENCE OF VALUE

The output of the conjoint analysis of the data collected in Step 2 might typically appear as in Figure 11.4. For each level of each attribute a 'utility' is computed and this can be graphed to give a visual indication of the importance of that attribute. More importantly, though, it enables the value of this arbitrary 'utility' measure to be given a price equivalence. It will be seen from Figure 11.4 that the difference in utility between a price of £5 and £5.50 is 0.25 (that is, 1.00–0.75); thus the price equivalence of one unit of 'utility' is (£5.50–£5)/ 0.25, that is, £2.

Using this information we can say, for example, that a 10 per cent improvement in saleable output is worth a price difference of £1 per pound (£2 [1.00–0.5]). Again, we can say that the benefit of a stable product with a long shelf life is worth an additional £0.5 per pound (£2 [0.75–0.5]) over a product requiring a high-level storage environment.

Given this information it is clear that the price decision-maker has a very powerful insight into the components of value in the customer's mind. The decision-maker can now also identify which product attributes have the biggest influence on value perception. In the case examined here, for example, availability and quality are seen as the two major components of value. A change from Level 2 to Level 1 in availability brings an increase in utility of 1.0, and a change from Level 2 to Level 1 in quality produces an increase in utility of 0.75 (worth £2 and £1.50 per pound respectively).

This information on the 'price-equivalence' of customer values can provide a basis for price determination that reflects the worth the market places

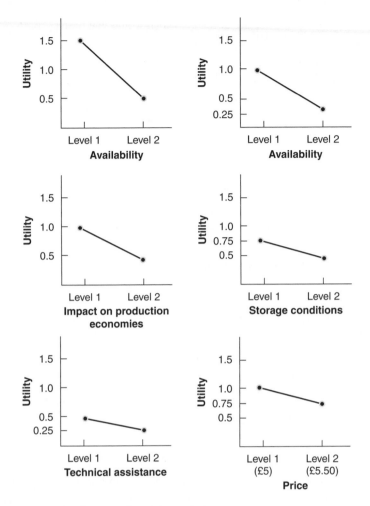

Figure 11.4 Graphical output of conjoint analysis

Note: Level 1 corresponds to the lowest level identified in the study for each attribute.

upon our offer. Perhaps one of the most important features of the value-in-use approach advocated here is that it focuses our attention on customer perceptions of product attributes and away from the narrower production orientation of suppliers' costs. In this sense it is very much a market-orientated approach to pricing.

There are also certain strategic issues raised by this approach to pricing, particularly with regard to marketing communications. It is well known that in many product/market fields there is a definite relationship between the price obtained and the perception of quality on the part of the customer. In other words, where there is a perception of 'added values', the demand/price relationship can be altered radically. Where added values are perceived by the customer to exist, the demand curve is, in effect, shifted to the right, as in Figure 11.5.

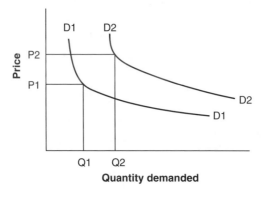

Key: D1D1   Original demand curve          Q1  Original demand
     D2D2   New demand curve               P2  New price
     P1     Original price                 Q2  New demand

Figure 11.5 The effect of perceived added values on the demand curve

So, in this particular case, the effect of these heightened perceptions of customer values has been to stimulate greater demand but at a higher price.

To make use of this fundamental model for profit improvement we must recognize two basic factors:

- *Perception*: to what extent does the customer/potential customer perceive that our product embodies certain attributes?

- *Value/utility*: to what extent does the current/potential customer consider these attributes to be important in the purchase decision?

In the first case, if the perception of product performance falls below that of competitive products, what can be done? It may be that the problem is largely one of communication. Perhaps we have not been forceful enough in our attempts to inform the market about the strengths of our product or, if we have, the message still has not come across. Alternatively, it may be that our product is deficient in these attributes and it may thus be desirable to institute a programme of product improvement.

If, on the other hand, we identify that our product scores highly, but on attributes that are perhaps given less weight by the customer (that is, their value/utility is lower), then we could downgrade the product on these attributes to improve overall profitability, or indeed reduce the price if appropriate. Similarly, recognizing the value/utility placed on the various product attributes should be of great help in designing and introducing new products, or in reformulating old ones.

From the point of view of marketing strategy, value-in-use can become the basis of a more effective segmentation strategy. Because different customers will have different perceptions of a product's attributes and will also differ in the value/utility they place upon those attributes, it will often be possible to target products to specific groups, or segments, in the market. Price is one of the simplest ways of segmenting markets, but price segmentation can become far more effective when based upon value-in-use. Recent research by Suk et al. (2012) indicates that consumer with lower levels of product knowledge may perceive higher initial value-in-use than more experienced consumers. Supporting Erdem et al.'s (2010) findings, Suk et al. (2012) also find inexperienced buyers more likely to use price as an indicator of quality. In practical terms, this suggests that buying experience could be a potentially effective segmentation variable for targeting price and promotional offers.

# COMPETITIVE PRICING STRATEGY

Most marketing activity takes place within the context of some level of competitive activity. Thus pricing decisions must clearly reflect competitive positioning, and the customers' perception of any differential values that are embodied in competitive offerings.

At one extreme is a market with one dominant supplier – say a 40 per cent market share to the nearest rival with 15 per cent – and where that dominant supplier has an offer that is high in perceived added values, it is likely that a substantial price differential could be obtained. On the other hand, if there is no single dominant player in market share terms, and the market is effectively a 'commodity' market with no perceived product differences, then it is highly unlikely that any single supplier could command a higher price.

In any competitive marketplace the following relationship will normally hold:

$$\frac{\text{Perceived benefits (market leader)}}{\text{Price (market leader)}} \geq \frac{\text{Perceived benefits (competitor)}}{\text{Price (competitor)}}$$

In other words, to maintain a position of market share leadership, the ratio of price to perceived benefits must exceed that of the competition. Using this relationship it will be recognized that it is not enough to have a high level of perceived benefits if the competition has a substantially lower price. It will sometimes be the case that a supplier may develop an offer with substantial added values and sell it at a higher price, but in so doing will provide competitors with a price umbrella under which they can shelter while developing 'me too' products. The plethora of the brands now competing directly with the Sony Vaio Ultrabook provides testament to this.

The position of the product in relation to the market life cycle will also be important in determining pricing strategy. Given the importance of maintaining or increasing market share in the early stages of the life cycle as a means of increasing the speed of movement down the experience curve – to ensure both higher profitability and cash flow as the market matures – careful attention must be paid to the benefit–price ratio.

In the past, marketing authors have distinguished between *skimming* strategies and *penetration* strategies, particularly in the context of pricing new products. It has been suggested that a penetration strategy (that is, a low relative price) is a route to early gains in market share if:

- demand is price sensitive;
- economies of scale exist; and
- competitive imitation is not difficult.

Commonly, penetration pricing can be effective where a core product is sold at penetration price, while money is made from the sale of associated products. For example, Hewlett-Packard sells printers at slim margins; profits are generated from the sale of ink cartridges. This can be taken to the extreme where the basic product or service is given away for free, but a premium is charged for additional features, functionality, services and so on. Known as 'freemium' pricing, this strategy is pursued quite commonly in the online environment, particularly in relation to music, video, news and magazine content.

Alternatively, it is argued that a skimming strategy (that is, a high relative price) could be appropriate, where:

- demand is not particularly price sensitive;
- there is a relatively flat cost curve (that is, unit costs at low volumes are not so much higher than unit costs at higher volumes); and
- there is limited danger of competitive imitation.

Apple is a good example of a company that employs a skimming strategy when new products are brought to market. Each time a new product is launched, Apple charges the highest price they know early adopters will pay. Once this category of buyer is saturated, the price is lowered. When the original iPhone first launched in 2007, the 4GB version sold for $499 and the 8GB version $599. Two months later, the latter was reduced by $200.

Figure 11.6 suggests the possible pricing strategies that may be appropriate given the opportunities for value enhancement or cost reduction. Value enhancement is a strategy based on building perceived benefits, while cost reduction can provide the basis for successful price competition. The rationale behind each of these options can be demonstrated by the use of the experience curve concept. As we have seen, it is usually the case that penetration strategies are more appropriate where the opportunity for cost reduction is greatest – that is, rapid movement down a steeply sloping experience curve can be achieved.

Figure 11.6 Appropriate pricing strategies

On the other hand, a skimming strategy is more likely to be appropriate where rapid cost reductions are unlikely – that is, the experience curve is less steep. Figure 11.7 outlines the logic of each of the four pricing options.

Ultimately, however, neither a skimming nor a penetration policy will lead to a position of substantial market leadership unless the benefit price ratio is maintained at a higher level than that of the competition. The achievement of a favourite ratio is obviously not down to pricing strategy alone but can only come about through a total focus of the marketing mix on differentiation while managing the operations of the business to provide a cost advantage.

# RELATIONSHIP PRICING

It has sometimes been suggested that we have entered the era of the 'value-driven' customer. This customer seeks even greater delivered benefits but at lower cost. Customers such as these can be found in every type of market, be it business-to-business or end-user. Price sensitivity seems to be as high as it has ever been, and customers are often quite willing to move from one supplier to another if the price–value equation does not appeal to them.

To counteract this tendency, companies such as Procter & Gamble have developed a philosophy of value-based pricing. Under value-based pricing, the customer (and the consumer) is offered a guaranteed lower price through the elimination of non-value-adding activities or strategies such as frequent promotions or brand extensions. The underpinning idea is that customers (or consumers) will not pay for non-value-adding activities or elements of a marketing offer. Thus, in the United States, Procter & Gamble used to offer over 20 variants of Crest toothpaste – different sizes, flavours and so on. Research highlighted that such variety did not create additional value for customers or

**(a) Follow my leader**

In this situation the industry price will follow costs and, in particular, the costs of the price leader

**(b) Penetration strategy**

Here price is set low by the early entrant to gain advantage of the price-sensitive market and thus gain market share and hence lower costs

**(c) Skimming strategy**

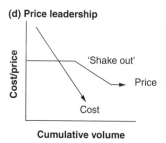

Under a skimming strategy it is assumed that the cost reduction opportunities are low, hence less steep experience curve

**(d) Price leadership**

Through a combination of high added value plus low cost, these companies are able to bring down the price 'umbrella' and shake out the less innovative or higher-cost competitors

Figure 11.7 Price and the experience curve

*Note*: All these charts assume logarithmic scales, hence the experience 'curve' is shown as a straight line.

consumers. In fact, the customers (the retailers) were not prepared to find shelf-space for such a range, and at the consumer level it only served to focus on the best-selling variants. This meant that significant complexity was taken out of the supply chain and hence costs came down without any loss of customer or consumer value.

In ways such as these, lower prices can be charged while margins are maintained. Customer relationships are built on many things, as we have observed throughout this book, but one of the strongest drivers of an enduring relationship is the perception by the customer that this supplier delivers 'more for less'.

Value-based pricing, or 'everyday low price' (EDLP) as it has been termed, is not just applicable in retail markets. In business-to-business markets the quest for value on the part of customers is just as great. Often this leads to 'deals' being offered by suppliers that are not based on cost reduction and are thus not sustainable. The key to 'everyday low price' in this environment is for both parties to collaborate in the search for genuine cost reduction through process improvement to enable prices to fall while margins are preserved. There is now a growing recognition in many industries that a partnership between buyer and supplier is a better way to achieve enduring cost reduction than the previous strategy of the customer playing one supplier off against another.

# DYNAMIC PRICING

Facilitated by new technology, companies increasingly are employing dynamic pricing models to hold their own in intensely competitive markets. Hinz et al. (2011) observe that although the technology has been around for some time, companies have been somewhat reluctant to move to pure dynamic pricing models for fear of a consumer backlash and potential negative publicity. In a high-profile case, Amazon had to apologize for using buyer profiles to charge varying prices for the same product and refund all customers who had paid higher prices. There is some evidence, however, that companies successfully employ dynamic pricing strategies without making it obvious to consumers (Baye and Morgan, 2002; Ellison and Ellison, 2004). In some industries, this has become the norm and has achieved consumer acceptance. For example, the travel industry has used dynamic pricing for some time, whether in relation to train companies charging premium prices during rush hour, or package holidays costing more during school holidays. More recently, this pricing model has found its way into other sectors and markets, and it has now become quite common in some B2C and B2B marketplaces.

The basis of dynamic pricing online is the pricing bot, which roams the web looking for the lowest, real-time price. Buyers (whether consumer or business) can simply trawl for the lowest price, and the transparency of the web enables prices to be compared quickly and easily. From the sellers' perspective, dynamic pricing enables experimentation and optimal sales; they can charge high prices, see how many consumers buy, assess the competition, reduce prices to sell more, and so on. It also allows sellers to charge different consumers different prices. Based upon consumer clickstream and previous purchase data, sellers have the opportunity to charge individual consumers whatever price they think the consumer will accept. As intimated however, there is a danger that brand equity could be harmed if consumers feel they are being manipulated, so the decision to use dynamic pricing must be made with care.

## CASE STUDY 11.1 DYNAMIC PRICING IN ACTION

Late in 2012 the English football Championship clubs, Cardiff, Derby and Bristol City announced that match tickets would be sold using dynamic pricing. Common in the United States, the basic premise of dynamic pricing is that the price of a match ticket can change, potentially quite significantly, in response to fluctuations in demand. Following the basic rules of demand and supply, the price of a ticket varies in line with the popularity of any particular match.

Within this framework, pricing follows two further, basic principles: firstly, the price of a ticket always increases as match-day approaches, therefore it is always more cost effective to buy well in advance. Secondly, the 'start' price for individual tickets is always set above the price paid by season ticket holders. Thereafter, the pricing bot simply tracks demand and suggests daily price changes.

The three clubs stated openly that they had two key objectives: to increase attendance (particularly at the less popular matches) and to maximize revenue from popular matches with high demand for tickets.

Thus far, all three clubs report improved attendance figures, and fewer empty seats, than in previous years.

### CASE STUDY QUESTIONS:

1. Dynamic pricing is based on simple demand/supply pricing, but marketers also need to consider psychological pricing. Discuss the role of psychological pricing in the dynamic pricing model.

2. As the case study illustrates, the three Championship clubs have succeeded in improving attendance figures by using dynamic pricing. What other industries might benefit from introducing dynamic pricing?

3. Discuss whether you think the (i) short-term and (ii) long-term outcomes of dynamic pricing might vary. If so, how?

# INTERNATIONAL PRICING MANAGEMENT

One of the most striking trends in recent years has been the rapid increase in the globalization of markets. Not only is this true in the case of well-established brands such as Coca-Cola, Marlboro and Gucci, but it is also apparent in markets as diverse as computing, motor cars and consumer electronics. Nor is the trend towards globalization confined only to products; we see similar transformations in services, whether it be banking, retailing or satellite TV.

At the same time, the corporations that have created and developed these global brands are refocusing their operations so that they too are global in their scope. What this means is that an electronics company, for example, may source some of its components in one country, sub-assemble in another, with final assembly taking place in a third country. Managing these complex global networks becomes one of the prime challenges to the achievement of profitability.

The impact of this move towards the globalization of business on the pricing decision is substantial. First, there are implications for the cost of the product or service, and second, it is quite likely that there will be significant differences from country to country in the price sensitivity of demand. Let us consider both of these issues in turn.

# COST IMPLICATIONS OF GLOBAL SOURCING

As we have noted, there is an increasing tendency for organizations to source materials and assemble and manufacture items offshore. The motivation for this is largely economic, based on the search for cost reductions. These lower costs may be available through lower labour rates, lower costs of material, lower taxes, lower costs of capital or government assistance. At the same time, these organizations may also rationalize production so that individual country operations no longer produce a full range of products for their own national markets. Instead, the company may now focus production on fewer factories making a limited range of items, but for a regional or even global market. The opportunities for enhanced economies of scale in production through such strategies may be considerable. Companies such as Unilever, for example, which previously manufactured soaps and detergents in local factories for local markets, have now rationalized their production on a regional basis with fewer factories producing for wider markets.

While the advantages of such strategies seem to be readily apparent, there are a number of implications for pricing.

## EXCHANGE-RATE FLUCTUATIONS

Given the volatility of exchange rates between currencies, there is a considerable inherent risk in companies committing themselves to long-term offshore supply arrangements. Companies with the ability to switch production from one location to another at short notice clearly have an advantage. For example, Heinz can increase or decrease production of tomato ketchup in their regional plants with a high degree of flexibility in order to take advantage of exchange-rate fluctuations. Companies that lack this flexibility can often find themselves faced with substantial cost increases as a result of changes in exchange rates.

## CHANGES IN FACTOR COSTS

Closely allied to the risk of exchange rate fluctuation is the problem of changes in factor costs such as labour, land or capital. Many companies decided to locate production in what were perceived to be low-labour-cost countries, often in South-East Asia, only to find that, with rapid economic development, the advantage proved to be transitory. Also to be taken into account is the way in which the costs of transport from the source of supply to the end market can change, in some instances eliminating any production cost advantage. Recently, container ships have slowed down to reduce costs (to the extent that, in 2010, the press reported that the world's largest cargo ships are now travelling at lower speeds than the Cutty Sark did over 130 years ago)!

## TRANSFER PRICING

In complex, multi-level production and distribution systems within a single company, the issue of internal transfer pricing arises. In other words, at what internal price should products or supplies be 'sold' to the next stage in the chain? Sometimes these decisions will be determined by tax considerations, but often there will be other factors influencing the transfer price, such as internal accounting practices that might allocate overhead costs on some arbitrary basis, hence distorting the cost that is passed on down the chain. There are countless examples of companies that have been forced to charge higher prices in end markets because of an accumulated cost that reflects the real costs of supply.

## PARALLEL IMPORTS

Often, identical products may be sold in different markets at different prices. This practice, known to economists as 'price discrimination', is made possible because of the different demand and supply characteristics in the different markets. However, once the price difference between markets exceeds the cost of acquiring and transporting those products from one market to another, then arbitrage or 'parallel imports' can become a serious problem for the company. This is a phenomenon that is encountered frequently in both consumer and industrial markets. One partial solution to this problem is to develop a unique brand for individual markets, but this may not allow economies of scale in sourcing, production and distribution to be achieved.

## GLOBAL/REGIONAL PURCHASING

In the same way that suppliers are tending to operate on a global, or at least regional, basis, so too are their customers. If a major European retailer, for example, sees that a product is being sold by a manufacturer at a lower price in one market (because of supply/demand considerations), then that retailer may insist on buying that product at a price for the markets in which it operates. This will become more of a problem for suppliers as increasing numbers of customers band together into regional or global buying groups. Across Europe, a number of such groups already exist, particularly in grocery retailing.

A further challenge to international pricing management arises where the same brand may be positioned quite differently in different national markets. Stella Artois is a premium-priced lager in the United Kingdom, for example, whereas in its home country of Belgium it is seen as a 'regular' beer sold at standard prices.

Given these potential problems, what are the options for a company seeking to develop an international pricing strategy? The overriding consideration, as with pricing decisions generally, is that the price must reflect the value proposition that is presented to the customer in each market in which the product is offered. Based on this, the 'target cost' for the market can be identified – that is, the achievable price less the desired profit margin. Decisions on sourcing must be taken in the context of that target cost, taking into account total supply chain costs – preferably undistorted by transfer pricing manipulations. No pricing strategy will eliminate the risks we have identified above, but careful and continuous management of the pricing decision on a global basis will help to minimize them.

# SUMMARY

The pricing decision is one of the most important issues to be faced by the marketing manager. Almost every market is influenced to some extent by the relative price of the products competing in that market. When customers buy products they are making choices based on their perception of the relative value of competing offers. The maximum price at which a product or service can be sold can be no greater than its perceived value.

It is proposed that price should be related to the value of benefits that our product or service delivers. Techniques such as trade-off analysis can be utilized to assist in the pricing decisions, particularly in the valuation of benefits.

# FURTHER READING

Rao, V. R. (ed) (2010) *Handbook of Pricing Research in Marketing*, Cheltenham: Edward Elgar.

An interdisciplinary compilation of perspectives on pricing strategies, decisions and issues by some of the leading academic writers in the field.

# REFERENCES

Baye, M. R., and Morgan, J. 2002. 'Information Gatekeepers and Price Discrimination on the Internet,' *Economics Letters*, Vol. 7 (1): 47–51.

Ellison, G. and Ellison, S. F. (2004) 'Search, Obfuscation, and Price Elasticities on the Internet,' NBER Working Papers 10570, Cambridge, MA: National Bureau of Economic Research.

Erdem, T., Michael L. K., and Baohong S. (2010), 'A Simple Test for Distinguishing Between Internal and External Reference Price Theories,' *Quantitative Marketing and Economics*, Vol. 8 (3): 303–332.

Hinz, O., Hann, I-H., and Spann, M. (2011) 'Price Discrimination in E-Commerce? An Examination of Dynamic Pricing in Name-Your-Own Price Markets,' *MIS Quarterly*, Vol. 35 (1): 81–98.

Suk, K., Lee, J. and Lichtenstein, D. R. (2012) 'The Influence of Price Presentation Order on Consumer Choice,' *Journal of Marketing Research*, Vol. 49 (5): 708–717.

# CHAPTER 12
# COMMUNICATIONS STRATEGY

IN THIS CHAPTER WE STUDY:

- the critical role of marketing communications
- the communications mix
- the difference between personal and impersonal communications
- the distinction between advertising and marketing objectives
- the implications of integrated marketing communications
- the corporate communications audit and the communication process
- the factors effecting media selection

# COMMUNICATIONS ARE CRITICAL

The role of marketing communications is to inform the market clearly and persuasively about the company, its products, services and brands. As businesses compete in progressively fiercer markets for a larger wallet share of an increasingly discerning and diverse customer base, they become ever more communication dependent. The emergence of customer relationship management (CRM), e-CRM and geo-locational mobile advertising underline this point.

The entire field of marketing communications has changed dramatically in recent years, due primarily to rapid developments in information and communications technology (ICT). Interactive dialogue has rendered market ignorance or complacency intolerable. Media bombardment and information overload, creating background 'noise', has numbed individuals' receptivity to messages. On the positive side, the shift from mass communications to individualized communications has seen greater customer involvement with particular goods and services, and better marketing use of a wider range of media channels and communication tools. Companies can now connect with current and prospective customers in far more ways than was possible some years ago, resulting in a paradigm shift from inform/persuade to a much more holistic model based upon listening to and interacting with consumers.

Consumer enthusiasm for new media, exemplified by the escalation in e-mail, social networking, consumer discussion groups, web- and mobile advertising and e-commerce websites all provide new means for developing, strengthening and influencing relationships with customers, other stakeholders and even competitors. The philosophical shift from persuasion to dialogue is considered by many as transformational (Hughes and Fill, 2007). That stated, there remains a place for transactional exchanges and mass communication, such that contemporary models of personalized, interactive communications must take their place alongside more traditional modes. Given this climate of changing consumer preferences and behaviour, constant innovation and growing market complexity, the imperative to communicate appropriately is immense. The evidence is unequivocal: marketing communications are complex and challenging – but absolutely critical to marketing success.

# THE COMMUNICATIONS MIX

In order to achieve its marketing objectives, an organization has to communicate with both existing and potential customers. It can do so in a variety of ways, either on a mass (impersonal) or a personal basis. Impersonal communication is accomplished indirectly, using advertising, sales promotion, point-of-sale displays and public relations, while personal communication is undertaken directly, either online or in traditional face-to-face settings.

The secret of powerful marketing communications is to optimize utilization of the armoury of communication tools at the organization's disposal. Used either singly or in combination, the promotional tools can be blended together into an effective and persuasive *communications* or *promotional mix*. The design of the communications mix represents the most cost-effective solution for achieving the organization's communication objectives. According to Sidhanta and Chakrabarty (2010), organizations have found out that advertising and sales promotion alone are not sufficient to achieve the ends, that is, generate profits. The firm has to unify the brand image and messages that come from different company activities. This is achieved through the promotional mix, which should be designed in relation to clear communication objectives, examples of which are shown in Table 12.1.

| Educating and informing | Create awareness | |
| | Promote understanding | |
| | Inform | |
| | Get enquiries | |
| Branding and image building | Get company name in file | The chosen communication objective(s) must contribute towards a total marketing programme, the objective of which is to achieve profitable sales |
| | Create company image | |
| | Reach personnel inaccessible to salespeople | |
| Affecting attitudes | Ease the selling task | |
| | Get editorial | |
| | Overcome prejudice | |
| | Influence end users | |
| Encouraging loyalty/affinity and reminding | Reduce selling costs | |
| | Achieve sales (including repeat sales) | |
| | Generate customer referrals | |

Table 12.1 Common communication objectives

# ADVERTISING

Advertising remains the most widely used tool in the communications mix. Often referred to as 'above-the-line expenditure', it includes measured media such as web-based advertising, mobile adverts, television, cinema, radio and print advertisements. To non-marketers, advertising may appear somewhat aggressive, in as much as it intrudes into consumers' individual space, often without their permission. But the most effective type of advertising is permission-based, where consumers have opted to receive the communication.

Far from being a somewhat primitive tool, when used correctly, advertising can be a reasonably sophisticated weapon in the marketer's armoury. Its role usually alters during the life cycle of a product. For example, the process of persuasion (awareness, interest, attitude formation, decision to act) cannot normally start until there is some level of awareness about a product or service in the marketplace. Creating awareness is therefore one of the most important advertising objectives in the early stages for the product life cycle (PLC). If the offer has been matched correctly with customer needs and is perceived to be superior to competitors' offers, through the astute use of such vehicles as branding, pricing or customer-convenient distribution, then advertising can tip the customer from initial awareness to a state of liking and preference.

The 'diffusion of innovation' curve discussed in Chapter 9 is relevant here. Experience indicates that once the first 3 per cent of innovators have adopted the product, the early adopters will probably try it, and once the 8–10 per cent point is reached, the rest will be likely to follow suit. This pattern demonstrates the need for different kinds of advertising for each category of customer, and thus different sets of advertising objectives and strategies for different stages in a product's life cycle. It is worth remembering too that, for optimum effect, advertising effort can be directed not only at consumers but also at all those who influence commercial success, including channels, shareholders, media, employees, suppliers and government.

There are two basic questions that advertising objectives should address: 'Who are the people we are trying to influence?' and 'What specific benefits or information are we trying to communicate to them?' Many companies use outside agencies to design their advertising. Advertising objectives, however, should *always* be set by the advertiser and *not* by an advertising agency.

There are many possible advertising objectives, such as to:

- convey information;
- alter perceptions;

- alter attitudes;

- create desires;

- establish connections (for example, the association of bacon with egg);

- direct actions;

- provide reassurance;

- remind;

- give reasons for buying;

- demonstrate; and

- generate enquiries.

Having defined and agreed the advertising objectives, all other steps in the process of assembling the advertising strategy then flow naturally from them. These subsequent steps address the following questions, which essentially form the process of producing the advertising plan:

| | |
|---|---|
| WHO | . . . are the target audience(s)? |
| (target) | What do they already know, feel, believe about us and our product/service? |
| | What do they know, feel, believe about the competition? |
| | What sort of people are they? How do we describe/identify them? |
| WHAT | . . . response do we wish to evoke from the target audience(s)? |
| (message-copy platform) | . . . are these specific communications objectives? |
| | . . . do we want to 'say', make them 'feel', 'believe', 'understand', 'know', about buying/using our product/service |
| | . . . are we offering? |
| | . . . do we not want to convey? |
| | . . . are the priorities of importance of our objectives? |
| | . . . are the objectives which are written down and agreed by the company and advertising agency? |
| HOW | . . . are our objectives to be embodied in an appealing form? |
| (creative platform) | What is our creative strategy/platform? |

(Continued)

| | |
|---|---|
| | What evidence do we have that this is acceptable and appropriate to our audience(s)? |
| WHERE (*media*) | . . . is/are the most cost-effective place(s) to expose our communications (in cost terms *vis-à-vis* our audience)? |
| | . . . is/are the most beneficial place(s) for our communications (in expected response terms *vis-à-vis* the 'quality' of the channels available)? |
| WHEN (*timing*) | . . . are our communications to be displayed/conveyed to our audience? |
| | What is the reasoning for our scheduling of advertisements/communications over time? |
| | What constraints limit our freedom of choice? |
| | Do we have to fit in with other promotional activity on: |
| |     other products/services supplied by our company? |
| |     competitors' products/services? |
| |     seasonal trends? |
| |     special events in the market? |
| RESULT (*performance success*) | What results do we expect? |
| | How would we measure results? |
| | Do we intend to measure results and, if so, do we need to do anything *beforehand*? |
| | If we cannot say how we would measure precise results, then perhaps our objectives are not sufficiently specific, or are not communication objectives? |
| | How are we going to judge the relative success of our communication activities (good/bad/indifferent)? |
| | Should we have action standards? |
| BUDGET (*investment*) | How much money do the intended activities need? |
| | How much money is going to be made available? |
| | How are we going to control expenditure? |
| SCHEDULE (*putting it all together*) | Who is to do what, and when? |
| | What is being spent on what, where and when? |

There are five key points to remember about advertising:

1. *Advertising is an integral part of the marketing effort and must never be seen as an isolated activity.* Its effectiveness will depend not only upon the persuasiveness of the message being conveyed to customers and consumers but also on the accuracy with which the target audience has been selected.

Clearly, any product or service can offer several different benefits; for example, it can be newer, safer, cheaper, more efficient, or unique. Each of these benefits will have more, or less, appeal to different customer groups. Targeting the right message to the right people is the key to successful advertising.

2. *The same rules apply to online advertising as offline.* Advertising works well at initial stages of the PLC, when consumers need to be made aware of a new product. Once awareness has been established, reminder advertising can encourage consumers to appreciate the key benefits on offer in relation to competitor products or services. Advertising alone seldom triggers a purchase, however (see 3 below). The ease of reaching target audiences online does not mean that the rules have changed. Sending unrequited online advertisement (spam) to consumers can not only damage their attitudes towards the product or service being advertised but also towards the brand or company sending the communication.

3. *New technology can shorten decision-making, but advertising alone is normally insufficient to trigger a purchase.* Online and mobile platforms are proving popular with companies and consumers alike. Around 30 per cent of all UK advertising expenditure is spent online of which approximately 60 per cent is paid search and 25 per cent on display advertising (including social media and video adverts) (www.smartinsights.com 2012 data). Mobile advertising is growing rapidly and accounted for almost 10 per cent of all digital advertising expenditure compared to 1.1 per cent three years previously. Benefits of direct online advertising include enhanced reach and frequency at relatively low cost; however, expenditure alone does not trigger a behavioural response. Quick response (QR) codes embedded in adverts might encourage consumers to take action, for example, getting more information about a product, or service, or accessing a website where the product may be purchased, but the decision to buy normally relies upon the interaction of several components of the communications mix (for example, advertising and sales promotion).

4. *The most impressive, elaborate and indulgent campaign will not convince customers and consumers to buy again if the product or service, whose virtues the advertising extols, is non-competitive.* Advertising alone rarely produces long-lasting marketing success. While it will encourage, reinforce a message and perhaps even encourage a positive attitude and help to develop a loyalty to a particular product or service, it will be no substitute for an offering that fails to bestow the necessary benefits on a customer.

5. *Advertising can be subject to controls or constraints from one country to another.* For example, in the Netherlands, confectionery advertisements must be

followed by exhortations to brush one's teeth, while cigarette and alcohol advertising is banned in many countries. Cultural mores and sensitivities have a part to play concerning what is and what is not acceptable.

# SALES PROMOTION

Sales promotion (often referred to as 'below-the-line expenditure') is non-face-to-face activity concerned with persuading consumers to make a purchase. It is essentially a problem-solving activity designed to encourage customers to behave more in line with the economic interests of the company – that is, to bring forward their decision to buy. Sales promotion involves the making of a featured offer to defined customers within a specific time limit. The offer must include benefits not inherent in the product or service, as opposed to the intangible benefits offered in advertising, such as adding value through appeals to image, reputation or relationships. Expenditure on sales promotions has grown rapidly during the current economic downturn, with competitions on Facebook being particularly favoured. Such initiatives not only generate consumer interest and 'buzz' but also provide companies with invaluable consumer data. Consumer enthusiasm for online sales promotions has helped to drive the rapid growth of sales promotions on social networking sites. Those with a degree of perceived exclusivity, that is, available only to 'fans' or 'followers', are known to be particularly popular with consumers.

Another growth area is the use of trade promotions in B2B marketing. Trade promotions expenditure continues to follow an upward trajectory as companies become increasingly cognizant of the need to push their products or brands through distribution channels. There is increasing recognition of the crucial role played by distribution partners, resulting in the development of a variety of trade promotions intended to accrue benefits to partners along the supply chain. In a study of trade promotions, Gomez et al. (2007) find that both manufacturers and retailers can influence the allocation of promotional funds, the former in favour of performance-based types (scanbacks/accruals and billbacks) and the latter in favour of off-invoice promotions, which allow them greater control over use of these funds. Trade promotions need to be negotiated and managed carefully as they can be a contentious issue between retailers and manufacturers as both parties seek to maximize their own profits.

Whether B2C or B2B, sales promotions fulfil a number of tasks, including controlling stock movement; counteracting competitive activity; encouraging repeat purchase; securing marginal buyers; getting bills paid on time; and inducing trial purchase. It is generally used as a short-term, tactical initiative, in contrast with advertising as a long-term, strategic activity that changes with the PLC. However, sales promotion does have a strategic role to play in helping to strengthen the bond between seller and buyer, and thus a sales promotion strategy is required to ensure that each promotion increases the effectiveness of the next in terms of impact and investment of resources.

Sales promotion seeks to influence:
Salespeople to sell
Customers to buy
Customers to use      more, earlier, faster, etc.
Users to buy
Users to use
Distributors to stock

In order to achieve these objectives, the promotion can take various forms. It might involve discounts (price reductions, coupons), instant rewards (competitions), goods (free goods – for example, two for the price of one, trade-ins, free trials, redeemable coupons and so on), services (guarantees, training, free services) or in B2B, performance-related rewards. When determining the nature of the sales promotion, the decision should be made first about which target group(s) need to be influenced most to make an impact on the sales problem, and, second, what type of promotion will have maximum appeal to that group. When considering the cost element, it must be remembered that the promotional costs have to be weighed against the benefits of reducing the sales problem – which the sales promotion is intended to solve. The cost-effectiveness of the sales promotion must be established and integrated into the overall marketing plan.

The objectives for each sales promotion should be stated clearly, such as trial, repeat purchase, distribution, a shift in buying peaks, combating competition and so on. Then the strategy to implement the objectives must be worked out, taking care to integrate offline and online tools. Sales promotion strategy should follow the standard route of selecting the appropriate sales promotion technique; pre-testing; mounting the promotion; and, finally, evaluating in depth. Spending must be analysed and categorized by type of activity (for example, special packaging, special point-of-sale material, loss of revenue through price reductions and so on).

As for the sales promotion plan itself, the objectives, strategy and brief details of timing and costs should be included. It is important that the sales promotion plan should not be too detailed, and only an outline of it should appear

| Heading | Content |
|---|---|
| Introduction | Briefly summarize the problem on which the promotion is designed to make an impact |
| Objectives | Show how the objectives of the promotion are consistent with the marketing objectives |
| Background | Provide the relevant data or justification for the promotion |
| Promotional offer | Briefly, but precisely, provide details of the offer |
| Eligibility | Who is eligible? Where? |
| Timing | When is the offer available (opening and closing dates) |
| Date plan | The dates and responsibilities for all elements of promotion |
| Support | Special materials, samples, etc. required by the sales force, retailers and so on |
| Administration | Budgets, storage, invoicing, delivery and so on |
| Sales plan | Briefing meetings, targets, incentives and so on |
| Sales presentation | Points to be covered |
| Sales reporting | Any special information required |
| Assessment | How the promotion will be evaluated |

Table 12.2 Sales promotion plan

in the marketing plan. Table 12.2 provides an overview of the key elements of a sales promotion plan.

# OTHER COMMUNICATION TOOLS AND TRENDS

There are a number of other indirect communication tools available to marketers. These range from conventional methods, such as point-of-sale displays, exhibitions and PR to a plethora of more contemporary techniques, such as direct mail, database marketing and interactive media. As Hughes and Fill (2007) observe, digital technologies have enabled organizations increasingly to seek out new ways of reaching smaller, more discrete audiences. For example, product placement (out of advertising), programme sponsorship (out of public relations and advertising), field marketing (out of sales promotion), events and hospitality (out of public relations), key account management (out of personal selling) and an increasing variety of direct marketing initiatives (out of advertising). The overall impact has been to splinter the promotional mix; for example, many companies have withdrawn completely from television advertising, switching their limited communications budgets to more direct methods of interacting and creating a dialogue with consumers.

## POINT-OF-SALE DISPLAYS

Point-of-sale displays are sometimes called 'the silent salesman'. They can communicate valuable marketing information as well as contributing to sales. Attractively presented and placed in strategic locations, they can be a low-cost means of catching the eye of potential customers. However, the products on display must be suitably packaged and the dispenser or showcase be designed for safety. It must also contain references to product price and how to obtain further information or advice.

## EXHIBITIONS

As the cost of exhibitions continues to rise, companies need to ensure that they get good value for their investment. While an exhibition offers the prospect of many potential customers making contact with a company without the sales team having to go out looking for them, this will not happen by chance. The stand will have to be designed to attract attention and interest; staff must demonstrate high levels of skill and involvement; supporting materials must be appropriate and impressive; and back-up systems must be in place to ensure that all prospects receive an appropriate follow-up.

## PUBLIC RELATIONS

Public relations, or PR, is concerned with an organization's relationships with various groups, or 'publics', that affect its ability to achieve its goals and objectives. The aspects of these relationships that act as a focus for public relations are the image and information a market holds about an organization (that is, its position in the market). At a simple level, this is achieved through publicity in various print and broadcast media. At a broader level, as encouraged by relationship marketing, this is achieved through activities that are more specific in their targeting and objectives.

PR includes the areas of news generation, events, publications, sponsorships and donations, 'expert opinion' (individual endorsement by a knowledgeable representative of the organization) and 'visual identity' (identification or association through product design, logos, trademarks and so on). Increasingly, the PR function is becoming as much a means of personal communication as it is of impersonal communication. Many PR opportunities are used to stimulate personal contact with customers as well as to attract an impersonal response. While PR messages can be far more influential than advertising, PR is unlikely to replace advertising or other means of communication and promotion.

## INTERNAL MARKETING

Internal marketing is gaining credence as a vital communication tool as internal communications play an increasingly critical role in changing, reinforcing or questioning prevailing strategy and corporate culture. The perceptions held by management, staff, shareholders and partners about the organization throughout the value chain have a profound impact on the nature and future of relevant business relationships. It is therefore essential that all members of an organization's 'sphere of influence' are aware of the organization's intentions and actions, and are working towards common goals.

A seamless customer experience relies on the operation of a shared 'corporate memory' of the customer, which replicates the customer's own memory of encounters with the business. This means that all messages sent must be coherent and consistent, as well as customer-relevant, and that all incoming messages must be lodged and responded to in a suitable, professional manner. The issue of messages that are conflicting or confusing, unnecessarily repetitive or outright inappropriate can do more harm than good. It is also important that all are invited to contribute constructive input through the appropriate processes. The role of internal 'people power' in corporate communications is developed later in this book.

## DIRECT MAIL

Direct mail is much less haphazard than it once was, because of advances in technology and marketing thinking. However, a direct mail campaign has to be conceived carefully to stand any chance of being successful. Traditionally, direct approaches through the post have had very low response rates, but in recent times companies have become more adept at targeting their mailshots. One reason for this is the growth of, and access to, sophisticated techniques for analysing target prospects. Most prominent among these is database marketing.

## DATABASE MARKETING

Database marketing has gained popularity as access to technology has made it cheaper and easier to store and manipulate massive amounts of data. With the fragmentation of market segments on the increase, it is increasingly important for organizations to treat customers as individuals. Marketing information held about both the company's customers and competitor's customers is now a vital part of the marketer's toolbox. More about database marketing and related activities is given in Chapter 21.

## INTERACTIVE MEDIA

The Internet as a marketing medium provides an ideal platform for one-to-one communication, enabling instantaneous, interactive exchange at relatively little cost. In addition to offering individualized benefits, such as convenience, 24/7 availability and self-service functions, the immediacy of e-mail and sychronous discussion groups mean that self-nominated alliances and networks (of suppliers or customers) can grow rapidly. The role of the Internet in marketing is covered in greater depth in Chapter 20.

## BRAND MANAGEMENT

Brand management might reasonably be included here as a significant communication tool. As discussed in Chapter 10, branding is a powerful means of communicating the values of an organization as well as the value delivered by its products or services. Corporate and brand image is being recognized increasingly as a major influence on sales. In the commercial world, where it can be technically simple and financially tempting to duplicate a competitor's offering, the creation of a favourable or distinct/different image may give the company a competitive advantage. Truly effective brand management not only communicates existing value but also works to create and communicate future value.

Having outlined some of the traditional and more recent tools found within the marketing communications toolbox, let us look at the development of integrated marketing communications (IMC) as a means of utilizing and managing these tools effectively.

# INTEGRATED MARKETING COMMUNICATIONS

Ultimately, IMC is the strategic co-ordination of all marketing messages and the alignment of all methods of communicating with customers, be they consumers or other targeted, relevant (external and internal) audiences. IMC has evolved as marketers have moved away from traditional mass-media-based communications strategies towards those that are more personalized, customer-orientated and technology-driven.

Perhaps the most useful way to define integrated marketing communications is to illustrate what happens when a marketing campaign is not integrated. The marketing communications activities of the personal computer and software markets provide such an example. Companies such as Apple and Microsoft spend millions of pounds on advertising and direct mail in order to increase consumer awareness of their brands. The point of sale, usually with a dealer, is full of sales promotion activities designed to persuade the customers to upgrade their equipment or purchase more powerful programs, and to benefit from improved software support and other ancillary services.

One of the main aims of IMC is to harmonize the promotional tools so that audiences receive a consistent and substantiated message. Integration within marketing communications works on two main levels: the creative and the strategic.

## CREATIVE INTEGRATION

The paradigm shift from a transaction to a customer relationship focus acknowledges that *all* marketing is about communication, because people form their images of brands and companies from information provided by a variety of sources. One of the most important aspects of IMC is that it encourages a view of marketing communications from the customers' perspective, or as a flow of information from indistinguishable sources. Therefore the 'message', as opposed to the delivery, has to be the central focus. If different types of marketing communications are used to support brand positioning, they must work together in a synergistic fashion. Case study 12.1 provides an example of an IMC campaign that set out to achieve this integrated creativity.

# CASE STUDY 12.1 CADBURY'S CRÈME EGG OLYMPICS

Companies that are confident about their marketing message have found that an integrated, creative approach to communicating it can bring real benefits. Cadbury's launched an Olympic and Paralympic themed campaign to support its sponsorship of the London 2012 Olympic Games. The media agency, Fallon, devised a series of light-hearted, 30-second adverts for the web and television featuring Crème Eggs in mock Olympics opening and closing ceremonies and taking part in various sports events, such as hurdles, diving, hammer-throwing, javelin and cycling. Also available on YouTube and the branded Crème Egg Facebook page the adverts proved hugely popular.

To support the adverts, 'the Goo Games' was launched for Facebook and mobile devices in which players were challenged to 'splat' Crème Eggs. In addition, Twitter and Google+ were used maintain interest and create a 'buzz' around the campaign. RFID technologies were employed to allow consumers to receive photos from the Cadbury Olympic Games, as well as automatically updating their photo, status or messages via a series of touchpoints.

The campaign proved extremely popular with target audiences. Cadbury reported that 2.5 million fans and followers were attracted specifically to its dedicated UK Olympic Games social media channels, making a total of 7.5 million following the brand on social media sites. The Twitter following was reported as the strongest growth area. The Head of Social Media at Cadbury commented, 'Because it is a digital Games, it is difficult to have predicated how it will impact brand traffic, but we've seen a huge uplift across every digital channel, not just social which includes higher traffic to the Cadbury website, higher CTR on email.'

See www.marketingweek.co.uk for full story

**CASE STUDY QUESTIONS:**

1. Employing communications theory, analyse and explain the reason for the success of the Cadbury's Crème Egg Olympics.

2. In communications terms, what, specifically, was the role and purpose of the Goo Games?

3. Based upon IMC principles, discuss what offline promotions could be employed to support the great success of the online campaign.

## STRATEGIC INTEGRATION

As well as requiring creative synergy, there are also managerial implications for adopting an IMC strategy. Although IMC is recognized as a distinct business process, the debate continues as to the role of IMC orchestrator. Should a client company place its entire marketing communications requirement with one agency, or should it instead engage a variety of specialists and retain control centrally?

The fact that agencies have been offering a range of communication services in-house is seen by many as a rush to diversify in order to retain profit margins as client spending shifts emphasis from advertising to 'below the line'. This trend has led some to argue that IMC is merely a repackaging of the full service agency ideal of the 1960s, similar to BBDO's 'seamless communications', or Young and Rubicam's 'whole egg' approach. But these were really more of a 'one-stop shopping' strategy by the agency suppliers, who understood that integration requires the overall marketing strategy, communication strategy and creative execution to be aligned.

Research has shown that the majority of marketers believe the orchestration of IMC should be undertaken by the marketers themselves. Success in this endeavour, however, is dependent on cross-functional collaboration in managing the marketing communications, preferably through the establishment of a functionally representative, dedicated team. It is also reliant on there being a 'corporate memory' of customer relationships, so that everyone in the organization has the same recollection and experience of the relationship as the customer, and no conflicting or repetitive messages are sent.

# THE COMMUNICATION PROCESS

The communication process can be illustrated simply by Figure 12.1. Essentially, the marketer is faced with similar communication problems to those experienced by any two people talking. The sender's message is determined largely by his or her values, knowledge, attitude and vocabulary; it could therefore be claimed to be worded in the sender's personal code. If the receiver is 'tuned in' to the sender's code, because he or she shares similar values, attitudes and language, then the 'decoding' process is relatively straightforward. If he or she is not attuned to the sender's wavelength, then it is very difficult for the message to get through. The communication process is further complicated by the 'interference' that can come between the two parties. For the marketer, this may mean that the receiver is distracted, his or her attention being focused on other matters. Alternatively, the receiver may be confused by conflicting messages from competing suppliers of products or services, or may be suffering from message 'overload'.

Fill (2009) The linear model of communication (based on Schramm 1955 and Shannon and Weaver 1962).

The lessons for the marketer that stem from this simple communication model are fourfold:

- Keep the marketing message relatively simple.
- Word it in the receiver's language.
- Choose a medium/mechanism for transmitting the message that gives minimal distortion and interference.
- Know the target audience.

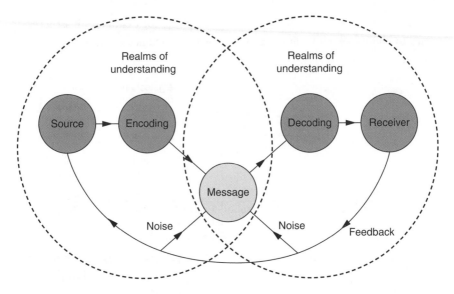

Figure 12.1 The communication process
*Source*: Fill (2009).

The important point is that, in order to design and achieve effective communication, the marketer must adopt the receiver's perspective. What types of media and messages appeal to the receiver? What mental processes take place in the receiver's mind on receipt of the message? There is evidence to suggest that the potential buyer goes through a thinking process something like this:

- becoming aware and developing understanding and knowledge (about the product or service and its supplier);
- developing interest, feelings, beliefs and preferences; and
- developing intentions, convictions and preparedness to try the product or service, or to dismiss it outright.

# THE CHANGING NATURE OF PROMOTION AND DISTRIBUTION

Nonetheless, in spite of the somewhat traditional approach to communications outlined above, promotion and distribution are changing in a number of respects. New channels such as the Internet are emphasizing an already growing trend from mass media such as advertising, through addressable media such as direct mail, to interactive media such as call centres and the web. Integrating these channels within a coherent strategy is not an easy task. Writers on IMC emphasize that, before engaging on detailed planning for each medium – writing sales plans or promotions plans, for example – it is necessary to choose which medium to use for which customer interaction. This is illustrated in Figure 12.2.

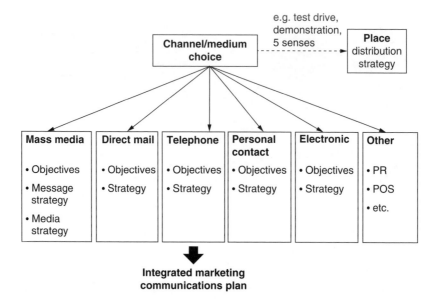

Figure 12.2 Defining promotion and distribution strategy
*Source*: McDonald and Wilson (2002).

## MARKETING OPERATIONS AND THE NEW SALES PROCESS

Once an overall marketing plan has been drawn up, including a plan for promotions, the plan must be implemented. This is the role of marketing operations – the delivery of the value to the customer that was specified in the planning process. But during the course of a year, plenty of finer-grained communications decisions need to be taken. To illustrate, consider the map of the marketing operations process in Figure 12.3.

The starting point for our analysis of the 'Deliver value' process was Porter's (1980) value chain. However, we suggest that there are a number of marketing activities that shadow these value chain activities, under the general heading of 'communicate the offer'. Porter placed 'Marketing' after 'Operations' in the value chain, but in the-modern one-to-one world, these communications can occur in parallel with all the tasks involved in value delivery. One might, for example, check a product with customers at the R&D stage. The product may be tailored by the customer, resulting in different components being bought in, assembled and delivered and so on.

Communicating the offer is managed typically by designing, implementing and monitoring a number of marketing communications programmes. A

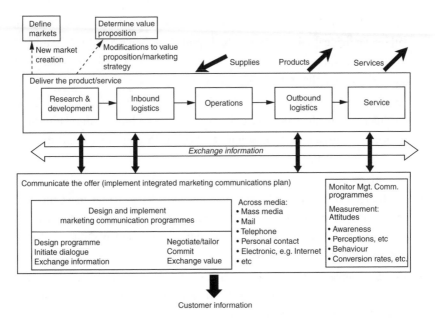

Figure 12.3 Delivering value – a map of marketing operations
*Source*: McDonald and Wilson (2002).

communication programme could be, for example, a direct mail campaign, an advertising campaign, a series of sales seminars, an in-store promotion and so on. Whatever the medium, the campaign will be aiming to contribute to one or more of the tasks within the 'Design/implement marketing communication programmes' box. The tasks may have an unfamiliar look: in order to represent the interactive one-to-one nature of twenty-first-century marketing we have renamed the classic steps in the sales process. Figure 12.4 illustrates traditional views of the sales and purchasing processes, with this revised interaction perspective between the two.

Traditional 'push-based' models of marketing, in which, after the product is made, prospects are found and persuaded to buy the product, are illustrated on the left of the figure. The delivery and service that follow are operational functions with little relationship to marketing. Traditional models of buyer behaviour, illustrated on the right of the figure, assume more rationality on the part of buyers but underplay the importance of what the buyer says back to the seller. The seller's offer is assumed to be predetermined, rather than developed in conjunction with the buyer.

The stages of the process of communicating value are therefore redescribed as follows:

- 'Recognize exchange potential' replaces 'category need' or 'problem recognition'. Both sides need to recognize the potential for a mutual exchange of value.

- 'Initiate dialogue' replaces 'Create awareness' or 'Prospecting'. The dialogue with an individual customer may be begun by either party. One feature of the Internet, for example, is that, on many occasions, new customers will approach the supplier rather than vice versa.

- 'Exchange information' replaces 'Provide information'. If we are to serve the customer effectively, tailor our offerings and build a long-term relationship, we need to learn about the customer as much as the customer needs to learn about our products.

- 'Negotiate/tailor' replaces 'Persuade'. Negotiation is a two-way process which may involve us modifying our offer in order to better meet the customer's needs. Persuading the customer instead that the square peg we happen to have in stock will fit their round hole is not likely to lead to a long and profitable relationship.

- 'Commit' replaces 'Close sale'. Both sides need to commit to the transaction, or to a series of transactions, forming the next stage in a relationship, a decision with implications for both sides.

- 'Exchange value' replaces 'Deliver' and 'Post-sales service'. The 'post-sales service' may be an inherent part of the value being delivered, not simply a cost centre, as it is often still managed.

| Supplier perspective | | Interaction perspective | | Buyer perspective | |
|---|---|---|---|---|---|
| Advertising | Selling | Marketing activity | Interaction | Decision theory | Consumer behaviour |
| | | Define mkt Understand value Create value proposition | Recognize exchange potential | Problem recognition | Category need |
| | | | | | Awareness |
| Brand awareness | Prospecting | Initial dialogue | | Information search | Attitude |
| Brand attitude ■ info re: benefits ■ brand image ■ feelings ■ peer influence | Provide information | Exchange information | | | Information gathering and judgement |
| Trial inducement | Persuade | Negotiate/tailor | | Evaluation of alternatives | |
| | Close sale | Commit | | Choice/ purchase | Purchase process |
| | Deliver | Exchange value | | | |
| Reduce cognitive dissonance | Service | ↓ | Monitor | Post-purchase behaviour | Post-purchase experience |

Figure 12.4 Rethinking the sales process
*Source*: McDonald and Wilson (2002).

One-to-one communications and principles of relationship marketing, then, demand a radically different sales process from that traditionally practised. The changing nature of the sales process clearly raises questions for the design of marketing communications, such as who initiates the dialogue, and how is the effectiveness measured of attempts to do so across multiple channels? How is the effectiveness measured, not only of what we say to customers but also what they say back? And how about the role of marketing communications as part of the value that is being delivered and paid for, not just as part of the sales cost? The trend towards multi-channel communications strategies has been underpinned by developments in CRM technology. This is discussed in greater detail in Chapter 14.

# SUMMARY

The organization has an armoury of communication tools that it can blend together into an effective and persuasive communications mix. Essentially, the communication strategy can be summed up as:

- What do we want to say?
- To whom do we want to say it?
- Why do we want to say it?
- How do we choose to say it?
- Where shall we communicate our message?
- When shall we say it?

These questions are deceptively simple, as answering them involves many important decisions affecting all levels of the organization.

Some communication tools might be more effective than others at conveying certain types of message to certain customers (or other stakeholders and competitors). Their appropriateness depends to a large extent on the potential purchasers' frame of mind and the stage they have reached in the buying decision process. The need to resolve any media conflict (that is, the sending or receiving of conflicting or confusing messages) and to pursue cost-effective communication strategies is a constant priority.

The two-way dialogue afforded by interactive marketing communications offers tremendous scope to improve the design and delivery of communication strategy, for the benefit of all concerned. The emergence of IMC is a response to the growing need for strategic co-ordination and customization of marketing messages and methods.

# REFERENCES

Fill, C. (2009) *Marketing Communications*, 5th edn, Harlow, Pearson.

Gomez, M.I., Rao, V.R. and McLaughlin, E.W. (2007) Empirical Analysis of Budget and Allocation of Trade Promotions in US Supermarkets, *Journal of Marketing Research*, Vol. 44 (3): 410–424

Hughes, G. and Fill, C. (2007) Redefining the Nature and Format of the Marketing Communications Mix, *The Marketing Review*, Vol. 7 (1): 45–57

McDonald, M. and Wilson, H. (2002) *New Marketing*, Butterworth-Heinemann, Oxford

Porter, M. (1980) *Competitive Strategy*, Free Press, New York

Sidhanta, S. and Chakrabarty, A. (2010) Promotional Mix and Corporate Performance, *Paradigm*, Vol. 14 (1): 97–110.

Schramm, W. (1955) *The Process and Effects of Mass Communication*, Urbana, University of Illinois Press.

Shannon, C. and Weaver, W. (1962) *The Mathematical Theory of Communication*, Urbana, University of Illinois Press.

# CHAPTER 13
# KEY ACCOUNT STRATEGY

IN THIS CHAPTER WE STUDY:

- stages of KAM development
- use of focus teams at the Integrated KAM stage
- bases for defining and selecting key accounts
- the significance of identifying the present position of KAM relationships
- development of key account objectives and strategies
- correlation between account relationship stage and account manager role
- factors that influence key account manager performance

# KEY ACCOUNT MANAGEMENT

Key account management (KAM) is a natural development of customer focus and relationship marketing in business-to-business markets. It can offer critical benefits and opportunities for profit enhancement for both seller and buyer if it is managed with integrity and imagination. Even in non-global firms, and small- and medium-sized enterprises (SMEs), attention to the key, or most valuable, business relationships can have a multiplier effect in creating sustainable competitive advantage.

The scope of KAM is widening constantly and at the same time becoming more complex. The main challenges affecting contemporary KAM stem from a gradual shift of power from suppliers to customers, which is a symptom of market maturity and globalization. In response, suppliers have to be much more stringent in their key account management (Woodburn and McDonald, 2011). In particular, key account strategy and the skills of those involved at both a strategic and an operational level need to be developed and updated continuously.

This chapter, which draws heavily upon the findings of unique research carried out at Cranfield School of Management, puts KAM relationships under the microscope. Cranfield's KAM Research Club, which has advanced some groundbreaking research since the 1990s, finds that the relationship between buyer and seller moves through observable phases. The challenges faced by key account managers vary at each stage as companies try to maximize the full potential of the KAM business approach. These insights provide a practical framework for better understanding and practising key account management.

The chapter is in three sections. The first section describes how key accounts can develop over time; the second section discusses how key accounts should be selected and categorized for the purpose of setting objectives and strategies; and the third section recommends how people and material resources should be allocated to get the most out of key account relationships.

# THE ORIGINS OF KAM

The roots of KAM can be found in various fields such as industrial marketing, sales management, purchasing management, the psychology of customer behaviour and relationship marketing. These disciplines share a marked emphasis on relationship-building within a transactional context, a quality characteristic of and crucial to effective key account management. The development of KAM has been gradual, evolving over time to meet changing needs and altered thinking. Significant changes in the context and constructs of marketing have highlighted the imperative of paying great attention to key account categorization, customer needs and profitability analysis.

The evolution of KAM is reflected in the KAM process itself, most commonly conceptualized as a progression of distinct stages of relationship maturity, as illustrated in Figure 13.1.

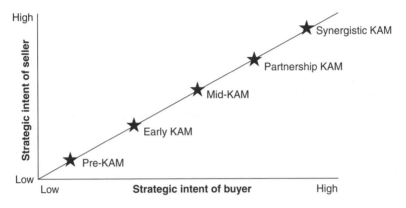

Figure 13.1 Millman and Wilson's (1994) original KAM evolution model

Subsequently, Millman and Wilson (1996) added a sixth stage: uncoupling KAM, in which companies disengage.

As the nature of the customer's relationship with the selling organization deepens from that of an 'anonymous buyer' to more of a 'business partner', the level of involvement between the two parties becomes correspondingly more complex.

Although Figure 13.1 shows an upward or positive development of the business relationship, a selling company should not always expect this to be the case. As with personal relationships, the business partnership can founder for a number of reasons, ranging from a relatively minor misunderstanding to a massive breach of trust. Additionally, the market position and priorities of the buying or selling company can change in ways that negate the strategic necessity for a close relationship. Figure 13.2 employs the labels chosen by the Cranfield KAM Research Club which highlight the existence of a transactional–collaborative continuum. In this model, each stage of KAM can be distinguished clearly by the issues having an impact on the relationship at the time.

At this juncture it is important to note that KAM cannot, and should not, be used with all customers; as Cheverton (2012: 4) observes, 'It is far better to be brilliant with a few than mediocre with many.' This is an important underlying principle if KAM is to work well.

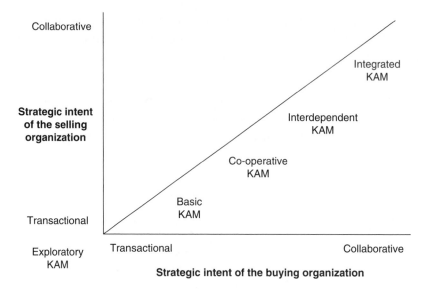

Figure 13.2 Re-labelled KAM evolution model
*Source:* Cranfield KAM Best Practice Club.

# KAM STAGES

Figures 13.1 and 13.2 are built on the premise that all goes well; assuming this to be the case, the KAM evolution model is a useful tool and therefore worth studying in more detail. At this point, it should be noted that the speed of progress through the stages is largely determined by the rate at which the buyer and seller can develop the necessary levels of trust. While some relationships may appear to 'stick' at one particular level for a long time, it is also possible for relationships to be held in a transitional phase, somewhere between any two consecutive KAM stages. In practice, it is therefore likely that an organization will have a variety of key accounts at different stages of evolution.

# EXPLORATORY KAM

Exploratory KAM can be described as the 'scanning and attraction' stage. Like a spaceship seeking its mother craft, both seller and buyer are sending out signals and exchanging messages prior to taking the decision to get together.

Broadly speaking, the aim of both parties is to reduce costs. The supplier prefers customers who are leaders in their respective markets and can offer high volume sales over lengthy periods, while the buyer is looking to safeguard the quality and quantity of supplies it purchases in future. Both parties instinctively know that any form of lasting commitment will be superior to *ad hoc*, tentative arrangements. Thus commercial issues such as product quality and organizational capability feature strongly in KAM. Expert selling and negotiating skills are also paramount in the inevitable discussions that take place about price.

As depicted in Figure 13.3, the key account manager and the purchasing manager must be capable of interacting effectively and on a regular basis in order to bring the two organizations closer together.

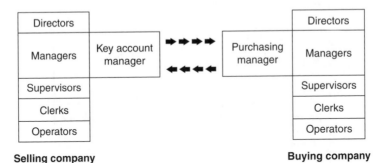

**Figure 13.3 The exploratory KAM stage**
*Source*: McDonald et al. (1996).

Successful bonding relies heavily on the key account manager's ability to encourage his or her company to become more customer-focused by improving production processes or internal procedures accordingly. All too frequently, other managers block proposed changes by putting their individual interests before those of the company. The key account manager must have high-level status (or top-level backing) to overcome such adversity. Moreover, the implications of KAM must be made blatantly clear throughout the supplying organization.

At this early stage, it is unlikely that either party will disclose confidential information, as no basis of trust has yet been established. A careful and concerted effort is required to protect and cultivate the fragile relationship.

# BASIC KAM

At the Basic KAM stage, transactions have begun and the supplier's emphasis shifts to identifying opportunities for account penetration. This means that the key account manager needs to have a greater understanding of the customer and the markets in which the customer competes.

The buying company, meanwhile, will continue market testing other suppliers for best price as it seeks value for money. It is therefore essential for the selling company to concentrate on packaging the core product or service and its surround into a customer-specific offer. Actions such as the simplification of 'paperwork' systems can contribute to a customer-friendly appearance.

At this primary stage, although there may still be a lack of trust, the relationship undergoes a subtle structural change. The key account manager and the customer's main contact are closer to each other, with their respective organizations aligned supportively behind them, as shown in Figure 13.4.

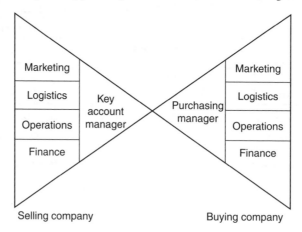

**Figure 13.4 The basic KAM stage**
*Source:* McDonald et al. (1996).

The single point of contact presented by the key account manager is a powerful benefit to the buying company in getting things done. To provide an effective customer interface, the key account manager must not only be highly skilled and approachable but he or she must also have the status to demand and obtain speedy responses from the selling company whenever it becomes necessary. Without such status, the key account manager will be bypassed and, for example, a more senior figure will be sought who can deliver the buyer's requirements.

# CO-OPERATIVE KAM

By now, an element of trust has developed, and the selling company may be a 'preferred' supplier. However, the buying company is rarely prepared to put all its eggs into one basket and will test the market periodically to check alternative sources of supply.

With increasing trust comes a greater preparedness to share information about markets, short-term plans and schedules, internal operating systems and other issues. Employees of the selling company enter into discussions with their counterparts in the buying company and vice versa, forging links at all levels from operations to the boardroom. This collaboration transforms the business relationship into a network with the key account manager and the purchasing manager at the core, as shown in Figure 13.4.

The multiple relationships portrayed in Figure 13.5 often extend beyond the workplace into the social arena. Interactions may take the form of organized events (such as golf days) or be less formal affairs (such as small dinner parties). This network arrangement brings new strength to the relationship, highlighting the fact that customer service operates on many levels and is driven by a desire not to disappoint personal contacts. It is this trust between people that gets results, rather than the somewhat patronizing statements of intent or customer charters favoured by many companies. However, as the willingness to co-operate is voluntary rather than contractual, the relationship is vulnerable to breakdown caused by staff turnover or random management.

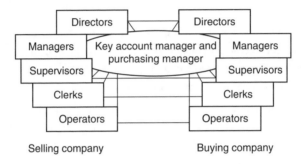

Figure 13.5 The co-operative KAM stage
*Source*: McDonald et al. (1996).

# INTERDEPENDENT KAM

At this stage, the buying company regards the selling company as a strategic external resource. The two companies are sharing sensitive information and engaging in joint problem-solving. Such is the level of maturity of relations that each party allows the other to profit from the partnership. Consequently, pricing is long-term and stable; perhaps even fixed.

There also exists a tacit understanding that expertise will be shared. Collaborative programmes to improve products or to simplify the administrative systems that support the commercial transactions provide evidence of this interdependence. The selling and buying companies are now communicating jointly at all levels, as shown in Figure 13.6. It should be noted that the main customer contact is by now not necessarily the purchasing manager, but may be someone more senior.

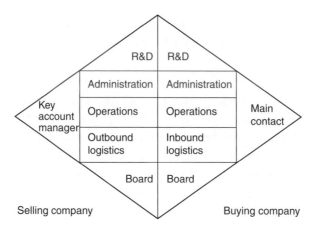

Figure 13.6 The interdependent KAM stage
*Source*: McDonald et al. (1996).

At this stage, the corresponding organizational functions communicate directly. The key account manager and the customer main contact adopt a more supervisory role, ensuring that the various interfaces are effective, and that nothing deters or disrupts the working partnership.

The partnership agreement is long term, extending to perhaps three or four years. Some buyers in our study asserted that in practice there is no limit. Even so, performance stipulations contained within partnership agreements may affect the longevity of commitment. The selling company will strive to uphold the 'spirit of partnership' by meeting all performance criteria consistently and to the highest possible standards. However, as there are no exit barriers in place at this stage, it is still possible for either party to end the relationship.

# INTEGRATED KAM

Integrated KAM refers to the companies relating so strongly and pervasively that they create a value in the marketplace over and above what either could achieve individually. In effect, the two companies operate as an integrated whole while still maintaining their separate identities.

At this stage, the key account manager's role changes fundamentally. The multiple linkages now function in a way that is largely independent of the key account manager. This is not to say that the role is redundant but rather that the incumbent can take a much more strategic approach than before. Figure 13.7 illustrates arrival at the integrated stage.

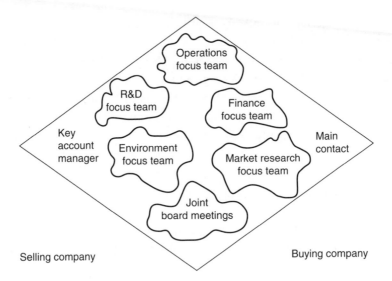

Figure 13.7 The integrated KAM stage
*Source:* McDonald et al. (1996).

The borders between buyer and seller become blurred. Focus teams made up of personnel from both companies assume responsibility for generating creative ideas and overcoming problems. The key account manager and the customer main contact merely co-ordinate the efforts of these teams.

The reason for constructing focus teams may be to tackle operational, market or project issues, or to introduce motivational forces. The respective teams will meet on a regular basis, setting their own agendas and objectives. Special project teams may be short-lived, existing only for long enough to serve their intended purpose.

At this advanced stage, the companies' electronic data systems are integrated, information flow is streamlined, business plans are linked and the erstwhile unthinkable is now willingly explored. About the only issue that remains sacrosanct for the selling company is its brand. Any requests from the buying company that might undermine the brand should be rejected.

# DETERMINING THE KEY ACCOUNT RELATIONSHIP

No one KAM stage is better than another; they are just different. The main question concerns the appropriateness of the relationship with a particular customer at a particular time. To illustrate this point, let us consider some of the relationships we experience in our personal lives.

Our relationship with passing acquaintances may not extend beyond an acknowledgement of familiarity such as nodding 'Good morning!', and at the other end of the scale are our close family and friends, with whom our relationship is warmer and stronger. The degree of intimacy in a relationship reflects the level of personal investment. A reversal of our behaviour with these two groups would be seen as highly inappropriate, verging on the insane. Similarly, we do not seek intense friendships with everybody we meet. To do so would not only be unsuitable but also impossible, as we do not have unlimited emotional reserves.

In the same way, organizations do not possess the resources to have all of their KAM relationships at the integrated level, even if this were deemed to be appropriate. Like people, organizations have a range of relationships that can be intensified, maintained or subdued. Naturally, investments of time, energy and resources must be justified and guided by strategic considerations. Of necessity, therefore, companies must choose which customers they wish to treat as key accounts. Although this appears straight-forward, according to Woodburn and McDonald (2011), it is surprising how many companies approach this task casually, only later to discover how many subsequent decisions are driven by their selection (and how awkward relationships can be to unpick).

Woodburn and McDonald (2011) advocate selecting key accounts by virtue of their alignment to the supplier's corporate strategy. Developing a portfolio approach along two dimensions: supplier's relative business strength as seen by the customer and key account attractiveness, they propose four kinds of key account customers, as follows:

1. Star key customers – with investment for growth prospects (high/high)

2. Strategic key customers – invest for strategic reasons (high/low)

3. Status key customers – requiring proactive maintenance (low/high)

4. Streamline key customers – managed for cash (low/low).

An alternative approach is proposed by Cheverton (2012): attractiveness and strength. According to Faucher (2013) this provides a useful way to map a key account portfolio based upon the relative attractiveness of a customer to the supplier and the strength the supplier represents to the customer. Cheverton (2012) identifies four customer classifications according to the customer/supplier attractiveness dimensions mentioned earlier:

1. Opportunistic accounts, where relative customer/supplier attractiveness is low.

2. Maintenance accounts, where customer attractiveness is low, but supplier attractiveness high.

3. Key development accounts, where customer attractiveness is high, but supplier attractiveness low.

4. Key accounts, where both dimensions are high.

Both the Woodburn and McDonald (2011) and Cheverton (2012) frameworks illustrate simple but effective ways of mapping strategic KAM, ensuring that resource allocation decisions are based upon maximizing the potential return on investment.

The significance of identifying the present position of key account relationships is that it allows companies to anticipate the development requirements of individual accounts as well as the collective demands of the account portfolio. Such knowledge and understanding is intrinsic to the setting of key account objectives and strategies, as is explained in the next section of this chapter.

# DEVELOPING KEY ACCOUNT OBJECTIVES AND STRATEGIES

Most companies are judged on the basis of profit, thus key accounts should be classified in accordance with their potential for growth in profits over, say, a three-year period. The criteria used by companies to measure potential profit growth are:

- available resources;
- available margins;
- growth rate; and
- purchasing policies and processes.

When each of these criteria are weighted and scored appropriately for each key account, the accounts can be evaluated in terms of profit growth potential on a 'thermometer' scale from low to high. There can be problems with this simple analysis – an obvious one being that it does not consider the maturity or business strength of the key account relationship. As discussed earlier, the KAM relationship can be anywhere between the Exploratory stage and the Integrated stage.

In order to define and select target key accounts accurately, a full profile of each account must be obtained. This is achieved by measuring profit growth potential in combination with relationship maturity. A comparative guide using these two dimensions, as shown in Figure 13.8 is helpful in setting realistic objectives and strategies for key accounts. It is worth noting that recent research by Ryals and Davies (2013) uncovered an interesting finding about supplier–customer relations. They find a misalignment of strategic intent

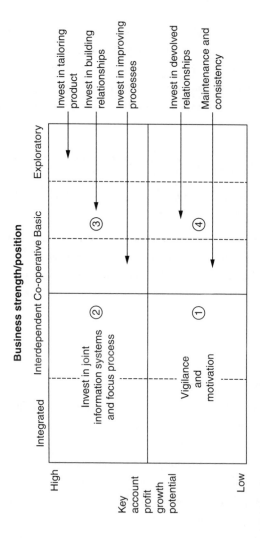

**Business strength/position**

Figure 13.8 Identifying target key accounts, objectives and strategies

*Source:* McDonald et al. (1996).

between supplier and customer, suggesting that strategic intent is unrelated to relationship type. In contrast, key buyer–supplier relationships were differentiated not by the level of strategic fit or intent but by contact structure and differentiated service. This highlights the imperative of focusing closely upon tactics to develop (and sustain) good relations with key account customers, once the strategic analysis is complete.

Taking the boxes in each quadrant in Figure 13.8 in turn and starting with the bottom left quadrant (Box 1: 'low potential/high strength'), it is possible to work out sensible objectives and strategies for each key account. Accounts meeting the profile of the bottom left quadrant are likely to continue to deliver excellent revenues for some considerable time, even though they may be in static or declining markets. Good relationships are already enjoyed and should be preserved. Retention strategies are therefore advisable, incorporating prudence, vigilance and motivation. More important, as the supplying company will be seeking a good return on previous investment, any further financial input here should be of the maintenance kind. In this way, it should be possible to free up cash and resources for investing in key accounts with greater growth potential.

The boxes in the top left quadrant (Box 2: 'high potential/high strength') represent accounts with highest potential growth in sales and profits. These warrant quite an aggressive investment approach, providing it is justified by returns. Net present value (NPV) calculations may be used as a basis for evaluating these returns, using a discount rate higher than the cost of capital to reflect the additional risks involved. Any investment here will probably be directed towards developing joint information systems and collaborative relationships.

Accounts situated in the boxes in the top right quadrant (Box 3: 'high potential/low strength') pose a problem, as few organizations have sufficient resources to invest in building better relationships with all of them. To determine which ones justify investment, net revenue streams should be forecast for each account for, say, three years, and discounted at the cost of capital (plus a considerable percentage to reflect the high risk involved). Having made these calculations and selected the promising accounts, under no circumstances should financial accounting measures such as NPV be used to control them within the budget year. To do so would be a bit like pulling up a new plant every few weeks to see whether it had grown! Achievement of objectives should instead be monitored using terms such as sales volume, value, 'share of wallet' and the quality of the relationship, enabling selected accounts to be moved gradually towards partnerships and in some cases towards integrated relationships. Only then will it become more appropriate to measure profitability as a control procedure. Accounts in which the company cannot afford to invest should be managed in a similar way to those residing in the final boxes to the bottom right.

Accounts found in the boxes in the bottom right quadrant (Box 4: 'low potential/low strength') should not occupy too much of a company's time. Some of these accounts can be handed over to distributors while others can be handled by an organization's sales personnel, provided that all transactions are profitable and deliver net free cash flow.

All other company functions and activities should be consistent with the goals set for key accounts according to the general categorization given in Figure 13.8. This rule includes the appointment of key account managers to key accounts. For example, some key account managers will be extremely good at managing accounts in the Exploratory, Basic and Co-operative KAM stages, where their excellent selling and negotiating skills are essential, whereas others will be better suited to the more complex business and managerial issues surrounding interdependent and integrated relationships.

The implications for key account managers are examined in the third section of this chapter.

# IMPLICATIONS FOR THE KEY ACCOUNT MANAGER

The fundamental challenge of the KAM task is to succeed in a matchmaking exercise; that is, to match the manager with the most compatible and complementary qualities with a specific account in order to maximize the return on investment. Durif et al. (2013) find that managers focus mainly on behavioural and results-based performance at the expense of return on investment (ROI) objectives. This can lead to a myopic approach that loses focus on the critical, strategic purpose of KAM. There are various elements of sound KAM, all of which require proactivity and consistency; in this section we address the key elements that have the greatest bearing upon success.

The correlation between the development of the account relationship and the development of the account manager's role is summarized in Table 13.1. Of course, real life is not quite so predisposed to split conveniently into neat boxes and the table merely encapsulates what is found to be the general experience. Clearly, the key account manager must be adept at balancing the growing expectations of both selling and buying companies. The roles and responsibilities of key account managers, and their ability to fulfil them, are critical to the success of any KAM strategy. So what is the personal specification of a key account manager?

As part of the Cranfield research, key account managers, their managers and their buying company contacts were all asked the same question, 'What

| | Exploratory KAM | Basic KAM | Co-operative KAM | Interdependent KAM | Integrated KAM |
|---|---|---|---|---|---|
| Selling company strategy | Invest in tailoring product | Invest in building relationship | Invest in improving administrative processes | Invest in sharing information and expertise | Invest in joint planning and development |
| Buying company concerns | Does supplier have product knowledge and industry expertise? | Does Key Account Manager demonstrate integrity? | Does Key Account Manager possess authority? | Does emphasis on key account teams mean loss of direct relationship? | Does autonomy of key account teams mean loss of direct control? |
| Key Account Manager's role | Identify prospective customers | Identify opportunities for account penetration | Facilitate formation of a network | Supervise relationship interactions and collaborations | Co-ordinate focus teams |
| Key Account Manager's skills | Technical knowledge, 'scouting' ability and communication skills | Product knowledge, selling and negotiation skills | Management skills, especially interpersonal skills | Full range of financial, marketing and consultancy skills | Full range of business skills, plus general management capability |

Table 13.1 Strategy, role and skills progression

essential skills/qualities does the key account manager need?' Surprisingly, there was little agreement among the three groups of respondents.

The selling companies involved in the study were unanimous in rating selling and negotiating skills as the chief essential attributes of successful key account managers. The buying companies, on the other hand, voted trustworthiness and strategic decision-making ability as the principal traits. Furthermore, the buyers disliked so intensely being sold to that they would not permit a salesperson to lead the key account team! The disclosed discrepancy between the comments of managers or key account managers and those of customer contacts is particularly alarming, considering that these senior managers are responsible for appointing key account managers to valuable accounts.

The skill area that prompted most dramatic disagreement is that of 'selling/negotiating'. While selling companies put great store on these skills (62 per cent and 67 per cent, respectively), only 9 per cent of buying contacts rated them as important. In simply repeating old patterns, selling companies show their perspectives to be more outdated than perhaps they care to admit.

# DEVELOPING KEY ACCOUNT PROFESSIONALS

It can be difficult to design appropriate training for key account managers, especially for those operating in global markets. In this section we consider how to develop good key account professionals.

## TRAINING AND DEVELOPMENT

The key challenge in this area is the need to develop a range of competencies in a number of traditionally specialist areas, such as:

- technical/product knowledge;
- relationship-building skills (interpersonal skills);
- finance;
- marketing/strategic thinking;
- business management;
- project management; and
- creative problem-solving.

Generally, the training of key account managers consists mainly of attending a number of short courses when deemed appropriate. On average, key account managers receive 5–10 days of training per year, excluding induction. Because recruits generally have a background in sales or marketing, training must deliberately set out to extend their skill bases in order to develop 'all-rounders' rather than better specialists. It seems unlikely that the *ad hoc* and limited approach to training identified here could ever create outstanding key account managers.

In terms of succession policy, selling companies do endeavour to ensure that the handover of a key account is managed with a sense of continuity. Where possible, new account managers are introduced to contacts by their predecessors, who then gradually pass over responsibility to the newcomers. Our study found that buying companies profoundly appreciate this smooth transition, and do not expect the new contact to be a clone of the old one. In fact, it was recognized that a new face can sometimes revitalize a flagging relationship.

## AUTHORITY AND STATUS

'We don't want to be dealing with a postman who has to trot back [to the boss] every time we ask a question' was the graphic view offered by one buyer on the autonomy of key account managers. The perception of key account managers as lacking status and authority, especially in the early stages of the KAM relationship, was a recurring theme among the buying companies. Selling companies would be wise to address this concern. Key account managers, it seems, are well aware of expectations and feel the pressure to make decisions and commit their company, even when they do not have the authority to do so. Paradoxically, although the KAM relationship is intended to develop unique arrangements with the buying company, it is on decision-related matters that account managers most often have to refer back to their company.

It is generally agreed that the one area in which the key account manager has least room for manoeuvre is on prices and margins. Any discretion that is allowed constitutes a 'freedom' to operate within carefully defined bands.

When dealing with key accounts, it is important to remember that the position of the key account manager can easily be undermined if the buying company is allowed to gain the ear of someone higher up in the selling organization. Therefore, more senior managers and directors should always be seen to defer to the account manager.

## REPORTING AND ACCOUNTABILITY

The Cranfield research revealed that 36 per cent of key account managers reported to directors within their companies. Reporting at a less senior level usually meant being accountable to a sales manager, sales and marketing manager, or business unit manager. All of the key account managers interviewed were, in effect, national account managers. Only four also held some global accounts, with responsibility for results achieved in other countries.

In most of the selling companies studied, key account managers did not have formal – or, for that matter, informal – teams assisting them. Working alone, they were expected to fulfil customer requirements solely by influencing their colleagues to mobilize the necessary resources, which would clearly make progression to interdependent or integrated stages extremely difficult, if not impossible.

Best practice key account management seeks to redress this operational weakness. As the KAM relationship matures, 'dotted line' project teams develop. Composed of functional staff, these teams report to the key account manager on specific matters of interest, while remaining responsible to their functional manager throughout the working day. Unsurprisingly, the dual reporting lines can be a source of tension. However, problems are not normally about questions of loyalty but about confusion over priorities. Where project teams are more formalized, team members are set specific objectives and time frames. In this team environment, it is imperative that the key account manager, as the main customer interface, keeps team members fully updated on all operational and strategic issues relating to their accounts.

## APPRAISAL AND REWARD

The majority of key account managers interviewed received a basic salary plus a bonus related to generated earnings, although a significant minority were employed on the basis of a straight salary. The level at which bonuses were set was a contentious issue.

Managers receiving 10–20 per cent of their income as a bonus felt that it was too low in relation to the importance placed on the volume of key account business. Other managers felt it to be unfair for bonuses to be linked closely to volume, since matters in the buying company such as market shifts, over which the key account manager has no control, could influence business volume.

In some of the selling companies, share options figured as a form of bonus, providing an incentive related to overall company performance. Many managers remained sales driven by a remuneration package based on 50 per cent salary and 50 per cent commission. Targets were set either by KAM directors or were the outcome of negotiations between the director and key account manager.

In addition to sales volume, the key account managers identified other performance criteria, including:

- customer satisfaction ratings;
- market share;
- account profitability;

- accuracy of forecasts;
- debt recovery;
- handling of complaints;
- number of new contacts; and
- new opportunities identified.

Where products were project based, key account managers were judged by the achievement of milestones and deadlines. In businesses marked by cyclical sales, such as capital equipment, the performance of key account managers was assessed against the total value of the selling company's product portfolio. This relative approach avoided the situation of having excessive bonuses one year and none the next.

# SUMMARY

It is important to understand key account management by finding out how selling companies operate, how their operations are perceived by buying companies and where there may be scope for improvement. From the evidence gathered in the Cranfield research, the following conclusions can be drawn:

- business success depends upon excellent processes as well as excellent people and products;
- KAM is not a 'quick fix' management process, and thus companies need to think in terms of long-lasting, ongoing relationships;
- despite the attraction of KAM, businesses have difficulty in implementing it;
- the KAM relationship is particularly vulnerable in the early stages of development;
- not all accounts can be developed beyond Co-operative KAM (preferred supplier) even though sellers may aspire to interdependent or integrated relationships;
- higher-level KAM relationships can only be achieved in customer-focused companies;
- organizing to meet the demands of global key accounts is particularly challenging;
- the key account manager is critical to the KAM relationship and requires skills considerably greater than those of a salesperson;
- the key account manager is likely to require ongoing training throughout his/her career as the role (and its inherent relationships) increases in complexity;

- in addition to training, selection, appraisal and remuneration policies influence the performance of key account managers;
- buying companies place a high value on the status and authority of key account managers and expect to deal with someone who can get things done; and
- account teams can enable a commitment to key accounts that transcends what key account managers can deliver working alone.

There remain some potentially far-reaching questions:

- If the KAM relationship is evolutionary, what is the next developmental stage likely to be?
- What is the best way to build key account teams?
- What are the special problems for key account managers who operate in complex supply chains or on a global basis?
- What are the organizational implications of global key account management?
- What kinds of decision support systems are required for key account management?
- How should the relationship between key accounts and non-key accounts be managed?
- How should the relationship between key accounts and non-key accounts be measured, particularly financially?
- At what level might the KAM relationship be seen to be a barrier to competition and fair trade?

Marketing professionals and business academics are not left unchallenged: the quest to maximize the potential of KAM is as long as the scope of KAM is wide.

Finally, it is clear that creating a value proposition for a key customer is just as crucial as it is for a market or a segment. Equally important, however, is to deliver the value proposition, once it has been agreed; this is where the greatest challenges lie.

# FURTHER READING

Woodburn, D. and McDonald, M. (2011) Key *Account Management: The Definitive Guide*, Oxford, Wiley

A comprehensive, practical book for 'thinking practitioners' providing a holistic view of contemporary KAM.

# REFERENCES

Cheverton, P. (2012) *Key Account Management: Tools and Techniques for Achieving Profitable Key Supplier Status*, London, Kogan Page.

Durif, F., Geay, B. and Graf, R. (2013) Do key account managers focus too much on commercial performance? A cognitive mapping application, *Journal of Business Research*, Vol. 66 (9): 1559–1567.

Faucher, H. (2013) Key vs. strategic account: A strategic orientation issue, *Velocity*, Vol. 15 (2): 25–29.

McDonald, M., Millman, T. and Rogers, B. (1996) *Key Account Management – Learning from Supplier and Customer Perspectives*, Cranfield University, UK.

Millman, T. and Wilson, K. (1996) Developing key account management competences, *Journal of Marketing Practice: Applied Marketing Science*, Vol. 2 (2): 7–22.

Ryals, L. and Davies, I. (2013) Where's the strategic intent in key account relationships? *Journal of Business Research*, Vol. 28 (2): 111–124.

Woodburn, D. and McDonald, M. (2011) *Key Account Management: The Definitive Guide*, Oxford, Wiley.

# PART III
# DELIVERING VALUE

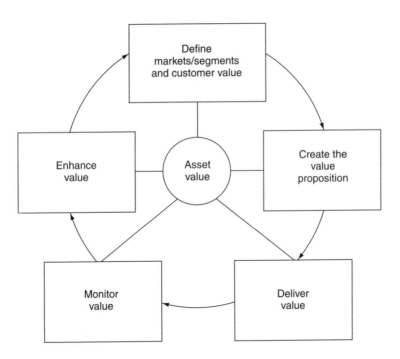

# CHAPTER 14
# MANAGING MARKETING RELATIONSHIPS

# THE VALUE CHAIN

In Chapter 6 we saw that adding value through differentiation can be a powerful means of achieving a defensible advantage in the marketplace. The extent to which this can happen is maximized if value is added throughout the succession of supply relationships, or value chain. This is evident in the fact that logistics and wider supply chain issues have become key sources of competitive advantage. Increasingly, it is supply chains that are competing rather than individual organizations.

In the highly competitive field of consumer marketing, many suppliers and retailers are paying closer attention to the value chain at whose head they sit. These organizations have recognized that advantage can be gained by exerting influence across all those who affect their products and their ability to supply. These advantages include lower cost, higher quality, better availability, product innovation, speed to market and a host of other important competitive factors.

In some industries, such as automotive manufacture, this management is sometimes delegated to a small group of key (Tier 1) suppliers who are expected to influence and co-ordinate the other suppliers in the chain. In others, such as the computer supply industry, many businesses are working directly with suppliers right down to component level and beyond in seeking efficiency and innovation in order to deliver superior value.

The process of delivering the value proposition can be analysed using Porter's value chain shown in Figure 14.1. Although Porter placed 'Marketing' after 'Operations' in the value chain, we have removed it here, since in today's one-to-one world, marketing activities can occur in parallel with all the tasks involved in value delivery. For example, it is common practice to check a product with customers at the R&D stage, which may result in the use of different materials, or assembly and delivery methods, than was initially envisaged. Taking this notion further, it could be argued that nowadays many stages occur concurrently, as companies increasingly move to interactive, co-creative business models involving the blurring of traditional boundaries between organizations, consumers, suppliers, distributors and retailers. Whether linear or networked, it is clear that the successful creation and delivery of value involves managing relationships effectively: relationships between people, processes and functions.

Figure 14.1 Porter's linear value chain

# A RELATIONSHIP MARKETING APPROACH

While it has long been acknowledged that the fundamental purpose of marketing is getting and keeping customers, the truth is that more attention has been paid, typically, to attracting customers than to keeping them. In recent decades there has emerged a recognition that marketing needs to encompass not only those activities necessary to capture business in the first place but also to develop processes that will enhance long-term customer loyalty. This viewpoint is the foundation for the development of the concept of relationship marketing, which is based on the belief that the fundamental purpose of marketing is the creation and development of long-term profitable relationships with customers (see Grönroos, 1997; Christopher et al., 2008; Grönroos and Ravald, 2011).

It should not be thought that relationship marketing is a replacement for traditional transactional marketing. Rather, it is an augmentation and refocusing of the marketing concept with the emphasis placed on strategies to enhance customer value, retention and loyalty. According to Grönroos (1997), relationships can enhance value by altering the ratio of perceived benefits to perceived sacrifice. Minimizing customers' relationship costs can lead to reduction in customer-perceived sacrifice, which, in turn, increases customer-perceived value. Thus, the relationship value between buyers and sellers is likely to affect value perception; an increase in relationship value also increases overall customer perceived value. Some of the major differences in emphasis between the traditional approach, which we label 'transactional', and the 'relationship' focus are summarized in Table 14.1.

| Transactional focus | Relationship focus |
| --- | --- |
| Orientation to single sales | Orientation to customer retention |
| Discontinuous customer contact | Continuous customer contact |
| Focus on product features | Focus on customer value |
| Short time scale | Long time scale |
| Little emphasis on customer service | High customer service emphasis |
| Limited commitment to meeting customer exceptions | High commitments to meeting customer expectations |
| Quality is the concern of production | Quality is the concern of all staff |

Table 14.1 The shift from transactional to relationship marketing

It will be seen from this table that the major difference between the relationship focus and transactional focus is the emphasis on a continuous commitment to meeting the needs of individual customers, with particular stress on service and quality. In practice, this philosophy translates into maximizing customer value by maximizing the value of the relationships involved in creating and delivering that value. Here the word 'relationships' can be seen to extend beyond relationships between people (employees, customers, suppliers and so on) to include the relationships between the inputs and outputs of the five key marketing processes, which are represented as arrows in our marketing map.

## CUSTOMER RELATIONSHIP MANAGEMENT

The ultimate business relationship is with the end-user. Even though the business may distribute its products through intermediaries, the challenge will always be to build an enduring relationship with the customer. Meeting this challenge will never be easy. There will always be competitive offers that can match performance on the 'fundamentals'. Therefore, much more than customer satisfaction with the product or service is required to secure a long-term consumer relationship.

In Chapter 15 we discuss ways in which customer retention might be improved, but it is appropriate to stress here the importance of customer relationship management (CRM) as a critical foundation for long-term, mutually profitable relationships. In CRM, technology is used to develop ongoing relationships with customers; vast databases enable companies to profile and build knowledge and understand about their customer groups. Thanks to the web, CRM has transformed the nature of marketing into an ongoing dialogue between value creators, vendors and buyers. The CRM revolution has created innumerable opportunities for businesses to reach, acquire, engage, satisfy and retain customers, as Peppers and Rogers (2011) observe, leading businesses to think about the process of value creation in light of their new technological capabilities to track and interact with customers on an individual basis.

The appeal of CRM technologies is the ability to collect and manage significant amounts of consumer data. Such data can enable customer insights, trend analysis and forecasting, allowing companies to tailor products and services to individual customers. Widespread adoption of web-enabled CRM has enabled the rapid spread of 'one-to-one marketing' or 'mass customization' in which organizations simultaneously pursue product/service personalization and economies of scope and scale. CRM is more than technology however (as many companies with off-the-shelf CRM 'solutions' bought to solve the 'problem' of customer interaction can attest); at its heart, it is a strategy to transform the organization from a traditional product/branding/selling focus to a customer orientation.

Ultimately, CRM has to be about *competitive advantage*. This is what organizations want and what the consultants can sell. There is also no doubt that

CRM can be a major factor in achieving competitive advantage, but it is an *enabler*, not a panacea. There are three basic principles of CRM: trust, commitment and reciprocity; customers will not engage if they feel they are being monitored or used in some way. Additionally, there are three legs to the CRM 'stool': strategy, marketing and IT. Take just one of the legs away and it will fall over. Try to build CRM on just one leg alone and it simply will not stand. The simple truth is, CRM creates enormous amounts of customer data. Whether the organization is able to make that data meaningful by turning it into information and then into knowledge depends on whether the organization knows what it wants to do with it. Imagine (and this is a real example) that you discover that the most important fact (correlation) about the heaviest users of your communication service is that they are likely to be cat owners. Then what? Joint promotions between telecoms and cat food? Too many companies believe that all they have to do is to collect large amounts of similarly pointless data and they will finally be able to meet those (ludicrous) cross-selling objectives.

Recently, a lot of attention has been focused upon 'big data', that is to say, data collected by an organization in the course of its day-to-day activities, including customer information. Modern information systems have huge data storage and manipulation capacity; many companies are now perplexed by the sheer volume and variety of data flowing into and around the organization. While big data can potentially be a key source of competitive advantage (McKinsey, 2011), allowing for greater in-depth customer data analysis and improved decision-making, it simultaneously raises numerous new challenges. Privacy, security and confidentiality are three key issues; it must be remembered that while CRM stands to benefit much from the big data explosion, nothing has the power to annoy more customers, faster and at greater cost than ever before.

## APPRECIATING THE ISSUES

All the CRM literature we have seen does (more or less clearly) state that the success of any CRM project depends on key strategic issues being agreed before any work is done. And, to be fair, those organizations marketing CRM solutions at the time of writing do mention the other things that need to be in place before (their version of) CRM will work. Unfortunately, these 'things' are neither small nor particularly easy to put in place. Of course, nobody writes this in red, or inserts health warnings at this point, but it needs to be done.

Perhaps it is time to learn from the pioneers of a previous technological age. Imagine CRM as the railway track. Lay the lines and it will get the train to its destination quickly and efficiently – you may have to knock down a few buildings standing in the way, but that is surely a small price to pay. The eighteenth-century entrepreneurs soon learned (sometimes the hard way) that success existed less in knowing how to lay the lines and more in knowing where people wanted the trains to go. Pushing the image as far as (or even beyond where) it will go, imagine the company trying to build the first, fastest and best line to, well, anywhere really. Customers are taken along for the ride and arrive where none of them ever wanted to be. Exit the customers and exit the business – faster than if it had done nothing in the first place.

The point is that, in order to realize the benefits of CRM listed in Table 14.2, the organization must first be clear on where it is intending to go and how it is going to get there.

- Identify most profitable customers
- Serve most profitable customers better
- Manage less profitable situations better
- Identify the lifetime value of customers
- Reduce customer 'churn'
- Find profitable prospects
- Market the right products
- Reduce selling and marketing costs
- Improve effectiveness of marketing communications and direct marketing
- Improve customer service
- Focus Internet/e-commerce on the right customers
- Focus marketing to the right customers
- Refine marketing strategy
- Obtain competitive advantage
- Win!

Table 14.2 The potential benefits of CRM

So these are still the fundamental questions that need to be answered:

- Where are we now? (industry and market);
- What do our customers want? (benefits, not features);
- What will our customers want tomorrow? (company objective/future role);
- Do different customers want different things? (segmentation);
- Which customers should we be targeting? (strategic segmentation); and
- How do we differentiate our company/brand(s)? (differentiation/unique market position).

The investment involved in agreeing the organization's longer-term ambitions (and therefore the objectives for a CRM project) will be minute compared to the cost of the CRM project itself. Experience has shown that the IT and organizational costs of CRM are likely to run to many millions – and that is without the potential business costs of getting it wrong. Very few companies would embark on a major capital project without a feasibility study, or an acquisition without 'due diligence'. CRM should be treated no differently, and will therefore require a CRM audit.

What is a CRM audit? As the name implies, it is an unbiased assessment of an organization's current customer position and requirements from any CRM process. An audit (shown in Table 14.3) represents an investment that pays off in two directions: it reduces the downside risks of disaster and increases the upside benefits from success.

- An identification of the market being served; 'What business are we in?'
- Quantification of the customer/process dynamics within this market
- An understanding of the competitive environment, including competitor positions and competitive dynamics
- An unbiased (*not* a priori!) segmentation of the market we are interested in serving
- An understanding of customer needs in each segment
- A realistic assessment of the organizational implications of introducing CRM
- An outline plan for the introduction of CRM
- An assessment of the likely costs and benefits of CRM for the organization
- An outline brief for CRM suppliers, especially IT

Table 14.3 The CRM audit

# TAKING THE CRM DECISION

Any organization contemplating introducing CRM into its relationship management strategy should first ensure that it has given full consideration to the following key issues:

*Customers:* Customers are the name of the game. Without customers there is no business. The purpose of marketing is to attract and retain customers. Achieving that is not easy, especially as most customers make emotional rather than rational buying decisions and, more often than not, have no idea what they want.

*Relationships:* How many 'relationships' does the firm have? How many of them are with commercial organizations? If the objective is simply to retain more customers for longer to make more money, this can probably be achieved by making fewer mistakes, so giving fewer excuses for customers to leave. Building a 'relationship' is quite another matter. Do customers want a 'relationship' in the first place? 'Please stop sending me birthday cards; just answer the phone when I ring' is a frequent customer complaint. Research indicates that supplier delusions about the state of the customer relationship have reached alarming proportions. It should also be remembered that, just as in our own personal lives the capacity to build close relationships with *all* our friends is limited, so too is it with major customers.

*Management:* Almost everything we read about CRM either talks about (or implies) the organization managing its customer relationships. Much as it might be the preferred route, it just does not work like that. As stated earlier in the book, 'You don't manage the customer; your customer manages you.' Most customers like to feel in control, so the organization helps them. Information flows, systems and processes designed from the customers' perspective might give the organization a better chance of achieving the desired results; happy customers spending more and more often.

Whether CRM provides any long-term solutions depends on how well those who use it apply a number of fundamental concepts. In order of most frequent mention, these are:

- A deep understanding of the market;
- Market segmentation (*not* 'your own database segmentation');
- Differentiation, positioning and branding; and
- Integrated marketing (marketing planning).

The extent to which CRM delivers success, optimizing the relationships between an organization's prospects, plans and performance will be influenced by the information derived from the organization's monitoring activity, by its proven level of professionalism, and by its recognized future potential. In short, CRM is simply one (albeit important) component of the marketing process. For marketing to work well, it needs to operate on a number of cross-related dimensions, and in so doing it draws on the involvement of various people and functional expertise from across and beyond the organization.

# MARKETING AS A CROSS-FUNCTIONAL ACTIVITY

One of the distinguishing characteristics of the relationship marketing approach is that it places the emphasis on a cross-functional, cross-organizational approach to customer satisfaction and lifetime value maximization (Christopher et al., 2008). It sees marketing as a cross-functional, as opposed to a functional, activity. In other words, marketing is an integrated process, not an isolated action. Figures 14.2 and 14.3 highlight this difference. Clearly, there will always be a requirement for the marketing function to manage such tasks as advertising, market research, pricing and so on. However, overlaying the traditional vertical organization are a number of cross-functional processes

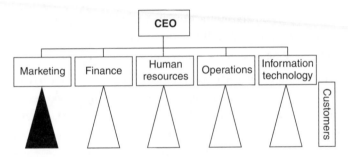

Figure 14.2 Marketing as a functional activity

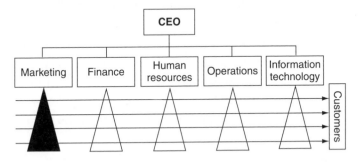

Figure 14.3 Marketing as a cross-functional activity

that must be managed if the business is to be truly market facing and value driven.

These processes include such activities as new product development, order fulfilment (that is, the physical satisfaction of demand), marketing planning and the management of customer relationships. As we shall see later, this integration is often extended beyond the boundaries of one organization; indeed, partnership networks are becoming increasingly common across a wide range of industries. The key point is that the marketing processes must add customer value, whether within one or across several organizations. What this means is making the product or service attractive to the customer because of the way things are done (and consequently more lucrative to the supplier, because it is selling well).

While customer value is perceptual, and different customers will clearly place value on different things, nonetheless by understanding customer perceptions of value companies can identify how to bind customers close to their preferred brand, product or retailer by engaging them in the process of value creation. (At this point, it is worth noting that in writing of the service sector, Grönroos (2011) observes it is not that customers are *always* co-creators of value, but that under certain circumstances the service provider may get opportunities to co-create value together with its customers.) According to Blois (2004), the way to understand value is for a supplier to construct value equations for its customers and seeks to perceive its own value equation from a customer's point of view. It will then gain insights into the way in which its product offering should be developed and presented to customers.

Involving customers in value creation may help to erect exit barriers; there is considerable evidence to suggest a high level of inertia in much buyer behaviour. This implies that as long as a relationship with a supplier is perceived to be delivering more customer value than competitive offerings for the same price, there will be little motivation for the customer to seek another source of supply. Creating and delivering superior customer value does not happen by chance, however – it requires continual focus on the processes whereby such value is generated.

This search for strategies that deliver superior customer value can be enhanced greatly by extending the concept of the 'market' beyond the traditional focus solely upon the end users or customers. In fact, it has been suggested that to succeed in building long-term relationships in the consumer market (the end-market) there are other markets that must also be considered.

# THE MULTIPLE MARKETS MODEL

The concept of marketing as a cross-functional process leads to the recognition that the achievement of enduring relationships with customers and consumers is dependent on other relationships too. This diversity of internal and external relationships can be described as identifiable 'markets' or 'market domains'. Christopher et al. (2008) assert that in relationship marketing the focus of marketing action needs to be upon multiple markets, as multiple market domains can directly or indirectly affect a business's ability to win or retain profitable customers. For example, the relationships that organizations have with their suppliers and employees clearly have an impact on the relationships they have with their customers. The thrust of the multiple markets model shown in Figure 14.4 is that organizations can best manage their network of relationships in different market domains by focusing on particular groups or market segments within them. There are, in effect, six main markets that must be addressed in a relationship marketing programme:

1. Customer markets;
2. Referral markets;
3. Internal markets;
4. Recruitment markets;
5. Influencer markets; and
6. Supplier and alliance markets.

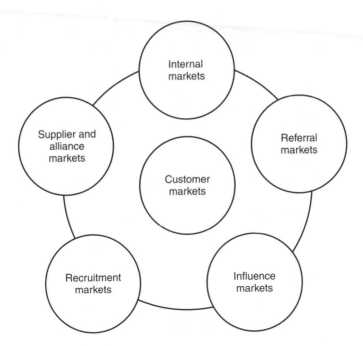

Figure 14.4 The multiple markets model

## CUSTOMER MARKETS

Customer markets are central to the multiple model, both because they remain the prime focus of marketing activity and because they are affected by the organization's success or failure in all the other markets. The customer market represents all the people or organizations that buy goods or services. It therefore includes intermediaries (retailers, distributors and so on) as well as end users.

In this market, the impact of customer service can be profound. Often the only source of competitive differentiation is the quality of the service provided. This is particularly the case when dealing with intermediaries or distributors. For example, the amount of shelf-space a retailer is prepared to give to one brand over another brand in the same category will often be determined by the supplier's ability to operate a just-in-time (JIT) delivery system, or by the supplier's ability to receive orders electronically and to link information systems together.

Experience has shown that the service and quality dimension can be especially critical in the case of marketing to end consumers. When faced with the decision about which television set or mobile phone to buy, the consumer will be influenced partly by the brand name, but it will be the specific added values, such as guarantees, after-sales service, customer support and off-the-shelf availability that will ultimately determine customer preference and 'clinch' the deal.

A key point in addressing customer and consumer markets is to give sufficient attention to *both* customer acquisition and customer retention. Many companies concentrate too much on winning new customers at the expense of keeping existing customers. This is a common weakness among organizations that view marketing as being 'transactional'. Other companies place an emphasis on growing relationships with existing customers without nurturing new sources of future custom. The danger is that a proportion of customers will defect naturally to competitors, or leave the fold altogether, and if this represents key customers, the company will have lost a vital, possibly irreplaceable, asset. Either way, intensifying competitive pressures mean that all organizations need to achieve a customer base including 'veterans' as well as 'new recruits'.

## REFERRAL MARKETS

The power of word of mouth is substantial. A purchase recommendation from a respected source is often worth more than any media advertisement. Referrals can come from sources of professional advice such as doctors, lawyers, bank managers and accountants as well as from existing satisfied customers.

Referral markets are often difficult to identify, but a start can be made by asking new customers what influenced their purchase decision. Referral markets must be researched carefully and the factors that influence their recommendations must be understood clearly. It is advisable to develop specific communication programmes that involve effective referral sources. For example, existing customers can be encouraged to act as 'recruiting agents' for the business. Often a small incentive is all that is needed to persuade a satisfied customer to encourage others to patronize the business. Once again, however, such strategies need to be planned and programmed so that they are not left to chance, but form a defined part of the overall relationship marketing plan.

## INTERNAL MARKETS

There is now widespread recognition that one of the major determinants of marketing success is the existence of a strongly felt and unanimously accepted 'corporate culture' within the business. Sometimes this set of commonly held beliefs is termed 'shared values', reflecting the commitment to customers subscribed to by the entire workforce. The creation of such a culture requires vision and leadership, which is communicated at every level in the organization, and also opens channels of internal communication. This is the realm of internal marketing.

Internal marketing involves regarding members of staff (and even shareholders and other stakeholders) as customers. In applying a customer focus internally, the needs, wants and desires of employees are identified, and pro-grammes are constructed to encourage and enable them to engage in exchange activities with colleagues. The aim is to inform and motivate all the members of the organization towards defined goals of customer and corporate satisfaction. The resulting collaboration improves not only internal morale and operational efficiency but also service levels to the external customer, thereby progressing the marketing campaign.

Seminars, workshops, team-building exercises, continuous and good two-way communication channels, newsletters, quality-improvement groups and, above all, a focus on the idea that everybody in the organization has and is a 'customer' are the ingredients of a successful internal marketing programme. In practical terms, however, internal marketing is limited in what it contributes to the wider issues of organizational culture, since it too often defaults to a communications exercise. Selling the need to value relationships with customers is a far more complex issue than just letting people know what is going on.

## RECRUITMENT MARKETS

The scarcest resource for most organizations is no longer capital or raw mate-rials: it is skilled people. An appropriately trained and experienced workforce is perhaps the most vital element in customer value delivery. But 'good people' are hard to find.

Global economics and the changing nature of employment have not helped to enlarge the recruitment pool, even if unemployment levels are climbing. The basic reason for the current lack of skilled workers is demographic trends. Most Western countries are experiencing a reduction in population growth, which means a relative shortage of new recruits entering employment. There is also the pressure constantly to seek economies and this has seen many Western industries rejecting domestic labour in favour of less expensive foreign labour, if only for partial operations, such as product assembly.

Because every organization is highly dependent on the quality of the peo-ple it employs, it is imperative that a high priority be given to recruiting and retaining employees who are likely to assist the company in achieving its overall marketing objectives. The aim should be to make the company into an organi-zation that is attractive to people (both the job-seeking and the career-minded employed) who share the values the company espouses. For many businesses, appealing to newly skilled workers is a key priority, whereas for others the focus may be on capturing specialists with years of experience.

Companies as diverse as Disney and the Ritz-Carlton chain of hotels have built up a reputation for service quality that owes a great deal to the care that is put into employee recruitment. Given the high costs of training new recruits in any business, it makes a lot of sense to ensure that the right people are recruited in the first place, and that, once in place, a strong emphasis is placed on min-imizing employee turnover. Companies with higher than the industry average of staff turnover will often be poor performers in terms of customer service.

Evidence exists in many markets that a 'virtuous circle' can be created whereby committed and satisfied employees result in loyal and satisfied cus-tomers, which further encourages and reinforces customer orientation among the employees. This is illustrated in Figure 14.5.

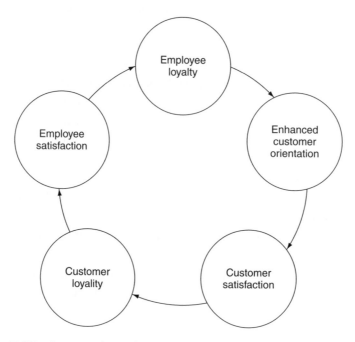

Figure 14.5 Employee satisfaction leads to customer loyalty

## INFLUENCER MARKETS

Clearly, there are many sources of influence on buyer behaviour, and so the definition of an 'influencer market' is not straightforward. In the context of relationship marketing, an influencer is an organization, entity or individual that, directly or indirectly, might cause a customer to buy a product or service. A critical part of a relationship-marketing programme may therefore involve seeking to work more closely with the influencers. An example might be a mar-garine producer that seeks to encourage an interest in low-cholesterol diets by supporting research into heart disease. Another example might be man-ufacturers of domestic smoke alarms lobbying the government to invest in public-information programmes on fire protection.

Much of what we call 'public relations' is often focused on developing a positive attitude among critical influencer markets. The ultimate aim is to try to ensure that the environment in which we market our offer is as favourable as possible.

Still more sources of influence are the 'innovators', or 'early adopters' (see Chapter 9), who are often used by others as a point of reference or guidance. Drug companies, for example, have long recognized the importance of building close relationships with general practitioners (GPs), who have a position of influence among other doctors when it comes to prescribing practice.

## SUPPLIER AND ALLIANCE MARKETS

Many companies have found that closer relationships with suppliers can lead to innovation in product design and functionality, quality improvements and lower purchasing costs. The move towards 'single sourcing' is also a part of this trend. The idea here is that the best way to gain the benefits of buyer–supplier collaboration is through working closely in a spirit of trust and long-term mutual commitment – a spirit that is unlikely to be engendered if the buyer insists on splitting his or her business between several competing suppliers. This type of collaborative relationship with supplier markets is known by various names. AT&T call it 'vendorship partnership', while the European electronics group, Philips, use the term 'co-makership'. In the United States it is referred to as 'reverse marketing'. Alliance markets have emerged, as organizations have adopted increasingly strategic relationships with one another. Alliances are recognized as a potential source of supply of capital, managerial expertise, market position, global coverage, technological skills and much more.

# RELATIONSHIPS AS PARTNERSHIPS

The basic philosophy underlying relationship marketing is that the goal of all marketing activity should be the establishment of mutually beneficial partnerships with customers. If customers perceive there is greater value in staying with a particular supplier than in moving to any other, then clearly they will stay. The challenge to management is to develop marketing strategies designed to create enduring customer partnerships and to combat customer churn and switching behaviour.

Ideally, the concept of partnership and value co-creation should be applied to each of the markets contained in the multiple markets model. Hence partnerships with employees, influencers, suppliers and customers enhance the prospect of greater long-term profitability for the business. Furthermore, it is worth remembering that partnership can operate between two or more parties, extending a 'win-win' situation to one of a 'win-win-win'. Many companies are benefiting from closer relationships with suppliers. What these companies are discovering is that by working alongside suppliers they can find ways to take costs out of the supply chain by focusing on such things as just-in-time (JIT) delivery systems and electronic data interchange (EDI). Resultant cost reductions can be passed on to customers, enhancing perceived added value. In addition, companies can build customer value by working together with suppliers *and* customers on product improvements and new product development. Indeed, numerous studies identify partnerships with suppliers, distributors and customers as major sources of innovation and value co-creation.

## SUPPLY CHAIN MANAGEMENT

What has emerged from this concept of 'proactive' partnership is the idea of the 'extended supply chain'. While traditionally companies have tended to see their strengths in terms of their own capabilities and resources, the notion of the extended supply chain looks beyond the legal boundaries of the company for new sources of competitive advantage. Supply-chain management can be defined as the management of upstream and downstream relationships with suppliers, distributors and customers so as to augment value for the customer as cost-effectively as possible for the organization. The result of a successful supply-chain management programme should be enhanced profit for all the partners in the chain.

Many companies have already found considerable benefit in developing partnerships in the supply chain. For example, as illustrated in Case study 14.1, Nokia has achieved significant improvement in its competitive position through developing a close partnership with Microsoft.

## CASE STUDY 14.1 NOKIA AND MICROSOFT

In 2011 Nokia was rapidly losing market share to its main rivals, HTC and Apple. One of the main reasons cited for the decline was Nokia's continued commitment to its Symbian operating system. As consumers now use their mobile devices for data consumption (web browsing and viewing) rather than simply voice and text communication, the Symbian OS was seen increasingly as overly complex and outmoded. To remain competitive, Nokia needed a platform to enable rapid development of music, video and entertainment applications for its new generation of smartphones.

Faced with falling sales, Nokia announced a partnership deal with Microsoft. Nokia would manufacture mobile devices that run the Windows OS while Microsoft would develop applications to run on Nokia phones. The benefits of Windows OS were cited as enhanced multi-platform functionality and flexibility, as well as the ability to incorporate social networks far more easily and comprehensively than Symbian. Windows was also anticipated to enable future software developments much more simply and cost-effectively than the old platform. The collaboration between the two companies provides Nokia with access to a highly expert development community, while Microsoft benefits from greater exposure and increased market share.

The driver behind the partnership was to improve the value proposition by creating market-leading mobile products and services while offering consumers, operators and developers unrivalled choice and simplicity and shortening development time. Value is created along the value chain by each partner focusing upon core competencies, integrating key assets to improve outcomes. Successful partnerships are made by focusing upon that part of the value chain where the firm has a competitive advantage and then seeking a partner(s) to manage the other parts of the chain where the partner(s) has (have) superior skills.

**CASE STUDY QUESTIONS:**

1. Employing value chain analysis, pinpoint where, exactly, added value is created by the Nokia/Microsoft partnership.

2. Discuss whether other components of the value chain could be leveraged further to create additional value.

3. Is there any potential merit in extending the Nokia/Microsoft partnership to include other partners? If so, explain why, and justify your reasoning.

Partnerships, whatever the type or the specific arrangements involved, lie at the heart of relationship marketing and in the complex business environment of the twenty-first century may often be the only means by which competitive advantage can be secured. The stronger the relationship with a value chain partner, the higher the barrier to entry presented to competitors.

# STRENGTHENING BUYER–SELLER RELATIONSHIPS

The traditional idea that buyers and sellers should maintain a distance from each other and only concern themselves with 'negotiating a deal' can no longer be sustained. Instead, the trend is increasingly towards a much wider, business-development-focused relationship, where the supplier takes a holistic view of the customer's needs. A good example of this is provided by recent developments in what is sometimes termed 'trade marketing'. While much of the emphasis in traditional marketing has been placed on end users to 'pull' the product through the marketing channel, trade marketing is concerned with gaining access to the marketing channel and increasing the 'opportunities to buy' experienced by end users; in other words, to ensure maximum shelf-space, distribution and availability is achieved. Occasionally these strategies are referred to as 'push' strategies; however, such a term implies a production orientation, and it is probably better to talk simply in terms of a 'relationship strategy'.

Let us revisit briefly the subject of key account management. Figure 14.6 highlights the difference between the two approaches. The conventional buyer–seller interface is a fragile connection, easily broken by competitors or the impact of market change. It is based on a motivation on the part of the buyer to maximize margin, and a motivation on the part of the seller to maximize volume.

In the relationship-based approach, the two 'triangles' are inverted to bring about a much stronger interface bond. Now there are multiple points of connection between the vendor and the customer. The objectives of the vendor are to develop the customer's business, to focus on the customer's return on investment and enhance the customer's own competitive capability. The benefit to the vendor if those objectives are achieved is the likelihood that it will be treated as a preferred supplier. At the same time, the costs of serving that customer should be lower as a result of a greater sharing of information, integrated logistics systems and so on.

Closer relationships between suppliers and retailers have led to the development of integrated EDI 'quick-response' or 'efficient consumer response' systems. The underlying principle behind these systems is that information on sales is captured at the point of sale and transmitted directly to the supplier. The supplier can then schedule production and distribution on the basis of known demand rather than on order projections, which are unpredictable in volume and frequency. The benefits to the supplier are greatly reduced logistics costs and improved production efficiencies, while the retailer needs to carry less stock

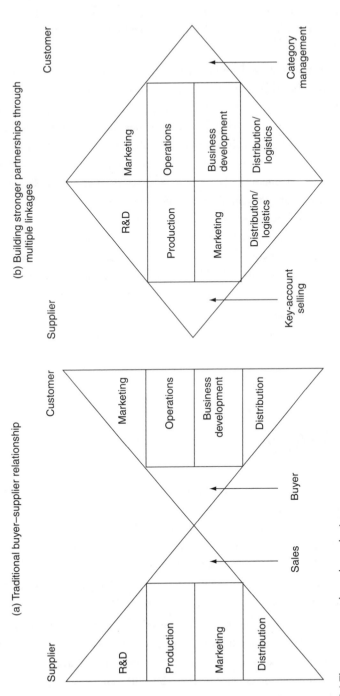

(a) Traditional buyer–supplier relationship

(b) Building stronger partnerships through multiple linkages

Figure 14.6 The move towards trade marketing

281

and run out of stock less often. Such relationships have resulted in the supplier being awarded 'preferred supplier' status, thus gaining increased shelf-space. For example, within the first year of integrating their information and logistics system in this way with Wal-Mart, Procter & Gamble's business with Wal-Mart grew by 40 per cent.

Cross-functional, cross-firm interactions that lead to value creation in B2B partnerships can be inherently complex and difficult to manage. Acknowledging this, Lambert and Enz (2012) assert that managers need actionable frameworks. They find that value co-creation between partners occurs during three cyclical and interrelated phases through which customers and suppliers interact, specifically: (i) the joint crafting of value propositions, (ii) value actualization and (iii) value determination. This necessitates a proactive approach in which business solutions are presented to the customer; that is, a value proposition rather than a sales proposition. For example, in B2B marketing a manufacturer might illustrate the impact of a proposed relationship in terms of a return on investment within the product or service category in question, while in B2C encounters, as well as product quality, communication, dialogue and post-purchase service might be key relationship-oriented attributes of value.

It is crucial, therefore, to develop marketing strategies that focus on optimizing channel relationships. This, and the role of intermediaries are discussed further in Chapter 17.

Because the issue of improving customer relations and customer loyalty is so crucial, we have devoted Chapter 15 to customer retention strategy.

# SUMMARY

As markets fragment and competition continues to intensify, traditional transaction-based approaches to marketing are replaced by a broader, relationship-based approach. Relationship marketing emphasizes that there must be at least as much attention placed on keeping customers as on getting them. This requires that marketing becomes a cross-functional, cross-organizational rather than an isolated activity and that managers proactively engage partners and customers in the process of value creation.

The development of successful relationship marketing strategies can be enhanced by a focus on multiple markets, namely customer and consumer markets; referral markets; internal markets; recruitment markets; influencer markets; and supplier and alliance markets. Specific, but complementary, strategies should be designed for each of these markets, the ultimate goal being to create a networked partnership approach to marketing that embraces the entire supply chain to achieve greater customer value at every level in the chain.

The adoption of a strategic approach to managing the organization's relationships should be preceded by a serious consideration of whether the purpose for which it intended can be achieved through alternative routes and whether the considerable investment that it is likely to entail is justifiable.

# FURTHER READING

Christopher, M., Payne, A. and Ballantyne, D. (2008) *Relationship Marketing: Creating Stakeholder Value*, Oxford: Butterworth-Heinemann.

An in-depth exploration of value creation and delivery, and relationship marketing management. Includes practical insights on how to implement a relationship strategy.

# REFERENCES

Blois, K. (2004) Analyzing exchanges through the use of value equation, *Journal of Business and Industrial Marketing*, Vol. 19 (4): 250–257.

Grönroos, C. (1997) Value-driven relational marketing: from products to resources and competencies, *Journal of Marketing Management*, Vol. 13 (5): 407–419.

Grönroos, C. (2011) Value co-creation in service logic, *Marketing Theory*, Vol. 11 (3): 279–301.

Grönroos, C. & Ravald, A. (2011) Service as business logic: implications for value creation and marketing, *Journal of Service Management*, Vol. 22 (1): 5–22.

Lambert, D. & Enz, M. (2012) Managing and measuring value co-creation in business to business relationships, *Journal of Marketing Management*, Vol. 28 (13/14): 1588–1625.

McKinsey Global Institute (2011) *Big Data: The Next Frontier for Innovation, Competition and Productivity*, Washington, McKinsey.

Peppers, D. & Rogers, M. (2011) *Managing Customer Relationships*, Hoboken, NJ: Wiley.

# CHAPTER 15
# CUSTOMER RETENTION STRATEGY

IN THIS CHAPTER WE STUDY:

- the link between customer retention and profitability
- the ladder of loyalty
- the key elements of a customer-retention strategy
- the customer-retention improvement process
- the need to research the causes of customer defection and customer loyalty
- the critical success factors and the critical failure factors
- the importance of correct market segmentation for customer-retention programmes

# CUSTOMER RETENTION AND PROFITABILITY

Customer-retention strategies have grown in popularity in parallel with increasing awareness of the costs associated with customer defection and acquisition. A company employing customer lifetime value (see below) as a key metric is more likely to focus upon creating value-added, personalized products, services and relationships. If done successfully, this can reduce defection and encourage positive word of mouth advocacy, ultimately leading to lower costs per customer, greater market share and enhanced competitive advantage.

Spurred on by evidence linking market share and profitability, companies often work hard to increase the former, without adequate consideration of the *costs* involved. While there is strong evidence of some correlation between market share and profitability, there is equally strong evidence to suggest that the *quality* is more important than quantity. Companies must ask themselves whether the customer base comprises predominantly long-established, loyal customers, or is there a high degree of customer turnover, or 'churn'? If the latter is the case, then the company is not as profitable as it might be. It has been known for some time that the longevity of customer relationships favourably influences profitability (Zeithaml et al., 1996) and it has been suggested that even a relatively small increase in retention can have a significant impact on profitability. Research by Bain and Co. indicates that, on average, an improvement of five percentage points in customer retention can lead to profit improvements of between 25 per cent and 95 per cent in the net present value of the future flow of earnings.

Why should a retained customer be more profitable than a new one? First, because of the costs of acquiring new business in the first place, it might take time to bring a new customer into profit. Second, the more satisfied customers are with the relationship, the more likely they are to place a bigger proportion of their total purchase ('share of wallet') with the company. Third, retained customers become easier to sell to, with consequent lower costs; also, in B2B environments, business clients are more likely to be willing to integrate their systems (for example, procurement, planning, scheduling and inventory) with the seller's, leading to further cost reductions.

Fourth, in some markets, effective customer-retention programmes can create satisfied customers who may act as advocates. It has long been known that word of mouth recommendations and referrals can lead to new customers, increased revenue and, ultimately, enhanced profitability. The popularity of customer referral programmes (CRPs), in which existing customers are incentivized to recommend a company, or brand, to non-customers, is increasing rapidly. Popular with customers, they are also found to be effective and cost-efficient way of attracting new customers (Schmitt et al., 2011). Additionally, Garnefield et al. (2011) find that customers who provide positive recommendations to others have positive loyalty intentions, while Garnefield et al. (2013) find that referral programmes influence behavioural loyalty.

Finally, loyal customers are often less price-sensitive and less inclined to switch suppliers when prices rise. All these elements combine to lead to the conclusion that retained customers generate considerably more profit than new ones. Figure 15.1 summarizes the relationship between customer acquisition costs and profit.

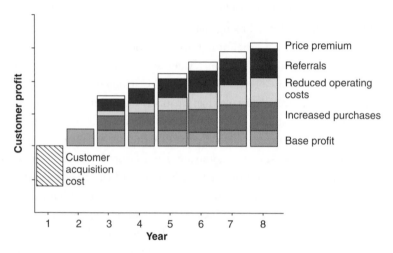

Figure 15.1 Customer profit contribution over time

There is a direct linkage between the customer retention rate and customer lifetime, as illustrated in Figure 15.2.

An important statistic that is not always measured is *customer lifetime value*. Put very simply, this is a measure of the financial worth to the organization of a retained customer. Measuring the lifetime value (LTV) requires an estimation of the likely cash flow to be provided by that customer over their lifetime with the company, for example, if a typical account lasts for ten years, the LTV equals the net present value (NPV) of the profit generated the over ten years. Once this is calculated, it is then possible to calculate the impact of increased customer retention rate on profitability, as well as the effect of extending the customer lifetime by a given amount. This information provides a good basis for marketing investment decision-making; how much is it worth spending, either to improve the customer retention rate or to extend the life of a customer relationship? This financially oriented perspective, often overlooked or executed inadequately, raises the complex issue of understanding, measuring and managing customer loyalty.

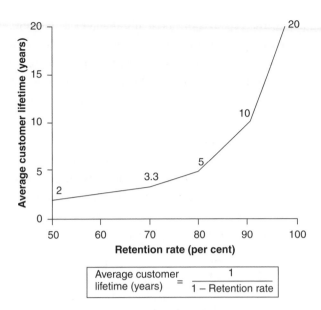

$$\text{Average customer lifetime (years)} = \frac{1}{1 - \text{Retention rate}}$$

Figure 15.2 Impact of customer retention rate on customer lifetime

# THE LOYALTY LADDER

It will be apparent from the previous comments that customer loyalty must become one of the principal objectives of marketing strategy. Customer loyalty is essentially a commitment to continue to do business with a company on an ongoing basis. Oliver (1999: 392) defines loyalty as 'a deeply held commitment to rebuy or repatronize a preferred product or service consistently in the future, despite situational influences and marketing efforts having the potential to cause switching behaviour'. It is generally measured in two dimensions: attitudinal and behavioural. Attitudinal loyalty concerns positive psychological attachment, whereas behavioural loyalty refers to the act of remaining with a particular firm, or brand (Dick and Basu, 1994). The aim of generating loyalty should be to seek to create committed customers, not customers who are 'locked in', for example, by contracts that demand a minimum service period (for example, telecoms and utilities). A customer who is figuratively 'held prisoner' is unlikely to stay with their current supplier if an alternative supplier makes a satisfactory offer.

It is perhaps worth highlighting here that this notion of encouraging customers willingly and voluntarily to make repeat purchases with a particular supplier underpins a key marketing principle: customer choice. Having the option to choose, and options to choose from, is crucial to marketing dynamics. Without choice, suppliers would be unable to create a unique selling proposition (USP) and to target their most promising opportunities; and customers would be unable to express their needs and purchase preferences, settling for something less-than-acceptable, or not at all. As suppliers' promotional activities become increasingly aggressive and personalized, marketers test the fine line between exercising reasonable pressure and exerting excessive force. The most successful marketing, in terms of building long-term, profitable relationships with customers, has always been founded on a basis of mutual interest, trust and respect.

When developing customer-loyalty-building strategies, it is helpful to think in terms of a supplier taking a customer up a 'ladder of loyalty', as portrayed in Figure 15.3. The bottom rung of the ladder represents the potential market for our product or service. At this stage we do not know the precise identity of these people (or companies) but we hope we know something of their characteristics – for example, their demographic profile, lifestyle and so on.

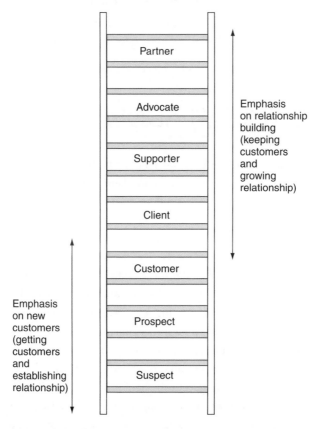

Figure 15.3 The loyalty ladder
*Source*: Christopher et al. (2002).

Once prospects have been identified, the sales process can begin. These prospects may first need to be 'qualified' to select those most likely to be in the market for our product or service, and to filter out those who are not. This can be achieved by a number of means, including direct mail, telephone interviews or even field sales visits, although the latter is usually reserved for use as a follow-up once enquiries have been received via other, more cost-effective means.

*Only when a sale has been made, do we have a customer.* For many companies, this closing of the sale is seen as the culmination of the marketing process. However, under the relationship marketing process, the conversion of a 'prospect' to a 'customer' should be seen as just the start of a journey of building customer loyalty.

To elevate the customer to 'client' status, we must establish a pattern of repeat buying by making it easy for the customer to do business with us. Being a client does not necessarily signal a *commitment*, however. Banks, for example, have regular customers who might be termed clients. Yet many of those clients may well express high levels of dissatisfaction with the service they receive, and if it were possible for them to move accounts easily, they would not hesitate to switch to another bank. In order to obtain seriously committed clients we must develop a customer-orientated approach that persuades our clients to become our 'supporters' – meaning that they are pleased with the service they receive and happy to provide continued custom.

If they are really impressed with the quality of service and if the relationship exceeds their expectations, they may turn into 'advocates' – meaning that they tell others about their satisfaction with our offer. Given the power of word of mouth, this type of advocacy can be worth more than any amount of advertising.

The final rung on the ladder of loyalty sees the customer as 'partner'. 'Partnership' is achieved where a mutually rewarding relationship exists, and neither party intends to leave the other. The concept of 'partnership' as a desirable goal of business relationships is fast gaining acceptance, particularly in industrial and business-to-business marketing. As stressed in Chapter 14, forging partnerships across the value chain can yield considerable benefits.

The loyalty ladder, while being a simple idea, can provide a practical framework around which to build specific customer-retention strategies.

# DEVELOPING A CUSTOMER-RETENTION STRATEGY

Customers continue to buy from a particular supplier because they perceive that the total 'value' they gain from the relationship is greater than the total cost that they incur. The challenge to the supplier, therefore, is to seek continually to improve the ratio between the perceived value the customer derives from the offer and the perceived cost. As intimated in Chapter 11, the perceived cost includes not only price but also switching costs and ongoing costs, such as maintenance, servicing and running costs.

If we wish to strengthen the relationship with our customers, it can be helpful to look more closely at *their* value chains. It is only by understanding their own processes that we can identify where in those processes it is possible for us as a supplier to have a positive impact. For example, if we identify that currently some customers are carrying high levels of inventory – say stocks of spares – the implementation of a rapid-response logistics programme might enable them to carry less inventory, thus their costs will be reduced and they will run out of stock less often. Such an initiative could therefore both raise customers' value and lower their costs.

A similar approach can often be applied in marketing to end users. For example, many modern consumers are 'time-sensitive' and products that can be augmented by a service dimension – for example, home delivery – can lead to a strengthened customer relationship. For example, Domino's Pizza, took a big share of the massive US market for pizza by basing its entire business philosophy around providing a reliable, speedy home-delivery service where customers receive their telephoned orders less than an hour after placing their call. Domino's expansion into the UK market shows similar success. The key elements of a retention strategy are outlined in Table 15.1.

# DEVELOPING A CUSTOMER-RETENTION PROGRAMME

Apart from striving continually to offer a superior product at a competitive price, with strong brand values (or corporate image), what else can a company do to stop its customers preferring to do business with the competition? Increasingly, organizations are realizing that they need to develop *active* customer-retention strategies as opposed to the more conventional passive approach to retention.

Figure 15.4 outlines an approach to developing a *proactive* customer-retention programme based on understanding not only what motivates customers to stay with suppliers but also what prompts them to leave suppliers. The average rate of customer retention that results from implementing the process represents the organization's customer-retention level. The customer-retention

- Retention strategy is based on clear and achievable retention objectives
- Retention objectives support and reinforce corporate and marketing objectives
- Visible leadership and commitment of senior management (personal enthusiasm and allocation of sufficient resources)
- Genuine empowerment of employees
- Valid endorsement of other stakeholders (shareholders, suppliers, legislators and so on)
- Relevant and accurate segmentation of customers (consider current and potential customer value)
- Meaningful and usable market information and intelligence
- Selective retention effort (grow most valuable customers/develop or drop least valuable customers)
- Design and development of proactive retention programmes (with goals of defection prevention and retention improvement)
- Organization-wide communication and implementation of retention programmes
- Continual monitoring of retention programmes performance and revision as necessary
- Regular review and reassessment of retention strategy

Table 15.1 Key elements of a customer retention strategy

improvement process can be viewed as working from the top of the figure downwards, with the output of early warning and remedial action feeding back into customer-retention level measurement.

## STEP 1 MEASURE CUSTOMER-RETENTION LEVEL

Any effort towards customer-retention improvement must be based on the current level of customer retention. Customer retention itself may be measured/defined in several different ways, depending on the circumstances. For example, in the case of long-term contracts such as insurance policies and bank accounts, retention is measured/defined by renewals. For more frequent transactions, retention is often used synonymously with customer loyalty, which may refer to customer attitudes, repeat purchase behaviour, or share of category requirements. Nevertheless, retention level measurement will necessarily take into account the customer retention rate, or percentage of customers at the beginning of the measurement period that remain at the end of the measurement period.

Customer-retention level measurement must also consider the reality that some customer relationships are more precious to the supplying organization than others. As limited resources dictate that no organization 'can be all things to all people', it is vital that marketing strategies are selective and prioritizing. The aim should be to retain the most valuable customer relationships and to

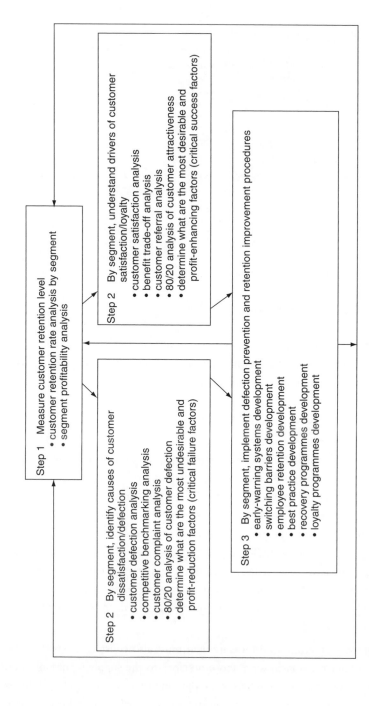

Figure 15.4 Customer-retention improvement process

develop or drop the least valuable ones. This involves rewarding 'valuable customer relationship' behaviour visibly while actively dissuading customers who up to that point have not met (in the case of existing customers) or are unlikely to meet (in the case of potential customers) the 'valuable customer relationship' criteria. Such criteria form the basis of segment profitability analysis.

Segment profitability analysis is an examination of different customer segments in terms of their present and future profitability. Its purpose is to increase customer retention among the segments of highest 'attractiveness' to the supplying organization. What defines 'attractive' will vary from organization to organization, as each will be unique in its situation and goals. However, critical aspects of customer attractiveness for any supplier will be customer lifetime value and customer life cycle position, as discussed earlier in the chapter.

## STEP 2 IDENTIFY DEFECTION CAUSES/UNDERSTAND LOYALTY DRIVERS

Measuring an organization's customer-retention level is not an easy task, but it is a critical one. The customer-retention level provides the springboard for launching improvements as well as the gauge for determining their effectiveness. Using the wrong measures, measuring the wrong things, or not monitoring customer retention sufficiently, can result in missing telling indicators of potential customer defection. It can also result in not recognizing potential opportunities for relationship growth. Let us consider more closely both sides of Step 2 in Figure 15.4, beginning with the left-hand box.

### Identify causes of customer dissatisfaction/defection

Astonishingly, few organizations research thoroughly the underlying causes of customer dissatisfaction and defection. Research into the loss of customer relationships can be carried out successfully through market investigation (telephone interviews, postal questionnaires and, where appropriate, in-depth interviews and focus groups), followed by careful data analysis and interpretation. The objective of such *defection analysis* is to dig as deeply as possible below the surface to identify the root causes of defection.

Because the decision to change suppliers or brands is not taken lightly by most customers, it will usually be cumulative dissatisfaction that confirms the decision to leave. It follows, therefore, that, if we can pin down the causes of dissatisfaction, specific actions can be taken to redress, and ideally remove, them. Over the years, businesses have accumulated a wealth of experience in what works for customers and what does not. Organizations that not only survive, but also thrive, embody valuable clues about the causes of customer dissatisfaction and defection.

Thus, one popular method of identifying the root causes of customer dissatisfaction and defection is *competitive benchmarking*. This involves using accepted standards of performance as reference points for comparing an organization with its competitors. Checking an organization's performance on critical elements – for example, sales per unit, market share or customer churn – against that of established or emerging rivals, provides a 'relative' index of performance success. However, this comparison of performance to the best achieved by competitors has met with criticism in some industries, where the performance of even the leading competitor is considered to be poor. Many choose instead to use *best practice benchmarking*, which compares the performance of a process to the best universal performance standard. Where the organization matches recognized best practice, natural delight should be accompanied by a determination to take the lead and do even better. Where the organization exceeds best practice, the focus should be on working constantly to sustain this achievement and help to guide others in a similar direction. It is strongly advised, however, that competitive benchmarking and best practice benchmarking be used only in conjunction with in-house market research: there is little point in following a leader blindly whose direction may be misguided or, in the circumstances, inappropriate!

*Customer complaint analysis* is another way of revealing the features of customer discontent. Often customer complaints will provide an indication of the source of dissatisfaction, but it must be remembered that only a minority of customers complain – the rest just 'vote with their feet'. There is something to be said for actively seeking criticism from customers. Customer feedback, be it a constructive comment or a venting of frustration, provides a means for gaining insightful knowledge that can then be acted upon to deliver improvement and even innovation. It also provides a way of demonstrating to customers that they are valued for more than just the contents of their wallets.

While there are many reasons why customers break off relationships with their suppliers, the 80/20, or Pareto, rule normally applies: that is, 80 per cent of customers leave for the same 20 per cent of reasons. A key component of the customer-retention improvement process is therefore an *80/20 analysis of customer defection*. The negative aspects of performance that customers most frequently nominate as having the greatest bearing on their decision to leave suppliers are termed 'critical failure factors' (CFFs). Common CFFs include:

- a product that fails to perform as promised;
- poor service (for example, long queues/waiting times, untrained staff, unreliable delivery and so on); and
- price (for example, perceived value/perceived cost ratio is unacceptable).

Organizations that are dedicated to identifying the most prevalent reasons for defection and to redressing those causal factors within their control clearly have a leading edge over their competitors. Organizations that do not get to the bottom of customer switching behaviour are condemned to continue losing customers and achieving an unnecessarily poor (business and customer) performance.

## Understand drivers of customer satisfaction/loyalty

The customer-retention improvement process is, in a sense, a two-edged sword: it cuts both ways. On the one hand it aims to reduce or eliminate the propensity for customers to leave a company, while on the other it aims to reshape customer perception and cut out the competition to some degree so that customers stay with the company longer. Thus, in addition to and at the same time as identifying the causes of customer dissatisfaction and defection, we must also be seeking to understand the drivers of customer satisfaction and loyalty. It is only by knowing what customers want that we can strive to meet their requirements better than our competitors. (Simply knowing what they *don't* want doesn't tell us what they *do* want.)

Here, we use the term 'customer loyalty' in its broadest sense – encompassing customer affinity, or an inspired sense of empathy or association with a supplier, and customer 'stickiness', or a reluctance to break the bond with a supplier. Again, it is understood that a customer's loyalty is not the exclusive domain of one supplier, and that a customer may be 'loyal' to multiple suppliers simultaneously. One customer-retention objective, therefore, is to shrink the customer's pool of preferred suppliers, while remaining firmly within it.

Effective *customer satisfaction analysis* requires organization-wide agreement about what exactly is meant by 'customer satisfaction'. For some suppliers, customers might be deemed to be 'satisfied' if they do not complain, while for others it might take a repeat purchase or two to be convinced. Yet others might adopt the stance that customers are *never* satisfied, and the best a supplier can do is to try not to *dis*satisfy them. So, the issue of measuring customer satisfaction levels is challenging, to say the least, especially as the factors that satisfy one segment may be inappropriate when applied to a different segment in the same market. Thus, great care is necessary in this crucial task, as can be seen from the case history at the end of this chapter.

The quest to identify the elements of performance that are most important to customers and that have the greatest influence on their relationship behaviour entails understanding customers from a customer perspective. *Benefit trade-off analysis*, or conjoint analysis allows different product/service or brand benefits identified by the customer to be 'traded-off' against each other to reveal the customer's benefit priorities. The resulting information and insights can then be used to develop more customer-orientated and customer-specific marketing strategies.

Customers also offer valuable insights into what characteristics they deem important in a supplier by the recommendations they give to others about specific products, services or brands. Increasingly, supplying organizations are asking new customers how they found out about the company, and whether a friend, family member or colleague who had already tried the product or service had spurred their interest. By studying the nature of such customer 'advocacy' through *customer referral analysis*, suppliers can work out to some extent what drives customer opinion to the point where customers need to share 'a good thing' with people they respect.

To summarize, understanding critical success factors (CSFs) is the very lifeblood of marketing, because if we can outperform our competitors on some or all of these points, we shall truly know why our customers prefer to buy from us rather than from whomever else offers competitive goods or services. Also, knowing CSFs will enable us to strive continuously for improvement.

## STEP 3 DEFECTION PREVENTION AND RETENTION IMPROVEMENT

The third step ensures customer retention improvement through taking both preventive and corrective action. Such measures are based on the knowledge and insights gleaned from the first two steps, and a commitment to do better.

A crucial feature of any retention-improvement programme is *early warning systems development*. The value of an early warning system is that it recognizes a potential danger immediately and alerts those who need to know so that they are able to act promptly and responsibly either to remove the threat or to reduce its impact. As supplying organizations increasingly interact with customers through multiple touchpoints, it is increasingly important to have real-time, organization-wide performance feedback and procedures for processing effectively. Customer empowerment and technological advances mean that in many cases customers can depart or switch suppliers at the click of a mouse. It is also important that everyone in the organization is vigilant to emerging problems, is kept up to date on problem areas relevant to their responsibilities and is invited to offer ideas for current and future problem-solving.

Customer defection prevention can also be obtained through *switching barriers development*. The idea here is to proactively dissuade the customer from leaving the relationship by erecting obstacles that make it especially undesirable or difficult to go. Strategic bundling, where groups of products or services are offered together as a package deal or 'bundle' of benefits, can prove irresistible to the determined bargain-hunter or convenience-orientated customer. Customer switching cost, or the cost to a customer of changing from using one product or service to using another can be an effective deterrent to customers who want to switch. However, it may also be a deterrent to potential customers who are wary that the cost of switching will be prohibitive if they find they are dissatisfied, so great care is needed here, and suppliers should adhere to a code of ethics that leaves them beyond reproach.

Team-based relationship management, or key account management (see Chapter 13), is a barrier often used in business-to-business marketing. It works on the basis that the more links that are forged between customers and supplier, the harder it will be for the customers to extricate themselves from the relationship. For example, a web of connections may be established between the supplier's production team and the customer's operations team, the supplier's marketing team and the customer's business development team, and so on. Any form of collaborative activity/investment can also be a 'tie that binds', providing a powerful disincentive to switch suppliers.

However, switching barriers should only be constructed if they serve the interests of both customers and supplier. If customers feel 'locked in' to an unsatisfactory relationship, or are offended by overt gestures that signal a degree of mistrust, this could lead to damaging publicity and greatly reduced profits.

Another major inhibitor to customer defection and dissatisfaction lies within the culture of the organization itself – *employee retention development*. We noted earlier that happy employees make for happy customers, and vice versa. This truism extends to employee and customer retention. Employees who are satisfied and motivated in their jobs, and based within an internal culture that they find exciting, challenging and worthwhile, are more likely to be retained than those who cannot claim to have such a positive work experience. Improved employee retention is likely to deliver improved internal and external service quality. This creates greater customer value, which in turn generates customer satisfaction and retention.

In addition to implementing measures to prevent customer dissatisfaction and defection, it is important to take corrective action where necessary to rescue a failing customer relationship and remedy any damage caused. This is the area of *recovery programmes development*. Because it is inevitable that, even in the best-run businesses, things will go wrong from time to time, there needs to be a policy of rapid response to customers' problems. The response should be the result of laid-down procedures combined with a high level of employee empowerment to put things right. The procedures should be based on the assumption that the customer is 'innocent' and that it is the company that is at fault. Unfortunately, many organizations have this the wrong way round – they assume that the customer is 'guilty'. Companies such as Marks & Spencer demonstrate that even though refunding the cost of purchases without question costs them money in the short term, in fact it makes them more money in the long term as customer satisfaction, and hence loyalty, is enhanced. British Airways has found that customers whose problems are resolved quickly and to their satisfaction are more likely to travel with British Airways the next time than those who had never experienced a problem with the airline.

The key to encouraging customer loyalty where problems occur seems to be in the simple concept of employee 'empowerment'. Organizations that are prepared to let all their employees – and in particular their front-line people – have complete responsibility for sorting out customer problems reap exponential rewards. As well as seeking to resolve customers' problems, organizations should endeavour to exploit the absence of customer problems; that is, to build on customer satisfaction and loyalty. *Loyalty programmes development* is a growing trend as the challenge of retaining existing customers becomes ever more difficult and significant.

Like customer defection, customer loyalty can be hard to define and the criteria used must be carefully thought through. The mobile phone market provides a good example. A substantial number of mobile phone customers use 'pre-pay' services and have no contract, so loyalty must be measured in terms of 'dormancy'. Normally, account dormancy means that the customer does not have any outbound calls for between 1 and 30 days. However, if the customer is purchasing a certain amount of vouchers a month as a way of controlling their costs, they may be an active customer but 'invisible' to the dormancy measurement. If the service provider were then to launch a marketing campaign to promote, say, handset upgrades to all of its 'loyal' pre-pay customers, this customer might inadvertently be left off the target list, even though he/she would probably take up the offer readily.

It is also important to understand that defection does not necessarily imply *disloyalty*; it may just be that a competing supplier offers a better deal or bundle of benefits for a particular customer. Thus the design of any loyalty programme should recognize and respect customer choice, as well as recognize and reward loyal customers.

Many 'frequent flyer' programmes are based on a recognition of the existence of a small core of customers who travel the most miles, usually paying the full (undiscounted) fare. For these 'Gold' customers there will be red-carpet treatment, upgrades, personalized service and tailored promotions. While the aim is to improve retention rates among all groups of customers, it is inevitable that there will always be a core group of customers providing the greatest profit.

It is worth emphasizing the important role played by senior management in taking the types of preventive and corrective action outlined here. Not only must top management approve any retention initiative, they must also be seen to endorse it actively through their enthusiastic commitment and support. Employees will only be inspired and encouraged to follow suit if strong leadership paves the way.

Customer-retention improvement is an ongoing and iterative process, as the arrows in Figure 15.4 indicate. The consequence of implementing Step 3 will have an impact on the retention-level measurement and thus require it to be reappraised and reviewed regularly. This in turn will influence efforts to identify the causes of customer dissatisfaction and defection and to understand the drivers of customer satisfaction and loyalty, the results of which will feed into the development of any preventive and corrective procedures.

Case study 15.1 indicates clearly the crucial importance of correct market segmentation as a precursor to understanding CSFs leading to effective customer-retention programmes.

# CASE STUDY 15.1 GLOBALTECH 'SERVICE SEGMENTATION'

This case history describes the use of market segmentation to assist in the development of a service product. Customer requirements were captured via qualitative research. The segmentation was completed through the use of quantitative research. The result was a set of segments that enabled the development of a new approach to delivering service while improving customer satisfaction. The process benefited from previous segmentations but was hampered by a changing market life cycle and internal barriers. The lessons learnt could be of interest to any organization having to care for large numbers of customers.

### Background

*A failed segmentation*
GlobalTech undertook a marketing audit, including market definition, segmentation and quantification. Each product division conducted their audit separately. They mainly used brainstorming techniques to define their markets and to produce the data required.
On completion, the results were compared across the divisions.
It rapidly became apparent that each division addressed almost all the markets. However, the market definitions they produced were different, with significant bias to just the products they offered.

Similarly, the segments each division identified were in conflict with the outputs from the other divisions.

On reflection it was agreed that the results were unreliable. They could not be used to help shape future strategies or marketing investments.

### Market research decision

GlobalTech were now in the uncomfortable situation of being in a market information vacuum. Any confidence they had in their understanding of the market had been destroyed. Consequently, the decision was taken that all future market analysis and understanding tasks would be supported by appropriate investments in market research.

### First market segmentation

The following year, the segmentation was redone, supported by extensive qualitative and quantitative market research. The objective was to understand and group into segments the product buyers in the overall market. The qualitative study produced a very clear picture and definition of the markets addressed by GlobalTech. It also provided the customers' view of the benefits they sought from the products, and the differences in their attitudes towards their suppliers. The questionnaire for the quantitative study was based on the results of the qualitative study. The result was seven clearly defined product buyer segments. This enhanced understanding of the market assisted with hardware and software product marketing but did not address service products or customer satisfaction and loyalty issues.

### The need

The market life cycle had matured, and all but the more sophisticated products were perceived as commodities. Consequently, the opportunities for effective product differentiation had diminished. GlobalTech, in common with its competitors, was finding that customers were becoming increasingly disloyal. For many years, product churns and upgrades from existing customers had accounted for some 70 per cent of GlobalTech's product revenues. Service and exhaust revenues (those revenues that follow on, almost automatically, from an initial product sale. These would normally include service plus training, consultancy, consumables, supplies and add-ons and so on) almost equalled total product revenues. Service was perceived to be a key influencer of loyalty. But the costs of delivering service were becoming unacceptable. Concurrently, service pricing was coming under increasing competitive pressures.

The challenge was to increase loyalty while achieving a step function improvement in margins. Therefore it was decided to invest in a better understanding of the service market as an enabler to delivering cost-effective differentiation and loyalty. This case history covers the project from inception to implementation.

## Service segmentation project overview

### Process

The project was divided into three main phases: a qualitative market research study was followed by a quantitative market research study and finally the strategy development as illustrated below:

The GlobalTech main board director responsible for Customer Service sponsored the project. This was a critical prerequisite, as the outcome would have a significant impact on the organization, its processes and behaviours.

Similarly, the project team included key members of Service, Marketing and Finance to ensure buy-in. However, at that time, it was deemed inappropriate to include representatives from all but two of the countries because of travel implications, costs and resource impacts. In retrospect, this was not a good decision.

### Business objectives

The project team agreed to/with the overall business objectives:

- To develop strategies for profitable increase in market share and sustainable competitive advantage in the service markets for GlobalTech's products.

- To identify opportunities for new service products and for improving customer satisfaction within the context of a robust customer-needs segmentation, which can be applied readily in the marketplace.

- To identify the key drivers of loyalty so that GlobalTech may take action to increase customer loyalty significantly.

- To provide the information required to help develop a new and innovative set of service products designed and tailored to meet differing customer requirements while reducing internal business process costs significantly.

### Results from the qualitative study

The output from the qualitative study was a 93-page report documenting the results, in line with the desired research objectives. Some of the more surprising aspects were supported by verbatims.

A key output was the polarization of very different attitudes towards service requirements that some buyers had in comparison with others. For example:

- Some wanted a response within a few hours, whereas many others would be equally happy with a response the next day.

- Some wanted their staff thoroughly trained to take remedial actions supported by a specialist on the telephone. Others did not want to know and would just wait for the service provider to fix the problem.

- Some wanted regular proactive communications and being kept up to date, while others wanted to be left alone.

- Some would willingly pay for a premium service, under a regular contract, while others would prefer to take the risk.

- The attitudes of professional buyers, procuring on behalf of user departments, were consistently different from those of the user departments.

### Results from the quantitative study

The output from the quantitative study was extensive, including a 168-page report that provided an almost infinite number of views of the information. Much of the output was detailed demographic data, opportunities information and competitive positioning comparisons. However, the focus was on a fairly extensive executive summary for internal communications within GlobalTech. What follows are summarized extracts from those outputs.

#### The segments

Six market segments were identified as a result of iterative computer clusterings. Initially, the clustering routines had identified more segments, but by careful analysis this was reduced to what was decided to be the most manageable level. Some previously very small segments were merged with very similar larger segments.

#### Polarizations in attitude

The computer clustering generated the segments by grouping customers with like attitudes and requirements. This resulted in some marked differences in attitude between segments. As illustrated below, the Koalas really did not want to know about being trained and having a go. But the Teddies, Yogis and Polars had an almost opposite attitude.

#### Satisfaction and loyalty

GlobalTech was measuring customer satisfaction for use locally, as a business process diagnostic tool, and globally, as a management performance measure. These satisfaction measurements were averaged across all customers, both by geographic Business Unit and by Product Division to meet internal management reporting requirements.

However, the outputs from the quantitative study showed clearly that these traditionally well-accepted measures were, in fact, almost meaningless. What delighted customers in one market segment would annoy customers in another, and vice versa. To make the metrics meaningful, they had to be split by key criteria and the market segments.

Loyalty was obviously highest where GlobalTech's 'one size fits all' service deliverable coincidently best matched a segment's requirement, as illustrated below.

### Correlation between loyalty and customer satisfaction

The market life cycle for many of GlobalTech's products was moving into the commodity phase. Therefore, not surprisingly, customers were becoming less loyal.

Each percentage point increase in loyalty translated into almost the same increase in market share. Each percentage point in market share added many millions of dollars of gross revenues. The cost of reselling to a loyal customer was about a sixth of the cost of winning a new customer. Consequently, each percentage point increase in loyalty had a significant impact on the bottom line.

Because of this, the quantitative study included correlating the key drivers of satisfaction and loyalty within each market segment. The qualitative study identified some 28 key customer requirements of their service provider. The quantitative study prioritized these to provide a shorter list of 17 common requirements. The correlation exercise reduced this to only two requirements that drew a significant correlation between satisfaction and loyalty:

- Providing service levels that meet customers, needs; and

- Providing consistent performance over time.

Although GlobalTech was achieving the second, it was really only delivering the first in two of the market segments.

### Market attractiveness

As an aid to deciding where best to invest, a market attractiveness factors chart was produced using EXMAR, the market-modelling tool. Market demographic data from the quantitative study were combined with internal GlobalTech financial data. Each factor was weighed to reflect the relative importance to GlobalTech.

This highlighted quite a few issues and some opportunities. For example, the highest margins were coming from some of the least loyal segments.

*Competitive positioning*

Fortunately for GlobalTech, its competitors did not appear to have an appreciation of the market segments or the differing requirements of their customers. They were also mainly delivering a 'one size fits all' service offering. However, there were some noticeable differences in their offerings. These resulted in each major competitor being significantly stronger in just one or two market segments where their deliverable best matched the segment needs.

The quantitative study provided detailed rankings of the CPIs and CSFs for each market segment. These were to prove invaluable during the phase, designing the service products and developing the strategy to achieve competitive advantage.

*Reachability*

Key to GlobalTech implementing successfully any strategies or communications that were to be market-segment-based would be being able to identify each customer by segment. As part of the quantitative study, two statistical reachability tasks were completed:

- A sampling of internal GlobalTech databases showed that there was sufficient relevant data to achieve better than 70 per cent accuracy, using statistical imputation methods, to code each customer record with its market segment. This was considered to be good enough measurably to enhance marketing communications, but might not be sufficiently accurate to ensure always making the most appropriate offer.

- Statistical analysis identified four questions that would provide acceptable accuracy in segment identification. These questions could then be used during both in-bound and out-bound call centre conversations until such time as all customers had been coded.

The recommendation was to use both methods in parallel so that accuracy would improve over time. Also, the coding of larger customers should be given a priority.

## Strategy development and implementation

*Market understanding and strategy development*

The challenge now was for the project team to absorb and understand all the outcomes from the two research studies. The team then had to turn that understanding into realizable strategies. To achieve this, a workshop process called OTIs (opportunities, threats and issues) was used.

Briefly, the process involved an extensive, but controlled, brainstorming session followed by a series of innovative strategy development workshops.

- A facilitator took the team systematically through every piece of relevant information available.

- Using brainstorming, the team tried to identify every conceivable opportunity, threat or internal issue associated with each item of information.

- The information was then also tested against a predetermined list of business behaviours and processes in an endeavour to entice additional and creative ideas out of the brainstorming.

- Using the CPIs and CSFs from the EXMAR market model, strengths and weaknesses were added, thus turning the process into a SWOT.

- Like ideas were merged.

- Each idea was given two scores in the range of 1–9. The first ranked the probable financial impact, where the second ranked the probability of success.

- The ideas were then grouped by like activity and where they had the same or an overlapping financial impact. This ensured that double counting was eliminated, and that opportunities and threats were offset as appropriate. Any one group of ideas would take on the highest single financial impact score and a reassessed probability of a success score.

- If the resolution of an internal issue was a prerequisite for capturing an opportunity or overcoming a threat, then the issue plus associated costs and resources was included in the same group as the opportunity or threat. The norm was for a single issue to be attached to many groups.

- The groups were named and then ranked, both by financial impact and by probability of success. This provided a prioritized short list of imperatives that should deliver the maximum realizable benefits to both GlobalTech and its customers.

- Iterative discussions developed this into an overall strategy with a number of prioritized sub-strategies.

- Each sub-strategy was supported by a documented description of the opportunity. At this stage, encouragement was given to creating innovative, yet simple, implementation options that would maximize the chances of success. Each implementation option was supported by market, revenue and organizational impact data, associated issues, resources, costs and required control metrics.

- Board members were involved in option selections and the investment approvals process.
- Finally, the implementation programmes and project plans were created.

### The strategy

The overall recommendation was to create a set of service deliverables tailored to the individual needs of each segment. These would be complemented by a set of premium add-ons that could be offered to the appropriate segments. By focusing on business process simplification during the design of the offering for each segment it was hoped to eliminate redundancy.

The objective of each offering was to increase customer satisfaction significantly with an emphasis on those items that would have a most positive impact on loyalty. Some offerings were quite different from others, both in terms of the deliverable and the internal processes that made it possible. This differentiation was also intended to create a measurable competitive advantage in a number of the market segments.

A key to the implementation of the project was a recommended change to the customer satisfaction measurements, so that they became an effective diagnostic tool for tuning the ongoing deliverables for each market segment.

### Implementation

Throughout the project, the same core team had been intimately involved with each stage of the project. They guided the work and took on board the results. They delved deeply into the analysis and did their best to understand the markets, their customer requirements and likely competitive impacts. Finally, they worked hard at developing the proposed strategies. They thought buy-in had been achieved by being sponsored by a main board director.

The implementation roll-out across country boundaries became difficult. Each country wanted their say. They had different views of their customer needs and how things should be done in their country. They did not understand easily or even accept the findings of the research and the meaning of the outputs.

The majority of these internal barriers were eventually overcome. Inevitably, there were compromises. These led the project team into believing that not all the market segments would be fully satisfied with the new offerings in all countries.

GlobalTech is the fictitious name of a real company marketing high-tech and service products globally. Customers are counted in hundreds of thousands. The markets are mainly business-to-business with a few very large customers buying thousands of items. Service is a major revenue stream measured in billions of USD.

### Lesson 1.

Markets transcend internally defined product divisions. Therefore it is best to understand the markets and monitor overall performance in those markets. To cut market information to meet the needs of internal reporting will lead to misinformation.

### Lesson 2.

Do not rely on the internally gathered opinions of Sales and Marketing staff to define markets and identify customer requirements and attitudes. Do invest in the necessary Market Research to provide a reliable segmentation and support for strategy and product development.

### Lesson 3.

Try to anticipate the scale of organizational change that a major segmentation project may demand. Then ensure the buy-in planned from the start of the project embraces all those who will eventually have a say in the final implementation.

CPIs (critical purchase influencers) are the needs (benefits) buyers are seeking to be satisfied by their choice of product or service.

CSFs (customer satisfaction factors) or KDFs (key discriminating features) are the buyer-perceived attributes by which the choice between suppliers is made.

### Lesson 4.

Understanding the different market segments helps in designing the required offers. But do not become fixated on reachability. It is not essential to code every customer to the right segment from day one.

Where you are not really sure, let them see different offers and thus position themselves.

Similarly, be willing to accept that within a large organization some buyers may fall into slightly different, though normally similar, market segments.

# SUMMARY

Retaining existing customers is more profitable than acquiring new customers, because:

- sales, marketing and set-up costs are amortized over a longer customer lifetime;
- customer expenditure increases over time;
- repeat customers often cost less to service;
- satisfied customers provide referrals; and
- satisfied customers may be prepared to pay a price premium.

The starting point for developing customer-retention strategies and programmes is research. Encouraging customers not to leave the relationship, but to stay and buy more, requires an in-depth understanding of both what causes customers to depart and what motivates customers to buy from our company rather than from competitors. These CFFs and CSFs will determine whether the organization can withstand any competitive comparison.

If customer-retention strategies are to succeed, they should focus on the two related, but separate, issues of customer defection and customer loyalty. If these two parallel strands of the retention strategies can be managed successfully, then the probability of an improved customer retention rate will almost certainly increase.

# FURTHER READING

Christopher, M., Payne, A. and Ballantyne, D. (2008) *Relationship Marketing: Creating Stakeholder Value*, Oxford, Butterworth Heinemann.

An in-depth overview of the key issues and themes in the area of relationship marketing, including practical application of key concepts.

# REFERENCES

Christopher, M., Payne, A. and Ballantyne, D. (2002). *Relationship Marketing – Creating Stakeholder Value* Oxford: Butterworth-Heinemann.

Dick, A. S. and Basu, K. (1994) Customer Loyalty: Toward an Integrated Conceptual Framework, *Journal of the Academy of Marketing Science*, Vol. 22 (2): 99–113.

Garnefield, I., Helm, S. and Eggert, A. (2011) Walk Your Talk: An Experimental Investigation of the Relationship Between Word of Mouth and Communicators' Loyalty, *Journal of Service Research*, Vol. 14 (1): 93–107.

Garnefield, I. Eggert, A., Helm, S. and Tax, S. (2013) Growing Existing Customers' Revenue Streams Through Customer Referral Programmes, *Journal of Marketing Management*, Vol. 77: 17–31.

Oliver, R. L. (1999) Whence Customer Loyalty, *Journal of Marketing*, Vol. 63, Special Issue: 33–44.

Schmitt, P., Bernd S. and Van den Bulte, C. (2011) Referral Programs and Customer Value, *Journal of Marketing*, Vol. 75 (January): 46–59.

Zeithaml, V. A., Berry, L. L. and Parasuraman, A. (1996) The Behavioural Consequences of Service Quality, *Journal of Marketing*, Vol. 60 (April): 31–46.

# CHAPTER 16
# SALES FORCE STRATEGY

IN THIS CHAPTER WE STUDY:

- the role of personal selling in the marketing mix
- the eight buy phases of the decision-making process
- the multifaceted role of the salesperson
- methods for determining the requisite number of salespeople
- quantitative and qualitative objectives for the sales force
- possible customer types and suggested selling postures
- key activities of sales force management

# THE IMPORTANCE OF PERSONAL SELLING

Many companies are finding that the 80/20 rule applies; 80 per cent of the business comes from 20 per cent of customers. As we saw in Chapter 13, this has led to a growth of interest in key account management. Combined with the imperative of nurturing customer relations, which we outlined in Chapters 14 and 15, it is not difficult to see why sales force management has become a key strategic issue in modern businesses. The sales force has a pivotal role to play in both KAM and CRM; whereas 50 years ago would undoubtedly have been on closing the next sale, nowadays the emphasis is on creating long-term, win-win relationships. This change in focus from sales to customer solutions has attracted a great deal of attention in recent years, with Sharm and Sheth (2010: 127) describing the contemporary salesperson as a 'consultant for the consumer'.

Companies that have been around for some time would certainly have had an organized sales force long before they introduced formal marketing activities of the kind described in this book. In spite of this, sales force management traditionally has been a neglected area of marketing management. There are several possible reasons. First, not all marketing and product managers have had the experience in a personal selling or sales management role. Consequently, these managers often underestimate the importance of efficient personal selling.

Secondly, sales personnel themselves sometimes encourage an unhelpful distinction between sales and marketing by depicting themselves as being at 'the sharp end'. After all, isn't there something slightly daring about dealing with real customers as opposed to sitting in an office surrounded by marketing surveys, charts and plans? Such reasoning is dangerous, because unless a good deal of careful marketing planning has taken place before the salesperson makes their effort to persuade the customer to place an order, the probability of a successful sale is much reduced.

The suggested distinction between marketing 'theory' and 'sales practice' is further invalidated when we consider that profitable sales depend not only on individual customers and individual products but on groups of customers (that is, market segments) and on the supportive relationship of products to each other (that is, a carefully planned product portfolio). Also, there is a constant need for the organization to think in terms of where future sales will come from rather than concentrate solely on present products, customers and problems.

Although its importance varies according to circumstances, in many businesses the sales force is the most important element in the marketing mix. In industrial goods companies, for example, it is not unusual to find very small sums being spent on other forms of communication and very large sums being spent on the sales force in the form of salaries, cars and associated costs. Recent surveys show that companies devote greater expenditure to their sales forces than to advertising and sales promotion combined. Personal selling, then, is a vital and expensive element in the marketing mix, and every effort should be made to maximize the investment.

The solution to the problem of poor sales force management can only be found in the recognition that personal selling is indeed a crucial part of the marketing process, and that it must be planned and considered as carefully as any other element. Indeed, it is an excellent idea for the people responsible to go out into the territory for a few days each year and themselves attempt to persuade customers to place orders. It is a good way of finding out what customers really think of the organization's marketing policies!

## THE ADVANTAGES OF PERSONAL SELLING

As stated in Chapter 12, personal selling can be seen most usefully as part of the communications mix. It has several advantages over other elements of the communications mix:

- Two-way form of communication, giving the prospective purchaser the opportunity to ask questions of the salesperson about the product or service.
- Sales messages can be made more flexible and can therefore be tailored more closely to the needs of individual customers.
- Salespeople can use in-depth product knowledge to relate their sales messages to the perceived needs of the buyers and to deal with objections as they arise.
- Most important of all, salespeople can ask for an order and perhaps negotiate on price, delivery or special requirements.

Once an order has been obtained from a customer, and there is a high probability of a repeat purchase occurring, the salesperson's task changes from persuasion to reinforcement. All communications at this stage should contribute to underlining the wisdom of the purchase. Where existing customers wish to place further orders, the salesperson might use the opportunity to cross-sell or up-sell, thus strengthening the relationship by highlighting other relevant products and services in the company's portfolio.

Good salespeople can ascertain quickly the requirements of a particular customer and identify to what extent these will be fulfilled by their company's offerings. Customers, for their part, can identify quickly whether the company understands their requirements fully, is a business of integrity and credibility and is able to provide the necessary service support. To survive such scrutiny, salespeople must have sufficient background knowledge of the customer's purchase decision-making processes and the particular pressures and influences at play. They must also have a sound appreciation of the inherent implications for their own role and a confident plan of how to manage such implications successfully.

# KEY CONSIDERATIONS FOR SALES FORCE STRATEGY

The development and implementation of an effective sales force strategy is founded on several key considerations. To begin with, the manager has to consider changes in the macro environment that impact upon sales force performance and productivity. Increasing competition, combined with the current economic downturn mean that the balance of power is shifting in favour of customers. Simply put, salespeople have to work harder to close deals. Secondly, web-based sales force technologies have become an integral part of the sales management process, helping to change the role orientation from *selling* to *solutions*. While sales force automation can reduce the volume of day-to-day administrative tasks, sales force CRM software has the capacity to fundamentally alter sales force reach and the frequency of interaction with clients. While this has numerous benefits, it has had the effect of raising customer expectations. Web 2.0 and the explosion of social media has changed the role of technology from simple reach/communication to developing deep relationships with customers. While positive, this can also be incredibly time consuming.

Numerous research studies indicate the sales force automation is beneficial. It is found to improve internal administrative performance (Hunter and Perreault, 2006). It is also found to be beneficial in terms of enhancing personal selling performance as well as relations with customers to the extent that using sales force CRM helps salespeople focus the direction of their activities and enhance the magnitude of their efforts (Rodriguez and Honeycutt, 2011). In Rapp et al.'s (2008) study, experienced salespeople gained more from CRM technologies than those less experienced and were found to be more likely to use adaptive selling techniques than their less experienced counterparts, presenting opportunities for improved performance through training. Overall, it is found that sales force automation is useful for reducing the volume of day-to-day tasks while CRM tools have a longer-term, strategic and relational focus.

As well as technology, to be successful the salesman or woman needs to be acutely aware of the readiness of the prospect to place an order (or existing client to re-order). This entails the ability to analyse at which stage the potential buyer is in the buying process in a clear understanding of their needs, wants and demands. To achieve this, the salesperson needs to consider the following: client information needs, buy phases, buy classes and pressures on the buyer.

## INFORMATION NEEDS

Before attempting to produce a sales force strategy, it is necessary to establish what information customers will require from the sales force. Communication efficiency depends on achieving a match between the information required and the information given. The selling organization must therefore identify the major influencers in each purchase decision and find out what information they are likely to need at different stages of the buying process. In the business-to-business context this may involve pinpointing relevant internal people as well as relevant members of the buying organization, in order to lay the groundwork for establishing links at multiple levels (see Chapter 14).

It will also need to know if the customer is buying for the first time or contemplating a repeat order. Customer information needs may range from details about the product range and product performance to price, running costs, guarantees, load sizes, competitor products, special offers, reordering and so on.

In order to source and supply the appropriate information for the appropriate people at the appropriate time, the selling organization must first be clear about the stages of the decision-making process (DMP) that will need to be gone through; the types of purchase that will apply; the myriad of forces that will act upon the buyer; and how all these factors will affect the salesperson's role and the allocation of the sales portfolio.

## BUY PHASES

The majority of salespeople operate in the field of industrial or trade marketing. However, the rapid growth in the service sector has enhanced the importance of personal selling in areas of consumer marketing. Whatever the arena, the tasks performed by the salesperson are essentially the same. The main difference is the added complexity of organizational buyer decision-making processes. For this reason, the focus here is predominantly on dealing with organizational purchasing as opposed to consumer purchasing.

As we have seen, the consumer purchase DMP typically follows five buying stages, or 'buy phases': need recognition, information search, evaluation of alternatives, purchase decision and post-purchase behaviour. The organizational purchase DMP, in contrast, is more complex and usually entails eight stages. This is because most organizational purchase decisions involve a large number of people (DMU) and take an extensive amount of time and consideration. A variant of Figure 3.1 is repeated here as Table 16.1 detailing the characteristics of each buy phase.

In looking at each buy phase of the DMP it is clear that different people and different numbers of people will be involved in each phase. A useful way

| Buy phase | Characteristics |
|---|---|
| 1 Problem recognition ↓ | Changing business needs |
| | Supplier review |
| | Current product/service dissatisfactions |
| 2 General need ↓ | Innovation |
| | Cost savings |
| | Improved performance |
| 3 Specification ↓ | Buyer/supplier dialogue |
| | 'Qualifying' criteria |
| | 'Differentiating' criteria |
| 4 Supplier search ↓ | Risk profile of purchase |
| | Information gathering |
| | Consideration set |
| 5 Proposals submission ↓ | Qualification of suppliers |
| | Choice set |
| | Proposal solicitation |
| 6 Supplier selection ↓ | Proposals reviewed |
| | Buyer/supplier negotiations |
| | Selection and ratification |
| 7 Order specification ↓ | Blanket contract/order |
| | Order fulfilment procedures |
| | Relationship development |
| 8 Performance review | Benchmark supplier performance |
| | Evaluation performance |
| | Endorse, modify or discontinue |

Table 16.1 The eight buy phases of the DMP

of identifying who is likely to be involved in the purchase decision, and at what stages, is to look at the purchase decision in terms of its 'unfamiliarity' to the buying organization. This 'unfamiliarity' can be broken down into two parts:

- Complexity of the product or service being proposed/considered; and
- Degree of commercial risk or uncertainty surrounding the outcome of the purchase.

Generally, the higher the 'unfamiliarity' in both these dimensions, the greater the number of people involved and the higher their status. For salespeople, high unfamiliarity means that the majority of their activity will be concentrated at the beginning of the DMP. They will have to involve themselves at an early phase if they are to influence the outcome effectively. This is because a growing commitment operates throughout the DMP: early decisions are reinforced and become successively more and more difficult to change. Salespeople, therefore, will need to know the degree of unfamiliarity involved so that they can direct their efforts towards the appropriate people. If product complexity is high, but commercial uncertainty low, then the design engineers and technologists will have the more important role. If unfamiliarity is low in both dimensions, purchasing officers will tend to dominate the DMP.

## BUY CLASSES

In using this concept of unfamiliarity in the purchase decision, the salesperson can divide the DMP of his prospective customers into types of buying situation, or 'buy classes'. These were referred to in Chapter 3. Each buy class tends to require that certain phases in the DMP be followed. By understanding at the outset what these phases are likely to be, salespeople can manage their role in the process better and increase the chances of a favourable outcome.

### New-task purchase

All eight phases of the DMP will normally be followed. Several functional departments of the buying organization will usually be involved: for example, manufacturing, design, finance, the company board and the purchasing department. People in all these departments can be influenced during the DMP, which, in the context of a new-task purchase, takes the longest time to reach a conclusion.

### Straight re-buy

A limited application of the eight phases will be followed. Only one or two functional departments, such as the user and purchasing department, may be involved. All phases will apply in that they will have been followed in the initial purchase routine but, since the technical specification of the product is now known and unchanging, no further technical involvement is needed in the buying process. The only factors likely to worry the buyer, provided that quality is maintained, are price and delivery, and these therefore become important negotiating points.

### Modified re-buy

Most of the phases will be followed. Changes in the product specification may be initiated by the salesperson (for example, an offer of improved performance or a reduction in price) or by the buying organization itself. The design and manufacturing functions may therefore become involved. The industrial salesperson should always endeavour to change a straight re-buy situation into a modified re-buy situation, as this could serve to strengthen the existing customer relationship and open up new opportunities (through customer referrals or resulting innovations) for establishing other customer relationships.

In addition to understanding the customer's DMP, the salesperson must also appreciate the pressures on the buyer and on the members of the DMU.

## IMPLICATIONS FOR THE SALESPERSON

The way the purchase DMP operates in different circumstances has important implications for industrial salespeople. They have to:

- recognize the buying situation they face and the stage it is at and determine how best to handle it;
- identify the DMU, or those people in the buying organization who are likely to be able to influence the purchase decision at that moment and during subsequent DMP phases;
- decide what benefits their product and their company can offer to each of these people and what technical help they can give in an attempt to influence the decision; and
- attempt to convert straight re-buys into modified re-buys by demonstrating that their product has significant additional benefits over products used at present.

From the range of people they have to influence, the uniqueness of each sales situation and the extended amount time the purchase DMP might take, it is plain that industrial salespeople have a complex and demanding role to fulfil.

# MANAGING THE SALES FORCE

To optimize the sales force and obtain best value for money from personal selling, an organization must resolve three basic issues. It must decide the requisite number of salespeople, their precise role and how they are to be managed. Therefore, let us consider the methods for determining the size of the sales force, establishing sales force objectives and ensuring sales force motivation.

## DETERMINING THE SIZE OF THE SALES FORCE
### Reviewing activities

The organization should begin its consideration of how many sales representatives it needs by finding out exactly how work is undertaken at the present time. It should start by listing all the things the current sales force in fact does. These might include opening new accounts, servicing existing accounts, demonstrating new products, taking repeat orders and debt collecting. This analysis should be utilized to explore if there are alternative ways of carrying out these responsibilities more cost effectively.

For example, telephone selling has been shown to be a perfectly acceptable alternative to personal visits, particularly in respect of repeat business. The sales force can thus be freed for more complex work, which is not so susceptible to the telephone approach. Can debts be collected by mail, e-mail or by telephone? Can products be demonstrated in showrooms or at exhibitions? It is only by asking these kinds of questions that we can be certain we have not fallen into the common trap of committing the organization to a decision of how best to undertake selling responsibilities and then seeking data and reasons to justify the decision.

## Measuring workload

Essentially, salespeople undertake three activities. They make calls, travel and carry out administration. These tasks comprise the *workload*. By analysing their current workload and considering alternative ways of undertaking these respon-sibilities, the organization can decide what constitutes a reasonable workload (that is, how many calls it is possible to make in a working day given the con-comitant time values for clerical tasks and travel) and how territories can be allocated equitably. Equally, an assessment of existing and potential customers should be made and the annual total number of calls calculated, bearing in mind that different customer categories need different call rates. The following formula is helpful in ascertaining how many salespeople are needed:

$$\text{Number of salespeople} = \frac{\text{Annual total calls required}}{\text{Annual number of working days} \times \text{all salespeople's calls per day}}$$

There are, of course, several ways to measure workload. One major consumer goods company used its Work Study department to measure sales force effec-tiveness. The results of this study are summarized in Figure 16.1, which shows how salespeople's time was spent and approximately how much of their time was in fact available for selling. One immediate action taken by the company as a consequence was to initiate a training programme, which led to more time being spent on selling as a result of better planning. A separate initiative sought to improve the quality of sales performance in face-to-face situations with customers.

Another method involves getting sales representatives to measure their own workload. Research shows that salespeople carry out this measurement task diligently over the prescribed measurement period. The method involves recording their daily starting time and the miles or kilometres on the car clock and repeating this throughout the working day for all calls. The only additional

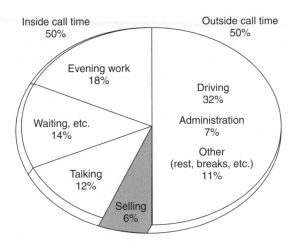

Figure 16.1 Breakdown of a salesperson's total daily activity

information required is the account category called on, and the time in and time out.

From this, it is possible to calculate over a two-month period, for example, the *average* time it takes to make a particular type of call (such as to a wholesaler, a chemist, a doctor, a hospital or a consultant). It is also possible to measure, given the type of territory (for example, town or country), how long it takes in travel to cover a given territory size. Finally, since administration is likely to be a fixed period of time for everyone, the organization has in its possession the vital information to measure, *territory by territory*, the precise workload of every salesperson. Territories can now be allocated equitably to all salespeople.

## Sales force productivity

There are, of course, many methods of calculating workload, but there is one further factor that is worthy of consideration here: the 'productivity' factor. This is a subject we have researched over a number of years, and which has proved extremely valuable in helping companies to allocate their salespeople more effectively.

Until recently, it was fashionable to predict the death of the salesperson as a key component in commercial success. Technology enthusiasts predicted that marketing methods would become so sophisticated and precisely targeted that the need for personal selling would vanish. This has proved inaccurate. Salespeople may be equipped with laptops and smartphones and sometime use email, Skype and conference calls instead of face-to-face meetings, but they are still around in abundance; indeed, many companies spend considerably more on personal selling than on all other forms of promotion put together. Despite their relatively high costs, no one has yet discovered a more effective agency than the human being for communicating the full benefit of product offerings and for addressing customers' concerns. The plethora of self-service options and automated information sources does not replace the need for person-to-person communication in conjunction with or in preference to other channels. Moreover, research indicates that, even in industries that doubt the usefulness of the personal selling process, customers see some inherent value; for example, despite some debate around the role and usefulness of sales people in the pharmaceutical industry, research indicates that doctors consider them to be a most valuable source of information about the latest developments.

As the pendulum has swung back towards personal selling, companies have invested heavily to improve the productivity of their sales forces. Indeed, modern salespeople, for the most part, are significantly more knowledgeable and skilled than in the past. They are now trained in KAM, CRM, problem solving and value creation, as well as product marketing and development. In addition, they must be comfortable and confident with technology. But, in terms of overall performance, it is not so much the quality of the 'reps' themselves that has changed as the quality of their direction and management.

Given the relatively high costs of a sales force compared with other communication methods, increasing the productivity of a sales force remains a major challenge for the most enlightened and results-orientated sales manager who is well aware that objectives such as increased sales are not the only yardsticks. Productivity is also affected by eliminating wasteful, valueless activities such as repeat sales calls spent trying to close a deal. In recent years, most companies have embraced mobile technologies as a driver of increased productivity, as illustrated in Case study 16.1.

## CASE STUDY 16.1 MOBILE SALES FORCE TECHNOLOGIES

In 2011 and 2012 companies rushed to equip their sales force with iPads and other tablet devices. Many now see it as a critical necessity. Tablet devices enable the sales force to maximize time spent with clients by providing access to data in real time and making the face-to-face experience more engaging. According to SAP, one of the major suppliers of sales force software, administration is reduced by task or process-oriented applications that embed critical information at the point of interaction. This augments meeting effectiveness and can also be an extremely useful element of CRM, as customer-specific data was always readily available and information can be obtained quickly and efficiently. Ideally, applications should be accessible from a variety of different devices. Tablets, in particular, are proving extremely popular, as the larger screen is more user-friendly than smartphones.

The pharmaceutical industry can be challenging for sales personnel, as physicians are often simply too busy to see sales representatives and increasing numbers prefer to do their own research (primarily via online physician networks). Sales personnel therefore need to ensure that meetings add value and are perceived to be of direct benefit to physicians. Tablets are seen as particularly effective in this regard. Traditionally, sales representatives used printed materials to promote their products; however, tablets enable the display of online visual aids. A 2012 study of the pharmaceutical industry by CSD on the relative usefulness, value and impact of various visual aids in sales meetings* reports that 2/3rds of meetings involved a visual aid; 55 per cent in traditional print format, 7 per cent on laptops and 5 per cent tablets. Meetings where laptops and tablets were used were shorter and outperformed print in terms of physicians' perceptions of the usefulness of the materials and their post-meeting prescribing intentions.

*Cegedim Strategic Data Promotion Audit report, 2012.

### CASE STUDY QUESTIONS:

1. SAP extols the benefits of 'task or process-oriented applications that embed critical information at the point of interaction'. Discuss what *specific* task or process-oriented information might be useful in a sales setting of your choice.

2. Evaluate the extent to which accessing data on the move reduces office-based administration for the salesman or woman.

3. The pharmaceutical industry can be challenging for salespeople as their clients are knowledgeable. Analyse the extent to which the personal selling function varies according to client knowledge, and specify exactly what has to be done differently when dealing with knowledgeable/unknowledgeable prospects.

# DIFFERENT CUSTOMER TYPES

As indicated in the case study, a firm's clientele normally consists of many types of customer: some large, some small; some experienced, some inexperienced.

Some represent a high sales potential, others do not. Some clients are loyal to the point of folly; others are sufficiently cynical to change patronage at the slightest provocation. Yet others are almost phobic about the supplying company and need superhuman persuasion to change their attitude towards it. Sheer common sense demands that customers of different potential should have different amounts of sales time invested in them.

The trouble is that, understandably enough, the average salesperson enjoys calling on the loyal customer and dislikes the prospect of being constantly rebuffed by the hostile one. The result, also understandably, is that salespeople tend to concentrate on loyal customers who will probably continue to buy from their company regardless. This is less worrying if those clients are among the 20 per cent that bring 80 per cent of the business, but in reality this is highly unlikely. Incestuous relationships can develop between salespeople and buyers; while both sides are quite happy to fête each other at frequent intervals, it may be little more than a 'mutual admiration society' from which little additional commercial and marketing value is derived. This needs to be managed and brought under control, yet the main difficulty is that if salespeople achieve their sales budget, little notice is normally taken of the fact that a lot of their time is directed unproductively – towards a customer who is literally 'in the bag'.

Salespeople would no doubt reply that, if they were neglected, even loyal customers might lose 'affection' for their favourite supplier. This is obviously true. However, it is no less true that the main thrust of communication with very loyal customers should be quite different from that which takes place with hostile prospects. In the former case, the main purpose of the sales call is to maintain contact to reassure the customer that his/her loyalty is wise and to cement a happy relationship. In the latter case, the aim is to try to understand the reasons for the hostility, to attempt to remove them, and then 'sell' the product. These are totally different tasks; they call for different approaches and should yield different results.

This notion can be taken a stage further. A firm's clientele can be divided into three major groupings: those who love the supplier (the 'Philes'); those who are totally indifferent to the supplier as long as the offering is right (the 'Promiscuous' companies); and those who are hostile to the selling company and reluctant to buy from it at all (the 'Phobes'). The point is that each of the three groups needs to be addressed with different selling and communication techniques. In fact, there is a strong case for developing individual sales processes for each case.

The situation is further complicated by the need to distinguish between the level of sales effort directed towards large, medium and small customers. Since each of the three Phile, Promiscuous and Phobe groupings can represent a large, medium or small prospect, there are a nine possible customer types (see

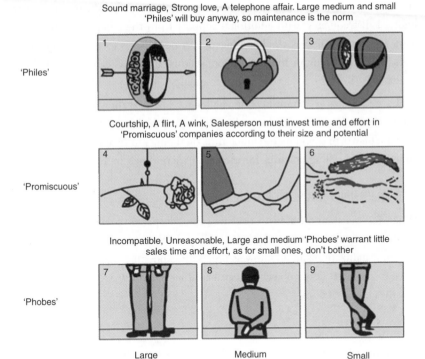

Figure 16.2 'Philes', 'Promiscuous' and 'Phobes'

Figure 16.2). Obviously, some of the cells of the matrix shown in Figure 16.2 represent better opportunities than others. A small Phobe is probably not worth bothering about, since the results of even a successful resolution of the phobia will not justify the effort involved. A small Phile, on the other hand, will probably buy from the supplier in any case. Since it only represents a small potential, however, the right approach is for the supplier to call infrequently, if at all, and then concentrate on assuring the customer that the affection is reciprocated. This can often be done by telephone. Spending any more time than the absolute minimum on such a client is unproductive.

Large Philes are both loyal and important. They should be handled with a maintenance policy, under which a representative should do only what is necessary to maintain the business. In practice, this might consist of a personal telephone call once a week only. The frequency of personal visits is a matter of management judgement, since there is always an element of vulnerability to strong competitive moves. The medium Philes can be handled according to the same principles, although obviously the call frequency will have to be less.

The most promising pay-off for the time invested by the representative clearly comes from the company that is both large and 'Promiscuous'. The appropriate treatment here is an investment policy that might mean a much higher call frequency, with additional support from the company in whatever ways are thought necessary. The objective, if possible, is to move it up to the status of Phile. Medium and small Promiscuous customers can be handled in a similar way, but with a decreasing call frequency.

Large Phobes are an interesting challenge. The first thing to establish here is the reasons for the antipathy to the selling firm. If that can't be discovered, it may not be worth spending too much time on them. The characteristic personas and suggested selling postures for each type are outlined in Table 16.2.

## ESTABLISHING SALES FORCE OBJECTIVES

Whatever the method used to organize the salesperson's day, there is always comparatively little time available for selling. In these circumstances, it is vital that an organization should know as precisely as possible what it wants its sales force to do. Sales force objectives can be either *quantitative* or *qualitative*, and usually a blend of both.

### Quantitative objectives

The principal quantitative objectives for the sales force are concerned with:

- how much to sell (volume);
- what to sell (product/service mix);
- where to sell (market segments and key customers);
- allowable costs; and
- profit margins.

The first three types of objective derive directly from the marketing objectives and constitute the principal components of the sales strategy. The sales plan is, in effect, a translation of these figures/products/customers into individual targets for each sales representative, taking into account special factors such as their territory size, the size of customers within a particular territory and so on.

### Qualitative objectives

Qualitative objectives should also be set. These will be related to the salespersons' skills in performing the job and can be appraised in terms of agreed standards of performance. The emphasis should be placed on measurable performance standards, such as expectations of work quality, efficiency, style and behaviour, rather than non-measurable factors, such as creativity, loyalty, interest and enthusiasm, which can easily be misconstrued as favouritism or unfairness. Given such standards, it is not too difficult for a competent field sales manager to identify deficiencies; to get agreement on them; to coach in skills and techniques; to build attitudes of professionalism; to show how to self-train;

| Customer type | Persona | Selling posture – main selling task consists of: | Key points about main selling task |
|---|---|---|---|
| Large/Phile (Box 1) | An important customer that has proved to be very loyal | (1) Maintaining contact – no more calls than absolutely necessary<br>(2) Communicating details of all new developments<br>(3) Responding to complaints (if any)<br>(4) Collecting information about general developments pertaining to the use of the product and/or competitive practices | (4) It is important that the client receives a copy of the company's annual report – and that salespeople are authorized to spend an appropriate amount on maintaining and developing the relationship |
| Large/Promiscuous (Box 4) | A fairly difficult customer, apt to change allegiance at the slightest opportunity and very sensitive to price. However, it is a large potential user and the business is worth having | (1) Identifying the motivational stimuli of the members of the decision-making unit in such companies (what makes them tick?)<br>(2) Planning sales presentations capable of demonstrating the cost/benefit and 'value-in-use' of the product<br>(3) Maintaining a careful record of competitive pressures likely to affect sales<br>(4) Demonstrating the selling company's ability and willingness to respond to problems and queries at all times<br>(5) Endeavouring to change the attitude of the prospect from Promiscuous to Phile | (5) Success in doing so will form part of the salesperson's performance appraisal system. Salespeople can be authorized to spend an appropriate amount on communicating with members of the client's decision-making unit provided they have identified the most appropriate people and can see a probability of a pay-off |

Table 16.2 Customer types, their personas and selling postures

| Customer type | Persona | Selling posture – main selling task consists of: | Key points about main selling task |
|---|---|---|---|
| Large/Phobe (Box 7) | A much more difficult customer to acquire and/or maintain. For some reason, known or unknown, it dislikes the supplying company to the point of phobia. It has large sales potential, but the amount of effort needed to convert the potential into results is probably prohibitive. This being so, the sales force should limit the time and effort it spends on such customers to the main tasks identified here | (1) Maintaining low-profile contact, if possible<br>(2) Endeavouring to diagnose the real reasons for the hostility and trying alternative solutions to any problems identified<br>(3) Monitoring changes in the company's ownership or personnel that might affect future relationships<br>(4) Keeping vigilant for serious let-downs or problems with other suppliers | (4) In general, salespeople must refrain from spending too much time or money on such unproductive clients until a change in attitude can be discerned |
| Medium/Phile (Box 2) | A loyal customer with a fairly good potential sales turnover. It is likely to buy without excessive sales effort | (1) Maintaining contact – no more than a few visits a year unless there are specific problems (strong telephone contact is preferred)<br>(2) Communicating details of all new developments – mainly by means of letters and/or personalized mailshots celebrations and Christmas | (2) Lavish expenditure should be discouraged, but customers in this category should be invited to fairs, exhibitions and other public promotional events. They should also be given preference for promotional items planned for anniversary |

Table 16.2 (Continued)

| | | | |
|---|---|---|---|
| Medium/Promiscuous (Box 5) | An awkward, fickle customer, but one whose business is not insignificant. Beware of wasting too much time on penetrating such accounts. The main objective must be to 'flirt' with them in a fairly low-key attempt to persuade them to mend their ways | (1) Identify the motivations of the decision-making unit to find what incentive is likely to convert its members from 'promiscuity' to loyalty<br>(2) Communicate at frequent intervals (although not through frequent personal visits) the great benefits of using the company's products | (2) Emphasis here is to be through mailshots, telephone calls and literature. Correspondingly, expenses must be kept to an absolute minimum and should only be used in exceptional circumstances |
| Medium/Phobe (Box 8) | A hostile customer with only medium purchasing justification for wasting too much selling effort on it | (1) Trying to determine the reason for the company's hostility<br>(2) Tracking and recording changes in the organization that might alleviate the phobia<br>(3) If the hostility stems from past mistakes, ensuring that any corrective measures are brought to the notice of the client<br>(4) Maintaining an up-to-date client dossier | (As for Large Phobe – Box 7) |
| Small/Phile (Box 3) | Although its loyalty is appreciated, the seller cannot reciprocate by giving it too much non-productive selling time | (1) Organizing an annual meeting to inform both all the small Philes of developments in the industry and the selling company (the meeting is a good opportunity for the small Philes and their friends in the sales force to demonstrate their mutual admiration) | (3) Happy communication can often be maintained through members of the sales administration team, who should be trained accordingly |

327

| Customer type | Persona | Selling posture – main selling task consists of: | Key points about main selling task |
|---|---|---|---|
| | | (2) Maintaining frequent (and less costly) telephone contact<br>(3) Ensuring that the restricted contact does not make the small and loyal customers feel unwanted | |
| Small/Promiscuous (Box 6) | This type of customer should mostly be ignored. They are small customers who feel that their limited purchasing power is sufficiently attractive to make selling organizations fight hard for their business. The only exceptions to this rule are when: | This type customer should mostly be ignored. They are small customers who feel that their limited purchasing power is sufficiently attractive to make selling organizations fight hard for their business. The only exceptions to this rule are when:<br>(1) There are indications that the firm is likely to become big in the future; and<br>(2) The customer is part of a larger organization that the selling company would like to penetrate | Very little time should be allocated to them. When they decide to become more loyal, they will receive more attention and affection. |
| Small/Phobe (Box 9) | Customers like these are more trouble than they are worth. Allow them to indulge their phobias in happy isolation. | Forget it! | |

Table 16.2 (Continued)

to determine which training requirements cannot be tackled in the field; and to evaluate improvements in performance and the effect of any past training.

## ENSURING SALES FORCE MOTIVATION

The key management activities involved in managing the sales force may be summarized as:

- setting performance standards (both quantifiable and qualitative);
- monitoring achievements;
- helping/training those who are falling behind; and
- setting the right motivational climate.

While monitoring what salespeople do can be accomplished largely through reports, sales figures and so on, assessing *how* they do things usually requires observing them in action. As a rule, the higher the uncertainty surrounding the salesperson, the territory, the product range, the customer and so on, the more frequently should performance be monitored. Having measurable standards of performance enables managers to identify the area and nature of help that salespeople need, and to respond appropriately. For example, they may need more information about prices and products, more support in terms of administration or joint visits, or more training to improve their skills set.

Perhaps most crucial of all is creating the right motivational climate. To maximize sales force performance it is necessary to achieve the optimal balance between incentives and disincentives. While remuneration will always be a key determinant of motivation, sales managers can improve sales force performance by clarifying performance expectations; providing rewards consistent with performance; giving due praise and recognition; ensuring freedom from fear and worry; and encouraging in their sales team a sense of doing a job that is worthwhile and valued.

Moreover, attractive remuneration does not necessarily mean paying the most money, although clearly, unless there are significant financial motivations within a company it is unlikely that people will stay. In drawing up a remuneration plan, which would normally include a basic salary plus some element for special effort such as bonus or commission, the following objectives should be considered:

- to attract and keep effective salespeople;
- to remain competitive;
- to reward salespeople in accordance with their individual performance;
- to provide a guaranteed income plus an orderly individual growth rate;
- to generate individual sales initiatives;

- to encourage teamwork;
- to encourage the performance of essential non-selling tasks; and
- to ensure that management can fairly administer and adjust compensation levels as a means of achieving sales objectives.

A central concept of sales force motivation is that the salespeople will exert more effort if they understand clearly what is expected of them, and what the concomitant rewards are for achieving their objectives.

Because of the uniqueness of each business situation and sales force make up, no two sales plans will be exactly the same. Nonetheless, some general guidelines can be given. Table 16.3 is an example of setting objectives for an individual salesperson. These objectives will be the logical result of breaking down the marketing objectives into actual sales targets.

# SUMMARY

Sales and marketing are clearly linked, yet require separate attention. The marketing process is only completed when a sale is made. It is essential that a sales force strategy be developed that is integrated closely with the overall marketing strategy. Where sales departments act independently of marketing, they often attain their short-term sales goals but fail to achieve the mix of products and markets consistent with longer-term strategic marketing objectives.

Personal selling offers the benefits of two-way communication, which advertising and sales promotion cannot provide. Sales messages can be made more customer-specific, questions can be asked and answered, and the salesperson can ask for an order and perhaps negotiate on price, delivery or special requirements. There is strong evidence that sales meetings can be enhanced by the use of mobile technologies, which enable sales personnel to access customer data and other information that can be a useful element of CRM.

Flexibility and personalization in communication can greatly enhance service levels and help to close sales, but it is worth noting that personal selling has a relatively high cost. When the total costs of recruiting, managing and providing salespeople with the necessary resources and support systems is considered, personal selling often accounts for more expenditure than advertising and sales promotion combined. It is therefore important to plan how personal selling will be integrated into the communications mix, and then to organize the logistics to ensure that the right results are achieved cost effectively.

| Task | Standard | How to set standards | How to measure performance | Performance shortfalls |
|---|---|---|---|---|
| 1. To achieve personal sales target | Sales target per period of time for individual groups and/or products | Analysis of<br>- territory potential<br>- individual customers' potential<br>Discussions and agreement between salesman and manager | Comparison of individual sales persons product sales against targets | Significant shortfall between target and achievement over a meaningful period |
| 2. To sell the required range and quantity to individual | The achievement of specified range and quantity of sales to a particular customer or group of customers within an agreed time period | Analysis of individual customer records of<br>- potential<br>- present sales<br>Discussion and agreement between manager and | Scrutiny of<br>- individual customer records<br>- observation of selling in the field sales person | Failure to achieve agreed objectives Complacency with range of sales made to individual customers |
| 3. To plan journeys and call frequencies to achieve minimum practicable selling cost | To achieve appropriate call frequency on individual customers. Number of live customer calls during a given time period | Analysis of individual customers' potential Analysis of order/call ratios Discussion and agreement between manager and sales person | Scrutiny of<br>- individual customer records<br>Analysis of order/call ratio. Examination of call reports | High ratio of calls to individual customer relative to that customer's yield. Shortfall on agreed total number of calls made over an agreed time period |

Table 16.3 Setting objectives for an individual sales representative

| Task | Standard | How to set standards | How to measure performance | Performance shortfalls |
|---|---|---|---|---|
| 4. To acquire new customers | Number of prospect calls during time period Selling new products to existing customers | Identify total number of potential and actual customers who could produce results. Identify opportunity areas for prospecting | Examination of<br>■ call reports<br>■ records of new accounts opened<br>■ ratio of existing to potential customers | Shortfall in number of prospect calls from agreed standard. Low ratio of existing to potential customers |
| 5. To make a sales approach of the required quality | To exercise the necessary skills and techniques to achieve the identified objective of each element of the sales approach | Standards to be agreed in discussion between manager and sales person related to company standards laid down | Regular observations of field selling using a systematic analysis of performance at each stage of the sales approach | Failure to identify<br>■ objective of each stage of sales approach<br>■ specific areas of skill/weakness<br>■ use of support material |

Table 16.3 (Continued)

The benefits to sales force management of following the strategic approach detailed in this chapter can be summarized as:

- Co-ordination of corporate and marketing objectives with actual sales effort.

- Establishment of a circular relationship between corporate objectives and customer wants that enriches the delivery of customer value.

- Improvement of sales effectiveness through an understanding of the corporate and marketing implications of sales decisions.

# FURTHER READING

Jobber, D. and Lancaster, G. (2012) *Selling and Sales Management*, Harlow: Pearson

A practical guide covering the nature and role of selling and sales management as well as practical, detailed advice on sales strategies and tools.

# REFERENCES

Hunter, G. and Perreault, W.D. (2006) Sales Technology Orientation, Information Effectiveness, and Sales Performance, *Journal of Personal Selling & Sales Management*, Vol. 26 (2): 95–113.

Rapp, A., Agnihotri, R. and Forbes, L.P. (2008) The Sales Force Technology Performance Chain: The Role of Adaptive Selling and Effort, *Journal of Personal Selling & Sales Management*, Vol. 28 (4): 335–350.

Rodriguez, M. and Honeycutt, E. (2011) CRM's Impact on B2B Sales Professionals' Collaboration and Sales Performance, *Journal of Business-to-Business Marketing*, Vol. 18 (4): 335–356.

Sharma, A. and Sheth, J.N. (2010) A Framework of Technology Mediation in Consumer Selling: Implications for Firms and Sales Management, *Journal of Personal Selling and Sales Management*, Vol. 30 (2): 121–129.

# CHAPTER 17
# CHANNEL STRATEGY

IN THIS CHAPTER WE STUDY:

- the link between communication channels and distribution channels
- alternative channels of distribution
- role, selection and development of channel intermediaries
- options and techniques for determining channel strategy
- types of channel objectives that need to be considered
- the impact of e-commerce on channel structure
- key elements of effective channel management

# THE LINK BETWEEN CHANNELS OF PHYSICAL DISTRIBUTION AND PROMOTION

Marketing channel strategy is one of the major strategic areas of marketing management. We begin this chapter by emphasizing the close link between physical distribution channels and promotional channels, as outlined in Figure 17.1. Promotion and distribution have been transformed by new channels such as the Internet, being simultaneously more transparent and more complex.

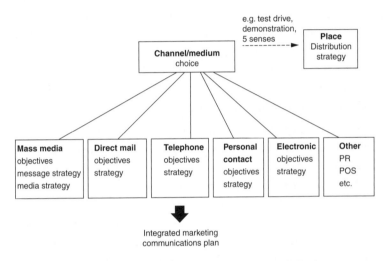

Figure 17.1 The link between communication and distribution channels
*Source:* McDonald and Wilson (2002).

Channel and medium choices are closely intertwined with distribution strategy, as distribution channels often have a mix of purposes, providing both a means of conveying a physical product to the customer and a medium for exchange of information. A car showroom, for example, provides information on car models, an opportunity for a test drive, a location where price negotiations can occur and a step in the physical delivery of the chosen car to the customer. A clothes shop provides a location where the information exchange of feeling a garment and trying it on can occur in a way that is difficult to replicate using direct marketing approaches. Similarly, the Internet can be both a promotional medium and a physical delivery outlet. So, the focus of promotion and information exchange is linked closely to the physical issues of distribution. In this chapter we focus exclusively on physical distribution channels, despite the web this is still a major domain in marketing and needs in-depth consideration in its own right.

# CHANNELS OF DISTRIBUTION

The fundamental role of a company's distribution function is to ensure that 'the right product is available at the right time'. This implies some organization of resources into channels through which the product moves to customers. A distribution channel may therefore be considered as the course taken in the transfer of the title of a product (or service) from its original source of supply to its ultimate consumer. It is necessary to consider both the route of exchange (and its administrative and financial control) and the physical movement of the product – as they may well be different.

As we have seen, distribution channels often have a mix of purposes, providing both a means of conveying a physical product to the customer and a means of exchanging information and ideas. For this reason, the selection, development and management of distribution channels are doubly important. When we consider that route-to-market decisions tend to be long term as they are difficult to change once established, we see that channel strategy is a significant and enduring aspect of marketing strategy.

Typically, many companies will not pay too much attention to the question of channel choice, as it is not regarded as a variable in the marketing mix. (*Place* emphasizes the actual sales outlet; that is, the 'destination' rather than the 'journey'.) More often than not, the distribution channel will have taken its current form as a result of unplanned and haphazard development. Such a disregard for this vital area of marketing discretion means that many opportunities for profitable market potential are passed over. For example, an international chemical company selling into Europe, using their own sales force to sell direct to customers, found that by using a chemical merchant they could reduce their own sales costs and take advantage of a ready-made sales organization with a host of local contacts.

Another British company, a carpet manufacturer, was perplexed by its falling sales as total carpet sales in the United Kingdom remained at a high level. It was felt that the company had in some way got its quality or pricing levels wrong. In fact, a deeper examination of the company's situation showed that the culprit was its continued policy of selling through small, traditional, high-street carpet shops. The new growth outlets were clearly the edge-of-town carpet warehouses, which often offered discounts. These distributors now accounted for the lion's share of carpet sales, and the manufacturer had missed a wonderful opportunity by failing to recognize the change in distribution patterns and respond accordingly.

These examples demonstrate the benefits of taking a fresh look at distribution channels. Each involved a reappraisal of the route by which the customer acquired the product, and a comparison of the costs and benefits of other distribution options.

Many companies do not rely on a single channel of distribution but prefer instead to use multiple channels. They may choose different channels to reach different market segments, or they may approach a single market via a mix of channels. In such cases it is important to ensure that no conflicts exist between channels, particularly in terms of price competition. For example, an insurance company that is seeking to set up a direct, telephone-based sales channel will have to be careful that its established business using insurance brokers is not affected adversely.

Ultimately, the choice of channel(s) must be based on the long-term balance of the benefits and the costs of that choice. As Figure 17.2 shows, each channel can have distinctly different cost and revenue profiles. The channels of distribution available run the gamut from direct to indirect, and from traditional media to the Internet. The choice of channel(s) will have an impact on the organization's current and future levels of service effectiveness, customer closeness, operational efficiency and corporate profitability. Any cost/benefit appraisal of channels therefore needs to be undertaken in the widest possible context. It needs to consider questions of marketing strategy, the appropriateness of the channel to the product, customer requirements and the question of the comparative costs of selling and distribution. Marketing channel decisions, then, are *key* decisions, which involve the choice of an intermediary (or intermediaries) and detailed consideration of the physical distribution implications of the alternatives.

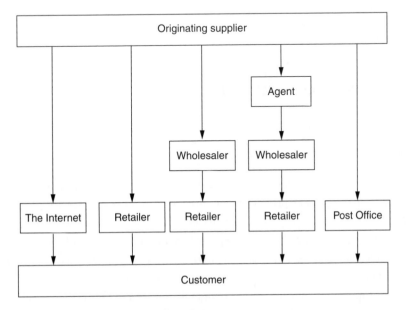

Figure 17.2 Alternative channels of distribution

# CHANNEL INTERMEDIARIES

The basic channel strategy decision is whether to sell direct to users, or to use some form of intermediary. The choice may be straightforward in that the costs incurred by selling direct may be just too high. When the decision is not so clear-cut, the choice will depend on an evaluation of the advantages and disadvantages of using intermediaries. The point is that the functions performed by intermediaries must be done by somebody in order that the final customer finds the overall offer worthwhile. Strategic decisions about channels are therefore concerned with who should perform these functions, and where they should be located.

## THE ROLE OF CHANNEL INTERMEDIARIES

The role of an intermediary is to provide the means of achieving the widest possible market coverage at a lower unit cost than would be possible by supplying direct. Many intermediaries hold stock, and thereby share some of the financial risk with the principal or supplier. They may also use the same transport and storage facilities for a number of suppliers' products, thereby spreading the overheads and thus reducing the costs of distribution for each supplier. This important consolidation role is highlighted in Figure 17.3.

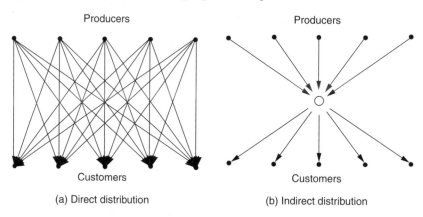

| Producers | Producers |

(a) Direct distribution  (b) Indirect distribution

Figure 17.3 Direct distribution and indirect distribution

Apart from being more cost effective, an intermediary should also complement the supplier's product range, pricing aspirations and service policies. Improved service response can be achieved by intermediaries who are closer to customers geographically, or who possess better local knowledge of the needs of customers in their area. In addition, intermediaries can enhance customer value through such means as one-stop shopping, systems integration, special packaging or supplying in smaller, rather than bulk, quantities. This is the concept of a 'value-added distributor'.

The potential benefits of using intermediaries include:

- access to markets;
- economies of scale through consolidation;
- final product configuration;
- selling and promotion;
- provision of trade credit;
- holding inventory; and
- installation and customer training.

While using an intermediary carries benefits for the manufacturer, it also involves significant 'costs', the most important of which is the *loss of control* that accompanies such a channel strategy. As Figure 17.4 shows, there is no guarantee that an intermediary will present or position the supplier's products in the most appropriate way, or that priority will be given over other suppliers' products. There is also a *loss of customer contact* and a risk that an intermediary may withhold customer information, either because of the inconvenience of passing it on to the supplier, or the advantage it provides in relationship negotiations. Often, too, disparity exists between the respective objectives of the supplier and the intermediary, leading to conflict and suspicion in the relationship. Clearly, then, the use of intermediaries is accompanied by a possible *loss of opportunity*.

Intermediaries also represent a real and measurable cost to the supplier in terms of *margin forgone*. It is important to remember that any margin allowed to intermediaries should not be seen as a sharing of the supplier's profit. Rather, the margin should be regarded as a recompense for the transfer of cost from the supplier to the intermediary. Thus, for example, if a wholesaler carries an inventory on behalf of a manufacturer, the wholesaler will incur a holding cost on that inventory. Since, presumably, this relieves the manufacturer of the need to carry that inventory, the wholesaler can be recompensed to the extent of the cost saved by the supplier. The concept of the *channel margin* is important in this context.

The channel margin can be defined as the difference between the price in the final market – the 'street price' – and the price paid to the supplier – the 'factory gate price': channel margin = street price – factory gate price.

One UK manufacturer of car batteries was surprised by what it learned when it commissioned a market research study on some of its Far East markets to see how high (and how variable) the street price was in comparison with the factory gate price. The question posed was: are the benefits we derive through our channel intermediaries – namely, market access, inventory carrying and so forth, greater than or equal to the cost we pay (the channel margin)? The company concluded that it should seek to establish a more direct channel to

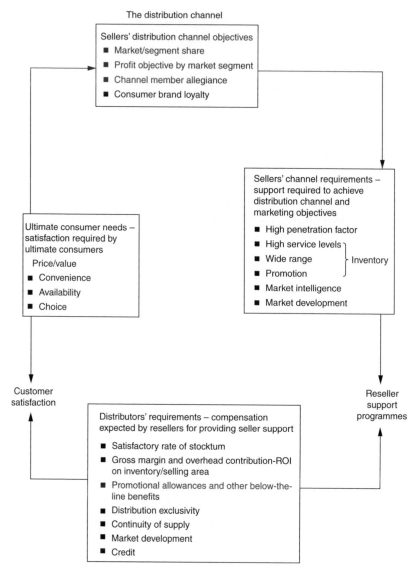

The distribution channel

Sellers' distribution channel objectives
- Market/segment share
- Profit objective by market segment
- Channel member allegiance
- Consumer brand loyalty

Sellers' channel requirements –
support required to achieve
distribution channel and
marketing objectives
- High penetration factor
- High service levels ⎫
- Wide range ⎬ Inventory
- Promotion ⎭
- Market intelligence
- Market development

Ultimate consumer needs –
satisfaction required by
ultimate consumers
Price/value
- Convenience
- Availability
- Choice

Customer
satisfaction

Reseller
support
programmes

Distributors' requirements – compensation
expected by resellers for providing seller support
- Satisfactory rate of stocktum
- Gross margin and overhead contribution-ROI
  on inventory/selling area
- Promotional allowances and other below-the-
  line benefits
- Distribution exclusivity
- Continuity of supply
- Market development
- Credit

Figure 17.4 The distribution channel

eliminate multiple steps in the chain from factory to consumer. A recent survey suggests that the channel margin can typically account for between 15 per cent and 40 per cent of the retail price of goods.

If the organization decides to sell indirectly through intermediaries, the next decision becomes one of which intermediary or intermediaries to use.

## THE SELECTION OF CHANNEL INTERMEDIARIES

A wide variety of channel intermediaries exist who will perform sales, distribution and service functions on behalf of a supplier. The major types are listed in

| Major types of intermediaries | |
|---|---|
| • Retailers in or out of town | • Direct mail retailers |
| • Wholesalers | • Franchised outlets |
| • Distributors | • Freight forwarders |
| • Dealers | • Merchandise clubs |
| • Agents | • Party sales organizers |
| • Value-added resellers | • Licensed manufacturers/service operators |
| • Original equipment manufacturers | • Websites |
| • Catalogue distributors | • Brokers |

Table 17.1 Major types of intermediaries

Table 17.1. A particular intermediary may be a single type, or a combination of two or more types. The appropriate number and types of intermediaries will vary according to the industry concerned.

For many companies, selecting an intermediary (or intermediaries) could prove to be one of the most important decisions they ever make. Without doubt, an efficient and motivated intermediary can be a priceless asset, while a lacklustre one could ruin the company. A multitude of factors could influence the choice decision. Table 17.2 shows the results of a survey conducted of a sample of UK firms to discover the criteria used for selecting intermediaries.

| Criteria | UK ranking |
|---|---|
| Knowledge of the market | 1 |
| Market coverage | 2 |
| Enthusiasm for the product | 3 |
| Number and quality of sales personnel | 4 |
| Knowledge of product | 5 |
| Frequency of sales calls | 6 |
| Previous success/track record | 7 |
| Costs involved | 8 |
| Extent of dealing with competitors | 9 |
| Service and stocking facilities | 10 |
| Quality of service staff | 11 |
| Executives' career history | 12 |

Table 17.2 Intermediary selection criteria

These factors are listed in order of rank, with the most important at the top of the list.

Clearly, these findings underline the fact that many of the key selection criteria relate to the intermediaries' marketing expertise and strength 'on the ground'. However, others would add the following considerations to this list and suggest that they should also figure in any selection process:

- Is the intermediary creditworthy?
- Does the intermediary create the right image?
- Are their policies regarding inventory and customer service compatible with our company's?
- Are their total promotion activities and budgets what we would expect for success?
- Are their locations consistent with our overall distribution strategy?
- Does the intermediary carry competitor lines?

And perhaps the most important of all:

- Is the intermediary someone we can trust and with whom we could develop a good working relationship?

If the answer to the last question is negative, then all the other criteria are largely redundant, because the secret of success is to select intermediaries who, in effect, become business partners. Implicit in this is that the relationship between the parties be conducted in an open and mature manner. For channel relationships to succeed, they must be forged with clarity of purpose and be fostered through mutual trust, commitment and gain.

# THE DEVELOPMENT OF CHANNEL INTERMEDIARIES

At a company conference, to which, for the first time, a manufacturer's overseas agents had been invited, discussion focused on communications. It is sad to report that the agents claimed unanimously that the only time they had ever had a visit from representatives of the company was 'when things went wrong'. Not only that, they also felt that they were kept 'in the dark' regarding future plans and new products.

The company in question was to be commended for taking such a bold step in organizing this conference as a means of integrating the agents more fully into the organization. The aim of the conference had been to learn how the agents perceived the company, and to use this knowledge to improve relationships. The company was surprised to find that, by seeming to focus on negative parts of the relationship, they had caused the agents to develop a defensive attitude: instead of trust, they had bred distrust.

The conference did, in fact, provide both the company and the agents with the opportunity to air difficult issues and to work through them amicably. Indeed, the event proved to be a watershed in the company's relationships with its overseas representatives.

So how can a supplier build a good relationship with an intermediary? Here are some tried and tested methods:

- *Understand the distributor's needs and problems.* This means getting out and talking to them regularly, not just when things go wrong. One company insists that its own sales representatives spend a set number of days per year 'working on the counter' in the distributors' premises.
- *Learn from distributors' experiences.* Monitor and feed back into internal knowledge management systems information about common problems, emerging opportunities, market trends and so on.
- *Conduct market research studies.* Encourage distributors to provide annual appraisals of the service they receive from supplier's and make recommendations about improvements. Alternatively, conduct customer surveys and share the results with distributors. Positive results will enable them to increase sales, while negative results will allow them to help address evident weaknesses.
- *Create a distributor panel.* Have a small group of specially selected distributors meet at regular intervals to act as a sounding board for future policies and to get feedback on current issues.
- *Invite distributors' input in the development of the marketing plan.* This will encourage them to 'buy in' to those parts of the plan that make an impact upon distribution.
- *Establish two-way communications.* Ensure dialogue at many different levels – for example, director to director, salesperson to salesperson, clerk to clerk and so on.
- *Demonstrate commitment to the distributor.* Refer customer enquiries and requests to the distributor and do not open up competing distributorships in their territory.

Later in the chapter we shall see how treating channel intermediaries as partners enhances channel management. First, however, let us consider the channel strategy options available, and understand that the use of intermediaries is not a foregone conclusion.

# CHANNEL STRATEGY OPTIONS

At first sight, the choice of channel strategy is deceptively easy. After all, there are basically only three options from which to choose:

1. Sell direct to the customer/user;

2. Sell to customers/users through intermediaries; or

3. Use a combination of 1 and 2 – that is, dual distribution.

However, the final choice of strategy will always be something of a compromise between the natural desire to keep control of the distribution of a supplier's products and the practical need to keep distribution costs to a bearable level. Pursuing a multiple-channel strategy (for example, using a direct channel alongside intermediaries) entails higher costs, but evidence suggests that consumers use different channels during their life cycle (Neslin and Shankar, 2009), so customer type (first time or repeat) needs to be considered alongside issues of complementarity and cannibalization.

The distribution channel algorithm given in Figure 17.5 can be helpful in deciding channels of distribution, in particular in determining whether intermediaries are required.

Growth in the number, type and sophistication of distribution channels is mirrored in the range of strategy options available. The addition of the Internet and mobile devices to the more conventional channels has expanded the choice of individual as well as integrated routes to market. And with greater channel choice has come stiffer competition. Companies such as Direct Line, First Direct, EasyJet, eBay and Amazon all compete by exploiting IT-enabled remote channels to add value, reduce costs or both.

The opportunities these IT-enabled channels present for building profitable customer relationships are huge. Witness the rapid take-up of packages for sales force automation, direct mail, telemarketing, customer service, e-commerce and marketing analysis, which are available both separately and together as integrated CRM suites. But these packages, while providing an essential infrastructure, need to be supplemented by managerial processes to address such fundamental questions as which channels to use and how best to use them to deliver customer value.

Our research suggests that companies can select from the following broad channel strategy options:

## SINGLE CHANNEL STRATEGY

The organization provides at least the bulk of the customer interaction through one channel. Direct Line and First Direct both started as primarily telephone

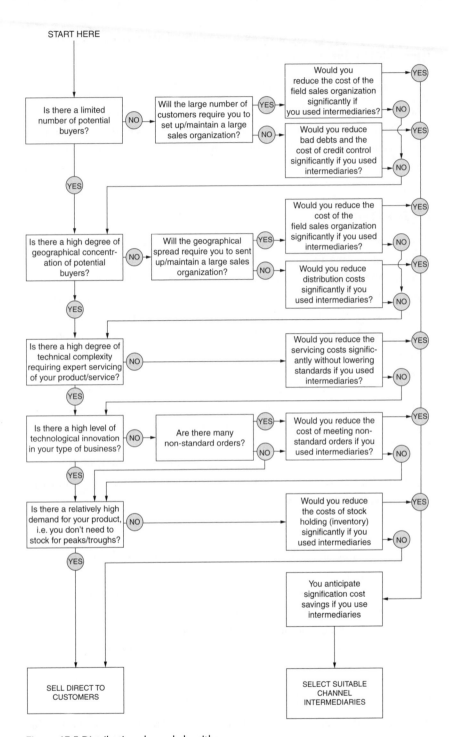

Figure 17.5 Distribution channel algorithm

operations, while in the Internet world the approach is referred to as 'pure play', represented by Amazon, eBay and so on.

## CHANNEL MIGRATION STRATEGY

The organization starts with one single channel, but is attempting to migrate its customer base on to another channel on the grounds of increased value or reduced cost. EasyJet initially sold tickets by telephone, but now provides financial incentives to its price-sensitive customers to buy online, most of whom now do so.

## INTEGRATED MULTI-CHANNEL STRATEGY

The organization offers different, interconnected channels to the customer without attempting to influence which one(s) the customer uses. A strategy based on the integration of multiple channels offers greater scope for respecting customers' channel preferences and propensities of use, thereby enhancing the organization's attractiveness and, ultimately, responsiveness to customers. It also works to ensure a 'seamless' customer experience, which will promote a stronger and longer customer relationship. Thomas Cook uses the Internet to generate leads and to take bookings, a direct sales force to sign up new major clients, a call centre to take orders and its shops to do all these things. The point here is that Thomas Cook empowers its customers to choose how to access them. First Direct provides both telephone and Internet banking as an integrated service. While the Internet has much lower unit costs, and also has proved better for cross-selling, First Direct chooses to position itself on customer service and accept the higher costs from those customers who primarily use the telephone without penalizing them or rewarding Internet users.

## NEEDS-BASED SEGMENTATION STRATEGY

The organization offers different channels to different customer groups to meet their varying needs. Each of these routes to market may use the same brand name, or different names. The insurer Zurich has multiple brands: Allied Dunbar, Zurich and Threadneedle. Each brand has strengths in different routes to market – the direct sales force, independent financial advisers and company pension schemes – in order to serve customer groups with differing needs and attitudes.

## GRADUATED CUSTOMER VALUE STRATEGY

The organization uses channels selectively according to the financial value of the customers. Many IT firms use account managers for high-value customers, and steer smaller customers to lower-cost channels such as the Internet, call centres or value-added resellers. The United Kingdom's clearing banks, however, are in danger of doing precisely the opposite; offering the high-cost branch network to the lower-value customers who prefer not to bank via telephone or the Internet.

The reason why channel strategy decisions are long term is because each party will require commitment from the other, and the creation of any arrangement will involve considerable investment of both time and money. The decisions will be based on trade-offs between control, cost and marketing objectives.

Selecting the most appropriate channel strategy for any given market at any given time means ensuring it is aligned to and supportive of both the needs and expectations of customers, and the requirements and capabilities of the supplier.

# DETERMINING CHANNEL STRATEGY

## VALUE ANALYSIS

When deciding on a channel strategy, the starting point must be the customers themselves. If we do not offer them the channels they would prefer to use, a competitor will. But with new channels, how can we predict customer take-up in advance? Figure 17.6 shows a simple technique for doing this, called *value analysis*. It operates in a similar vein to benefit analysis (see Chapters 4 and 8). Value analysis amounts to plotting the relative strength of those factors that exert greatest influence on customer purchase preference for each type of channel used.

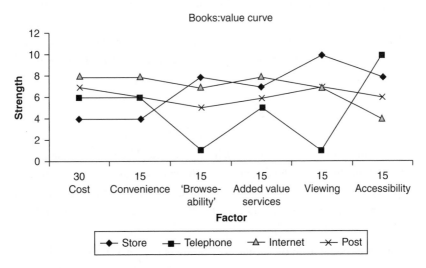

Figure 17.6 Value analysis: the book market
*Source*: McDonald and Wilson (2002).

Value analysis begins with an identification of the customers' buying factors – the factors that determine which supplier gets their business. These are listed on the horizontal axis of Figure 17.6, along with weights out of 100, which represent their relative importance in the purchase decision. These factors will vary by customer segment, so the analysis must be done for each one. In the segment illustrated here, the customers are most interested in the cost they pay – the price plus any other charges such as delivery – but are also concerned with such factors as convenience of purchase and the ability to browse for the book they want.

The ability of each current or future channel to deliver against each factor is then assessed judgementally on a 1–10 basis. In this hypothetical example, the various means by which a book can be purchased are compared. It can be seen that taking all the factors together, the Internet and physical stores have the best matches to this particular segment. In reality, different segments of the book market are clearly best matched to different channels.

The score of a channel against price-related factors, such as 'cost' in this example, will be affected by the channel economics, which will determine the price that any competitor using the channel chain will be able to offer. Channel economics should be assessed by transaction, acquisition and retention costs; the dot.com arm of a retail chain recently discovered that customer acquisition through banner advertising was costing them £700 per customer, while the average sale was only £50. The good news for this bricks-and-clicks retailer in its competition with pure-play dot.coms was that it could leverage its physical stores for customer acquisition at a cost of just £13 per customer.

This example of physical stores and the Internet working together illustrates a complicating factor. In many markets, customers do not use a single channel. Rather, they use a number of channels in combination to meet their needs at different stages of their relationship with the supplier. To help define how this can best be done, we suggest using a tool termed *channel chain analysis*, which is portrayed in Figure 17.7.

## CHANNEL CHAIN ANALYSIS

Channel chain analysis involves describing which channels are used at which stages of the purchasing and value delivery process. The stages of the process are listed on the left of the diagram, and the channels used to accomplish the stage are listed against each stage. The channel used for one stage will often affect which channel is likely to be used at the next stage, so the relevant boxes are joined with a line.

In this example from the business-to-business PC market, three of the common channel chains being offered by the various competitors are illustrated. The channel chain on the left shows the traditional account management

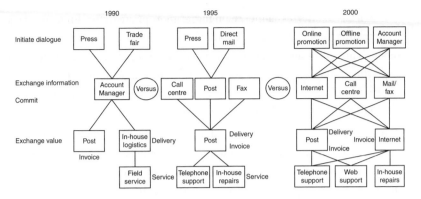

**Figure 17.7 Channel chain analysis: the PC market**
*Source*: McDonald and Wilson (2002).

approach in which the sales process is largely handled face-to-face by account managers. Nowadays, this model tends to be complemented by other channel chains that offer better channel economics for smaller deals.

One of these new channel chains was the direct model, illustrated in the centre of Figure 17.7 under the heading '1995'. Here, press advertising formed the dominant marketing tool, with further information being provided by product brochures and call centre staff. The actual order could be placed via a number of means – often a traditional fax or mail order placed by the accounts department.

More recently, many competitors have added the Internet to the channel mix, as illustrated on the right of the diagram. But most of these are far from pure-play Internet providers. Account managers might serve major accounts via building relationships and negotiating discount levels. This frees them from the details of product configuration and pricing by the website, while the order itself is as likely to be placed by fax or post as it is on the web.

Different channels, then, are needed at different points in the sales cycle, and different competitors may adopt different approaches. It is easy to imagine a fourth, pure-play Internet channel chain, which has a low-cost structure and is appropriate to certain price-sensitive segments. Indeed, there are competitors adopting this e-channel approach.

Having drawn the channel chains in current use, the next step is to consider possible future channel chains. This requires experimentation with channel chain diagrams to think through not only how the sale is to be made but also how every other aspect of the customer's needs is to be satisfied. Will a mobile phone purchaser buying over the Internet be able to return a faulty phone to a nearby store? Will an e-hub be able to handle not just price negotiations but also information flows on stock levels, complaints, returns and product development – and if not, what additional channels will be needed?

The trick is to offer a channel chain that is appropriate to the differing needs of a company's target segments. In other words, the acid test as to whether a channel chain will flourish is whether it represents a better value proposition to a specific group of customers. To test this, we recommend drawing the value curve we described earlier under value analysis, but comparing channel chains rather than the individual channels themselves.

There is a timing issue to be considered as well. Even if a channel chain offers a theoretically better proposition to customers, they may not yet be ready for it. A channel chain innovation, like a product innovation, is likely to proceed along the lines of Rogers' bell-shaped diffusion of innovation curve (see Figure 9.1). For example, in order to encourage customers to purchase online, it is necessary to consider what proportion of the customer base has Internet access, and a preference and proficiency in using it to make purchases.

## CHANNEL OBJECTIVES

The underlying purpose of the distribution channel is to reach the customer in the most appropriate and cost-effective way. This means giving consideration to both the customer's buying objectives and the supplier's selling objectives and achieving a productive balance of the two.

# CUSTOMER OBJECTIVES

While the requirements of the customer might vary from market to market, it is possible to generalize customer objectives relating to the decision of where to buy the product.

## PRICE/VALUE

This dimension is present to a greater or lesser extent in all markets. It implies that the customer is seeking a certain level of value or utility from the product or service, but there is an implicit trade-off between that value and the price charged. In this way, shoppers in the United Kingdom have a wide choice before them. At one end of the spectrum they can buy their groceries at Harrods; and at the other end they can choose the no-frills approach of Lidl or Aldi.

In industrial service markets the same principles of price/value optimization apply; the only difference is that professional buyers are likely to use formalized evaluation techniques, such as value analysis, to help them to reach their purchase decision.

## CONVENIENCE/AVAILABILITY

It has long been recognized that these factors can play a key role in competitive markets. For example, in the United Kingdom, estate agents who traditionally played the role of 'marriage broker' between seller and buyer, now offer a range of ancillary services, providing prospective buyers with convenient one-stop shopping. The recognition of this simple truth has led to some major financial service companies buying into estate agencies as distribution outlets for their products.

On the industrial front, manufacturers of high-density polyurethane foam plastic, which is used extensively in furniture upholstery, often set up plants where there is a high concentration of furniture manufacturers. Not only does this reduce the high transport costs of shipping 'bubbles of air' around the country, which would be the case if they were to move blocks of plastic foam great distances, but it also virtually guarantees supplies 'on tap' for the furniture companies.

## CHOICE

Choice of channel is, of course, a key component of competitive differentiation. The range of distribution channels made available to customers will not only determine how the supplier interacts with customers, and vice versa, but also how the supplier is perceived by customers. Customers who believe they are being valued in the treatment they receive, and their needs are being reflected in product or service offerings, are more likely to feel an affinity towards the supplier and to reward the supplier with their custom.

Issues underlying customer perception might include the following questions: Is it a 'customer-orientated' supplier, demonstrably aware of customer channel preferences and accessibility? Is it a 'technologically current' supplier, dedicated to channel innovation and investing in the introduction of new or improved channels where relevant? Is it a 'future-thinking' supplier, actively planning for long-term sustainability rather than short-term gain? Is it a 'market-smart' supplier, visibly adept at exploiting the competitive environment in order to provide consistently superior customer value? Such concerns underline the significance for suppliers of appreciating and acting on manifestations of customer discernment.

# SUPPLIER OBJECTIVES

The selection of distribution channels must fit the requirements and capabilities of the supplier in addition to meeting the objectives of the customer.

Essentially, the supplier's channel objectives embrace *market, institutional* and *marketing* considerations.

Here is an example of how market considerations might influence the choice of channel. Suppose we were marketing financial services to individuals in the high tax bracket. It would not be appropriate to set up a network of door-to-door salespeople. Instead we would be likely to choose an indirect channel of distribution that might rely upon intermediaries such as accountants and bank managers to connect us with our target customers. Clearly, we would also be faced with making decisions regarding geographical coverage and penetration of our market, but these decisions are far less difficult to make once we are clear about our distribution channels.

Institutionally, the supplier should be concerned with issues such as image and appropriateness of the channel. For example, if we produced top-quality goods with a somewhat elitist image, then we will be wise to seek distribution channels that are consistent with this image. It would be counter-productive to do anything less.

Suppliers must also decide where to focus marketing efforts. They have two main marketing strategies open to them if they want to maximize the flow of their goods through the channel:

1. *Push strategy*. Here the supplier focuses attention on the distributor and uses an armoury of different approaches to 'sell-in' more of their products. They might use their field sales force, advertising and special promotions aimed at the distributor and their special incentive schemes. The use of 'trade marketing', whereby the supplier works closely with the distributor in developing joint marketing programmes, has become widespread since the 1990s.

2. *Pull strategy*. Here the focus of attention is the customer, and the objective of the strategy is to stimulate the level of demand so that the distributor is encouraged to stock the product. Marketing techniques used could include TV advertising, national press advertising and promotions and in-store demonstrations and exhibitions.

In practice, most manufacturers would probably use a combination of push and pull strategies consistent with their marketing objectives and their capabilities.

The marketing strategy might also involve the development of different channels over time. For example, a direct sales force can help an organization to prove that a market exists through obtaining early market penetration, but is then replaced by dealers to obtain intensive distribution as a market grows. This may be followed by a move to exclusive distribution to create brand value in a mature market. Since the Internet revolution, it has become common to add a web-enabled direct channel to the existing channel mix. In some cases, this has been very successful; in others, some cannibalization and logistical problems have occurred. In studying the impact of adding a new channel, Avery et al. (2012) find that both the type of channel being added and the composition of the existing channels already in the channel mix matter because different channels have different capabilities. Thus, the outcome of adding a direct channel (the Internet) to a retail store channel differs from the addition of a retail store to an Internet channel. Managers need to be cognizant of such detail when planning an extension to their channel strategy. The decisions involved in determining channel strategy are not easy but can influence success in the market significantly.

# CHANNEL MANAGEMENT

Having devised a channel strategy, it must then be managed expertly if optimal return on investment is to be achieved. One element of good channel management is understanding the different contributions of customers (in terms of revenue streams, lifetime value, customer referrals and so on) and exploiting this individuality. Where indirect selling is used, suppliers have to develop appropriate relationships with their intermediaries so that working arrangements complement their marketing objectives and minimize the problems of control and access to market information. Organizations can ensure effective channel management through attention to channel structure, channel motivation, channel partnership, channel conflict and channel performance.

## CHANNEL STRUCTURE

Until relatively recently there was relatively little innovation in the structure of distribution channels. Organizations have assumed that distribution channels are, by their nature, fixed and not easily changed. However, the phenomenal impact of the Internet and other technologies has challenged traditional thinking and paved the way for new ideas about how products and services should reach the marketplace. This has led to rapid development of multi-channel and cross-channel strategies.

The Internet has been particularly significant. With the advent of the web, many companies pursued a strategy of disintermediation, in which one or more intermediaries were removed along the supply chain. In some industries, this has produced real cost and time benefits for consumers, for example, buying books or music online, purchasing travel tickets and holidays. Self-service banking has eroded the need for high-street branches, and telephone-based insurance companies have diminished the need for field sales representatives. But intermediaries have not disappeared completely; on the contrary, new types of intermediaries have emerged offering specialist knowledge and expertise across a range of services, for example, finance, law, business consultancy.

Organizations seeking to redesign channel strategy must revisit and redesign their market maps, evaluating the implications of consequent changes in the value chain. There are five main ways in which the market map can be reconfigured, as outlined in Table 17.3.

When reviewing or revising channel structure, an organization should consider whether alterations to channel structure are advisable in the light of existing relationships and are sustainable given the inevitability of market and technological change. Which channel structure will be appropriate for the organization, for a particular channel type, will depend on which method can best attract end consumers in the target market/segment. This in turn will depend on the organization's ability to create and deliver value relevant to those customers' needs – and thus to the commercial requirements of intermediaries.

## CHANNEL MOTIVATION

The prime focus of intermediaries is satisfying their own customers, since they are their source of income. Intermediaries will also be concerned with issues of stock turnover and profit margin and will tend to concentrate their efforts on the products that sell most easily. Suppliers must therefore actively encourage their intermediaries to give priority to their products and not those of competitors'. Intermediaries can be motivated to act in the supplier's interests (as well as their own) through reducing prices or making the margin available more inviting. Suppliers should endeavour to minimize the risk of stock-outs on the part of the intermediaries, which may result from their reluctance to hold large inventories. At the same time, suppliers must stimulate intermediaries to promote their products rather than just wait for customers to turn up.

Perhaps the most important aspect of motivating intermediaries is to remember that they are, themselves, a market, and not just someone in the middle being paid to provide a service for the supplier. As a market, intermediaries' problems need to be solved in ways that recognize their perception of value. This will encourage them to be advocates for their suppliers. Areas of value to intermediaries include:

- sales support materials;
- market research about intermediaries' markets;
- advanced information about product development;
- fast responses to technical queries;
- the creation of market pull;

| Ways to redraw market maps | Inherent questions | Examples |
| --- | --- | --- |
| *Product substitution/reconfiguration:* The underlying need for a product or service is replaced by a better option | Does an electronic channel enable the underlying customer need to be satisfied in a different way ('substitute products') or to be bundled into different product configurations ('reconfigured products'), which adds value? | A newspaper (bundled product) competes with web services that also provide news, job adverts, weather updates, etc. |
| *Disintermediation:* There is one less link in the chain by removing an intermediary whose primary function of information transfer can be performed more effectively by using the Internet | Does the removal of an intermediary improve physical flows? If so, can information flows or other value-adding services provided by the intermediary be handled as effectively by others in the chain? | Telephone and Internet banking |
| *Re-intermediation:* A previous intermediary is replaced by a new on-line intermediary, rather than bypassed | Does the replacement of an existing intermediary with a new on-line intermediary afford advantages in terms of cost-effectiveness and customer value? Do these advantages outweigh the negative implications of stopping one relationship and starting another? | On-line sites which search automatically for the cheapest car insurance compete with telephone-based car insurance brokers |
| *Partial channel substitution:* An intermediary's role may be reduced but not eliminated, with some of its value being provided remotely by the supplier to the intermediary's customer | Does the addition of an Internet communication channel improve information flows (e.g., faster, easier and cheaper communication with the customer)? | Car manufacturers' websites build the brand and provide customer information while pointing customers to traditional outlets for their actual purchase |
| *Media switching/addition:* Links in the chain may remain the same, but communication between them may be partially or fully switched to the Internet from previous media | Within the current structure, can the Internet reduce costs or add value for some communications? | RS components added a web channel to its dominant telephone sales model while still selling to the same customers |

Table 17.3 Evaluating potential changes to the market map/value chain

- rapid fault tracing; and

- product training.

## CHANNEL PARTNERSHIP

An organization's relationships with its intermediaries are often better managed if they can be formed into partnerships. Under a partnership arrangement, intermediaries are more likely to regard themselves as a meaningful part of their supplier's enterprise. The essence of 'partnership' will be *agreement* between supplier and intermediary about the supplier's general market policies, plus positive demonstrations of *commitment*. A significant signal of commitment to channel relationships is to devote a specific part of the supplier's marketing management structures to channel marketing.

This is not to say that channel partnerships cannot be changed, because they can be, and will often need to be. As a product matures through its life cycle in the market, different arrangements may be required to match different market developments. As a simple example, mass markets need to be addressed in a different way from niche markets, and products that are tending towards commodity status do not require the same level of dealer sophistication in order to be competitive. Similarly, as the competitive status of a product improves through, for example, brand development, different types of intermediary may be required to maintain product positioning.

## CHANNEL CONFLICT

Since channel members are normally independent organizations, there is always the potential for conflict, either between channel members themselves, or between an intermediary and its supplier. Resolution of such conflict is vital if intermediaries are to remain responsive to efforts to motivate them and a partnership relationship can be maintained. According to Sahama et al. (2011) perceived unfairness is a key driver of channel conflict, directly damaging channel relationships and aggravating the negative effects of both conflict and opportunism, and undermining the benefits of using contracts to manage the distribution channel. Conflicts between channel members may arise from perceived supplier favouritism, or by the appointment of too many intermediaries within one geographical area, resulting in them fighting each other for a worthwhile portion of a finite business 'pie'. Alternatively, there may be a feeling that an individual channel member is 'letting the side down' through over-vigorous competitive activities or reductions in quality standards.

It is important, therefore to manage potential conflict by addressing neglect or inconsistent channel management. Conflict, and the resulting likelihood of a reduced return being experienced by all, can to a large extent be eliminated if someone within the distribution chain exercises a leadership role. It can therefore be in the manufacturer's interest to set out deliberately to take the initiative and strive for channel leadership, thereby bringing a sense of order and fairness to what could be a volatile and mutually destructive situation. However, leadership can only be sustained if suppliers can back up their stance with economic power, or with a unique, highly desirable product that is in great demand.

It is quite conceivable that channel leadership can pass to anyone else in the chain. Wholesalers, distributors or agents can, if they exploit their power according to their circumstances, influence the channel 'politics' to their advantage. An example of this can be found in the agricultural market in Western Europe, where some distributors have become more dominant and more powerful than their suppliers.

## CHANNEL PERFORMANCE

Since the success of manufacturers using indirect selling is heavily dependent on the effective performance of their intermediaries, it is necessary to have a general framework against which to assess channel performance. In recent years, marketers have used the concept of *performance auditing* of distributors increasingly. One way of doing this is to monitor outlets on a day-to-day basis, making a check on their sales, either in total or through the range. This information can be useful as a rough control mechanism for management, but a detailed performance audit will go further than this. Some of the elements that should be reviewed are:

- Sales performance:
    - current sales compared with historical sales;
    - sales compared with other channel members;
    - sales compared with target sales; and
    - sales growth trends.

- Inventory maintenance:
    - levels compared with contractual (if any) arrangements;
    - levels though the range;
    - levels compared with market trends;
    - number of 'stock-out' situations;
    - levels of competing stocks;
    - condition of inventory and facilities;
    - old stock on hand/attempts to shift it; and
    - stock-keeping records/control efficiency.

- Commitment:
    - enthusiasm/motivation of staff;
    - general housekeeping;

- displays of products/sales material; and
- number of suggestions/queries initiated by distributor.

- Competition:

    - competition from other intermediaries compared with sales figures; and
    - competition from other product lines stocked by the intermediary.

- General growth prospects:

    - Does the track record indicate future growth? Is it keeping pace with that projected for the region, trade area, and so on?
    - How does current performance compare with local yardsticks?
    - Is the intermediary's organization expanding/shrinking? Why?
    - What record of investment in their business does the intermediary have?
    - What are the qualifications/experience of their staff?
    - What continuity is likely, for example, through management succession plans and health of key staff members?
    - What evidence is there of adaptability to change?
    - What are the intermediary's own business plans?

Having developed a set of criteria such as these, it ought to be possible to evaluate the performance and longer-term prospects of any distributor. More accurate assessment, for comparative purposes, can be attained by weighting the individual criteria according to their importance. Also 'point-scoring' techniques can be used in conjunction with the weighting if they serve a clear purpose.

The performance audit not only provides the marketer with valuable information about the current effectiveness of the distribution channel, it also establishes the basis upon which a distributor development strategy can be formed.

Too often, suppliers see themselves as *selling to* rather than *selling through* the intermediary. No small wonder then that, with this perception, suppliers are frequently dissatisfied with distributor performance. Four areas have been identified as being sources and symptoms of problems common among various types of intermediaries. These should be monitored closely by the supplier.

1. *Diversification*. The intermediary is spreading its limited resources over too wide a range of products or markets.

2. *Capitalization*. There is inadequate funding/cash flow to sustain the business unless tough management decisions are made.

3. *Market share*. Falling market share can be a valuable pointer to the fact that the intermediary is failing to be competitive.

4. *Attitude*. There is a negative attitude on the part of the intermediary towards the supplier company and its products.

In addition, field sales personnel should monitor the intermediary's performance in:

- financial management;
- sales personnel training;
- planning;
- network management;
- market development; and
- sales management.

It is in these areas that huge strides can be made in terms of enhancing channel performance. However, few suppliers have a sales force of sufficient calibre either to identify needs or to provide business counselling to intermediaries.

Some enlightened suppliers have set up separate specialist teams of advisers to fulfil such an intermediary development role, thereby overcoming what might be seen in some quarters as a dilution of the field sales activity. The results stemming from this type of investment indicate that distributors become more flexible, adaptive and successful, thus safeguarding the supplier's long-term strategic interests. In addition, considerable goodwill can be generated by this approach to intermediary development.

It must be remembered that the development of intermediaries can be costly, and the decisions regarding the depth and breadth of such improvement activities should not be taken lightly. However, there is an alternative approach to securing more effective control of a distribution channel and this is through a process called *vertical integration*. Vertical integration is also a common phenomenon in distribution channels. Such integration could involve a company merging with or absorbing those firms who are its sources of supply (*backward integration*), or taking similar steps to gain control of those intermediaries closer to its markets (*forward integration*). Such a movement, either forward or backward, can sometimes be accomplished without taking over the ownership of the firms in the chain.

## CASE STUDY 17.1 BIG DATA IN THE UK GROCERY SECTOR

Nowadays, 'big data' is news. McKinsey (2011) has identified it as 'the next frontier' for innovation, productivity and competition. 'Big data' is the content of the millions of databases around the world, which is increasing both in terms of volume and dept on a daily basis. Its potential value is great, *but only* if it is used in an intelligent, discriminating way to the benefit of companies, partners and consumers alike. The McKinsey study identified five key ways that big data can add value:

i. Making information transparent and usable at much higher frequency;

ii. Providing more accurate and detailed performance data, thereby offering opportunities to expose variability and improve performance;

iii. Ever-narrower segmentation of customers, therefore much more precisely tailored products and services;

iv. Sophisticated analysis can improve performance;

v. Improve the development of the next generation of products and services.

In the UK supermarket sector, Aimia has run the Nectar scheme for numerous brands and retailers for some years, creating insights from customer and transactional information. Sainsbury's use the insights provided by Aimia to inform its Wesupply B2B hub. Suppliers can exchange data with Sainsbury's automatically, using the electronic data interchange (EDI) platform, or manually via a web browser. They can submit shipping information, print barcodes to attach to shipments and monitor shipment progress. Wesupply focuses upon technically integrating all their supply chain partners, providing on-demand software functionality to directly measure and improve supply chain performance.

### CASE STUDY QUESTIONS:

1. Numerous retailers have switched to Wesupply's fully integrated EDI system. Discuss the decision criteria of such a move and outline the key benefits of switching to a fully managed EDI service.

2. What are the advantages and disadvantages to suppliers?

3. From the retailers' perspective, what could be the disadvantages of switching to an external EDI service?

# SUMMARY

Getting products or services to the market is a regulated dimension of the marketing mix. It is vital for the success of the supplier that customers should have access to the product or service through channels that meet their requirements as well as the supplier's.

In response to e-commerce, routes to market are being reconfigured in five main ways:

- product substitution/reconfiguration (such as e-mails instead of physical post);
- disintermediation (e-commerce can make intermediaries redundant);
- re-intermediation (a previous intermediary is replaced by a new online intermediary);
- partial channel substitution (an intermediary's role may be reduced, but not eliminated – as in the case of a car manufacturer providing customer information, but pointing customers to particular outlets); and
- media switching/addition (the links in the chain may remain the same, but communication between them may be partially or fully switched to the Internet from the previous mechanisms).

Developing relationships with channel intermediaries based on partnership can be a powerful means of building competitive advantage. The aim should be to develop marketing programmes that are attractive to all members of the distribution channel and not just to end users. In a *push strategy*, attention is concentrated on the intermediary to 'sell-in' more products, whereas in a *pull strategy*, the supplier emphasizes the creation of demand so that intermediaries are encouraged to deal in that product.

# FURTHER READING

Rosenbloom, B. (2012) *Marketing Channels: A Marketing View*, Mason, USA: South-Western Cengage Learning

An exploration of marketing channel strategies and systems combining theoretical perspectives and practical application.

# REFERENCES

Avery, J., Steenburgh, T.J., Deighton, J. and Caravella, M. (2012) Adding Bricks to Clicks: Predicting the Patterns of Cross-Channel Elasticities Over Time, *Journal of Marketing*, Vol. 76 (May): 96–111.

McDonald, M. and Wilson, H. (2002) *The New Marketing*, Oxford, Butterworth-Heinemann, 2002.

McKinsey (2011) *Big Data: The Next Frontier for Innovation, Competition, and Productivity*, McKinsey Global Institute. Available at www.mckinsey.com/insights.

Neslin, S. A. and Shankar, V. (2009), Key Issues in Multichannel Customer Management: Current Knowledge and Future Directions, *Journal of Interactive Marketing*, Vol. 23 (1): 70.

Samaha, S., Palmatier, R.W. and Dant, R.P. (2011) Poisoning Relationships: Perceived Unfairness in Channels of Distribution, *Journal of Marketing*, Vol. 75 (May): 99–117.

# CHAPTER 18
# DISTRIBUTION STRATEGY

# THE IMPORTANCE OF DISTRIBUTION AND LOGISTICS

For many businesses, distribution plays a small part in their marketing plans. When it *is* considered, the prime concern seems to focus on the physical aspects: the logistics of getting tangible products transported from the supplying company to the customer. The physical distribution function of an organization provides the time and place dimensions that represent *Place* in the marketing mix. This is depicted in Figure 18.1, in relation to the other utility-producing elements. The importance of 'place' is simple: if a product is not available when and where a customer wants it, it will surely fail in the market.

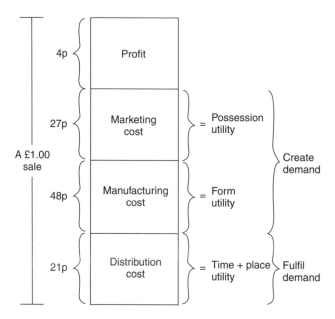

Figure 18.1 Distribution provides time-and-place utility

However, distribution embraces a much broader concept than just the delivery of goods. Chapter 17 emphasized how it takes into account the strategic importance of distribution channels and the potential value of channel intermediaries. The next chapter will highlight how it also ensures that customer service is kept in the forefront of the company's deliberations about its marketing policies. Both channel strategy and customer service strategy are key sources of competitive advantage. What renders and releases this advantage is the distribution and logistics strategy that underpins them. The purpose of this chapter is to establish a sound understanding of the role of distribution and logistics, and how this role is evolving from the province of the supply chain to realm of the value chain.

# SUPPLY CHAIN MANAGEMENT

The distribution process seeks to optimize the flow of materials and supplies through the organization and its operations to the customer. It is essentially a planning process and an information-based activity. Nowadays it is generally demand led; requirements from the marketplace are translated into production requirements and then into material requirements. Terziovski and Hermel (2011) emphasize the imperative of customer-centricity and customer-driven metrics in supply chain management. In their analysis, the selection and development of suppliers with a long-term view towards improving product quality, speed of delivery and responsiveness to customer needs are the key imperatives for integrated supply chain performance. This customer-centric approach, requiring an extension of the logic of logistics upstream to suppliers and downstream to final customer is generally accepted as pivotal. Underpinning this view is the recognition that the distribution process delivers time and place utility for customers, as illustrated in Figure 18.1, and that all parties from suppliers to retailers need to be involved.

Supply chain management is a fundamentally different philosophy of business organization. It is based on the idea of partnership in the marketing channel, where a high degree of linkage exists between entities in that channel. Traditional models of business organization have been based on the notion that the interests of individual firms are best served by maximizing their revenues and minimizing their costs. If these goals are achieved by disadvantaging another entity in the channel, then so be it. Under the supply chain management model, the goal is to maximize profit through enhanced competitiveness in the final market; a competitiveness that is secured by a lower cost to serve, reached in the shortest time frame possible. It is generally accepted that such goals are only attainable if the supply chain as a whole is integrated closely (Narasimhan and Kim, 2001; Christopher, 2005) in order to minimize total channel inventory, remove bottlenecks, compress time frames and eliminate quality problems.

Interestingly, empirical research confirms that supply chain integration is related to performance, but most supply chains are not well integrated (Childerhouse and Towill, 2011). Companies do appear to follow a similar route in a quest for seamless operation however, beginning with an attempt to improve internal effectiveness followed by upstream streamlining and then finally downstream integration. Encouraging practitioners not to despair, Childerhouse and Towill (2011: 7441) observe that 'indifferent practice is indeed the norm'. How can this be, and what can be done about it?

## SUPPLY MANAGEMENT

Historically, companies generally have paid scant attention to the management of supply. Even though the costs of purchases represent the largest single cost for most businesses, procurement has not been seen as a strategic task. It is only relatively recently that this view has begun to change as the realization grows that not only do procurement decisions and procedures have a dramatic impact on costs but also that innovation and response-to-market capability are affected profoundly by supplier relationships.

The philosophy of *co-makership* is founded on the notion of a mutually beneficial relationship between supplier and buyer, rather than the more traditional adversarial encounter. With this partnership approach, companies will identify opportunities for taking costs out of the supply chain, instead of simply pushing them upstream or downstream. Through EDI, paperwork can be eliminated, information shared, problems solved jointly, collaboration enhanced and quality improved. By its very nature, co-makership will normally involve longer-term relationships based on single-sourcing, rather than multiple supply points. A major benefit of working more closely with suppliers can be gained through involving them in the new product development process. A great deal of innovation now is supplier originated, and closer partnerships with suppliers can often lead to significant opportunities for new product breakthroughs.

## MANUFACTURING

The key word in manufacturing today is *flexibility*. The ability to produce any variant in any quantity, without a significant cost penalty, has to be the goal of all manufacturing strategies. In the past, and even now, much of the thinking in manufacturing has been dominated by the search for economies of scale. This type of reasoning has led to the formation of mega-plants, capable of producing vast quantities of a standardized product at incredibly low unit costs. It also has led many companies to opt for so-called focused factories, producing a limited range of products for global consumption.

The downside of adopting a flexible approach is that it can have the reverse effect by producing 'diseconomies of scale'. These diseconomies might take the form of a build-up of large inventories of finished products ahead of demand, an inability to respond rapidly to changed customer requirements or a reduction in the variety of products that can be offered to the customer. Instead of pursuing economies of scale, the search is now on to identify strategies that will reduce total supply-chain costs, not just manufacturing costs, and that will offer maximum flexibility against changing customer requirements. The goal of manufacturing must be 'the economic batch quantity of one', meaning that, in the ideal world, we would make things one at a time in response to known customer demands.

Time has become a major competitive issue in most industries, and hence manufacturing and marketing strategies need to be closely coupled.

## DISTRIBUTION

The role of distribution in the supply chain management model has extended considerably from the conventional view that it is concerned solely with transport and warehousing. The critical task that underlies successful distribution today is *demand management*.

Demand management is the process of anticipating and fulfilling orders against defined customer service goals. Information is the key to demand management: information from the marketplace in the form of medium-term forecasts; information from customers, preferably based on actual usage and consumption; information on production schedules and inventory status; and information on marketing activities, such as promotions that may cause demand to deviate from the norm.

Quick response logistics has become the aim of many organizations, enabling them to achieve the twin strategic goals of cost reduction and service enhancement. In essence, the idea of 'quick response' systems is based on a replenishment-driven model of demand management – as items are consumed or purchased, information is transmitted directly to the supplier and this immediately triggers an appropriate response. Often, high-speed, smaller-quantity deliveries will be made, the trade-off being that any increase in transport costs will be more than covered by reduced inventory in the pipeline and at either end of it, yet with improved service in terms of customer responsiveness. Certainly, information technology has been a major enabling factor in quick response logistics, linking instantaneously the point of sale or consumption with the point of supply.

In addition to quick response logistics, a further visible trend in distribution is the search for *postponement* opportunities. The principle of postponement dictates that the final configuration or form of the product should be delayed until the last possible moment. In this way, maximum flexibility is maintained, but inventory is minimized. The distribution function takes on a wider role as the provider of the final added value. What is apparent is that distribution in the integrated supply chain has now become an information-based, value-added activity, providing a critical link between the marketplace and the factory. This closer connection with the marketplace not only makes the company more responsive to customer demand, and hence more agile, it can also reduce the cost of financing the supply chain. For example, at Cisco Systems, the vast majority of orders come through Cisco.com web portal. While this proved adequate for small orders, more complex orders involving multiple products and components are dealt with by the Manufacturing Connection

Online hub through which Cisco can immediately communicate orders to suppliers and contract manufacturers who then build customized products on a just-in-time (JIT) basis. At the same time, the third-party logistics service provider is informed of the impending shipment requirements. As a result, customized products can be delivered and installed in much shorter time frames than previously. This enables Cisco to outsource 70 per cent of its production, quadrupling output without adding capacity, and shortening time to market for new products by 66 per cent in just six months.

While B2B hubs certainly aid information-sharing processes, the critical factor is not so much the EDI, *per se*, but the willingness of all parties in the supply chain to act as partners and to communicate openly and honestly. Some of the biggest improvements in supply chain agility have occurred through a change of attitude among the parties involved, where 'win-win-win' thinking has replaced the traditional adversarial approach. Table 18.1 summarizes the main differences between these old and new models of supply chain management.

| Traditional approach | Agile approach |
|---|---|
| Stock is held at multiple echelons, often based on organizational and legal ownership considerations. | Stock is held at the fewest echelons, if at all, with finished goods sometimes being delivered direct from factory to customer. |
| Replenishment is driven sequentially by transfers from one stocking echelon to another. | Replenishment of all echelons is driven from actual sales/usage data collected at the customer interface. |
| Production is planned by discrete organizational units with batch feeds between discrete systems. | Production is planned across functional boundaries from vendor to customer, through highly integrated systems, with minimum lead times. |
| Majority of stock is fully finished goods, dispersed geographically, waiting to be sold. | Majority of stock is held as 'work in progress' awaiting build/configuration instructions. |

Table 18.1 Agile supply chain management versus traditional approach

# THE IMPACT OF LOGISTICS ON CUSTOMER VALUE

The potential impact that logistics can have on customer value is considerable. As set out earlier in the book, customer value can be defined as the benefits the customer perceives to flow from the supplier relationship compared to the perceived costs. The benefits will typically comprise both tangible and intangible aspects. Tangible elements of the benefit 'bundle' might include product features and 'hard' service elements, such as on-time delivery. The intangible components of the offer might include the corporate image as well as 'soft' service elements, such as the helpfulness of the customer service call centre.

The cost that the customer incurs will be more than just the price charged for the product or service. Sometimes there can be significant transaction costs involved in placing orders, actioning progress, checking and remedying quality defects, checking invoices and making payments. There may also be ongoing costs, termed life cycle costs, such as maintenance and running costs. It is the totality of these costs – often referred to as the total cost of ownership – that the customer evaluates against the perceived benefits.

Figure 18.2 draws these different ideas together and suggests that logistics, directly or indirectly, can have an impact on all the component elements of customer value. For example, to a retailer, product packaging can have a significant effect on in-bound distribution costs and shelf-space profitability. Suppliers who include logistics considerations in their product or pack design decisions can thus greatly improve customer value. A good example of this type of forward thinking is provided by Procter & Gamble (P&G), who redesigned the pack of their global shampoo brand, Head & Shoulders, and as a result, enabled 25 per cent more product to be moved and stored on a pallet. This initiative

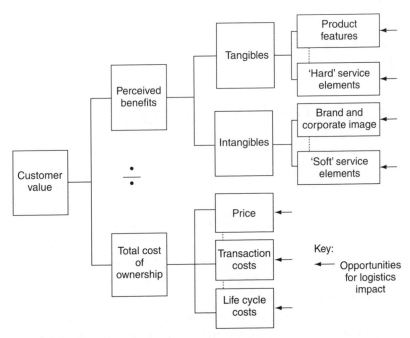

Figure 18.2 The impact of logistics on customer value

benefited P&G's retail customers as well as the company itself, with a further significant benefit accruing to the retailer through better shelf-space utilization.

Suppliers' logistics processes can also deliver enhanced customer value through ensuring more reliable delivery, thus reducing the customers' need to carry safety stocks. The supplier can provide further benefit to the customer by actively managing the customer's inventory – a concept known as vendor managed inventory (VMI). Under VMI, the supplier monitors the customer's inventory levels and, using this information, decides when to replenish stocks and in what quantities. The customer pays only when they use or sell the product. Large retail chains, for example, form partnerships with their suppliers to facilitate these types of collaborative and mutually beneficial logistics arrangements.

From the standpoint of competitive advantage, this type of value-adding logistics activity can be very positive. The more the customer's processes become integrated with the supplier's processes, the greater the barrier to entry that is erected against competitors. Companies with integrated supply chains are known to be more competitive; value is added by simplifying material flow through the supply chain in response to replenishment requests. This, in turn, enhances the customer experience, and the connection between logistics processes and superior customer service is self-evident. Transparency has engendered an acceptance that customer service is much more than simply a question of motivating employees or producing generalized mission statements and slogans. Delivering superior service means having detailed understanding of customer needs and developing strategies for effective service delivery in parallel with supply chain strategies.

## CASE STUDY 18.1 BAOSTEEL

Baosteel is an enormous enterprise with interests in the construction, trade, real estate, transportation and IT industries. It sought to develop an integrated global business platform for its companies, partners, suppliers and distributors to improve communications and processes among supply chain partners, as well as reduce costs. Its 'Unified Enterprise Collaboration Platform' (UECP) enabled all parties to work collaboratively even if their EDI standards were implemented in a different way. The platform connects parochial systems together so they can exchange information without human intervention. This resulted in greatly improved supply chain operating efficiency: inventory management processing time was cut from two days to two hours; orders could be tracked; logistics, inventory and payment activities monitored across the value chain, detect problems and delays and identify sudden demand peaks or stock shortages. The EDI platform has allowed Baosteel to significantly grow the number of online transactions, both internally and externally, improve operational efficiencies across their extended enterprise and connect with new suppliers. Overall, user-friendly EDI has helped to improve the competitive position of Baosteel in an increasingly tough economic environment.

Adapted from *BSteel establishes Global IT Integration Platform* by GXS. Available at www.gxs.com

### CASE STUDY QUESTIONS:

1. Discuss how Baosteel's UECP promotes a customer-centric approach to supply chain management.

2. The case study mentions logistics, inventory and payments management specifically. What other functional processes could be bolted on to enhance performance?

3. What supply chain performance metrics would you suggest to judge the efficacy of the UECP?

In order to ensure that the supply chain is delivering value, it is crucial to put in place a robust quality assurance system. Supply chain quality management (SCQM) is increasingly recognized as an important concomitant to supply chain management. SCQM can undoubtedly provide benefits but, as Foster et al. (2011) point out, it is not easy to achieve. Organizational structure, culture, reward systems and the difficulties of communicating across functional and specialist boundaries have all been cited as barriers to SCQM (Pagell, 2004) while Foster et al. (2011) find that operations managers and quality managers approach quality management issues from differing perspectives. It can be difficult to achieve consensus. Companies need to work hard to remedy this as, as we have observed, distribution is an absolutely fundamental element of the marketing mix.

# THE CRITICAL ROLE OF LOGISTICS SERVICE

The importance of logistics in marketing strategy is that it is the *process* that delivers customer service. As markets take on increasingly the characteristics of 'commodity markets', where customers perceive little difference between products at a functional or technical level, customer service can provide a powerful means of differentiation. In markets as disparate as industrial chemicals or personal computers, the struggle is to find ways to avoid the commodity trap. For many companies, the solution to this problem has come through enhanced service performance. Modern customers are service sensitive, requiring availability of supply at short notice, for they often operate on a JIT basis, whether they are a manufacturing business, a retailer or an end user.

Customer satisfaction at a profit is the goal of any business organization, and the role of the logistics system is to achieve defined service goals in the most cost-effective manner. The establishment of these service goals is a prerequisite for the development of appropriate logistics strategies and structures. There is now widespread acceptance that customer service requirements can only be determined accurately through research and competitive benchmarking. Customer research may also reveal the presence of significant differences in service preferences among customers, thus indicating alternative bases for market segmentation in terms of service needs.

Tailoring customer service strategies to meet the precise needs of customers can be a powerful means of differentiation leading to enduring competitive advantage – service segmentation is a key means to achieving this end.

Understanding customers' service preferences is the starting point for re-engineering logistics processes to ensure greater cost effectiveness; thus customers' service preferences should be the starting point for the development of logistics and supply chain strategies. The challenge to the organization then becomes one of how to re-engineer processes and to restructure conventional, functional systems to achieve these service goals at minimum cost.

Key to the achievement of these customer service goals is closer collaboration with downstream partners in the distribution channel. As discussed in Chapter 17, the way in which distribution channels are structured, and the relationships within them are managed, is crucial to competitive performance in any industry.

# THE SERVICE-LEVEL DECISION

One of the fundamental cost trade-offs in logistics that has an impact on marketing performance is the question of *service levels*. The level of service is a measure of the extent to which the organization plans to make the product available and to support it in use; for example, with the provision of after-sales service.

The simplest measure of service is stock availability, usually measured as the percentage of demand that can be met from stock. Clearly, there is more to service than this, as we shall explore in Chapter 19. However, it can be regarded as the foundation of the service 'package'.

Naturally, the customer seeks maximum availability and the company will normally endeavour to supply it. However, the problem is that, as we increase the planned level of availability, the necessary investment in inventory rises more than proportionately. Figure 18.3 highlights the relationship between inventory and service levels. The reason the curve rises so steeply as the planned level of availability increases is that, even though the chance of running out of stock may be remote, additional safety stock must be held to cater for that eventuality.

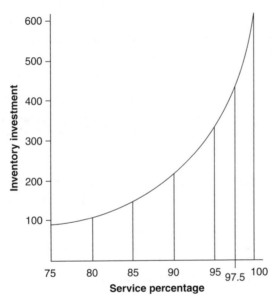

Figure 18.3 The cost of 'availability'

Many companies frequently underestimate the true costs of holding stock. It is a fair estimate to account for a 25 per cent per annum holding cost for inventory (that is, 25 per cent of the book value of the stock) if we include the cost of capital, storage, obsolescence and insurance. Since most medium-to-large organizations carry millions of pounds worth of stock at any time, the annual cost at 25 per cent is clearly substantial.

The trade-off that has to be considered, therefore, is: 'What is the cost of holding stock compared with the cost of running out?' If stock runs out too frequently, the outcome can be a substantial fall in sales revenue. At best, the company will forfeit the immediate contribution to its cash flow, while at the same time incurring some degree of customer hostility. At worst, the customer will not delay the purchase but will buy from a competitor instead. Clearly, the cost of running out of stock will vary from product to product, and will to some extent be dependent on the nature and availability of competing products.

Poor stock availability also antagonizes channel intermediaries. In a survey carried out in the United States, it was estimated that, if a supplier decreased stock availability by 5 per cent, nearly a quarter of intermediaries indicated that they would purchase elsewhere. Unaware of this reaction, supplying companies estimated that such a reduction of service would at worst lose them 'only about 9 per cent' of their outlets!

## Profit implications of stock management

Because we are dealing with aspects of human behaviour as well as economics when faced with an out-of-stock situation, there is no precise way of measuring the impact on profit. Instead, we have to evaluate the probabilities of stock-exhaustion consequences, estimate the frequency at which each of these consequences is likely to occur and make a weighted judgement about the financial consequences. Table 18.2 is an example of how this might be done:

| Consequence of service failure | Profit penalty |
|---|---|
| • Loss of sale to competitor<br>• Order processing cost<br>• Loss of sale of related goods<br>• Shipment of goods from supplier<br>• Expediting of rush orders<br>• Customer's ill-will | • Gross margin of item<br>• Customer reordering<br>• Gross margin on all items<br>• Expediting and other depot's transport cost<br>• Non-standard production cost<br>• Possible lost customer |

Table 18.2 Cost & profit implications of service failure

Ideally, a market experiment should be conducted to measure more precisely the effect of non-availability on market share. There have been a number of reported studies suggesting that over a certain range of service improvement there can be a significant impact on sales. However, once 'saturation' level is reached the customer may find it difficult to distinguish small improvements in stock availability. Thus, as in Figure 18.4, it is suggested that there comes a point where diminishing returns to service improvement are encountered.

The task of marketing management when seeking to develop appropriate levels of stock availability is to balance the known cost of service against the estimated market response. Figure 18.5 depicts the basic trade-off between the cost function and the response function.

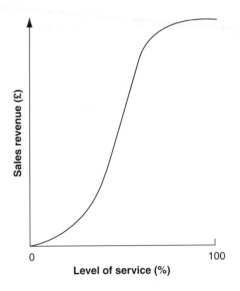

Figure 18.4 The market response to service

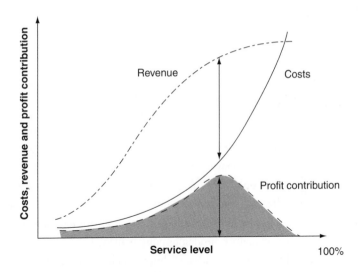

Figure 18.5 The cost/benefit of service

# DISTRIBUTION PLANNING

As in the development of the other tactical plans, distribution planning should begin with the distribution audit, from which distribution objectives and strategies can be established. Distribution objectives can be many and varied, but the following are considered basic for marketing purposes:

- objectives related to outlet penetration by type of distribution;
- objectives related to inventory range and levels to be held;

- objectives related to distributor sales and sales promotion activities; and
- objectives related to other specific customer development programmes, for example, incentives for distributors.

A simple, iterative approach to distribution planning can be summarized as the steps listed below, the content of which will shape the distribution and logistics strategy:

1. Determine marketing objectives.
2. Evaluate changing conditions in distribution at all levels.
3. Determine the distribution task within overall marketing strategy.
4. Establish a distribution policy in terms of type, number and level of outlets to be used.
5. Set performance standards for distributors.
6. Obtain performance information.
7. Compare actual with anticipated performance.
8. Make improvements where necessary.

The interrelationship between developing the marketing plan and developing the distribution plan is usefully depicted in Figure 18.6.

# SUMMARY

Today there is a much greater recognition of the importance of distribution and logistics in the overall marketing strategy of businesses. Not only does the material flowing through the firm attract substantial costs (for example, inventory holding charges, transport and storage) but the way in which the flow is managed can have a considerable impact on customer value as identified in customer service. More fundamentally, it provides the added value of 'time-and-place utility' to the product, without which the product is worthless.

Unless there is a formalized distribution structure, distribution-related activities may be spread across production, marketing, procurement, finance and so on, leading to conflicts of interest between distribution decisions. A more centralized, interrelated distribution system, often referred to as 'logistics', will ensure that one distribution activity is traded off against another to arrive at the most efficient system overall.

The person responsible for distribution therefore has several variables to contend with in the search for trade-offs; taken together these constitute the *logistics mix*. There are five components to manage in the physical distribution of tangible products:

1. *Facilities* – the number, size and geographical location of storage and distribution depots.

2. *Inventory* – the stockholding levels throughout the distribution chain consistent with customers' service expectations.

3. *Communications* – the flow of information, for example, order processing, invoicing, forecasting and so on.

4. *Unitization* – the way in which goods are packaged and assembled into large units, for example, palletization, containerization and so on.

5. *Transport* – the modes of transport, delivery schedules and so on.

'Integrated logistics management' gives the logistics concept managerial application. It is an approach to distribution planning, implementation and control whereby two or more of the functions involved in moving goods from source to user are integrated and viewed as a coherent and cohesive system.

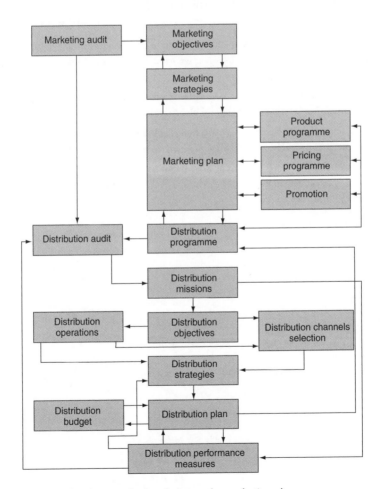

Figure 18.6 The distribution plan in relation to the marketing plan

# FURTHER READING

Ellis, N. (2011) *Business-to-Business Marketing: Relationships, Networks and Strategies*, Oxford University Press.

A comprehensive introduction to the key managerial issues and strategies in the area of B2B marketing. Includes detailed consideration of the role of the manager and the organizations they represent.

# REFERENCES

Childerhouse, P. and Trowill, D.R. (2011) Arcs of supply chain management, *International Journal of Production Research*, Vol. 49 (24): 7441–7468.

Christopher, M. (2005) *Logistics and Supply Chain Management*, London: FT Prentice Hall.

Foster, S.T., Wallin, C. and Ogden, J. (2011) Towards a better understanding of supply chain quality management practices, *International Journal of Production Research*, Vol. 49 (8): 2285–2300.

Narasimhan, R. and Kim, S.W. (2001) Information system utilization strategy for supply chain integration, *Journal of Business Logistics*, Vol. 22 (2): 51–75.

Pagell, M. (2004) Understanding the factors that enable and inhibit the integration of operations, purchasing and logistics, *Journal of Operations Management*, Vol. 22 (5): 459–487.

Terziovski, M. and Hermel, P. (2011) The Role of Quality Management Practice in the Performance of Integrated Supply Chains: A Multiple Cross-Case Analysis, *Quality Management Journal*, Vol. 18 (2): 10–25.

# CHAPTER 19
# CUSTOMER SERVICE STRATEGY

# ELEVATION OF THE CUSTOMER SERVICE ROLE

Modern organizations appreciate the need for good customer service. There is even an Institute of Customer Service specifically set up to promote it. The Institute reports that customer service in the United Kingdom has reached a plateau, with retailers (John Lewis, Waitrose, First Direct) scoring high while utilities languish at the bottom of the annual league table (Customer Satisfaction Report, 2013).

Three factors have perhaps contributed more than anything else to the growing importance of customer service as a competitive weapon. One is the continuous heightening of customer expectations. Consumers are becoming increasingly demanding and sophisticated in their service requirements and expectations, and able to defend their bargaining stance/purchase position. Greater access to information, growth in self-assisted services and the widespread change from a sellers' to a buyers' market are just a few of the drivers of consumer empowerment. Similarly, in industrial purchasing situations, buyers are expecting higher levels of service from vendors, particularly as more manufacturers convert to JIT manufacturing systems.

The second factor is the inexorable transition towards 'commodity' markets, as the customer perceives little technical difference between competing offers. The power of the brand is diminishing as the technologies of competing products converge, thus dulling or destroying product differentiation. Take, for example, the current state of the laptop market. There are many competing models and these are substitutable as far as most would-be purchasers are concerned. Unless a buyer is particularly expert, it is difficult to use product features as the basis for choice.

The third factor is the commercial realization that increases in customer satisfaction and retention levels can have a significant positive impact on corporate profitability and prosperity levels. It will be recalled from Chapter 15 that an improvement of five percentage points in customer retention can lead to profit improvements of between 25 per cent and 95 per cent in the net present value of the future flow of earnings. It will also be recalled that poor customer service can have a devastating effect on future opportunities in terms of negative publicity by word of mouth and unresolved problems through unregistered complaints.

Customer service is often seen as the focused handling of customer complaints, rather the holistic value-creating management of customer relationships. Regrettably, such a perspective ignores the research finding that 98 per cent of dissatisfied customers never complain when they receive poor service; they simply defect. ABA Bank Marketing (2013) reports that 30 per cent of bank customers whose local branch closed moved their accounts to another institution, while Tatikonda (2013) observes that failure to identify the financial impact of customer defection can cost a company millions in potential profit – without anyone knowing. Highlighting gaps in current knowledge, Tatikonda (2013) calls for better understanding of the relationships between customer satisfaction, customer retention and improved performance.

In addition to defect costs, reactive 'fire fighting' is more costly and much less productive than proactive 'fire prevention'. Experience has shown that companies that systematically attempt to improve customer satisfaction, through well-developed customer relationship management practices, reap the rewards of happy customers, employees and other stakeholders and healthy profit margins.

This connection between good levels of customer service and good levels of customer satisfaction and retention underpins the common association of customer service with keeping, rather than winning, customers. Customer service therefore plays a pivotal role in relationship marketing. Getting this role right, and to a standard of expertise that is superior to that of competitors and sustainable in the longer term, requires an in-depth understanding of the nature and nuance of customer service.

# WHAT IS CUSTOMER SERVICE?

Customer service is a concept that applies equally in the world of physical products as service industries. It can be conceptualized as a system organized to provide a continuing link between the first contact with the customer, through to the time that an order is received and the goods/services are delivered and used. The objective is to satisfy customer needs continuously. In relation to manufacturing, Grönroos and Helle (2010) contend that it is necessary to adopt a service logic for the entire manufacturing business, not separately for industrial service activities only, which is the traditional approach to studying service in manufacturing. Only by adopting a service logic can companies create and deliver sustainable value, a key determinant of competitive advantage. In relation to value sustainability, it is worth noting that different customer segments will require different levels of customer service, and these may well fluctuate over time. From this, it can be seen that managing customer service provision is a complex and critical activity.

It is also expensive. Operating service levels at 100 per cent can be crippling to the supplier, yet to drop below an acceptable level is to surrender one's market share to a competitor. Research has shown that once the service level (defined as the percentage of occasions the product is available to customers, when and where they want it) increases beyond the 70–80 per cent mark, the associated costs increase exponentially. In many cases, such high levels of customer service are not necessary.

The provision of high levels of customer service involves understanding what the customer buys and determining how additional value can be added to an offer to differentiate it from competing offers. Thus, customer service can be seen as an activity that provides time-and-place utilities for the customer: in other words, there is no value in a product or service until it is in the hands of the customer or consumer. It follows, therefore, that making the product or service 'available' to the customer is a key ingredient in the provision of customer service.

Availability is, however, a complex concept, as it is affected by a range of factors that together constitute customer service. For example, availability may be influenced by delivery frequency and reliability, stock levels and order cycle times. In fact, it could be said that customer service is determined ultimately by the interaction of all those factors that affect the process of making products and services available to the customer.

In practice, there are many definitions of customer service. One major study found the following range of descriptions of customer service among the industries surveyed:

- All activities required to accept, process, deliver and bill customer orders and to follow up on any activity that erred.

- Timeliness and reliability of getting materials to customers in accordance with the customer's expectations.

- A complex range of activities involving all areas of the business which combine to deliver and invoice the company's products in a fashion that is perceived as satisfactory by the customer and which advances our company's objectives.

- Total order entry, all communications with customers, all shipping, all freight, all invoicing and total control of repair of products.

- Timely and accurate delivery of products ordered by customers with accurate follow-up and enquiry response, including timely delivery of invoice.

Clearly, while a variety of perspectives exist on the subject, what all definitions of customer service have in common is that they are concerned with relationships at the buyer–seller interface. Customer service may therefore be seen to be related to the building of relationships with customers and other markets or segments to ensure long-term relationships that are mutually trusting and profitable, and that reinforce the other elements of the marketing mix.

# THE ELEMENTS OF CUSTOMER SERVICE

Nowadays, it is widely acknowledged that customers are looking for, and expect companies to provide, solutions. The product is no longer all-important; customer perceptions and evaluations are based upon the whole experience of interacting with a given provider. Customer service attends the buyer–seller interface at all stages of decision-making and purchase. As such, it can be examined under three headings that relate to three distinct phases of the buying process:

- pre-transaction;
- transaction; and
- post-transaction.

The *pre-transaction* elements of customer service relate to corporate policies or programmes, involving written statements of service policy, and the planning of customer lifetime strategies and appropriate organizational structures and systems flexibility. *Transaction* elements comprise the customer service variables that are involved directly in performing the physical distribution function, such as product availability, order cycle times, order status information and delivery reliability. *Post-transaction* elements work to support product usage and include product warranties, parts and repair services and customer complaint procedure. It is at this post-transaction stage that cross-selling initiatives and managing the customer life cycle become essential to the establishment of long-term customer relationships. The key elements of customer service for each buying stage are outlined in Figure 19.1.

In any product/market situation, some of these elements will be more important than others, and there may be factors other than those listed that will feature significantly in particular markets. It is therefore imperative to understand customer service in terms of the differing requirements of different market segments, and to recognize that no universally appropriate list of customer service elements exists. A company may serve multiple markets, each with its own unique service requirements and priorities.

The multivariate nature of customer service and market segments means that it is essential to have a clearly defined customer service strategy.

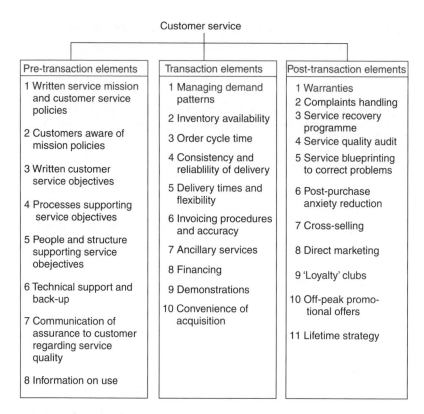

Customer service

| Pre-transaction elements | Transaction elements | Post-transaction elements |
|---|---|---|
| 1 Written service mission and customer service policies | 1 Managing demand patterns | 1 Warranties |
| | 2 Inventory availability | 2 Complaints handling |
| 2 Customers aware of mission policies | 3 Order cycle time | 3 Service recovery programme |
| 3 Written customer service objectives | 4 Consistency and reliablility of delivery | 4 Service quality audit |
| 4 Processes supporting service objectives | 5 Delivery times and flexibility | 5 Service blueprinting to correct problems |
| 5 People and structure supporting service obejectives | 6 Invoicing procedures and accuracy | 6 Post-purchase anxiety reduction |
| 6 Technical support and back-up | 7 Ancillary services | 7 Cross-selling |
| | 8 Financing | 8 Direct marketing |
| 7 Communication of assurance to customer regarding service quality | 9 Demonstrations | 9 'Loyalty' clubs |
| | 10 Convenience of acquisition | 10 Off-peak promotional offers |
| 8 Information on use | | 11 Lifetime strategy |

Figure 19.1 Elements of customer service

# DEVELOPING A CUSTOMER SERVICE STRATEGY

Customer service should be viewed as strategic rather than operational because it has a key role to play in creating sustainable competitive advantage. According to Grönroos (2007: 6), organizations should have a holistic *service perspective* which entails serving customers with goods and services of a core solution, additional separately billable services and other non-billable services such as invoicing, complaints handling, advice, personal attention, information and other value-enhancing components. Framed by a service-oriented philosophy, the organization should develop a customer service strategy which, in Christopher's (1992) analysis, comprises four key steps:

1. *Identifying a service mission* – the company should articulate its service pledge and values within its corporate mission, and/or in a separate customer service mission statement. This declaration should focus on the unique and distinctive elements of the company's offer while reflecting the company's philosophy and commitment to customer service.

2. *Setting the customer service objectives* – the company's objectives, or goals, must be clearly defined and fully understood if effective strategies are to be developed. In terms of customer service, this involves answering questions such as:
   - How important is customer service compared with the other marketing mix elements?
   - With whom do we compete in the customer's mind?
   - Which are the most important customer service elements – that contribute most to overall customer satisfaction and market share?
   - What dimensions of service are seen as priorities by customers when they choose suppliers?
   - How do we perform against the competition?
   - In considering levels of performance in setting these customer service objectives, service providers must consider the importance of service quality variables such as:
   - Reliability – the ability to perform the promised service dependably, accurately and consistently over time;
   - Responsiveness – prompt service and a willingness to help customers. Speed and flexibility are essential here;
   - Assurance – knowledge and courtesy of staff and their ability to inspire trust and confidence;
   - Empathy – caring, individualized attention to customers; and
   - Tangibles – for example, physical facilities, equipment and staff appearance.

3. *Customer service strategy* – most markets consist of market segments that seek different combinations of benefits. As all customers do not require the same level of service, segmentation can be a powerful means of creating appropriate service packages for each relevant market segment. Christopher's approach to developing a service-based strategy consists of four steps: identify the service segments and their specific requirements, identify the most important products and customers using Pareto analysis, prioritize the service targets and develop the service package.

4. *Implementation programme* – once the most effective service package has been developed for each segment, the service package should then become part of an integrated marketing mix.

As with any other marketing strategy, for a customer service strategy to succeed, it must be well informed, well devised and well executed. What distinguishes customer service strategy from its marketing counterparts is the pervasive nature of its impact and importance. Customer service touches everyone and every aspect of an enterprise. Its influence extends from internal and external perceptions of the business to current and potential realities of commercial viability. Its role as the principal source of added value is confirmed by the growth of the service sector in many Western economies. Given the formidable responsibility attached to customer service, it is crucial that customer service strategy is based on meaningful market research and suitable and sustainable service-level decisions.

## CASE STUDY 19.1  JOHN LEWIS

Over recent years, John Lewis has won numerous customer satisfaction awards, thanks to a well-developed strategy for customer service. Its multi-channel service strategy is designed to ensure customers receive excellent service, regardless of whether they shop in one of the department stores, Waitrose supermarket or online. A spokesman for John Lewis stated,

> For us service is not a thing. It is everything.... It's really important that customer service is not seen as a commodity but it is different for companies with different business models and strategies. For example, John Lewis is big on personal service but Amazon also has a great reputation for customer service, yet I don't know anyone who has spoken to a single one of their people.

John Lewis regards partners, customers and profits as equally important. In this, it has been observed to be very different from public companies who put shareholders first. The company attributes its success to a mixture of culture, training and process, involving technology investments that make it easier for its partners to delight customers at every touchpoint. Online sales are growing rapidly and in that context the priority is 'to serve multi-channel customers better than anyone else'. The company stands for 'trust, loyalty and looking after the customer'. Two contact centres in Manchester and Glasgow have 1000 partners handling 4.5 million calls a year. A knowledge management solution provides the ability to share knowledge across its service operations. John Lewis has also invested in desktop automation technology to drive operational efficiency. The system was enabled to store and recall information intuitively, making it easier for staff to access the information required to solve customers' problems. Complexity and language ambiguity was removed from the process of information retrieval, making it easier to 'multicast knowledge across multiple channels'.

**CASE STUDY QUESTIONS:**

1. Discuss how a customer might measure service quality at John Lewis.

2. How has John Lewis managed to turn customer service into a key differentiator? Why don't competitors simply emulate what John Lewis is doing?

3. What is the role of, and how important is, the knowledge management system in assuring high-quality customer service at John Lewis?

# CUSTOMER SERVICE RESEARCH

There is a great premium to be placed on gaining an insight into the factors that influence buyer behaviour (see Chapters 2 and 3) and, in the context of customer service, which particular elements are seen by the customer to be the most important. The use of market research techniques in customer service has lagged behind their application in such areas as product testing and advertising research, yet the importance of researching the service needs of customers is just as great as, for example, the need to understand the market reaction to price. In fact, it is possible to apply standard, proven market research methods to gain considerable insight into the ways that customers will react to customer service.

The first step in research of this type is to identify the relative source of influence on the purchase decision. If we are selling components to a manufacturer, for example, who will make the decision on the source of supply? This is not always an easy question to answer as, in many cases, there will be several people involved. For example, the purchasing manager of the company to whom we are selling may only be acting as an agent for others within the firm. In other cases, the individual's influence will be much greater. Alternatively, if we are manufacturing products for sale through retail outlets, is the decision to stock made centrally by a retail chain or by individual store managers? The answers to these questions can often be supplied by the sales force (see Chapter 16).

With a clear indication of the source of decision-making power, the customer service researcher at least knows *who* to research. The question still remains, however: which elements of the vendor's total marketing offering have what effect on the purchase decision? Ideally, once the DMU in a specific market has been identified, an initial, small-scale research programme should be initiated, based on personal interviews with a representative sample of buyers. The purpose of these interviews is to elicit, *in the language of the customer*, first, the importance they attach to customer service vis-à-vis the other marketing mix elements such as price, product quality and promotion; and second, the specific importance they attach to the individual elements of customer service.

Assuming that through research we can identify the appropriate elements of the customer service mix for the specific market segments we are targeting, how do we decide on where to place this emphasis? Some kind of formalized logic needs to be adopted to guide the development and implementation of cost-effective service policies. This is the realm of the service-level decision.

# THE SERVICE-LEVEL DECISION

As stated at the beginning of the chapter, customer service is a system organized to provide a continuing link between the first contact with the customer through to the time the order is received and the goods/services delivered and used, with the objective of satisfying customer needs continuously. Customer service thus encompasses every aspect of the relationship and is likely to involve the commitment of considerable resources.

In fact, as intimated in Chapter 18, once the level of service (defined here as the percentage of occasions the product is available to customers, when and where they want it) increases beyond the 70–80 per cent mark, the associated costs increase exponentially. Figure 18.5 demonstrates the typical relationship between service level and the cost of providing it. From the diagram it will be observed that the cost of increasing the service level by a small amount – say, from 95 per cent to 97.5 per cent – results in a sharp increase in inventory costs.

Significantly, many companies appear to be unaware of the level of customer service they are offering – that is, there is *no* customer service policy as such. Even where such a policy does exist, the levels are quite often set arbitrarily and are not the result of a careful market analysis. The question then arises: what level of availability *should* be offered? This question is relatively simple to answer in theory, but very difficult to quantify and achieve in practice, since different product groups in different market segments could well demand different levels of customer service.

In theory, at least, it is possible to say that service levels can continue to be improved so long as the marketing advantage that results continues to outrun the additional costs incurred. Conceptually, it is possible to draw an S-shaped curve, as shown in Figure 19.2, which suggests that, at very high levels of customer service, customers are unable to distinguish small changes in the service offered. When a company is operating in this region, it is quite possibly incurring more costs than are necessary for the level of sales being achieved. For example, marketing and sales managers who insist on offering maximum service to all customers, no matter what the profitability and location of those customers, are probably doing their company a disservice.

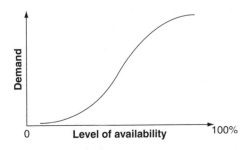

Figure 19.2 Customer response levels to increasing levels of availability

## COST–BENEFIT ANALYSIS

By reviewing customer service policy carefully, and perhaps even introducing differential service levels for different products or different customers (at least on a trial basis), marketing can enhance its contribution to corporate profitability.

Somewhere between the costs and benefits involved in customer service, a balance has to be found. It will be at the point where the additional revenue returns for each increment of service are equal to the extra cost involved in providing that increment. To attempt to ascertain this point of balance, certain information is required. For example:

- How profitable is the product? What contribution to fixed costs and profits does this product make, and what is its sales turnover?

- What is the nature of the product? Is it a critical item as far as the customer is concerned, where stock-outs at the point of supply would result in a loss of sales? Does the product have characteristics that result in high stockholding costs?

- What is the nature of the market? Does the company operate in a sellers' or a buyers' market? How frequently is the product purchased? Are there ready substitutes? What are the stockholding practices of the purchasers? Which markets and customers are growing and which are declining?

- How profitable are the customers constituting each segment?

- What is the nature of the competition? How many companies are providing an alternative source of supply to customers? What sort of service levels do they offer?

- What is the nature of the channel of distribution through which the company sells? Does the company sell direct to the end customer or through intermediaries? To what extent does the company control the channel and the activities of its members, such as the stock levels and order policies?

This basic information is the raw material for the service level decision. To take an example, the level of service offered is less likely to have an effect on sales if, in fact, the company is the sole supplier of the product and there are no substitutes. This is the case in some industrial markets, and from a short-term point of view to offer a higher level of service of, say, 90 per cent instead of 85 per cent, would probably have the effect of reducing the total profitability of the product.

The correlation between customer satisfaction, customer retention and customer profitability was discussed in Chapter 15. In financial terms, this link is explained by the fact that, as the relationship extends, the initial 'contact' costs, such as checking creditworthiness, no longer figure on the balance sheet. In addition, the more that is known about the customer as the relationship develops, the more offers can be tailored effectively to meet their needs. Thus the customer gets greater value, which in turn encourages more frequent and larger purchases. It follows, therefore, that when a company lowers its defection rate, average customer relationships last longer and profits climb. Viewed in this way, the costs of providing enhanced customer service could be seen as an investment in customer retention.

## CUSTOMER SERVICE TRADE-OFFS

While, ideally, the customer would like to have the best of everything – for example, 100 per cent availability from stock, 24-hour delivery, reliable on-time deliveries and emergency ordering, it will probably not be cost-effective for the supplier to offer such a service. In the customer service decision, therefore, we are forced to make trade-offs. (The technique of trade-off analysis was introduced in Chapter 11.) The question is, which elements of service to trade-off against each other? A simple analogy is the decision to buy a car. A customer might ideally like a car with the appearance of a Lamborghini and the performance of a Ferrari, but with the miles-per-gallon of a Fiat, the spaciousness of a Volvo estate and perhaps at the price of a Nissan! Clearly, not all these things are achievable in one car. The actual purchase decision can be viewed, therefore, as a reflection of the importance an individual attaches to each aspect of the purchase – that is, appearance, performance and price.

Thus, in the service-level decision, the marketer needs to research the service priorities of the company's target markets and to assemble a customer service package that is optimal for those markets and for the company.

# DEVELOPING A CUSTOMER SERVICE PACKAGE

The key to developing a successful customer service 'package' (the customer's perception of logistics performance) is ensuring that it embraces product availability, with attractive order cycle times and mechanisms for minimizing customer inconvenience arising from order cycle times. This necessitates a dynamic knowledge of both customer needs and preferences, and the company's ability to satisfy them.

The starting point, then, is to establish those elements of the customer service mix that have the greatest impact on the buyer's perception of the supplier. This thinking needs to be carried right through into the design of the customer service package, because it will most probably contain more than one element. The following list contains the major elements of customer service that should be researched (with reference to Figure 19.1, it will be noted that these elements span all three buying stages):

- frequency of delivery;
- time from order to delivery;
- reliability of delivery;
- emergency deliveries when required;
- stock availability and continuity of supply;
- orders filled completely;
- advice on non-availability;
- convenience of placing order;
- acknowledgement of order;
- accuracy of invoices;
- quality of sales representation;
- regular calls by sales representatives;
- manufacturer monitoring of retail stock levels;
- credit terms offered;
- customer query handling;
- quality of outer packaging;

- well-stacked pallets;
- easy-to-read use-by dates on outer labels;
- quality of inner package for in-store handling and display;
- consults on new product range regularly; and
- co-ordination between production, distribution and marketing.

This will almost certainly mean designing different customer packages for different market groups. At present, very few manufacturers/suppliers bother to do this. Basically, six steps are involved in this process:

1. Define the important service elements (and sub-elements).
2. Determine customers' viewpoints on these.
3. Design a competitive package (and several variations, if necessary).
4. Develop a promotional campaign to 'sell' the service package idea.
5. Pilot test a particular package and the promotional campaign being used.
6. Establish controls to monitor performance of the various service packages.

The design of the package will also need to take into account the differing needs of various market segments, so that the resources allocated to customer service can be used in the most cost-effective way. Too often, a uniform, blanket approach to service is adopted by companies, which does not distinguish between the real requirements of different customer types. This can lead to customers being offered too little customer service or too much.

The precise composition of the customer service package for any market segment should depend on the results of the market research described earlier. It will be determined by budgetary and cost constraints. If alternative packages can be identified that seem to be equally acceptable to the buyer, it makes sense to choose the least costly alternative. For example, it may be possible to identify a highly acceptable customer service package that enables the emphasis to be switched away from a high level of inventory availability towards improved customer communication. Once a cost-effective package has been identified in this way it should become a major part of the company's marketing mix – 'using service to sell' is the message here.

If the market segments we serve are sensitive to price, then the service package must be promoted actively. One way in which this can be achieved with great effect is by stressing the impact on the *customer's* costs of the improved service package, such as, for example, what improved reliability will do for their own stock planning; what shorter lead times will do for their inventory levels; and how improved ordering and invoicing systems will lead to fewer errors. All too often the customer will not appreciate the impact that improved service offered by the supplier can have on their own 'bottom line'.

# STRATEGIES FOR SERVICE

Beyond the simple presentation of a marketing message based around an improved customer service package lies the opportunity to develop tailor-made service offerings, particularly to key accounts, based on 'negotiated' service levels. The idea here is that no two customers are alike, whether in terms of their requirements or, specifically, in terms of their profitability to the supplier. One United Kingdom-based company in the consumer electronics field identified that while three of its major customers were roughly equivalent in terms of their annual sales value, there were considerable differences in the costs generated by each. For example, one customer required delivery to each of its 300-plus retail outlets, while the others took delivery at one central warehouse. Similarly, one company paid within 30 days of receiving the invoice, while the others took nearer to 40 days to pay. Again, one of the three was found to place twice as many 'emergency' orders as the others. Careful analysis of the true costs showed that the profitability of the three customers differed by more than 20 per cent. Yet each customer received the same levels of value-related discounts and customer service.

Conducting such a 'customer account profitability' analysis can provide the supplier not only with a basis on which to negotiate price but also a basis for 'negotiating' service. While companies in the United States tend to be familiar with the importance of relating price discounts to customer-related costs, because of the Robinson–Patman legislation, it is rarely used elsewhere in a positive way. Thus, while the concept of paying more for an airmail letter than a surface mail letter is well established, it is less common to find a supplier offering different 'qualities' of service at different prices. Interestingly enough, business managers who accept the difference between Business Class, Economy Plus and Economy on the airline they fly with to see their customers, might never think of how that same principle could be applied to their own business!

# DEVELOPING A CUSTOMER SERVICE CULTURE

In our eagerness to develop a customer service strategy, it would be a mistake to focus exclusively on the 'external' dimension of service; that is, customer perceptions. Of equal importance is the 'internal' dimension; that is, how do our people, our managers and workforce, view service? What is their attitude to customers? Do they share the same concept and definition of service as our customers?

It would be a truism to suggest that ultimately a company's performance is limited more by the vision and the quality of its people than it is by market factors or competitive forces. However, it is perhaps only belatedly that we have come to recognize this.

Much has been written and spoken about 'corporate culture'. We have come to recognize that the shared values held throughout the organization can provide a powerful driving force and focus for all its actions. More often than not, though, we have to admit that most organizations lack a cohesive and communicated culture. Even if there is a defined philosophy of the business, it may be little understood. This lack of shared values can have an impact on the company in many ways, and particularly on its approach to customer service.

One viable way to assess the customer climate within the firm is to 'take its temperature' by means of an employee survey. One such method begins with identifying all personnel who have a direct or indirect impact on customer service. A useful device here is to consider all the points of customer contact, whether personal or impersonal, and to ensure that all the people involved in the different departments who influence the customers' perceptions have been identified. The focus of the survey should be on these key people's perceptions of service: what do they think is important to the customers? And how do they think the company performs, service-wise?

What quite often emerges from these internal surveys is that different employees hold quite different views as to what constitutes customer service. Similarly, they may often overrate the company's actual performance compared with the customer's own rating. Making such comparisons between customers' perceptions and employees' perceptions can provide a powerful means of identifying customer service problems and their sources.

This 'audit' of internal perceptions and attitudes towards service can form the basis of a programme of action aimed at developing a customer service culture. However, such a process, which almost inevitably will involve a major reorientation within the firm, cannot work without the total commitment of top management. The service culture must grow outwards from the boardroom, and the chief executive must be its greatest champion.

Within the customer service function, one very practical step is to set up the equivalent of a 'quality circle'. Such a scheme might involve looking at the total order-processing and invoicing cycle and selecting individuals from all the sections involved. This group would meet at least once a week with the expressed objective of seeking improvements to customer service from whatever source. A further task that might usefully be given to this group is the handling of all customer complaints that relate to service.

Underpinning all these initiatives should be a company-wide education pro-gramme. Increasing numbers of organizations have come to recognize the key role that in-company education can have in developing a sense of shared val-ues. Furthermore, because it is a basic tenet of psychology that attitude change must precede behavioural change, education can lead to a measurably improved performance. Another technique used for measuring and improving service per-formance is competitive benchmarking. As discussed in Chapter 6, competitive benchmarking seeks to assess customers' perceptions of the company's perfor-mance against other suppliers from both within and outside the industry. Some financial services organizations, for example, benchmark themselves increas-ingly, not against other banks, but against companies such as Disney and Virgin who excel in customer service provision. These organizations believe that they can learn much more from comparing themselves with such companies rather than from other companies in the financial services market. Figure 19.3 shows an example of competitive benchmarking for a manufacturing firm.

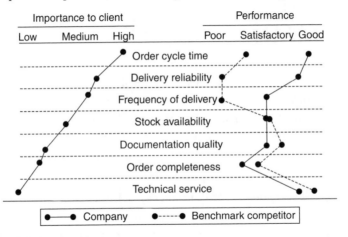

Figure 19.3 Customer service profile

It can be seen from the example that the elements of service that the client rates most highly are perceived to be delivered better, or better matched, by the company than by the competitor. The competitor's performance profile is poor in the areas that the customer values, and good in the areas that are not important to the customer. Companies that use competitive benchmarking find that it provides them with a clear guide for helping to develop business strategy, as it can often point to areas for improvement that have previously not been identified.

It is surprising, perhaps, that so few companies have defined policies on customer service – let alone an organization flexible enough to manage and con-trol that service – when it is considered that customer service can be the most important component in the company's marketing mix. By way of addressing this weakness, it is suggested that three basic actions are required for the creation of a service culture and the management of customer service:

1. Define an overall company philosophy of customer service in terms of attitude, organization and responsibilities, and encourage everyone within the company to 'live and breathe' it.

2. Develop internal standards for customer service on careful studies that have explored the quantitative trade-offs between various levels of customer service and the costs of achieving such levels so as to identify the most profitable policy for each customer segment.

3. Inform customers of what they might expect by way of customer service (perhaps in more general terms than the company defines its policies internally), and ensure these expectations are upheld. Where they are not upheld, the company, and not the customer, should be regarded as the party at fault.

# SUMMARY

Customer service is perhaps the most powerful dimension in the marketing mix of any company. In one sense, the development of targeted customer service strategies is only the logical extension of the marketing concept: customer service is about recognizing the specific needs of the customer and developing a strategy that focuses the resources of the organization towards meeting those needs cost effectively.

As such, the development of a customer service strategy requires a corporate culture that extends beyond slogans and involves all levels of the organization in working together to ensure that, for customers, doing business with the company becomes a regular habit of choice.

To achieve the most effective deployment of corporate resources in developing a customer service policy, a number of prerequisites exist:

- the differing perceptions of the various parties to the purchasing decision in terms of customer service must be recognized;
- the trade-off potential between the various components of the customer service mix must be evaluated; and
- the unique customer service requirement of each product/channel/market segment must be identified.

The choice of service level for a particular product should balance supplier costs and customer benefits, the point of balance being reached when the costs equal the extra revenue gained by the extra level of availability. Service level decisions will be tempered by other influential factors, such as:

- The contribution to fixed costs – for example, can it bear the cost of an upgraded service level?
- The nature of the market – for example, are there substitute products?
- The nature of the competition – for example, do they offer better service levels?
- The nature of the distribution channel – for example, does the company sell direct or through intermediaries?

The proven direct correlation between customer retention and profitability suggests that the costs of providing enhanced customer service could be seen as a justified investment in customer retention.

# FURTHER READING

Grönroos, C. (2007) *Service Management and Marketing: Customer Management in Service Competition*, Chichester: Wiley

The principles and practice of contemporary customer service management; managing services, relationships and quality.

# REFERENCES

ABA Bank Marketing (2013) Warning! Branch Closures Result in Customer Defections, *ABA Bank Marketing*, Vol. 45 (6): 3.

Christopher, M. G. (1992) *The Customer Service Planner*, Oxford: Butterworth-Heinemann.

Grönroos, C. and Helle, P. (2010) Adopting a Service Logic in Manufacturing, *Journal of Service Management*, Vol. 21 (5): 564–590.

Institute of Customer Service (2013) *UK Customer Satisfaction Index: The State of Customer Satisfaction in the UK*, London: ICS.

Tatikonda, L. U. (2013) The Hidden Costs of Customer Dissatisfaction, *Management Accounting Quarterly*, Vol. 14 (3): 34–43.

# CHAPTER 20
# ELECTRONIC MARKETING

IN THIS CHAPTER WE STUDY:

- the fundamentals of electronic marketing
- how value is created online
- the '6Is' framework and add a seventh 'I'
- the e-marketing plan
- strategic e-marketing business models
- social media marketing

# INTRODUCTION

The Internet and the world wide web have the capacity to transform relations between organizations and stakeholders. 'Electronic marketing' is commonly interpreted rather narrowly as a means of reaching new consumers in new markets, more frequently and intensely than by traditional means. Rushing to get online, companies often ignore consumer preferences and notions of value creation, focusing instead on the mechanics of establishing a branded website, Facebook or Twitter account before contemplating purpose and content. In this chapter we pose a number of fundamental questions: what is the role and purpose of technology in marketing; how does it create value, and for whom; what strategic options are available; how might electronic media be exploited in marketing to the mutual benefit of companies, customers and other key stakeholders? Obvious questions, perhaps, but questions that many organizations fail to pose.

# FUNDAMENTALS

The first issue to be addressed is whether or not the Internet and web necessitate a completely new approach to marketing. According to Christensen (1997), a disruptive innovation is anything that creates an entirely new market through the introduction of a new type of product. Generally, disruptive technologies underperform established products in mainstream markets, but they have features that a few (generally new) customers value. Over time, the benefits accruing from disruptive innovations are recognized by an increasing number of customers and eventually they render existing products obsolete. According to Christensen (1997), disruptive innovations have three key characteristics: they are radical (as opposed to incremental); the pace of disruption outstrips market needs; existing financial structures of successful companies often preclude them from adopting disruptive innovations. If we consider the impact of the Internet upon traditional ways of doing business, the emergence of new products, distribution and communication strategies and revenue models, web-based companies such as Google, Amazon, eBay, Apple and Facebook that have sprang up and quickly dominated the online space, the phenomenal success of social networking sites (SNSs) and the difficulties existing companies have had in responding to new challenges, then it can easily be argued that the Internet and web may indeed be considered disruptive innovations. Consumers have embraced web technologies enthusiastically leaving little doubt that organizations need to approach marketing with the web in mind.

In a seminal article published in the Harvard Business Review, Michael Porter writes;

> Many have argued that the Internet renders strategy obsolete. In reality the opposite is true. Because the Internet tends to weaken industry profitability without providing proprietary operational advantages, it is more important than ever for companies to distinguish themselves through strategy. The winners will be those that view the Internet as a complement to, not a cannibal of, traditional ways of competing.
>
> (Porter, 2001:2)

Porter highlights the relationship between the Internet, strategy and profitability, which is a sound starting point for our consideration of the role and purpose of electronic technologies in marketing. Electronic marketing, for our purposes, concerns any type of marketing activity that is facilitated by Information and Communications Technology (ICT).

The terms 'Internet' and 'web' are used interchangeably in everyday speech, however the former refers to the technological infrastructure and the latter the language; HyperText Transfer Protocol (HTTP) being the protocol that enables communication and HyperText MarkUp Language (HTML), the language of the web. Initially, it was anticipated that the web would enable companies to interact more extensively with prospective customers; however, the impact has been far more pervasive, fundamentally affecting both B2C and B2B relations, expectations and behaviours. New types of products and services have been created, such as digital music tracks and online intermediaries, and entire industries and markets have changed fundamentally, such as the music distribution and publishing industries. The ultimate impact of the web is unknown; however, by providing a new channel for communication, transactions and distribution, it has already been instrumental in reshaping relations between companies and consumers, suppliers, distributors and retailers.

Our primary focus is the web, as the concept of e-marketing was established and widely understood with the advent of web-enabled e-commerce at the turn of the millennium. It is useful to conceptualize the systems that support electronic marketing as 'front-end' and 'back-end', the former being the client-facing interface (for example, a company website) that brings an organization into contact with buyers (also encompassing consumer-to-consumer [C2C] interaction) and the latter being processes and relationships that enable companies to bring products and services to market. The focus of back-end systems is the marketing information system (MIS) database, which is often linked to external partners by extranet technologies and applications.

Figure 20.1 provides a very simple overview of the three basic levels of web-enabled e-marketing.

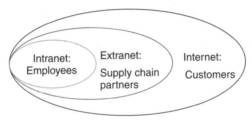

Figure 20.1 Intra-, extra- and Internet

An Intranet is essentially a closed, firewalled electronic network that enables employees within an organization to communicate. Nowadays Intranets apply Internet principles and protocols, making them relatively accessible, flexible and scalable. An Intranet can be a critical platform for internal marketing, promoting core organizational values through information dissemination, shared discussions and co-created content. If exploited well, Intranets can be instrumental in enhancing employee satisfaction, feedback and, ultimately, engagement.

Extranets enable both data processing and communication with key partners. Adoption has grown rapidly, driven by the prospect of lower costs, fewer human errors and improved communications between partners, typically along the supply chain. Extranets also use Internet protocols, so they too are relatively accessible, flexible and scalable. Transparency is a key benefit, in that sharing information and knowledge with key partners can eliminate the need for extraneous communications, multiple phone calls and face-to-face meetings. With partners accessing one shared source, errors can be reduced and processes accelerated, thereby enhancing productivity and competitiveness. Studies of organizations that prefer not to use extranets identify a number of barriers to adoption however, including reluctance to share knowledge, the need for a high level of detailed information and requirements for in-depth discussions/extensive communications.

The Internet, as intimated, provides the infrastructure for web-based communications with a variety of stakeholders; from an e-marketing perspective, we are concerned primarily with consumers and customers. Unlike parochial information systems, Internet standards and protocols are universal, offering a number of benefits compared to traditional marketing channels. The key benefits of the Internet are accessibility and 'always on' availability; for consumers, this means being able to access a wide range of products, services and information at a convenient time, while for organizations it provides global access consumers and other stakeholders, with more frequent interactions than traditional offline channels permit.

For any business, the web can enhance its role as vendor (86% of UK consumers research a company online before purchasing something from it offline), or as buyer (85% of UK B2B buyers use the web in their procurement decision-making). Yet, ICT contributes to marketing success *only* if objectives are clear and specific, accompanied by sound strategic planning, meticulous operationalization and continuous monitoring, measurement and management. Technology is never an end in itself; it is a means of improving consumer engagement and, ultimately, enhanced profitability.

The rapid advance of the web is driven by a number of macro-level factors, specifically globalization, increasing competition and significant economic advances in the developing BRICS and EAGLES countries. In response, companies in the developed world are engaged in an ongoing quest for lower operating costs, greater efficiency and productivity gains alongside improved customer and partner relations. The web offers solutions, seducing the optimistic or naïve with the prospect of a quick fix. In order to secure ongoing, sustainable benefit from technological advances, however, organizations need to understand how they might be exploited to create value for consumers and other key stakeholders.

# VALUE CREATION

The success of the web, in many respects, is illustrative of two of the fundamentals of marketing; appearing 'in the right place, at the right time'. During the 1980s and 1990s, a key economic, political and societal shift occurred, in the form of globalization, laying the foundations of and setting the scene for new ways of doing business. Accompanied by neo-liberal discourses and axioms promoting borderless markets and the supremacy of capitalism and the individual, globalization enabled companies to enhance marketing reach and the frequency and depth of marketing communications. Offering the potential of global reach and customization, the web was embraced enthusiastically by both businesses and consumers from the late 1990s onwards.

Enabled by rapidly developing database and electronic information transfer technologies which became increasingly accurate, scalable and cost effective, organizations were able to establish internal systems which create value for multiple stakeholders. For example, supplier and distributor-facing electronic corporate interfaces (extranets) create value by enabling each member to specialize in the area where it has strong core competence. A software developer could, for instance, release an update directly over the Internet to the consumer, thus releasing the distributor to focus on supplementary service provision. Value is created for the consumer by reducing lead time, providing opportunities to benefit from supplementary services and, potentially, lower prices if some of the cost savings are passed on.

The web creates value for consumers in other ways, too. Compared to traditional forms of marketing, it has a variety of value-adding attributes that can be leveraged to bind consumers closer to a company or brand. At a generic level, the web has six key value-adding attributes for consumers, formulated by McDonald and Wilson (1999) as the 'Six Is' framework and is still valid today.

## INDEPENDENCE OF LOCATION ('ANYWHERE')

To begin with, a website offers independence of location, meaning that consumers can reach the online store, regardless of geographic location. The benefits of this are obvious; from the consumer's perspective, purchase decisions and transactions can be accomplished from the comfort of their own home, while from the company's perspective, there is no need to invest in expensive premises or have a large network of branches; consumers can access the virtual store wherever they are in the world. For mass market companies, such as supermarkets or FMCG brands, the web offers the prospect of even greater massification, economies of scale, lower costs and, ultimately, increased profits. Companies serving niche markets can find value in the web, by reaching and serving their target markets even if they are geographically disperse. Even high-end brands which in the past established websites to showcase rather than sell products, shying away from transactional functionality for reasons of diminishing allure and damaging brand equity, are increasingly introducing transactional functionality. For example, at www.uk.burberry.com a classic trench coat can be purchased for just over £1090 (bewilderingly, an additional £7 is charged for postage).

## INDEPENDENCE OF TIME ('ANYTIME')

Value is created further by 'always open' availability. Compared to the past, consumers have unprecedented access to companies' products and services at a time that suits them. The ultimate retailing convenience is to be able to shop 'at the right time'. Being able to reach consumers whenever they (the consumer) wish has the effect of widening choice and extending consumer power. Unconstrained by standard opening hours, it is now feasible for products and services to become truly global, necessitating a global strategy and approach. Time independence is particularly relevant for service industries or industries with a high level of self-service. For example, Oxford Brookes University's MBA programme offers 'anytime' learning, including module descriptors, video and audio lectures, seminars, groupwork, assignments and self-assessment exercises all provided online, and accessed at the convenience of the individual learner.

## INTERACTIVITY

The web enables consumers to interact on a continuous basis with companies and each other. Moving from traditional *push* strategies in which messages are broadcast unilaterally, web technologies encourage *pull* techniques, in which consumers literally pull information from companies, creating the potential for highly interactive communications. For example, even a traditionally low-involvement product such as Fairy washing-up liquid has its own website and Facebook page where consumers can access information about the Fairy product range, as well as a selection of dishwashing tips, ideas for family time. In addition, they can share photos and recipes, watch commercials, download coupons, enter competitions, become a 'Fairy Ambassador' or donate to charity.

## INDIVIDUALIZATION

A key feature of the web is its ability to identify, profile and track individual users. While potentially raising a number of privacy issues, trackability simultaneously presents numerous opportunities for one-to-one or *micro-marketing* which is defined conceptually as companies serving 'segments of one'. Individualized communications essentially involve sending different messages to each customer, according to his or her requirements. Typically, the process is triggered by an online consumer allowing a website to download a cookie onto his or her computer. A cookie is a small file, typically of letters and numbers; once downloaded on the user's computer, it is then sent back to the originating website on each subsequent visit, allowing the company to track site usage and behaviour. Interestingly, although cookies are commonplace and reasonably well known, a 2011 survey of 1000 UK web users by PriceWaterhouseCoopers on behalf of the Department of Culture, Media and Sport found 41 per cent unaware of the different types of cookies and 37 per cent admitting ignorance of how to manage cookies on their computer.

More proactively, consumers can register with a website to receive personalized communications; though, in practice, these are not unique to each individual, but contain generic information of interest to a particular segment – known as 'mass customization'. In addition, collaborative filtering, which employs a relatively simple algorithm to recommend relevant offers to customers based upon mapping past choices, can create the impression of a high level of personalization (at relatively low cost). In the United Kingdom, Amazon and Tesco have gained formidable reputations for exploiting mass customization to great effect, creating significant value for their customers.

## INTEGRATION

In order to manage customer relationships, organizations need information about the customer purchase cycle from initial contact through pre-sales, order placement and delivery to post-sales service. Such data must be available across the various communication media employed and should be easily updated across multiple sources. Without this, customer experiences will vary across the different channels; important information may be lost, or opportunities to improve information squandered. Managing customer data in this way is referred to as data integration. Although many organizations have client-facing websites, back-end systems are often not fully integrated; for example, sites are often used simply to provide details of the products or services, purchase facilities and/or collect email addresses for direct mail purposes. By failing to integrate front-end and back-end technologies, opportunities are missed to glean key consumer insights. A common illustration of front- and back-end integration is when a product search result indicates how many items remain in stock, thus indicating that the ordering and inventory systems are connected.

## INDUSTRY RESTRUCTURING

The web has had a major impact upon numerous industries, in some cases resulting in a wholescale rethink of long-standing business models (for example, music, books and films), to less dramatic but nonetheless significant effects (for example, the travel industry). In the early days of the web, many companies became enthralled with the idea of disintermediation or 'cutting out the middle man'. The potential benefits were obvious (shorter supply chains, removing the costs of intermediaries, getting closer to the customer). Some industries have managed to adapt successfully to the web environment by exploiting two key characteristics: (i) the potential for customers to self-serve and (ii) the ability of electronic technologies to standardize and automate processes. easyJet, for example, succeeded in circumventing travel agents by requiring passengers to self-serve, booking flights directly through the website and printing their own boarding cards. Other industries, such as banking, insurance, sports, entertainment and leisure, have similarly managed to essentially outsource process costs to customers. This has attracted little complaint, as customers perceive value in the ability to shop online and make choices at a convenient time and place.

To the 'Six Is' framework we add a seventh:

## INTELLIGIBILITY

One of the key benefits of the web to consumers is its transparency and intelligibility. Consumers value highly the ability to compare product information and prices before making a purchase decision. Websites provide a vast amount of information for consumers, making it relatively easy to compare product specification and prices quickly and with minimal effort. This has been found to have a levelling effect, as unintelligible prices cannot survive long in the hypercompetitive online arena. In response to the need for transparency and intelligibility, new intermediaries, in the form of consolidator or 'aggregator' sites, have become widespread. Aggregators allow consumers to search the web for specific items and the range of prices available, in effect outsourcing a time-consuming activity. Examples of aggregator sites can be found in almost any industry, ranging from B2C aggregators focusing upon a single industry, such as hotels.com, through multi-sector sites such as moneysupermarket.com, to massive B2B aggregator portals like www.alibaba.com. Value is created for consumers by the 'one stop shop' approach that aggregators offer.

# THE E-MARKETING PLAN

Emergent technologies indisputably offer new opportunities for growth, either through the invigoration of traditional companies and brands, product or service digitization, access to new markets, reaching new segments, expansion of consumer touch-points and so on. In addition, new technologies provide organizations with trackable, measurable results, making it relatively simple to measure effectiveness of specific campaigns or, more broadly, return on e-marketing investment. Nonetheless, not all companies are well placed to capture the numerous benefits arising from rapid technological advances. To understand the potential contribution of technology to marketing, organizations must possess some knowledge of various ways in which it can be exploited. Once this is mapped, an e-marketing plan can be produced. There are two diametrically opposing views of the e-marketing plan; either that it should be done separately to the main marketing plan, or fully integrated within it. From an integrated marketing communications perspective, in terms of efficacy of time and effort, it is preferable to adopt a holistic approach even though some activities will be offline and others online.

## MARKETING OBJECTIVES

The first, most important starting point is to set clear, achievable objectives. These may vary quite widely according to context; however, they should be set in relation to broader marketing and organizational objectives. Rushing online in a bid to keep abreast of competitors is *not* a sound objective (but may be more common than one might imagine). Broadly speaking, e-marketing objectives can fall into one of six generic categories (see Dann and Dann, 2011):

Cost-oriented: in which the goal is to reduce costs. This is a popular objective, given the perpetual downward pressure on costs in increasingly global markets.

Sales-oriented: in which the objective is to increase both the amount sold and sales revenue. Transactional websites, search engine optimization (SEO) incorporating both paid and organic search, subscription-only sites and affiliate marketing are all potentially important drivers of online sales.

Behavioural change: where the objective is to change the behaviour of customers or partners, most typically by automating some aspect(s) of the purchase process. Examples are numerous, ranging from fully automated self-service such as online banking, travel bookings, gas and electricity meter readings and payments to partially automated processes, such as buying groceries online.

Information dissemination: where the web is used as either a supplement or substitute to traditional channels. The objective is to streamline and improve the quality and reach of information flowing from the organization to its target audiences.

Promotional objectives: in which the objective is to improve the promotion of products and services to target audiences. From a marketing communications perspective, these would typically be stated in terms of reach and frequency and could incorporate simple factual provision aimed at the cognitive level of more persuasive messages aimed to elicit an affective response.

Entertainment-oriented objectives: these are becoming more common due to rapid adoption of social media technologies and applications. Evidence indicates that consumers like to be entertained and recall entertaining messages or activities more easily than other forms of promotional communications.

We know that successful marketing relies upon offering clear value to consumers and it can be tempting to set marketing objectives in terms of 'what the customer would like'. This is to underplay the role of marketing objectives in defining also how value might be created *for the organization*. It is sensible not to rush setting marketing objectives; they require forethought and discussion in order to ensure they are defined in terms that offer overt value both to consumers and the organization.

## STRATEGY

Once objectives are set, the next step is to devise a strategy to move from the current to the desired position. This step requires in-depth knowledge of the marketing planning process and e-business/e-commerce/e-marketing strategy options. Organizations with little knowledge or ability often confuse strategy and tactics, focusing at this stage upon setting up a website, Facebook pages or Twitter account, with little strategic sense. This is unlikely to achieve a successful outcome. What is needed at this stage is the classic planning approach: situational analysis, including market and competitor analysis and trend data; primary and secondary market research; consumer feedback and user statistics.

At the strategy stage, the *target audience* should be clearly in focus. Market segmentation should be undertaken such that there is a clear definition of who is being targeted. Online technologies enable much more sophisticated segmentation than in the past. Organizations can now monitor, track and measure consumer interaction, providing valuable data for use-based segmentation. In addition, the general propensity for modern consumers to be relatively liberal with their personal data means that companies can relatively easily build up segmentation profiles based upon a variety of characteristics, such as demographics, behaviour, attitudes, preferences, psychographics and so on. Once segments have been evaluated against the usual criteria (homogeneity, size, measurability, accessibility, actionability, responsiveness), decisions can be made about which segments to target and how best to reach them.

With all the above data at hand, a number of strategic options can be considered. Strategically, the web might support the marketing activities of an organization in one or more of four key ways:

1. Showcasing (non-transactional)

   In which a company uses its website to display its products, or services, but without any communications or transactional functionality. It is appropriate for exclusive or bespoke offerings that are not aimed at mass market consumption.

2. Communication (with suppliers, customers, partners)

   Encompassing anything from a simple 'contact us' email facility on a company website to fully integrated, extranet-enabled Electronic Data Interchange (EDI) between numerous partner organizations up- and downstream along a supply chain.

3. Transaction/processing (involving some level of integration)

   Ranging from, at one extreme, a relatively unsophisticated 'buy now' facility to a sophisticated multi-product, multi-company B2C portal or B2B portal or hub.

4. Relationship-building (to/from and among consumers [B2C & C2C])

   Encompassing everything from basic asynchronous email correspondence via a website to extensive, interactive, frequent, vibrant social media marketing.

For some years, e-commerce and e-marketing theory has been predicated on the basis of linear, sequential development from 1 to 4 above, however consumers' enthusiastic embrace of social media technologies has disrupted this sequence and it is now common to find parallel evolution of all four stages.

When making strategic decisions therefore, rather than adhere to the linear model of development, it may be more beneficial to conceptualize the process as an electronic value chain, in which a series of value-adding activities connect an organization's buy-side (inbound materials, logistics, information flows, production processes etc.) with its sell-side (marketing, sales, distribution, order fulfilment). In design terms, buy-side comprises numerous suppliers and one buyer, while sell-side consists of one seller and numerous buyers. Most newcomers to e-marketing focus primarily upon sell-side, which typically is conceptualized as a website on which products or services are displayed and made available to buyers (either by ordering online and distributing either physically or virtually). Nonetheless, the bulk of activity and the greatest impact upon profitability has been achieved by strategic investment in B2B buy-side systems. Before going any further, it may be useful to explain the key features of buy-side and sell-side systems.

## Buy-side

Embracing extranet technology, businesses across all industries have exploited the web, reshaping business processes to improve operational efficacy. Buy-side systems are used primarily for procurement and, although much of the e-marketing literature focuses upon e-commerce websites, B2B procurement accounts for the bulk of e-business (and, thereby, e-marketing) transactions. Numerous industries (for example, chemical, mining and car manufacturing, and health care) use cloud-based data exchange services to securely and reliably share information across technological platforms and systems. Companies operating in industries that use data exchange applications for procurement purposes have achieved significant cost savings by working collaboratively, leveraging their bulk buying power to push down procurement costs. Suppliers, in turn, have had to become increasingly price competitive, in many instances having to organize themselves into hierarchical networks in which Tier 1 suppliers who cannot fulfil orders themselves take responsibility for sourcing supplies for the client from Tier 2 and so on.

The procurement process is typically initiated and completed electronically. Far from being a simple process of search, locate, identify, buy, the procurement process can be quite extensive and complex, involving price comparisons, formal tendering, negotiation, purchase approval, contract entry and payment. Barriers to adoption include integration and operability issues across multiple systems for multiple clients and unwillingness to share information/become completely transparent. Nonetheless, the benefits of e-procurement, in particular, enabling the procurement process to be structured, organized and executed relatively smoothly and efficiently, and nowadays, cloud-based, on-demand (Software as a Service [SoaS]) services permit even small- and medium-sized enterprises (SMEs) to benefit from web-enabled e-procurement.

## Sell-side

Sell-side systems are designed primarily to facilitate the product presentation and sales process. They can be used for any one or all four of the purposes outlined earlier. Typically, a sell-side website seeks revenue from advertising and selling online, although in some cases the financial model may be based upon subscriptions and membership fees, such as online versions of newspapers, journals or magazines. Sell-side websites may also be used solely for showcasing and brand-building, or indeed may start as such and over time transform into a different model. For example, the high-end brand, Chanel, until relatively recently maintained only a showcasing presence on the web, featuring brand history, photoshots and 'behind the scenes' news and storytelling features. Embracing social media, Chanel now has a multichannel presence; as well as the website it also has a presence on Facebook, Twitter, YouTube and Google+, showcasing, communicating and building relationships with its target audience. Congruent with its exclusive market positioning and distribution strategy however, Chanel has eschewed transactional functionality on its website, relying instead upon a 'store finder' facility.

Whatever the purpose of an organization venturing onto the web, and regardless of whether it is engaged primarily in buy-side or sell-side commerce, the key questions to be addressed at this stage should not be focused on the technology, *per se*, but on generic marketing issues:

- What is our USP?
- How can technology help to support it?
- Are we trying to create or responding to demand?
- How can we keep ahead of the competition?
- What should our 'product' be?
- Do we have the resources to trade successfully online? If so, which business model would be best?

To evaluate and answer these key questions, organizations need at least a basic understanding of online business models.

## BUSINESS MODELS

A number of strategic choices must be made. If we assume that a company exists already in the physical world and is contemplating using the web to augment its marketing activities, then a choice must be made concerning the underlying financial model. Many organizations worry that moving online might cannibalize sales through existing outlets, so it is important to understand strategic business models and the accompanying issues. There are two basic financial models: (i) revenue-generating, normally incorporating transactional functionality and (ii) shareholder value, focused more upon promoting the brand, building brand equity and reputation over the medium term. The revenue-based model has a large number of variants, as follows:

1. Transactional e-commerce and m-commerce sites
2. Direct selling (manufacturer to consumer, cutting out the middle man)
3. Subscription-based sites (fee-based, members-only services)
4. Broker models (online auction sites, exchanges, distributors and aggregators)
5. Infomediaries (advertising networks, online service providers)
6. Advertising (search engines and portals)
7. Affiliate marketing (pay per click/view/download)
8. Community (open source, social networks, co-created content)

Marketing has an important role to play in supporting each of these, requiring the development of a detailed e-marketing plan which clearly identifies how to appeal to the target audience at each stage of the customer life cycle (Figure 20.2). In contrast to traditional marketing, online marketing is much more reliant upon consumers taking proactive action, for example, to reach a website, download and use a mobile app, co-create content on Facebook or a sponsored YouTube page, or follow a branded Twitter feed.

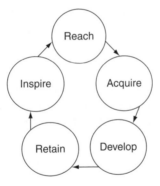

Figure 20.2 Customer life cycle

The initial 'reach' stage is therefore of utmost importance. Almost all businesses, regardless of size, have a presence on the web which, theoretically at least, enables them to reach their target audience. It is easy to overlook the fact that competitors are likely to be playing exactly the same game, and unless there is a clear USP and some attention-grabbing messaging, efforts can simply be lost in the noise. For revenue models, the initial challenge is to reach the target audience, for example, by employing online or offline channels that work in parallel with the branded website (for example, a print advert in a targeted medium, such as a special interest magazine or newsletter, advert at a special interest event, perhaps incorporating a QR code, radio advertising etc.) or online media, such as a product review on a third-party review site, QR code in a picture on a partner site, Facebook pages, targeted blog, or a viral video advertising campaign.

Acquiring customers is done either by creating compelling communications at an individual level or by targeted advertising or SEO. SEO can be either paid in which organizations bid to be near the top of the search engine results page (SERP) (see Google Adwords tutorials at accounts.google.com) or organic search in which results appear in order of relevance to a particular keyword search. Search engines work by crawling the web looking for tags and meta-tags, which it then indexes. The underlying decision-making algorithm is based upon two key attributes: relevance and authority. Relevance is based upon keywords, so care must be taken when designing web pages, with particular attention paid to tagging page titles and descriptors, inclusion of URL, text used for linking (in and out). Authority is based upon the number, and quality, of citations and links to a particular page are important (see later section on SMM). Google+, though a social networking site, should not be overlooked as a strand in SEO as Google indexes and ranks activity on Google+ pages, thus, in effect, ensuring it features strongly in SERPs.

Customer acquisition has become big business online, with many third parties aggregating and selling leads. While data protection legislation is designed to assure the privacy, confidentiality and security of personal data, there have been numerous newspaper exposés of malpractice involving data being bought and sold. The majority occur across international jurisdictions, making it difficult to charge the culprits. Other ways of acquiring customers involve communicating unilaterally with target audiences by posting useful information on a branded website, mobile site or blog and driving traffic to the site either by means of a compelling, value-based appeal (such as offering customized products, special offers, knowledge acquisition, breaking news, opportunities to co-create and share relevant content and so on) or by means of affiliate marketing programmes.

## CASE STUDY 20.1 AFFILIATE MARKETING

Affiliate marketing has grown rapidly in popularity. Sometimes called 'zero-risk advertising' its commission-based model is extremely attractive to online retailers. Affiliates display advertisements on their site with the objective of creating sales leads or driving traffic to the merchant's site. The revenue model is commission-based, with the amount of commission payable based solely upon performance. The web, by its inherent nature, enables both parties to track and monitor performance with minimal effort. The merchant pays only when a lead is passed through from the affiliate site.

Amazon was one of the first online retailers to recognize the potential of affiliate marketing, launching its 'Associates Program' in 1996. Exploiting its first mover advantage, it rapidly established a network of affiliates to drive traffic to the Amazon website. Displaying links, banners or widgets that direct users to Amazon products, affiliates are paid when the customer orders, and Amazon dispatches, 'qualifying products'. As well as the revenue stream generated from affiliate marketing, an additional attraction for the affiliates is the halo effect of being connected in consumers' minds with the trusted Amazon brand.

In addition to Amazon, other affiliate networks have been established and have grown rapidly in size, scope and popularity, among them eBay Partners, Commission Junction and Trade Doubler. These networks also act as affiliate managers, minimizing for retailers the work involved in finding appropriate affiliates, updating product and pricing information, tracking activity and making payments. For websites that have a limited presence and sell little or nothing online (for example, a blog), affiliate marketing can be a useful source of income.

### CASE STUDY QUESTIONS:

1. Outline the key benefits of affiliate marketing to (i) retailers and (ii) affiliates.

2. Employing marcoms theory, analyse the place (role, purpose and relationship with other marcoms tools) of affiliate marketing in the communications mix.

3. Some e-commerce retailers have abandoned affiliate marketing. Discuss why you think they have taken this course of action.

Customer development entails creating various opportunities to engage customers with interesting content that compels them to become repeat customers. This could be something quite basic, such as inviting customers to sign up to regular email newsletters, or encouraging feedback by embedding an email or discussion facility in the customer interface (website or mobile site). Most commonly, however, companies are turning increasingly to mobile technologies, using Facebook, Twitter, Google+, YouTube and mobile apps. Nowadays, it is rare to find a company not using the web to engage, develop, retain or inspire customers. Walmart, for example, recognizes that its customers are price-conscious value-seekers; it therefore sends SMS alerts to inform customers (who have opted to receive them) about special offers and promotions, and a link embedded within the message connects recipients to Walmart's mobile site. Sony uses a range of social media channels to engage consumers, and by monitoring discussions and question and answer sessions about the VAIO laptop, found 'love, design, style and colour' to be the most commonly used words. Sony then revamped its marketing plans, replacing planned campaigns that emphasized technical specification, speed, memory and weight with communications that emphasize stylishness, colour options and a new range of accessories that enabled customers to personalize their VAIOs. Other companies are using value-added communications, with tangible outcomes, which have proved extremely popular. London City Airport, for example, has launched a Twitter tool enabling followers to access real-time flight data by tweeting their flight number to @lcyflightinfo. It is a relatively simple matter to extend this basic communication to transactional functionality/revenue generation. The British Airways mobile app enables users to book a flight, view live flight information, check-in, download boarding card and board their plane.

Though not directly concerned with revenue generation, the shareholder value model can reap great benefits in terms of customer acquisition, retention and inspiration, ultimately resulting in improved sales performance. The Ogilvy group, for example, formerly used its website for showcasing, thereby building brand equity. Embracing social media channels, Ogilvy now has a blog as well as a Facebook, YouTube and Twitter presence. In addition, the website is exploited to promote Ogilvy's corporate social responsibility credentials by showcasing an advertisement created for the World Wildlife Fund (WWF). One of the most successful examples in recent years of the shareholder value model is the Old Spice 'The Man Your Man Could Smell Like' viral video, featuring the NTL athlete, Isaiah Mustafa. Launched at the 2010 Super Bowl and posted on YouTube, it achieved 80,000 Twitter followers in 2 days and became the most viewed sponsored video on YouTube (236 million views). Additionally, interaction with the brand on Facebook increased by 800 per cent. In response to the unprecedented fan reaction on Twitter, Proctor & Gamble (the brand owners) commissioned 116 'response' videos to fans tweets. Featuring Mustafa, the videos were filmed and posted on YouTube within 24 hours of tweets being received. Using multi-media, multi-channel exposure, running in parallel to the branded website, constantly updating content, and welcoming the numerous parodies that appeared on YouTube, P&G were rewarded by 107 per cent increase of sales of Old Spice. In addition, supporting the social media activities, the branded website features the latest branded YouTube videos as well as downloadable wallpaper, screensavers and ringtones. Visitors to the website can also use a store locator, or use the 'swag' tab to browse and buy products online from the P&G online store.

All the major brands have invested heavily in multi-channel communications platforms to retain and inspire customers. Highly tangible branded products, such as Coca-Cola, have become as skilled as intangible brands at embracing the networked properties of the web to create relationships with consumers, reinforce brand values and build brand equity. As well as the country-specific websites, national www.coke zone websites are packed with news, special offers, rewards, personalized merchandise, ringtones, videos – as well as links to the Coca-Cola Twitter, Facebook and YouTube sites. The Coca-Cola 'Crabs and Penguins' mobile app for Apple devices is a game designed to encourage long-term engagement with the brand. Players work through various levels, negotiating obstacles to return a football to penguin characters. The key message of the game is to 'spread happiness', thus reinforcing brand values. Other brands are relying increasingly upon mobile apps to add value to the customer experience. For example, Mercedes-Benz's Mbrace app for iPhone and Android devices offers a range of value-added services, such as locating the vehicle on a map, sounding the horn and flashing the lights when trying to find it in a car park, lock and unlock the vehicle, call roadside assistance or the Mercedes-Benz information call centre, and send directions to the in-vehicle global positioning service (GPS) device. Meanwhile, BMW has developed an in-car navigation system to guide drivers to the nearest available parking space and a mobile app that alerts drivers of parked cars to the amount of time left on their parking ticket. BMW have also launched 'Mini TV', a mobile app containing latest news videos about the iconic Mini brand.

*Social media marketing.*   In recent years there has been a rash of books about 'how to do' social media marketing (SMM). Often regarded as a tactic, it should be conceptualized as a strategic concomitant to any existing e-marketing. In fact, the fundamental principles of e-marketing apply equally to SMM: the product or service offering must still have overt value; USP must be clear; activities must be focused upon marketing objectives and strategy; detailed segmentation is still required. In many ways, though, the emergence of Web 2.0 (second generation web) represents a second disruptive innovation. Web 2.0 is essentially a set of collaborative networking technologies that encourage collaborative peer-to-peer communications and co-created content. The unique, disruptive characteristic of SMM is that it is largely *user-controlled*. This means that organizations must accept relatively little control over marketing communications once they have been let loose into the social media domain. Over the years there has been a gradual relaxation of corporate control of marketing messages, due in part to consumers becoming increasingly well travelled, well educated, sophisticated and demanding, and partly due to eager embrace of technology for work and play. SMM takes this to a new level. It might be argued (as many have been doing for some years) that we are witnessing a substantive rebalancing of power relations between commercial organizations and consumers, with the latter in the ascendency. Certainly, there is evidence that consumers value the facility to post comments on the products and services they consume and co-create content with their preferred brands. Thus, organizations have little choice but to accept the new landscape; whether or not they set out to engage with consumers in the social media domain, they can be reasonably certain that their products, services and brands will be discussed openly and visibly in C2C communications.

The success or failure of SMM to a large degree depends upon a thorough understanding of the structure of the web and importance of critical mass. To be successful in the social media domain, a company (or organization) needs to have a large number of people reading, communicating and posting content about it and its products, services or brands.

## Structure of the web and importance of critical mass

Barabási, renowned from his work on network theory, developed the concept of scale-free networks. According to the Barabási-Albert model, large-scale networks follow a scale-free, power law distribution. In contrast to the more common Poisson Law random distribution, a Power Law distribution means that there is a number of large, well-connected nodes and a long tail of small, increasingly isolated nodes (see Anderson's 2006 textbook, *The Long Tail*). This has two critical features directly applicable to SMM; firstly, that networks expand continuously by the addition of new vertices, and, secondly, *new vertices attach preferentially to sites that are already well connected*. Contrasting with earlier theories, the implication of this is that the development of large networks is governed by robust self-organizing phenomena that go beyond the particulars of the individual system (see barabasilab.com for more detailed information). The key implications are that networks are fundamentally dynamic, growing and changing constantly and new nodes connecting to an existing network (in this case, the web) do so on a *non-random* basis. These principles are absolutely crucial to the development of SMM, indicating that the web expands hierarchically and structurally comprises relatively few main hubs and a large number of isolated nodes. Barabasi describes the structure of the web as a bow-tie, with a 'strongly connected' component to which, and from which, pages are connected. Success breeds success, such that the strongly connected nodes go from strength to strength. This is in keeping with preferential attachment theory which holds that nodes with many existing incoming links have a higher probability of receiving additional incoming links compared to nodes with only a few existing incoming links. For SMM, therefore, connectivity is king. Links to and from highly connected content (for example, a popular branded website or social media content) are crucial. Somewhat surprisingly, in our experience, awareness and understanding of the implications of Power Law distribution among marketing practitioners is generally rather poor (Figure 20.3).

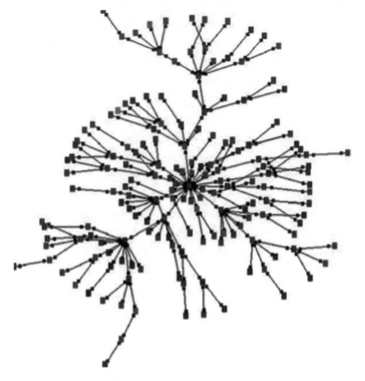

Figure 20.3 Structure of the web

Once we understand the non-random structure of the web, we can appreciate more easily the importance of word-of-mouth (WoM) marketing, which involves consumers passing on perceptions and opinions to others in their network. There exists a plethora of reports and articles in both the academic and practitioner press which acknowledge the power of WoM on consumer perceptions and purchase decisions. Within WoM, opinion leadership is acknowledged as critical. Preferential attachment links and the number and perceived quality of the reviews or comments posted by an opinion leader are found to be significant drivers of new incoming links. Currency is also known to be relevant, such that if opinion leaders cease to post content for a period of time, the number of incoming links and general interest in their views diminishes quite rapidly. Opinion leaders can be either individuals with a strong reputation in a particular field, such as George Soros (see www.georgesoros.com), or websites recognized as having something useful to say, such as www.motleyfool. co.uk. Because the web is non-random, the effects of WoM vary markedly. It has been identified as highly influential in strongly connected hubs (such as Nike Soccer on YouTube, Facebook and Twitter and Nike's Pro-Direct Soccer Zone mobile app) which, due to critical mass of visitors, co-created content and news about/advice straight from top footballers have gained a formidable reputation. WoM is also influential in situations where consumers are buying a product for the first time, or the purchase decision involves a high level of risk. It is expected to continue to be a main influence on purchase decisions, as it is now perfectly normal for consumers to look for product reviews, either by other consumers or third-party reviewers (independent review websites or opinion leaders' blogs or videos), before making a purchase.

To exploit SMM successfully, organizations need to have specific objectives for social media usage. As with e-marketing objectives, SMM objectives can vary widely, relating to one or more stages of the customer life cycle. SMM objectives can be concerned with customer acquisition, enhanced engagement, customer retention or advocacy. Once objectives are clear, SMM strategy can be developed. It goes without saying that the SMM strategy must underpin and support the e-marketing strategy (and, in turn, the broader marketing and corporate strategies). At this stage, it is useful to understand the key characteristics and attributes of the most widely used SNSs for B2C, Facebook, Twitter and YouTube.

Facebook is the most widely used SNS globally, providing a potentially powerful means of engaging target audiences. Evidence suggests that, like Facebook for private use, consumers expect branded Facebook sites to be relatively informal, friendly and packed with useful content. It has been suggested that Facebook can be a useful way of 'humanizing' a brand, as well as a useful communication tool for 'family news' about a brand and a distribution channel for special promotions and offers for 'fans' who follow and 'like' the brand on Facebook. The look and feel of Facebook pages lend themselves to visual content, such as photographic and video content, presenting new opportunities to promote unique brand attributes, personality and characteristics.

In contrast to Facebook, Twitter provides limited scope for engaging consumers with humanizing brand features. The purpose of Twitter is to keep a brand 'live' by reminding consumers of its presence in both the physical and digital worlds. Twitter works best as a viral marketing tool, creating a 'buzz' around a brand, or around events, or news items posted in cyberspace. *Where it gains critical mass*, it can be immensely powerful. The key attribute of Twitter is the instantaneousness of messaging, coupled with ease of use (the limit of 140 characters means relatively little effort required to engage with a brand on Twitter). Audiences can be incited to action relatively easily, for example, to attend events, enter competitions, visit video content on an accompanying website or SNS. Although Twitter is relatively anonymous (it does not humanize brands as Facebook can), some companies, such as McDonald's provide introductions to the Twitter team on their website, thus presenting a human face to Twitter feeds.

YouTube is growing rapidly as a key communication platform for brands. Recently, there has been a surge of consumer interest and enthusiasm for video content, which YouTube is perfectly placed to provide. Evidence suggests that brand loyal consumers enjoy engaging with visual content. Video commercials and associated content on YouTube which provides information to viewers and equips them with new knowledge ('how to' videos) have proved extremely popular. Additionally, consumers respond well to opportunities to engage interactively with a brand on YouTube, for example, by co-creating content or entering competitions. One of the main benefits of YouTube is the ability to embed video content in other channels, such as in blogs or other SNS, thereby extending reach and target audience exposure.

Organizations need to plan the media to be used and identify adequate resources to keep content and communications up to date. It is well known, but often overlooked in busy periods, that out-of-date content is a 'turn-off' – and nowadays what constitutes 'out-of-date' is changing (shortening) continually. Generally, a mixture of 'push' or 'pull' strategies is used to distribute content and create interest and enthusiasm for, and 'buzz' about, a brand or organization. The starting point is to create interesting, highly relevant content. Content for the site can be created in a number of ways, potentially involving the whole networked community, rather than just the host organization. It can include the main website and associated branded sites (such as YouTube, Facebook and Flikr) can be produced in a number of ways, for example, online video and photo sharing, podcasts and blogs. It would be a mistake to assume that consumers will find their way to a website; this is the single most important reason for the failure of a website to meet expectations. A content-rich site is just the starting point. Once there is sufficient content offering overt value to the target audience, strategies can be developed to push consumers to interact with, and co-create, content. WoM becomes important at this point, and can be exploited by using any one, or several, of the multifarious social networks that exist online, for example, Facebook, Twitter, LinkedIn, question and answer forums such as Quora, social bookmarking sites such as Reddit, or branded mobile apps. Push and pull strategies can then be used in tandem, for example, if a visitor allows cookies, or signs up for an email newsletter, then new content can be pushed out to them as and when it becomes available. In relation to email newsletters, although these are used by numerous companies for CRM purposes, there is plenty of evidence indicating that subscribers are motivated primarily by special offers and discounts.

The success of SMM is largely dependent upon the networks and channels selected for brand promotion, the amount and nature of social media participation and the level and quality of community engagement. Social media monitoring can track how communications about a company's products or brands is being spread across the web as well as identifying opinion leaders. Recently, there have been numerous examples of successful SMM campaigns (i.e. campaigns designed specifically for social media channels). Nike's 'My Time is Now' campaign remains top of the 'most watched adverts on YouTube' in 2012, engaging 21 million viewers for an average of 6 minutes 18 seconds. The Nike Football brand has over 25 million followers on Facebook, 1.5 million Twitter fans and almost 7 million fans across other online social networks. Mobile video is emerging as the most popular SMM tool. The Vyclone iPhone app which enables friends to co-create, edit and share video is growing rapidly in popularity, while for Android users SnapChat, which enables non-permanent messages to be exchanged without creating a trackable record, is also experiencing rapid adoption. For business and B2B users, numerous mobile apps have appeared recently to facilitate collaborative content creation, editing and sharing. Cloud-based and updated in real-time, they are anticipated to grow rapidly in volume and popularity in the coming years. At the beginning of 2012 Gartner identified mobile apps as *the* key growth area to watch, specifically: location-based services, mobile social networking, mobile search and transaction, end-to-end mobile commerce including easy-to-use payment functionality, context-aware services (based upon personalized consumer profiling), object recognition functionality, mobile video and mobile instant messaging and email (see www.itbusinessedge.com). It is widely anticipated that mobile technologies, particularly user-friendly mobile apps for smartphones will become the norm for business use also, with multiple, independent processors dividing the device into discreet silos, one for work, the other for private use, implying that mobile apps will become mainstream in B2B communications in the not too distant future. In 2012 Standard Charter bank distributed iPhones to its employees, enabling rapid communication both with back-end systems and consumers wishing to engage via its mobile app, Breeze.

# SUMMARY

E-marketing should be conceptualized as an extension of traditional marketing. Although the Internet can be considered a disruptive innovation, the fundamentals of marketing planning remain. In order to evaluate how technology might help achieve marketing objectives, an organization needs set clear objectives and make a series of strategic choices with a specific target audience in mind. The poverty in much of the e-marketing rhetoric resides in the propensity to rush online without a clear strategy with a 'me too' mindset. Technology is never an end in itself yet, particularly with the rapid advancement of social media channels, it can be tempting to focus on the vehicle to the detriment of content or even the desired outcomes.

If e-marketing strategies are to succeed, they should be focused clearly upon creating value for stakeholders along the electronic value chain which includes employees, suppliers, wholesalers, distributors, aggregators and retailers, as well as customers. The digital marketspace is cluttered and increasingly competitive, so it becomes imperative to cut through the noise with communications that not only contain value-added messages but opportunities for consumer activation. Through SMM consumers can be become more powerful, animated and engaged to the benefit of all in the virtual value chain.

# FURTHER READING

Dann, S. and Dann, S. (2011) *e-Marketing: Theory and Application*, Basingstoke: Palgrave Macmillan.

A practical, user-friendly introduction to the theory and practice of electronic marketing.

# REFERENCES

Andersen, C. (2006) *The Long Tail*, London: Random House.

Barabási, A.-L. and Reka, A. (1999) Emergence of Scaling in Random Networks, *Science*, Vol. 286 (5439): 509–512.

Christensen, C. M. (1997) *The Innovator's Dilemma: When New Technologies Cause Great Firms to Fail*, Boston: Harvard Business School Press.

Dann, S. and Dann, S. (2011) *e-Marketing: Theory and Application*, Basingstoke: Palgrave Macmillan.

McDonald, M. and Wilson, H. (1999) *e-Marketing: Improving Marketing Effectiveness in a Digital Age*, Harlow: Pearson Education.

Porter, M. (2001) Strategy and the Internet, *Harvard Business Review*, Vol. 79(3): 62–78.

# PART IV
# MONITORING VALUE

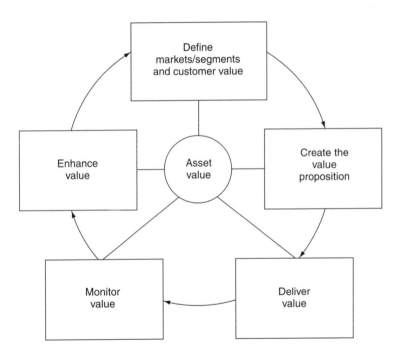

# CHAPTER 21
# MARKETING INFORMATION AND CONTROL

IN THIS CHAPTER WE STUDY:

- main areas for monitoring value
- marketing audit as a management information tool
- the importance of establishing a marketing information system
- the purpose of database marketing, data warehousing and data mining
- objectives of information management and control systems
- the marketing budget as a management control tool

# THE MEANING OF
# MONITORING VALUE

In the marketing map, the key marketing process of 'monitor value' appropriately follows the output of 'deliver value', or performance. The need to maintain regular surveillance over marketing performance is as important as that over any other aspect of business performance and should not be underestimated. A laissez-faire attitude to management of customer value is not only dangerously irresponsible but also ignores the central of pillar of the marketing concept: that marketing is a *matching process*. Achieving a match between the wants and needs of customers and the objectives and capabilities of the supplier cannot be left to chance if it is to be a commercially viable and sustainable aim. Instead, it must be a deliberate, concerted effort based on realism and commitment.

There are four main areas where monitoring can occur. These correspond to the main types of information dealt with in the strategic marketing planning processes of 'define value' and 'create value proposition', and derive from the implementation process of 'deliver value'. They may be summarized as:

1. *Value required* – (by customers at the latest indication) versus the expectations used in planning;

2. *Value delivered* – (to customers) versus the value proposition;

3. *Value received* – (by supplier) versus the corporate and marketing objectives;

4. *Value perceived* – (by customers in terms of product/price/place/ promotion) versus the marketing plan.

## VALUE REQUIRED

First, the organization can monitor whether the value the customers require is consistent with the previous analysis of customer requirements carried out as part of 'define markets/segments and customer value'. The information for this may be obtained partly from the information gained in the 'deliver value' process, or it may require special activity such as market research (see Chapter 4).

## VALUE DELIVERED

Second, the value delivered to customers can be monitored against the value proposition that was determined during the 'create the value proposition' process. As all aspects of customer value delivery are measured by the customer's perception, this will again involve asking the customer by some means.

## VALUE RECEIVED

Third, the organization will also wish to monitor the value it receives against the marketing objectives established in the 'create the value proposition' process. This is the area of regulation that most organizations are best at, through monthly analysis of sales by product, channel and so on (though analysis by segment or customer is often poorer than analysis by product, with customer profitability or lifetime value being generally difficult to obtain). But as the financial results are an indication of customer satisfaction, monitoring the value delivered to the customer is equally important and, for many organizations, one of the simplest ways of improving performance.

## VALUE PERCEIVED

Finally, the overall effectiveness of the marketing strategies by which the value was delivered may be evaluated. The four 'P's of the marketing mix – product, price, place and promotion – provide the main criteria for gauging perception. The information on which such insight is acquired should be a synthesis of customer data, including customer purchase behaviour and customer feedback (both solicited and unsolicited), as well as trade press commentary and industry ratings in the case of industrial purchasing.

In practice, the predominant mechanism for monitoring these areas is the marketing audit. The marketing audit provides the basis on which performance can be appraised, so that the firm can seek further professionalization of its organization and operations in order to grow its competitive potential.

# THE MARKETING AUDIT

Clearly, any marketing plan will only be as good as the information on which it is based, and the marketing audit is the means by which information for planning is organized. As stated in Chapter 7, a marketing audit is a systematic, critical and unbiased review and appraisal of all the external and internal factors that have affected an organization's commercial performance over a defined period. It answers the question: 'Where is the organization now?' By providing an understanding of how the organization relates to the environment in which it operates, the marketing audit enables management to select a position within that environment based on known factors.

## THE NEED TO AUDIT

Often the need for a marketing audit does not manifest itself until things start to go wrong for the organization, such as declining sales, falling margins, lost market share, underutilized production capacity and so on. However, without knowing the cause of these danger signs, management can easily treat the wrong symptoms and fail to address the root problems. For example, the introduction of new products, restructuring of the sales force, reduction of prices or cutting of costs are unlikely to be effective measures if more fundamental problems have not been identified. Of course, if the organization survived for long enough, it might eventually solve its problems though a process of elimination. Either way, the problems have first to be properly defined, and the marketing audit helps to define them by providing a structured approach to the collection and analysis of data and information on the complex business environment.

## THE FORM OF THE AUDIT

Any organization carrying out an audit will be faced with two kinds of variable: those over which it has no direct control and those over which it has complete control. The former includes economic and market factors, while the latter usually concerns the organization's resources, or operational variables. This division suggests that the marketing audit should be structured in two parts:

- external audit – the uncontrollable variables (business and economic environment, the market and the competition); and

- internal audit – the controllable variables (organization's strengths and weaknesses, operations and resources *vis-à-vis* the environment and competitors).

The key areas that should be investigated under these two headings are outlined in Table 21.1.

Each of these headings should be examined with a view to isolating those factors that are considered critical to the organization's performance. It is important to omit at this stage any information that is unrelated to the organization's specific problems, so that the marketing plans that are eventually prepared are pertinent to the organization's future development. Inclusion of such things as brand-switching analyses or over-detailed sales-performance histories by company and product that lead to no logical actions whatsoever, only serve to cloud focus. The auditor's initial task, therefore, is to screen the enormous amount of information and data for validity and relevance, so that all extraneous information is removed. Some data and information will have to be reorganized into a more easily usable form, and judgement will have to be applied to decide what further data and information are necessary for a proper definition of the problem.

Thus there are basically two phases that comprise the auditing process:

1. Identification, measurement, collection and analysis of all the relevant facts and opinions that impinge on an organization's problems; and

| External audit (opportunities and threats) | Internal audit (strengths and weakness) |
|---|---|
| Business and economic environment | Marketing operational variables |
| economic | Own company |
| political/fiscal/legal | Sales (total, by geographical location, |
| social/cultural | industrial type, customer, product) |
| technological | Market shares |
| intra-company | Profit margins/costs |
| The market | Marketing information/research |
| Total market, size, growth and trends | product management |
| (value/volume) | price distribution |
| Market characteristics, | |
| developments and trends | promotion |
| products | operations and resources |
| prices | |
| physical and virtual distribution | |
| channels | |
| customers/consumers | |
| communication | |
| industry practices | |
| *Competition* | |
| Major competitors | |
| Size | |
| Market share/coverage | |
| Market standing/reputation | |
| Production capabilities | |
| Distribution policies | |
| Marketing methods | |
| Extent of diversification | |
| Personal issues | |
| International links | |
| Profitability | |
| Key strengths and weaknesses | |

Table 21.1 The marketing audit checklist

2. The application of judgement to uncertain areas remaining after this analysis.

It will be recalled from Chapter 7 that the findings of the marketing audit then need to be formatted as a SWOT analysis in order to illuminate the business's key strengths, weaknesses, opportunities and threats. This 'information-turned-intelligence' will then provide the basis on which appropriate and realistic marketing objectives and strategies can be set.

Some of the principal points about the *marketing audit* are:

- A checklist of questions must be agreed and issued.
- Checklists need to be customized according to level in the organization to make them meaningful and relevant.
- It is essentially a database of all relevant company/market-related issues.
- It should be continuous and dynamic.
- Do not hide behind vague terms, for example 'poor economic conditions'.
- Do incorporate product life cycles (PLCs) and portfolio matrices. Diagrams and corresponding words should match.
- It is a valuable 'transfer device' for incoming personnel.

## 'WHEN' AND 'WHO' CONSIDERATIONS

Along with considering *what* the marketing audit should cover, *when* the audit should be undertaken and *who* should undertake it are also crucial to the effectiveness of the resulting marketing plan. Many people hold the mistaken belief that the marketing audit should be a last-ditch attempt to define an organization's marketing problems, or at best something done by an independent body from time to time to ensure that an organization is on the right track. However, since marketing is such a complex function, it seems illogical not to carry out a pretty thorough situation analysis at least once a year at the beginning of the planning cycle (see Figure 7.5). Many highly successful companies, in addition to using normal information and control procedures and marketing research throughout the year, also undertake an annual self-audit of everything that has had an important influence on marketing activities, as a discipline integrated into the management process. Such practice reinforces the role of the marketing audit as a planning as well as a monitoring tool.

This self-audit can be achieved, first, by institutionalizing procedures in as much detail as possible so that all managers involved in the audit, from the highest to the lowest levels, conform to a disciplined approach, and, second, by providing thorough training in the use of the procedures themselves.

# MARKETING INFORMATION SYSTEMS

Sound marketing plans rely on sound marketing evidence, and this requires the organization of information into a coherent structure so that planners can match external facts about the market to internal facts and figures. In other words, good marketing centres around a good marketing information system (MIS). The role of the MIS is to aid managerial decision-making, thus system design and operation are absolutely crucial. It is important not to be side-tracked by the technology; web-enabled advances make it relatively simple and cheap to collect, store and cross-reference huge amounts of data, but without an overarching plan of what data to collect, for what purpose, an MIS can end up being a massive, unwieldy mess.

Exponential advances in system functionality and storage capacity have made both marketing research and CRM much easier than in the past, but they can also conceal or divert attention from the reality of a situation. It is tempting to collect data for the sake of it, rather than for specific purposes, leading to an over-accumulation of 'big data' without any clear idea of purpose or application. There is also often an assumption that computerized analysis gives definitive results, whereas in some cases the data used for analysis may be incomplete, out of date, irrelevant or flawed in some way. Recent advances in 'in-memory analytics', in which data are pulled up from a system's RAM rather than from the traditional storage on physical disks, shortens query time and enables more rapid integration of operational and analytical data. Rather than the marketing manager having to analyse numerous data records from multiple systems, they can simply run real-time queries against the most up-to-date customer data. Acker et al. (2011) cite the benefits of in-memory analytics as performance improvements (response time, calculation performance, handling complexity, modelling capabilities); customer value creation (instant, self-service access if required, enhanced customer service); and lower costs (data stored in one place, simpler set-up and maintenance). As technology continues to evolve rapidly, it behoves marketing managers to keep abreast; the use of information, and the use of technology, must be guided by good judgement and a systematic, strategic approach to marketing information management.

## INFORMATION NEEDS

Information is not the same as technology, nor is it necessarily derived from information technology. There are many myths associated with the use of computers to hold marketing data, as Table 21.2 reveals.

| Myth | Reality |
|------|---------|
| The database collects what we need | We collect what is easily available |
| The database measures what matters | We measure what is least embarrassing |
| The database users understand what data they need | We know what we used last, what the textbooks say and what might be interesting on a rainy day |
| The database needs to hold more and more data | We feel safer with loads of data, even when we haven't a clue how to use it |
| The database must integrate the data physically | We like neat solutions, whatever the cost |
| The database will save staff time | We need more and more staff to analyse data |
| The database will harmonize marketing, finance and sales | We all compete for scarce resources, and this involves fighting |
| The database is the one source of information | We haven't really coordinated our data and market intelligence |

Table 21.2 Myths and realities about databases

*Note:* Thanks are due to Dr Robert Shaw for his contribution to this section.

As has already been established, information is not all hard, objective data; and companies will not necessarily become better informed by collecting more and more raw data and storing it until it knows 'everything'. Accounting systems are often seen as a source of hard facts, since most accounting transactions have to be audited and therefore must be reasonably accurate. Yet most accounting data have little direct relevance to marketing strategy.

What information is needed to support marketing strategy? The answer to this question is something of a conundrum, since the information needs depend on the marketing objectives that form the strategy. Unlike accounting or manufacturing, which have fixed information needs, the information needs of marketing keep changing as a consequence of the evolution of the marketing strategy.

## COMPONENTS OF A MARKETING INFORMATION SYSTEM

For all the problems, there are, in practice, a limited number of basic underlying marketing issues with which all companies have to contend. Furthermore, the solutions usually adopted can be seen as variations on relatively few themes. Essentially, information flows into the central marketing information database from a number of sources. Some data may be purchased from specialist external agencies, market research firms or government sources. Other data may be generated in the course of the organization's day-to-day activities or specific market research conducted by the organization. As well as current data, obviously over a period of time the database will build up valuable historical data that can be used to inform current and future practice. The basic model of information flows to support a MIS are illustrated in Figure 21.1. The main components of an MIS are explained in Table 21.3.

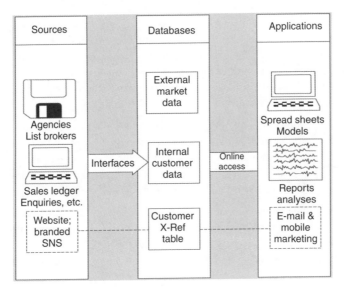

Figure 21.1 Information flows in a marketing system

The critical issue, then, when building a MIS is that it will need an interface that draws data from internal systems used in other functional areas of the organization (such as finance or sales). It should not be assumed that raw data from other departments will be adequate; such data will have to be handled, formatted and presented in a way that is of direct relevance to the marketing department. In addition, it will need to capture appropriate data-feeds from external sources to provide other supporting information.

Critical success factors include:

- Understanding the information needs of marketing, and in particular how internal and external views of a market will be reconciled.

- Developing a strong cost–benefit case for the development of information systems, given that other systems, including financial ones, will have to be altered to accommodate the needs of marketing.

- Working continuously with internal IT staff until the system is built, while recognizing that they are/will be under pressure from other sources, especially finance, and that unless marketing maintains momentum and direction, other priorities will inevitably win.

**External market data:** purchased from external agencies. These include governmental agencies, market research firms, list brokers and so on.

**Internal customer data:** collected from the sales ledger and other internal sources such as customer service, field sales, interactive TV, company website, branded social networking sites etc. It is coded and segmented in such a way that various metrics (for example, market-share) can be created by comparison with external data.

**Customer reference table:** needed to make the system work effectively. It identifies customers (as defined by marketing) and provides a cross-reference to sales ledger accounts. Whenever a new sales ledger account is created, the cross-reference table is used to determine the customer associated with that account. It is also used by marketing applications as a standard reference table for customers.

**Databases:** refer to all three of the above data types. They need to be structured using a technique known as *data modelling* which organizes the data into the component types that marketing wants, and not the structure that finance or anyone else provides. Usually, the data are held using *relational database* software, since this provides for maximum flexibility and choice of analysis tools.

**Interfaces:** refers to the computer programs that grab the data from the source systems and restructure it into the components to go on to the marketing database. These programs have to be written by the in-house IT staff, since they obtain and restructure data from the in-house sales ledger, and other in-house systems.

**Applications:** the software programs that the planners use to analyse the data and develop their plans. They include data-grabbing tools that grab the items of data from their storage locations, reporting tools that summarize the data according to categories that marketing defines, spreadsheets that carry out calculations and 'what-if' analyses on the reported summary data.

Table 21.3 The main components of a marketing information system

*Source:* Reproduced with the kind permission of Dr Robert Shaw of Shaw consulting, London.

# THE MARKETING DATABASE

The database is at the heart of contemporary marketing. Good databases enable profiling and personalization and micro-segmentation based on criteria such as buying patterns, customer-initiated communications, fine-tuned demographics and other, normally difficult to discern characteristics. As Wehmeyer (2005) observes, the marketing database supports decision-making concerning the entire marketing mix. It is therefore of strategic importance. For information and communications technology (ICT) to enhance marketing, there needs to be a fit between IT support and marketing requirements at both strategic and operational levels. Disjuncture between the two will render even the most sophisticated, expensive MIS useless.

Like any other information system, the marketing database should follow some simple rules. It should support *strategic* goals; have clear objectives; be planned carefully to contain high-quality data which can be accessed and analysed easily. Decisions about who should access the database and for what purpose (access rights) and issues of maintenance, currency and relevance need to be addressed early on the design process. The database is created, populated and manipulated by the database management system (DBMS). Nowadays, most databases are *relational* (rather than hierarchical), which means that tables are created using data that are related in some way; each table is stored independently, making it relatively straightforward to add, retrieve, manipulate or delete data. Since relationships between tables are created as part of the manipulation process, relational databases are well placed to support one-to-many and many-to-many relationships; a valuable attribute in today's networked environment.

In practice, databases often represent a compromise between the strategic requirements of an organization's planners and the tactical requirements of other managers. They can also fall prey to the pitfalls illustrated earlier in Table 21.2. The consequence of these problems is that databases often hold data that do not fit the purposes of the tacticians, far less the needs of strategic planners. One of the most acute problems is that of reconciling the internal and external views of markets. The usual problem is that data retrieved from the sales ledger rarely possess the details needed to link customer records to market segments. Some of the problems are described in Table 21.4 against the key issues involved in identifying a market segment: what is bought, by whom, and for what reason? Fusing together data from external sources and internal

| External audit variable | Problem with internal audit |
|---|---|
| What is bought | Internal systems have rich detail on accounts and stock-keeping units. However, information about products such as colour, style etc. can often be missing. Information on the outlets or channels through which they were sold is also very often lacking. |
| Who buys | Internal systems record who paid the invoice and who received delivery of the goods. They rarely record who made the buying decision or who influenced it. Even when buyer details are on the system, it is rarely easy to determine their characteristics such as age, sex and so on. |

Table 21.4 Problems of reconciling internal and external market audits

| External audit variable | Problem with internal audit |
|---|---|
| Why | Internal sources of information on why people purchase is scarce. Enquiries can be qualified, using survey techniques, to provide some clues about why people respond to an advertising campaign. Customer satisfaction surveys may also yield clues. Call reports from field sales and telesales can also provide valuable clues, especially if survey disciplines can be observed by the sales staff. |
| Reconciling variables | Reconciling external with internal variables involves:<br><br>matching accounts to customers;<br><br>matching stock-keeping units to products;<br><br>matching external variables to internal records;<br><br>collecting data from sources other than the sales ledger (e.g. from surveys of sales representatives). |

Table 21.4 (Continued)

data, or 'data fusion', is becoming increasingly common as a solution to this internal–external problem. Where large volumes of data are involved, computer programmes, known as *deduplication routines*, are used to automate the matching of the data.

# DATA WAREHOUSING

Data warehousing is a way of combining and holding data from many corporate systems and external sources in a consolidated database, or data warehouse. The data can then be accessed by end users using online analytical processing (OLAP) tools. Thus a data warehouse is essentially an MIS that stores all external and internal information in a user-friendly, efficient and current format. Some key points about data warehouses are:

1. Data warehouses aim to integrate data from all operational systems, such as order processing and billing, into one database using a single data model. That is, there is a single consistent view of such things as customers and products. So, for example, a customer's name and address will only be stored once, and all the products purchased by that customer can readily be ascertained. The data are refreshed regularly from the operational systems – typically overnight – to keep it up to date. So just as the operational systems at the customer interface are becoming better integrated, data warehousing represents the desire to better integrate information for purposes of management information and analysis.

2. Data warehouses typically hold historical information, not solely the current information needed for billing and so on. This has become possible because of the rapidly decreasing cost of computer power and data storage.

3. Similarly, increasing capacity allows the information to be held at a fine level of detail. Information can be stored about individual purchases, even for mass consumer markets, over substantial periods.

Taken together, these developments provide a rich store of information which, at least potentially, integrates the two key levels of data: customer/product level data and aggregated data at the level of markets and product groups.

# DATA MINING

Data mining is the process of discovering previously unknown information from the data held in data warehouses. Data mining software allows users to access the data warehouse to search for correlations between data that can be used in decision-making. Some of the analyses of particular relevance to marketing are:

1. *Segmentation*: subdividing markets using tools such as clustering analysis, a statistical technique which groups a large number of objects into few clusters with similar characteristics, where there are fewer differences within individual groups than among groups.

2. *Causal, econometric or predictive modelling*: predicting the effect on, say, future sales based on predictions of various 'independent variables' such as future price, advertising spend, competitors' prices and so on.

3. *Undirected searching for correlations*: asking the system to search for significant correlations between a large number of potentially connected variables, such as consumers' purchases of particular product lines. The revelation of patterns can be useful in strategy formation – for example, evident multi-purchase behaviour might suggest improvements in shelf management.

Marketing should take place as close to the customer as possible. Marketing planners must therefore secure cross-functional understanding and co-operation if they are to develop the systems they require to ensure that the company's products meet present and future customer needs. They must build interdepartmental bridges to acquire data, information and knowledge on an ongoing basis. They must also ensure that such intelligence is meaningful and usable by management, for the chief purposes of measuring and improving performance, while upholding standards of quality, responsibility and accountability.

# INFORMATION AND CONTROL
# DATA OBJECTIVES

Just as there is a hierarchy of corporate and marketing objectives, so there has to be a hierarchy of information and control data. For example, at the macro level in an organization, information will have to be generated to show overall sales volume, while at the micro level varying degrees of individual account detail will have to be generated according to the needs of the organization.

At the next level down, each department or function will need to generate its own specific control data, so that, for example, if an advertising objective is to achieve an attitude change over a given period, it will require an attitude survey in order to ascertain whether this particular objective has been achieved, and whether it possibly could, and should, be achieved better. Or, if the objective was to convey a particular piece of information to a specific target market, then again research would be necessary to establish whether this objective had been achieved and whether it could, in future, be maintained through a more cost-effective alternative strategy. The same principle would also apply to the sales function, which ideally will have a series of control data generated and distributed according to need, as well as establishing its own specialized control procedures when circumstances demand information that cannot be generated by the general company information and control system.

Any information system should be related closely to the company's organization and objectives so that relevant information for decision-making can be presented to each level of management. The important fact that emerges from any review of information and control procedures is that its purpose should be to provide management with the necessary information to enable it to monitor its progress towards its predetermined objectives, thus providing the necessary loop in the planning cycle.

Nonetheless, the basic tool for controlling the marketing effort is the budget, which itself derives from the marketing plan.

# THE MARKETING BUDGET

One of the most vexing questions for any marketing manager, or indeed, any marketing organization, is 'How much should we spend on marketing, and where?' The question is difficult because it requires an understanding of what should be included in a marketing budget, the way in which costs are generated and the relationship between marketing expenditure and the results sought. As Fischer et al. (2012: 51) observe, very often marketing practitioners allocate budgets on 'gut instinct' or some 'rule of thumb' basis, or in response to the negotiating skills of individual managers. Budget decisions should, however, not be taken lightly as such a random approach can easily result in allocations that are sub-optimal in terms of potential profit-maximization. Budget allocation decisions should be based on fact rather than intuition. Fischer et al. (2012) advocate a highly formalized approach, using a heuristic decision-support tool that accounts for dynamics in marketing effects over a period of time. Linking budgets firmly to financial outcomes, such a structured approach provides a series of budget scenarios along with their implications for the development of market shares and profits over the coming five-year period. There is certainly merit in reducing complexity and employing sophisticated financial information and analytical tools for the development of profit-maximizing budgets.

## BUDGETING PRACTICES

Unfortunately, for many organizations, such information and tools are not readily available. In their absence, the most appealing approach is to use the previous year's figures as the base and to project forward. This, of course, takes into account inflation and prevailing market conditions, and adds on an amount that senior controllers will deduct at the budget review!

### Zero-based budgeting

More preferable is an iterative zero-based approach which starts with marketing objectives and the programmes designed to achieve these objectives. Once activities have been identified, the incremental cost of these can be calculated and a budget established. If these are deemed to be too expensive, alternative activities or structures can be investigated. If these prove equally unacceptable, then a review of strategy is required and so on. In this way, every item of expenditure can be traced back to specific objectives, and indeed, the overall corporate objectives of the organization.

### Variable cost budgeting

A less wide-ranging approach is to base the budget on variable costs, particularly for short-term budgeting, since certain costs, such as human resources and physical activities, can only be altered significantly over the longer term. Periodically, however, this would require a zero-based approach to be used to review all products, markets and related activities. This would enable organizations to abandon obsolete and unnecessary features, and to make appropriate structural alterations. Such reviews have resulted in many firms refocusing much more clearly upon category or business process management.

## Life cycle budgeting

Budgeting for marketing can also incorporate life cycle costing. This involves assessments of the total costs involved in managing products over their lifetime in the market (see Chapter 8). Such an approach requires marketing managers to plan ahead in terms of product upgrades, changing promotional activities, service and distribution support, and the way price is likely to alter over the life of a product. Long-term assessments of return on investment, payback and cash management can therefore be made, which will help both short-term budgeting control and organizational financial planning.

## Operating and opportunity budgeting

A further approach to structuring a budget utilizes the notions of operating budgets versus opportunity budgets. Operating budgets cover those activities that are a continuation of existing programmes. The key issues here are in terms of efficiency and the maintenance of expected performance levels. This highlights the fact that marketing managers should be seeking constant cost-reduction and better ways of managing the marketing mix and obtaining marketing information, while at the same time countering adverse developments. An opportunities budget should be developed for unexpected circumstances that can yield financial and marketing benefits for the organization. One of the critical roles of marketing managers is to spot such opportunities and to feed them into the general management of their enterprises.

## Human resources budgeting

Most budgets only provide for money, and specify where it should be spend. They do not contain the necessary provisions to make reasonably sure that the expected results can be obtained. They do not provide for the only resource that can produce results: accomplished people. This is particularly relevant to marketing managers, where skilled sales representatives, market researchers, advertising personnel and public relations executives are crucial to the survival of the company. Recruitment and training must be accounted for both in terms of time and money resources.

## Sales budget

While the overall marketing commitment is the responsibility of any marketing manager, it may be that in smaller companies considerations such as product research and development, testing and extensive marketing research are not relevant in terms of a young or comparatively small operation.

It may be that the sales budget will be central to the marketing manager's objectives.

# SUMMARY

Marketing information is crucial to marketing planning and performance development. It can be seen to anchor marketing activities firmly in reality, while also giving marketing aims the wings to move beyond 'the acceptable' towards 'the exceptional'. The process of monitoring value, so that plans and performance can be evaluated and improved, focuses on four areas: value required; value delivered; value received; and value perceived. Each area can be examined using the distillation of key information and data provided by the marketing audit.

The marketing audit is a critical and unbiased appraisal of all the external and internal factors that have affected an organization's commercial performance over a defined period. As such, it offers a valuable management tool for diagnosing problems, as well as identifying potential solutions. Dynamic information feeds and flows are best kept open via a MIS, which often benefits from exploiting the power of information technology. Any MIS should reflect the company's organization and objectives, and should not be self-contained within the marketing department.

All budgets, no matter how they are constructed, enable managers to pull together their commitments, plans and projects, and all the costs involved, into one comprehensive document, thus providing a point of reference and control. A budget is a managerial tool, not just a financial device. While budgets are expressed mainly in monetary terms, these should be regarded as a kind of shorthand for the actual efforts needed. In other words, the marketing budget is an aid to thinking through the relationship between desired results and available means. The numbers can be worked out with comparative ease once the criteria for expected results has been explored fully and marketing management have a clear brief as to what they are accountable for, and what marketing objectives must be satisfied.

# FURTHER READING

McDonald, M. and Wilson, H. (2011) Completing the Marketing Audit (parts 1 and 2) in *Marketing Plans: How to Prepare Them, How to Use Them*, Chichester, Wiley.

A comprehensive overview of marketing planning theory and application; issues, process, execution and pitfalls.

# REFERENCES

Acker, O., Gröne, F., Blockus, A. and Bange, C. (2011) In-memory Analytics: strategies for real-time CRM, *Journal of Database Marketing & Customer Strategy Management*, Vol. 18 (2): 129–136.

Fischer, M., Albers, S., Wagner, N. and Frie, M. (2012) Dynamically allocating the marketing budget: How to leverage profits across markets, products and marketing activities, *GfK Marketing Intelligence Review*, Vol. 4 (1): 50–59.

Wehmeyer, K. (2005) Aligning IT and marketing – The impact of database marketing and CRM, *Journal of Database Marketing & Customer Strategy Management*, Vol. 12 (3): 243–256.

# CHAPTER 22
# MEASURING MARKETING EFFECTIVENESS

IN THIS CHAPTER WE STUDY:

- the need for marketing accountability
- imperative of strategic marketing and value creation
- three levels of marketing measurement
- Marketing Due Diligence

# INTRODUCTION

The ultimate test of marketing investment is whether it creates value for shareholders. But few marketing investments are evaluated from this perspective, and many would argue that it is almost impossible to link financial results to any specific marketing activity. Increasingly, boards of directors and city analysts the world over are dissatisfied with this lack of accountability for what are, very often, huge budgets. Marketing's lack of accountability is seen increasingly as being harmful not only to an organization but marketing's place within the organization. Park et al. (2012) find that inadequate accountability leads not only to a weakening of the department's influence within the organization, but also threatens the department's legitimacy within the organization.

There is an urgent need for measurement frameworks, not only to answer the widespread accusations of poor performance, but so that corporate and financial strategists can understand how to link marketing activities to the wider corporate agenda.

# GROWING NEED FOR GREATER MARKETING ACCOUNTABILITY

Growing understanding of the importance of marketing has had a number of consequences. Firstly, the classic textbook treatment of strategic issues in marketing has finally caught up with reality. Topics such as market and customer segmentation, product and brand development, databases and customer service and support are now regularly discussed at board level, instead of being left to operational managers or obscure research specialists. CEOs are recognizing that they must support the role of chief marketing officer if they want to create truly customer-led organizations. Additionally, because of their 'new' mission-critical status, marketing investments are attracting the serious attention of finance professionals. As part of a wider revolution in thinking about which corporate assets are crucially important in today's business environment, intangibles such as knowledge about customers and markets, or the power of brands, have assumed a new importance.

The academic world too has turned its attention to the link between the use of marketing metrics and outcomes. Abramson et al. (2005) find that using metric-based information influences profits; Schulze et al. (2012) identify a link between metric usage and shareholder value, while Mintz and Currim (2013) find that the use of metrics improves marketing mix outcomes. Against this background, the race is on to find robust methods of quantifying and evaluating such assets for the benefit of corporate management as well as the wider investment community.

# THREE DISTINCT LEVELS FOR MEASURING MARKETING EFFECTIVENESS

The problem with marketing accountability has never been about measuring the effectiveness of promotional expenditure, but rather to convince folk that marketing is not all about promotion. In world class organizations where the customer is at the centre of the business model, marketing is responsible for defining and understanding markets, for segmenting these markets, developing value propositions to meet the researched needs of the customers in the segments, getting buy-in from all those in the organization responsible for delivering this value, playing a role in delivering this value and for monitoring whether the promised value is being delivered. As such, marketing is an important function for strategy development as well as tactical sales delivery.

This is represented in Figure 22.1, which illustrates how to identify three distinct levels of measuring marketing effectiveness.

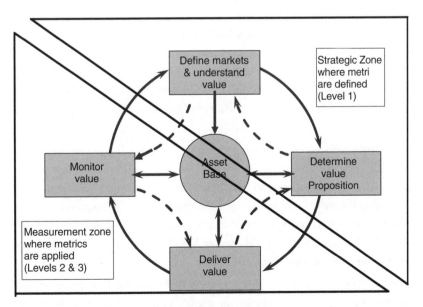

Figure 22.1 Map of the marketing domain and the three-level accountability framework

## LEVEL 1 MARKETING DUE DILIGENCE

Companies that recognize the importance of value creation through intangible assets are well positioned to undertake Marketing Due Diligence. This involves the careful assessment of a business plan and the supporting information behind it, discounting subjective opinions and the spin of investor relations. The output of the Due Diligence process is a number, in other words, a tangible measure of the risk associated with a chosen strategy. This number is then applied in the tried and trusted calculations that are used to work out shareholder value. In place of a subjective guess, we have a research-based and objective answer to the all-important question: does this plan create shareholder value?

Too often, the answer is no. When risk is allowed for, many business plans create less value than putting the same money in a bank account or index-linked investment. Such plans, of course, actually destroy shareholder value because their return is less than the opportunity cost of the investment. An accurate assessment of value creation would make a huge difference to the valuation of the company. The result of carrying out Marketing Due Diligence is, therefore, of great interest and value to both sides of the capital market. For the investment community, Marketing Due Diligence allows a much more informed and substantiated investment decision, providing a standard by which potential investments may be judged and a means of seeing through the vagaries of business plans. Additionally, portfolio management is made more rational and transparent and the growth potential of a company is made more explicit, easier to measure and harder to disguise.

For those seeking to satisfy investors, the value of Marketing Due Diligence lies in two areas. Firstly, it allows a rigorous assessment of the business plan in terms of its potential to create shareholder value. A positive assessment then becomes a substantive piece of evidence in negotiations with investors and other sources of finance. If, on the other hand, a strategy is shown to have weaknesses, the process not only pinpoints them but also indicates what corrective action is needed.

For anyone involved in running a company or investing in one, Marketing Due Diligence has three messages. Firstly, business needs a process that assesses shareholder value creation, and hence the value of a company, in term of risk rather than the cost of replacing intangible assets. Secondly, business risk can be dissected, measured and aggregated in a way that is much more accurate than a high-level judgment. Finally, Marketing Due Diligence is a necessary process for both investors and companies.

Eventually, we anticipate that a process of Marketing Due Diligence will become as de rigueur for assessing intangible value as financial due diligence

| Key background facts |
|---|
| Risk and return are positively related (i.e. as risk increases, investors require a higher return) |
| Risk is measured by the volatility in returns (i.e. high risk entails either very good returns or losing the initial investment. This can be described as the 'quality of returns') |
| All assets are defined as having future value to the organization. Hence, intangible as well as tangible assets should be included in the calculation (i.e. key market segments) |
| The net present value (NPV) of future cash flow is the most acceptable method to value assets. NPV is increased by:<br>• increasing future cash flows;<br>• bringing forward future cash flows;<br>• reducing the risk in these cash flows;<br>hence, reducing the required rate of return |

Table 22.1 Calculating SVA using Marketing Due Diligence process

is for its tangible counterpart. Tables 22.1 and 22.2 provide a summary of how shareholder value should be calculated using the Marketing Due Diligence process. The output of SVA has very practical implications. Figure 22.2 shows how the output of the shareholder value analysis (SVA) can be applied to the strategic decision-making process. By understanding how shareholder value is created, and undertaking appropriately detailed analysis, marketing managers will be well equipped to make investment decisions based upon sound financial analysis rather than gut feeling. Until such a rigorous approach is widely understood and accepted among marketing managers, early adopters will be able to use the 'due diligence' approach as a source of competitive advantage.

As we have seen, SVA is profit after tax, minus net capital employed multiplied by the cost of capital. There are only three things you can do to affect SVA:

- increase revenue
- decrease costs
- decrease the amount of capital tied up in the business.

All of these are highly influenced by the strategic marketing plan.

A very simple example of how SVA can be calculated follows: A has £15,000 invested in the company. The cost of capital is 10 per cent. The company makes a net profit of £2000. Therefore, the company has created £500 SVA (£15,000 × 10% − £2000 = +£500).

1. Identify key market segments. It is helpful if they can be classified on a vertical axis according to their attractiveness to the company. 'Attractiveness' usually means the potential of each for growth in profits over a period of between 3–5 years (see matrix).

2. Based on current experience and appropriate planning horizon (between 3–5 years), project future net free cash flow from each segment. Base calculations upon:

   - Revenue forecasts for each year;
   - Costs forecasts for each year;
   - Net free cash flow for each segment for each year.

3. Identify factors that are likely to increase or decrease cash flow. These factors are likely to be assessed according to the following:

   - Riskiness of the product/market segment relative to its position on the Ansoff matrix;
   - Riskiness of the marketing strategies to achieve the revenue and market share;
   - Riskiness of the forecase profitability (i.e. the cost forecast accuracy).

4. Now recalculate the revenues, costs and NPV for each year, having adjusted the figures using the risk factors in (5) above.

5. Accountant should provide the overall SBU cost of capital and capital used (including tangible and intangible assets).

6. Deduct the proportional costs of capital from the free cash flow for each segment for each year (e.g. £1m capital required at 10% required rate of return (RRR) = £100k minimum return).

7. An aggregate positive NPV indicates that shareholder value is being created, i.e. achieving overall returns greater than the weighted average cost of capital (WACC), having taken into account the risks associated with future cash flows.

Table 22.2 Suggested approach to calculating SVA

Level 1 is the most vital of all three, because this is what determines whether or not the marketing strategies for the longer term destroy or create SVA. Corporate assets and their associated competences are relevant only if customer markets value them sufficiently highly that they lead to sustainable competitive advantage, or shareholder value added. This is our justification for evaluating the strategic plan in terms of what is to be sold, to whom and the projected profits. In this way, it is possible to assess whether shareholder value will be created or destroyed.

How much is a company really worth? As shown in Figure 22.3, intangible assets play a significant role in enterprise value. Acknowledging this, numerous

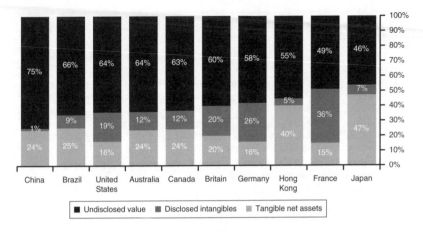

Figure 22.2 Application of SVA to strategic decision-making

ways have been developed to measure the true value of intangibles and good-will. These stem mostly from a cost-accounting perspective however, involving estimates of the cost of re-creating the brand, intellectual property or any other basis of intangible assets. Our research into companies that succeed and fail suggests that approach is flawed, because what matters is not asset ownership, but *use*. We therefore need to get back to the basics of what determines company value.

Figure 22.3 illustrates the importance of intangible assets, and the following examples illustrate the discrepancy between balance sheet tangible assets and the real value of companies: Philip Morris bought Kraft and its portfolio of brands for $12.9 billion, four times the value of its tangible assets. Grand Met bought Pilsburg for $5.5 billion, a 50 per cent premium of is pre-bid value and several times the value of its tangible assets.

Nestle paid $4.5 billion, more than five times Rowntree's book value. More recently, Proctor and Gamble paid $31 for Gillette, of which only $4 billion was for tangible assets. At the end of 2011, Coca-Cola was valued at $70.4 billion, Microsoft at $60.8 billion, Google at $43.5 billion and McDonald's at $33.5 billion, most of this value residing in intangible assets such as brand names, relationships with channels and the like.

This high-level process for marketing accountability, however, still does not address the dilemma of finding an approach which is better than the plethora of metrics currently available. To resolve this effectively, the following questions need to be addressed:

- What needs to be measured?
- Why it needs to be measured?
- How frequently it needs to be measured?

### Valuing key market segments
### Background/Facts

- Risk and return are positively correlated, i.e. as risk increases, investors require a higher return

- Risk is measured by the volatility in returns, i.e. high risk is the likelihood of either making a very good return or losing all your money. This can be described as the quality of returns

- All assets are defined as having future value to the organisation. Hence assets to be valued include not only tangible assets like plant and machinery, but intangible assets, such as Key Market Segments

- The present value of future cash flows is the most acceptable method to value assets including key market segments

- The present value is increased by:
  - increasing the future cash flows
  - making the future cash flows 'happen' earlier
  - reducing the risk in these cash flows, i.e. improving the certainty of these cash flows,

  and, hence reducing the required rate of return.

---

### Suggested approach

- Identify your key market segments. It is helpful if they can be classified on a vertical axis (a kind of thermometer) according to their attractiveness to your company. 'Attractiveness' usually means the potential of each for growth in your profits over period of between 3 and 5 years. (See the attached matrix)

- Based on your current experience and planning horizon that you are confident with, make a projection of future net free cash in-flows from your segments. It is normal to select a period such as 3 or 5 years.

- These calculations will consist of three parts:
  - revenue forecasts for each year;
  - costforecasts for each year;
  - net free cash flow for each segment for each year.

- Identify the key factors that are likely to either increase or decrease these future cash flows.

- These factors are likely to be assessed according to the following factors:
  - the riskiness of the product/market segment relative to its position on the ANSOFF matrix;
  - the riskiness of the marketing strategies to achieve the revenue and market share;
  - the riskiness of the forecast profitability (e.g. the cost forecast accuracy).

- Now recalculate the revenues, costs and net free cash flows for each year, having adjusted the figures using the risks (probabilities) from the above.

- Ask your accountant to provide you with the overall SBU cost of capital used in the SB. This will not consist only of tangible assets. Thus £1,000,000 capital at a required shareholder rate of return of 10% would give £100,000 as the minimum return necessary.

- Deduct the proportional cost of capital from the free cash flow for each segment for each year.

- An aggregate positive net present value indicates that you are creating shareholder value - i.e. achieving overall returns greater than the weighted average cost of capital, having taken into account the risk associated with future cash flows.

Figure 22.3 Asset breakdown for top ten countries by enterprise value (2011)

Source: Brand finance plc.

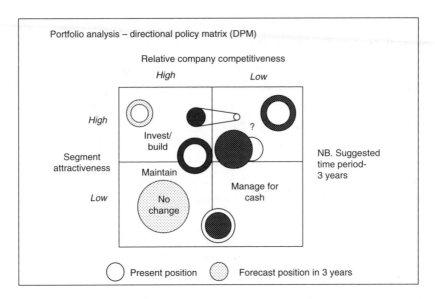

Figure 22.3 (Continued)

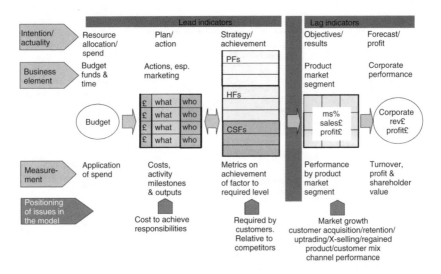

Figure 22.4 High-level process model for measuring marketing accountability

- To whom it should be reported?
- What is the relative importance of each?

Metrics can be driven from a company's strategy. This is illustrated in Figure 22.4, which demonstrates the link between Lead Indicators and Lag Indicators.

The model is explained in detail in *Marketing Accountability* (McDonald and Mouncey, 2009), so here we provide a brief summary of the key points only.

## LEVEL 2 MARKETING EFFECTIVENESS: LINKING ACTIVITIES TO OUTCOMES

Few academics or practitioners have addressed the link between marketing actions and outcomes in a holistic way. To begin with, it is important to destroy once and for all one of the great myths of measurement – marketing return on investment. Implying 'return' divided by 'investment' and, for marketing expenditure such as promotional spend, it is a notion that is difficult to defend intellectually. It is analogous to demanding a financial justification for the wings of an aircraft! At the same time, we note that the budget and all the energy employed in measuring it are not an acceptable proxy for measuring marketing effectiveness.

So, how do we set about linking our marketing activities to our overall objectives? We start with the Ansoff Matrix shown in Figure 22.5. Each of the cells in each box (cells consist of products for segments) are planning units, in the sense that objectives will be set for each, volume, value and profit for the first year of the strategic plan.

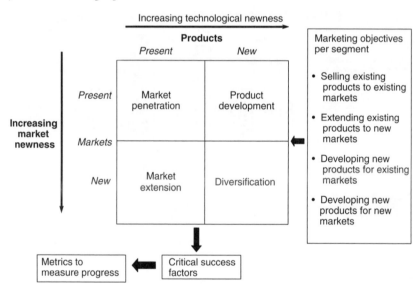

Figure 22.5 Ansoff Matrix

Having set objectives for each of the products for segment cells, the task is then to determine strategies for achieving them. The starting point for these strategies is Critical Success Factors (CSFs), the factors critical to success in each product for segment, which will be weighted according to their relative importance to the customers in the segment. See Figure 22.6.

In these terms, a strategy will involve improving one or more CSF scores in one or more product-for-segment cells. It is unlikely though, that the marketing function will be directly responsible for what needs to be done to improve a

| Critical success factors | Weighting factor | Your organization | Competitor A | Competitor B | Competitor C |
|---|---|---|---|---|---|
| CSF 1 | | | | | |
| CSF 2 | | | | | |
| CSF 3 | | | | | |
| CSF 4 | | | | | |
| Total weighted score (score x weight) | 100 | | | | |

*In the centre of the table (spanning Your organization to Competitor B columns, over CSF 1 and CSF 2 rows):*
- Strategies to improve competitive position/achieve objectives over time (4Ps)
- Metrics (each CSF) to measure performance over time in achieving goals

Figure 22.6 Critical success factors in each segment, defined by segment

CSF. For example, issues like product efficacy, after-sales service, channel management and sometimes even price and the sales force are often controlled by other functions, so marketing needs to get buy-in from these functions to the need to improve the CSF scores.

It is very rare for this information to be perfectly available to the marketer. While models such as price sensitivity, advertising response or even marketing mix or econometric approaches may help to populate the CSF form, there are generally several other factors where information is less easy to gather. Nevertheless, a CSF analysis indicates where metrics are most needed, which can steer the organization towards measuring the right things.

Figure 22.7 shows the actions that have to be taken, by whom and at what cost in order to improve the CSFs.

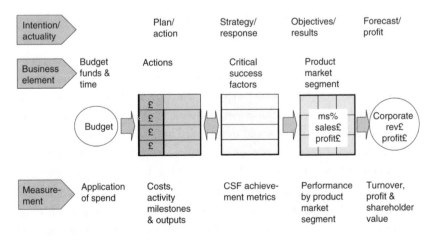

Figure 22.7 Marketing metrics model

Figure 22.8 shows how these actions multiply for each box of the Ansoff matrix.

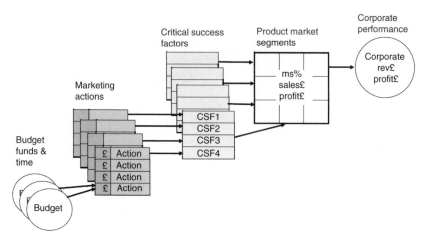

Figure 22.8 Cascading actions from the Ansoff Matrix

There are other factors, of course, that influence what is sold and to whom. These may be referred to as 'Hygiene Factors' (HF) – that is, those standards that must be achieved by any competitor in the market. Other factors may be referred to as 'Productivity Factors' (PF) – that is, those issues which may impact on an organization's performance unless the required productivity is achieved in its relevant activities.

Thus, it can be seen how the expenditure on marketing and other functional actions to improve CSFs can be linked to marketing objectives and, ultimately, to profitability and it becomes clear exactly what must be measured and why. It also obviates the difficult-to-justify assumption that a particular marketing action can be linked directly to profitability. It can only be linked to other weighted CSFs which, if improved, should lead to the achievement of volumes, value and, ultimately, profits (Figure 22.9).

Figure 22.4 is repeated here, as it summarizes all of the above in one flow chart, illustrating the difference between 'Lag Indicators' and 'Lead Indicators'. Lead indicators are the actions taken and the associated expenditure that is incurred. Lag indicators are the *outcomes* of these actions and expenditures and need to be carefully monitored and measured. Thus, retention by segment, loss by segment, new customers, new product sales, channel performance and the like are *outcomes*, but these need to be linked back to the appropriate *inputs*.

There is one other crucial implication to be drawn from this model. Most operating boards on scrutinizing profit and loss accounts, typically see only one line for revenue, while costs are covered in considerable detail and it is around costs that most of the discussion takes place. In the view of the authors, there

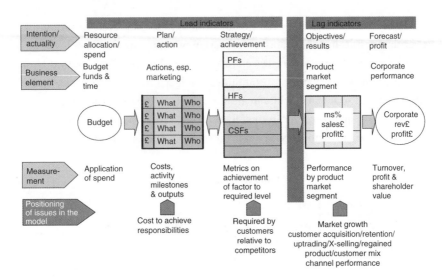

Figure 22.9 Overall marketing metrics model

should be at least two sets of figures – one to detail where the sales revenue has come from, as outlined above, another to detail costs. A key task of marketers, rarely carried out, is to link the two documents together.

## LEVEL 3 PROMOTIONAL EFFECTIVENESS

Level 3 is the fundamental and crucial level of promotional measurement. It would be surprising if marketing as a discipline did not have its own quantitative models for the massive expenditure of fast moving consumer goods companies. Over time, these models have been transferred to business-to-business and service companies, with the result that, today, any organization spending substantial sums of shareholders' money on promotion should be ashamed of themselves if those responsible could not account for the effectiveness of such expenditure.

Nonetheless, with the advent of different promotional methods and channels, combined with an empowered and more sophisticated consumer, the problems of measuring promotional effectiveness have increased considerably. Consequently, this remains one of the major challenges facing the marketing community today. For example, in fast moving consumer goods, supermarket buyers expect and demand a threshold level of promotional expenditure in order to be considered for listing. Indeed in most commercial situations, there is a threshold level of expenditure that has to be made in order just to maintain the status quo – that is, keep up the product or service in consumer consciousness to encourage them to continue buying. We refer to this as 'maintenance' expenditure.

In most situations, however, not to maintain existing levels of promotion over time results in volume, price and margin pressure, market share losses and a subsequent declining share price. The graph in Figure 22.10 shows that, in one experimental scenario, a promotional budget was cut to zero for a year, then returned to normal, while in another, the budget was cut by 50 per cent. Sales recovery to pre-cut levels took five years and three years respectively, with cumulative negative impacts on net profits of £1.7 million and £0.8 million.

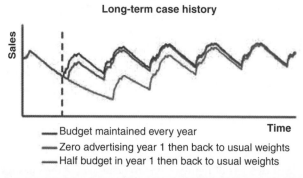

**Long-term case history**

— Budget maintained every year
— Zero advertising year 1 then back to usual weights
— Half budget in year 1 then back to usual weights

| | Budget saved | Sales foregone | Profit on foregone sales | Impact on bottom line | Time to recover |
|---|---|---|---|---|---|
| Zero budget year 1 | £1.8m | £8.6m | £3.5m | £1.7m | 5 years |
| Half budget year 1 | £0.9m | £4.3m | £1.7m | £0.8m | 3 years |

ROI defined as the incremental revenue generated from advertising per unit of spend

Data 2 decisions

Figure 22.10 ROI long-term case history

It is important to make one final point about measuring the effectiveness of promotional expenditure in taking account of 'maintenance' expenditure. This point relates to the tried and tested method of measuring the financial impact of promotional expenditure; net present value (NPV). As can be seen from the following, by not taking account of the expenditure to maintain current sales and by including total promotional expenditure in the NPV calculations, a totally false result ensues. However, by taking account of maintenance expenditure, a much better result emerges.

Discounting a future stream of revenue into a 'Net Present Value' assumes that a rational investor would be indifferent to having a dollar today, or to receiving in some future year a dollar plus the interest that could have been earned by investing that dollar for those years. Thus, it makes sense to assess investments by dividing the money to be received in future years by $(1 + r)$, where $r$ is the discount rate (the annual return from investing that money) and

$n$ is the number of years during which the investment could be earning that return.

PV, or NPV or DCF is denoted as:

$$PV = \frac{\Sigma C_t}{(1+r)^n}$$

$\Sigma$ is the sum of the cash flows in years t (1, 2, 3, 4 etc)

This summation of the cash flows is then divided by $(1+r)^n$ where $r$ is the discount rate and $n$ is the number of years the investment could be earning that return.

Hence, for a net free cash flow of $2 million a year over 4 years and a cost of capital of 10 per cent, the net present value is:

$$\frac{2}{(1.1)} + \frac{2}{(1.1)^2} + \frac{2}{(1.1)^3} + \frac{2}{(1.1)^2} = \$6.4 \text{ million}$$

Minus an initial investment of, say, $5 million, the NPV of this investment is $1.4 million.

However:

A promotional investment of, say, $7 million, using the above figure, would produce a loss of $0.6 million.

If, however, a company needs to spend say $6 million just to maintain current sales, the investment is only $1 million and the NPV would then be:

$$-\$1 \text{ million} + \frac{2}{(1.1)} + \frac{2}{(1.1)^2} + \frac{2}{(1.1)^3} + \frac{2}{(1.1)^4} = \$5.4 \text{ million}$$

The research issue facing marketers is how to estimate what might be classified as 'maintenance' promotion as distinct from 'investment' promotion. This is complicated by the different forms of promotion and the many different channels available today, but it is not impossible.

# SUMMARY

It is important to measure marketing results and to understand the relationship between inputs and outputs. This has been a much discussed and difficult area, but of late there is evidence that organizations are starting to make it a priority. In this chapter we have covered the key issues and provided a practical approach to measuring marketing effectiveness. The key questions are what to measure, why, when, how, how frequently, by whom, to whom the results should be reported, and at what cost. Increasingly, marketing is having to become more accountable and demonstrate due diligence. There are three crucial levels at which marketing effectiveness can be measured, as the three-level accountability framework illustrates. In measuring outcomes, marketing should be defined, disaggregated and measured as a process that creates value for consumers and other stakeholders alike. We predict that such an approach, grounded in sound financial management practices, will become the norm; until then, companies adopting this approach will benefit from a competitive advantage in their chosen markets.

# FURTHER READING

McDonald, M., Smith, B. and Ward, K. (2013) *Marketing and Finance: Creating Shareholder Value*, Chichester, Wiley.
An examination of the mission-critical interface between Marketing and Finance, from a combined perspective that incorporates leading knowledge in both disciplines.

# REFERENCES

Abramson, Charles, Imran S. Currim, and Rakesh Sarin (2005) An Experimental Investigation of the Impact of Information on Competitive Decision Making, *Management Science*, Vol. 51(2): 195–207.

McDonald, M. and Mouncey, P. (2009) *Marketing Accountability*, London, Kogan Page.

Mintz, O. and Currim, I.S. (2013) What Drives Managerial Use of Marketing and Financial Metrics and Does Metric Use Affect Performance of Marketing-Mix Activities? *Journal of Marketing*, Vol. 77 (March): 17–40.

Park, H-S., Auh, S., Maher, A. and Singhapakdi, A. (2012) Marketing's Accountability and Internal Legitimacy: Implications for Firm Performance, *Journal of Business Research*, Vol. 65 (11): 1576–1582.

Schulze, C., Bernd S. and Wiesel, T. (2012) Linking Customer and Financial Metrics to Shareholder Value: The Leverage Effect in Customer-Based Valuation, *Journal of Marketing*, Vol. 76 (March): 17–32.

# PART V
# ENHANCING VALUE

# CHAPTER 23
# ORGANIZATIONAL STRUCTURE AND CULTURE

IN THIS CHAPTER WE STUDY:

- importance of marketing professionalism
- impact of organizational structure on marketing effectiveness
- phases of organizational evolution
- options for organizing at board and operational levels
- challenges for determining marketing organization
- why the marketing process requires a conducive organizational culture
- essential features of good marketing organization

# GROWING PROFESSIONALISM TO YIELD POTENTIAL

For marketing to succeed, it needs to be placed centrally in an organization and those working within it need to pursue the very highest professional standards. In 2009, Verhoef and Leeflang observed that marketing as a functional area in corporate organizations was in decline. As we explored in the previous chapter, the key issue perceived was lack of accountability and the absence of metrics against which to judge a performance. Other reasons cited were limited innovativeness, creativity and poor connection with customers.

As intimated in Chapter 22, in recent years there has been greater acknowledgement among marketers and senior executives that marketing is, in fact, of strategic importance, hence the shift of emphasis to financial 'bottom line' outcomes and shareholder value analysis. In this sense, it can be argued that marketing has a window of opportunity to move to a key strategic role. However, to achieve positive financial outcomes and be seen as a key value-creating activity, it is crucial to achieve high professional standards as a driver of competitive advantage.

Despite this, it is notable that the quest to professionalize marketing still does not take precedence on all business agendas, despite the fact that marketing professionalism is the hallmark of commercial success. The reasons for this lie squarely with organization itself, and may be defined as the main organizational barriers to effective marketing planning. These are summarized as:

- *cognitive* – not knowing enough about marketing planning;
- *cultural* – the company culture is not orientated towards marketing planning;
- *political* – the culture 'carriers/leaders' feel threatened by marketing;
- *resources* – not enough resources are allocated to marketing;
- *structural* – lack of a plan and organization for planning; and
- lack of an effective MIS.

The difficulty in acknowledging and overcoming these barriers does not, however, mean that it cannot be done. Experience has shown that leadership and entrepreneurial skills, combined with well-honed marketing skills, is what characterizes the 'market leaders' from the 'wannabes' and 'has-beens'. Such professionalism, however, must be earned and embedded in organizational structure and culture.

Marketing professionalism requires the courage to question strategic priorities that do not appear to have been defined or refined adequately. It requires conventional wisdom to be challenged if it appears to be no longer relevant. It requires the discipline to follow the logical processes of strategic analysis and planning rather than jumping at the first good idea that comes along. But at its base, it also requires professional marketing skills and formal training in the underlying concepts, tools and techniques of marketing as a management discipline. The core professional curriculum comprises:

- market research;
- gap analysis;
- market segmentation/positioning;
- product life cycle analysis;
- portfolio management;
- The marketing mix;
  - product management;
  - pricing;
  - place (channel management, customer service); and
  - promotion (selling, sales force management, advertising, sales promotion).

As has been emphasized throughout this book, marketing's role as a driver and deliverer of value emanates from the competitive stance adopted by the organization. If the organization is truly committed to acquiring and retaining mutually profitable long-term customer relationships, this will be reflected in all its activities, and not just those for which marketing is directly responsible. If the organization levies the bulk of expectation on the marketing function, in the absence of appropriate information and control systems, management practices and resource allocations, marketing will undoubtedly fail the test, and ultimately bring down the rest of organization with it. The point being reiterated here is that marketing forms an intrinsic part of organizational success. As such, it cannot be separated or isolated from other business activities, nor can it be seen to carry 'the hopes and dreams' of the organization without proper support and recognition.

This raises the fundamental issues of organizational structure and culture in the relentless pursuit of superior professionalism within marketing, and the organization as a whole. Thus a key step in the marketing process is 'Enhance value', where current levels of professionalism are strengthened and extended through assimilated learning to produce greater, *realizable* potential. This potential is then manifested in a myriad of ways throughout future iterations of the marketing process. Ideally, this process, which in this book has been depicted as a cycle, becomes an upward spiral, reaching ever-higher dimensions of value.

# ORGANIZATIONAL STRUCTURE AND MARKETING

Given all the principles of measurement outlined in the previous chapter, regarding the necessity and accuracy of monitoring value, it is nonetheless a fundamental truth that customers are generally indifferent to the ways in which suppliers are organized. The structure of suppliers' management and operations generally attracts little customer attention or interest; all customers want is the delivery of perfect products or services, on time, in full, whenever and wherever they want them, and preferably at the same price everywhere in the world where they operate.

Inconsequential though it may seem to the customer, the window of opportunity hinges firmly on matters of organizational structure. Chapter 18 endorsed the notion that, increasingly, it is supply chains, rather than the individual efforts of organizations, that compete in the marketplace. This transformation has profound implications for how companies organize to create and deliver customer value. Consider for a moment how difficult, if not impossible, it is to meet customers' expectations where the company organizes as follows:

1 Around 'production' units, such as factories. Each unit will endeavour to optimize its profitability, justifiably making its profit from production rather from action based on exploiting market forces.

2 Around 'functions'. With every function focused on achieving its own objectives, it is extremely difficult, if not impossible, for departments, individually or collectively, to take into account customer needs in any consistent or coherent way.

3 Around geographical groupings, such as the United Kingdom, France, Germany and so on. Here, country 'barons', each with their own profit and loss account, frequently relegate the needs of global customers and markets to their own narrow profit-maximizing motives.

There are, of course, many other possible combinations, none of which will be perfect.

Organization for effective marketing is a subject fraught with difficulty, largely because all companies and all markets are different. The complexities arising from the possible combinations of product, market, geography, function and size make it impossible to be prescriptive about the way a company should organize for marketing. Nonetheless, despite these complexities, it must seek to find the optimal structure in the interests of performance and profit maximization.

Comstock et al.'s (2010) study of how GE reorganized its marketing to deal effectively with a high level of complexity is of some interest. Faced with increasing competition and declining market share in a number of product categories, GE gave marketing a new revenue-generating role. Marketing was given the challenge of 'commercial innovation' which required collaboration on a number of 'initiatives' across various organizational boundaries. A number of CMO posts were created for all GE's SBUs and at the corporate level. Comstock et al. (2010: 98) observe that 'for the first time, GE is treating marketing as a critical function – one for all seasons'.

While there is no single recipe for success, there are some abiding general precepts concerning strategic options that involve decisions at two levels; at the macro level the key issue is centralization/decentralization of management control, and at micro level, the structure of marketing operations.

## CENTRALIZING AND DECENTRALIZING MARKETING ACTIVITIES

For organizations which have expanded so that they operate in several regions, the first choice is between centralizing or decentralizing their marketing activities. Some method has to be found of planning and controlling the growth of the business in order to utilize effectively the evolving skills and emerging reputation of the firm, and so avoid an uncontrolled dissipation of energy and talent.

Centralized operations make co-ordination much easier and are better at avoiding duplication. From the depiction of centralized organization in Figure 23.1, it will be seen that there is no strategic level of management in the subsidiary units, particularly with respect to new product introductions. This kind of organizational form tends to lead to standardized strategies, especially with regard to product management. For example, when a new product is introduced, it is often designed at the outset with as many markets as possible in mind, while the benefits of market research in one area are passed on to other areas and so on. The problem here, of course, is that unless

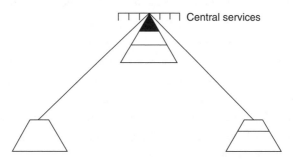

Figure 23.1 A centralized company

great care is exercised, subsidiary units can easily become less sensitive to the needs of individual markets, and hence lose flexibility in reacting to competitive moves.

Decentralization allows for more flexibility and better exploitation of local opportunities. As Figure 23.2 shows, central services, such as market research and public relations, are repeated at subsidiary company level. It can also be seen that there is a strategic level of management at the subsidiary level, the acid test being whether subsidiary company/unit top management can introduce new products without reference to headquarters. The point about this kind of decentralized organizational structure is that it leads inevitably to duplication of effort and differentiation of strategies, with all the consequent problems, unless a major effort is made to get some synergy out of the various systems by means of a company-wide planning strategy.

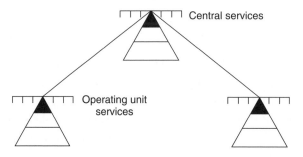

Figure 23.2 A decentralized company

In respect of achieving a flexible and enterprising organization, there are no 'right' or 'wrong' options. The choice will depend on the organization's product diversity, the need for local variations and the management's ability to get a good balance between co-ordination and control. The latter is necessary to avoid fragmentation and to prevent managers feeling that they have no effective freedom of choice.

Sadly, in many international organizations, it is not uncommon for local (that is, decentralized) marketing personnel to find themselves with no influence over product decisions, price or delivery, and they then become frustrated at having to manage a marketing mix over which they have little control.

An ideal arrangement, of course, is to organize around a combination of both in order to gain the benefits of each. This involves putting marketing as close to the customer as possible, while also having some kind of centralized marketing function. In this way, the potential for costly and unnecessary duplication is minimized, and the possibility of achieving economies of scale and effective knowledge transfer is optimized.

For organizations with marketing departments, the second area of choice is the methodology for structuring the department's activities. The main decision is whether to organize around functions, products, markets, key accounts, geographical areas, channels, or some combination of two or more of these options. A functionally organized department would separate activities such as new product development, market research, customer service, advertising, market analysis, public relations, sales promotions and so on.

Alternatively, a marketing department could be organized around a series of product managers who would be responsible for the whole range of activities associated with their products or brands. This would include stimulating activity within the sales force and third-party resellers, as well as intra-company co-ordination. Organizing around markets would involve the creation of market managers, whether geographically, by sector, or by segment. Variations on this theme have been referred to as vertical marketing, trade marketing and industry marketing.

In some cases, such as, for example, where there are very few customers, it is sensible to organize around key account management. In others, it is appropriate to have marketing specialists with responsibility for all activities within a definable area. Many organizations use a combination of approaches to minimize the dangers inherent in any single approach. As examples, some businesses organize around brand managers, but separate the functions of public relations, customer service and planning, while others use both product and market managers in a matrix-type relationship.

Whatever organizational form is employed, it should be able to deal successfully with the spectrum of issues, including those surrounding marketing information, analysis and interpretation, and those regarding how best to organize for marketing planning and implementation. *How* the marketing process is managed must be congruent with the current level of organizational development. This is to say that marketing planning organization must reflect the organizational evolution of the company as it passes through characteristic life phases.

# ORGANIZATIONAL EVOLUTION

As depicted in Figure 23.3, organizational growth is propelled by reaction to crises. At start-up the firm is often organized around the owner, who tends to know more about customers and products than anyone else in the company (creative evolution). However, as the firm grows in size and complexity, and

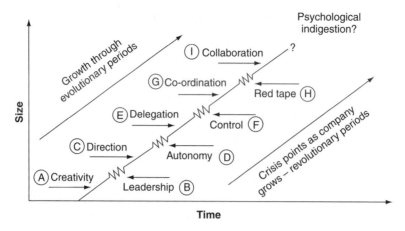

Figure 23.3 Organizational evolution
*Source:* Greiner (1972).

new products and markets are added, the organizational form breaks down and the owner must either sell up or allocate certain functional duties to specialized departments (directed evolution).

Eventually, these departments seek greater autonomy and a more delegative style of leadership prevails, which generates more autonomy at lower levels (delegated evolution). As growth continues, senior management become concerned about the high levels of autonomy lower down in the organization and try to regain control by establishing better co-ordination between the various parts of the organization (co-ordinated evolution). Ultimately, these co-ordinated practices become institutionalized, and thus planning procedures become ritualized and procedures seem to assume precedence over problem solving. To redress the stifling effects of oppressive bureaucracy or 'red tape', the company strives towards a new phase of collaboration, with greater emphasis on teamwork, creativity and spontaneity (collaborative evolution).

Clearly, each solution to an organizational development problem gives rise to the next evolutionary phase. Since the key to successful marketing is to have a suitable organizational structure, understanding this pattern of structural change can indicate in a useful way appropriate organizational and planning frameworks. Figure 23.4 attempts to encapsulate the types of organizational structure as they relate to company size and complexity, and the associated degree of formality in the marketing planning process. (To evaluate the appropriateness of your own organizational structure, place an x on each of the four lines to indicate where your organization currently lies.)

## ORGANIZATIONAL TRAITS AND TRENDS

No single organizational form can be recommended, as common sense and market needs are the final arbiters.

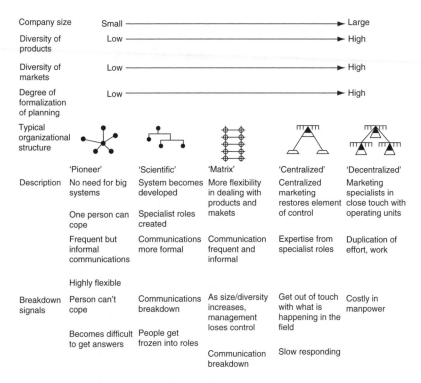

| Company size | Small ————————————————→ Large | | | | |
| Diversity of products | Low ————————————————→ High | | | | |
| Diversity of markets | Low ————————————————→ High | | | | |
| Degree of formalization of planning | Low ————————————————→ High | | | | |
| Typical organizational structure | | | | | |
| | 'Pioneer' | 'Scientific' | 'Matrix' | 'Centralized' | 'Decentralized' |
| Description | No need for big systems | System becomes developed | More flexibility in dealing with products and makets | Centralized marketing restores element of control | Marketing specialists in close touch with operating units |
| | One person can cope | Specialist roles created | | | |
| | Frequent but informal communications | Communications more formal | Communication frequent and informal | Expertise from specialist roles | Duplication of effort, work |
| | Highly flexible | | | | |
| Breakdown signals | Person can't cope | Communications breakdown | As size/diversity increases, management loses control | Get out of touch with what is happening in the field | Costly in manpower |
| | Becomes difficult to get answers | People get frozen into roles | Communication breakdown | Slow responding | |

Figure 23.4 Types of organizational structure

However, the following factors always need to be considered:

- marketing 'centres of gravity';
- interface areas (for example, present/future; salespeople/drawing office and so on);
- authority, responsibility and accountability;
- ease of communication;
- co-ordination;
- flexibility; and
- human factors.

As these basic traits indicate, an organization's marketing planning effectiveness, (demonstrated through its performance and assessed through constant monitoring), is affected significantly by the way it organizes for marketing. The typical evolutionary pattern for an organization that has grown over time will lead it from being a 'one-man-band', where one person will perform all tasks, and where sales essentially involve order-taking with small amounts of prospecting or advertising, to the multi-functioning super-department incorporating a whole range of specialist activities, as illustrated in Figure 23.5. As an organization grows and becomes more sophisticated in its approach to

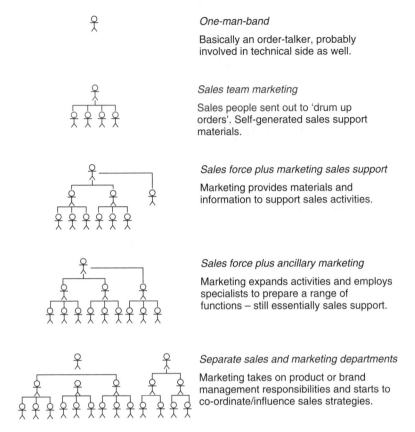

One-man-band

Basically an order-talker, probably involved in technical side as well.

*Sales team marketing*

Sales people sent out to 'drum up orders'. Self-generated sales support materials.

*Sales force plus marketing sales support*

Marketing provides materials and information to support sales activities.

*Sales force plus ancillary marketing*

Marketing expands activities and employs specialists to prepare a range of functions – still essentially sales support.

*Separate sales and marketing departments*

Marketing takes on product or brand management responsibilities and starts to co-ordinate/influence sales strategies.

Figure 23.5 Typical evolutionary pattern of marketing

marketing, it is faced with a number of options for structuring its range of marketing activities. Wherever practicable, it is sensible to organize around customer groups, or markets, rather than around products, functions or geography, so that personnel, accounting, production, distribution and sales policies are tailored to unique sets of market needs.

Increasingly, firms are organizing their operating units around customers or core processes or initiatives (see the GE case study). The process orientation entails each process being managed by a team that has responsibility for delivering efficiency in that area, and for meeting the objectives appropriate for competitive advantage. The key difference between conventional structures and a core process, team-based approach, is that the team becomes multi-functional with responsibility for, say, inbound logistics, production, sales and supply, rather than each activity stage being a distinct and separate operation. Marketing works best when it is treated as an integrated philosophy, discipline and function within the enterprise. It can, and should, both drive and support all other organizational activities in helping to achieve the overall corporate objectives. Research into the future of marketing indicates that the world's front-running organizations base their structures on customer groups and processes rather than on products.

It is also better to put sales and marketing under the supervision of one person, to ensure proper co-ordination of these distinct but interrelated functions, as shown in example (b) in Figure 23.6. Separation of sales and marketing at board level can cause a disparity between what marketing is planning and what sales is doing out in the field. Lack of a suitable organizational structure for an integrated marketing function, compounded by lack of meaningful information about market segments, means that marketing planning is unlikely to be successful.

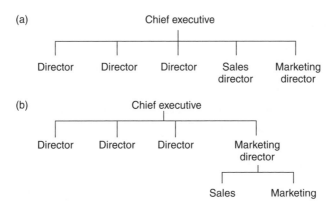

Figure 23.6 Organizing for marketing at board level

Experience has shown that, above all, the very best marketing plans in terms of direction and performance emerge from an organizationally *inclusive* process. Fundamentally, marketing planning is simply a process, with a set of underlying tools and techniques, for understanding markets and for quantifying the present and future value required by the different groups of customers within these markets – what marketers refer to as segments. It is a strictly specialist function – like accountancy or engineering – which is proscribed, researched, developed and examined by professional bodies such as the Chartered Institute of Marketing in Europe and Asia, and the American Marketing Association in the United States. Sometimes customer-facing activities such as customer service, selling, product development and public relations are controlled by the marketing function, but often they are not, even though many of them are included in the academic marketing curriculum.

In the model in Figure 23.7, representatives from appropriate functions are members of market planning teams, with the main body of work being done by the marketing representative, who has the professional skills to accomplish the more technical tasks of data and information gathering and market analysis. The team might also include a representative from product

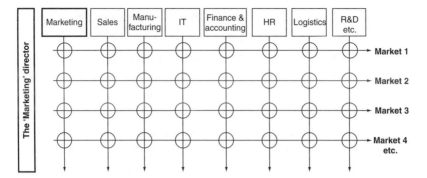

Figure 23.7 Organizing for marketing at operational level

development, brand managers, key account managers and so on, depending on circumstances.

The advantages of this team-based approach to marketing planning are as follows:

1. Any plans emerging are based on a deep understanding of the organization's asset value (tangible and intangible assets) and capabilities.

2. Members of the team 'own' the plan, thus preventing implementation problems later on.

3. The marketing director, or whoever is responsible to the board for integrating and co-ordinating all the plans emanating from this process, can be sure that he or she is not foisting unwanted plans on to reluctant functional heads.

4. Any strategic functional plans, such as IT, logistics, purchasing, R&D and so on, will be genuinely market driven or customer-needs driven rather than production driven.

5. Any business or corporate plans that emerge at a higher level will also be market driven.

## ORGANIZATIONAL CHALLENGES FOR MARKETING

The position and structuring of marketing within organizations is being challenged and impacted by developments throughout the value chain. The first of these is the decline of traditional brand management as retailers become more powerful and, in some cases, substitute brands. Rather than a brand's franchise in the market influencing the choice of supplier, retailers are much more interested in costs, strategy alignment and response to regional differences, as a basis for choosing suppliers.

The second development is the advancements being made in micro-marketing, which are encouraging marketing managers to look at differences between consumers in more elaborate ways, and to use sales promotion activities and database marketing for more accurate targeting (see Chapters 5, 12 and 21, respectively).

The third is the reduction in the effectiveness of mass advertising as media channels proliferate, and as it becomes harder to reach mass markets. These trends will support moves away from national and international brand management as a basis for organizing marketing, towards market-focused management structures, either as part of a process team, or as a framework based on relationships.

Fourth, the current popularity of category management as a basis for organizing consumer goods marketing is also affecting how suppliers organize their marketing activities. To match their retail customers, suppliers are organizing brand portfolios and appointing category managers, or 'champions', whose focus is on maximizing profit from a category for the retailer rather than developing brand franchises.

In the end, however, it must be remembered that structure is of only secondary importance in establishing marketing as an effective force within an organization. Of greater significance is the attitude of the managers working within the structures, and the ways in which they are able to influence other managers towards a market-orientated approach to their own responsibilities. If a market orientation is well embedded and stretches across its range of activities, it is almost possible to argue that structure is irrelevant to marketing effectiveness.

# ORGANIZATIONAL CULTURE AND MARKETING

While the marketing process in terms of the five key sub-processes remains more or less consistent throughout, how that process is managed must be congruent with the current organizational culture. The alternative to this would be to take steps to change the company culture and make it more amenable to a particular planning process.

Since culture tends to act to maintain the existing power structure and hence the status quo, marketing planning and implementation interventions in companies must be recognized as having a 'political' dimension; that is to say, the motivations behind them are not purely educational or commercial. Not least among the political issues is the question of whether or not a company's management style can adapt sufficiently to enable the marketing process to deliver the rewards it promises. For example, can managers who have led a company down a particular path suddenly change track? The iconoclastic books would claim that they can, because this is a much more optimistic message with which to sell copies. However, those who have carried out academic research, or are experienced consultants, would have some reservations. We remain open-minded about this issue, believing that, if the business pressures on a company are sufficient, intelligent behaviour will win the day.

Marketing's role in bringing the organization closer to customers, and thus in growing long-term and profitable customer relationships, is crucial to the success of the organization. Iglesias et al. (2011) find that if relationships with customers are to endure successfully, there are two critical values that need to be shared throughout the organization (in other words, become cornerstones of organizational culture). These are client orientation and a high degree of concern for employees. The two are interlinked and there is little point in promoting the former without the latter.

Thus, creating and maintaining a culture and climate within the organization that is conducive to value-based initiatives is the responsibility of marketing as much as, if not more than, any other aspect of the business. We suggest that the following are essential features of a healthy culture: innovative, engaging, inclusive, rewarding and empowering.

## INNOVATIVE

As discussed earlier, resistance to change and discouragement of creativity are the foremost obstacles that face organizations seeking growth and prosperity. They can derive from a number of factors:

- the desire to maximize returns from existing capacity products and services;
- the desire to defend current patterns of behaviour, systems and procedures;
- the desire to minimize losses on existing plant and equipment (and people) through enforced obsolescence;
- the desire to protect status derived from past experience;
- the desire to avoid risk consequences; and
- fear of the unknown.

While sources of improvement and innovation (here defined as providing new solutions that offer value to customers) can be found almost anywhere in the organization, real change tends to come from the top. The visible enthusiasm and commitment of the chief executive and senior management towards exploring and implementing new ideas, be they situated in product, policy, management or operational development, is what promotes commercial vibrancy and adds customer value. Without such stewardship and affirmation, employees and other stakeholders are unlikely to mirror the direction and investment in innovation shown by their 'leaders'. In this way, the company can overcome fears and potential stagnation, and capitalize on its strengths by being able to respond to new situations. It is a flexible approach such as is that is the hidden strength of the small company.

Many organizations have turned to merger and acquisition in pursuit of growth and shareholder value. While this strategy may provide short-term performance improvements, it is unlikely to generate long-term shareholder value. The reason is that sustainable growth generated by continuous innovation is based on the capabilities and attitudes of the people within the company and depends on a culture that encourages entrepreneurship and processes that enable individual and team-based creativity to surface and flourish. At 3M, which invests over 7 per cent of its turnover in research and development, the link between its astonishing growth in sales and shareholder value is very clearly based on a vision that identifies innovation as a core company process.

## ENGAGING

Every company should endeavour to be attractive and enticing at every customer touch point – not just to customers, but also to its current and future workforce and wider supply chain network. Happy employees and other company representatives tend to indicate that the organization's policies on employee recruitment and selection, employment and retention, in addition to those surrounding business operations, are sound and acceptable. In other words, a corporate culture that demonstrates integrity and is consistently engaging in its various expressions, will generally reveal an employer whose 'true colours' include openness, fairness, equality, diversity and a work opportunity well worth taking.

## INCLUSIVE

Creating an organizational culture which ensures that thoroughness and innovation go into developing the value proposition and communicating it throughout the organization is not easy, but once the culture is right it is very difficult for competitors to replicate it, and as such it becomes a source of sustainable competitive advantage. Cross-functional co-operation and company-wide involvement in steering the business towards appropriate goals can be obtained through well-considered and established procedures. Organizations contain enormous potential in terms of information and insight contained within its people, information systems and operational approaches. This can be harnessed through employee development, inclusive business practices and targeted business development activities.

## REWARDING

Creating an organizational culture that rewards its members justly for their contributions to the business can be seen to encompass all stakeholders, including employees, distributors, shareholders and even customers. Indeed, corporate culture is reflected in company partnership programmes as well as customer loyalty and affinity schemes. For example, in some strategic alliances, working partners are offered special access to company information in return for their willingness to share ideas. Companies which value customer feedback often stimulate customer comment by inserting questionnaires in regular communications or as part of online-ordering processes or by offering prizes for the best responses to statements such as: 'I like this product because...' in competitions. While promotional inducements seek to attract new business, information-gathering incentives support value-building activities.

## EMPOWERING

A challenging and exciting corporate climate is produced by the culmination of the above characteristics, together with a heavy dose of empowerment and entrepreneurial spirit. The need for balance between control and creativity was mentioned earlier in the chapter. Organizations that can reach and maintain a productive equilibrium will benefit from the strength provided by disciplined practices and the energy derived from positive reinforcement of individual and collective creativity. Employees need to have 'breathing space' to allow them to understand and contribute to organizational performance, as well as the power to take decisions that influence organizational direction and performance.

As intimated, the fundamental aims of internal marketing are to develop awareness among employees of both internal and external customers, and to remove functional barriers to organizational effectiveness. By regarding every employee and every department as internal customer and/or an internal supplier, it is possible to ensure that every individual and department provides and receives high standards of internal service. It also promotes internal buy-in to the organization's mission, strategy and goals, which produces a more collaborative and cohesive working environment.

## CASE STUDY 23.1 MARKETING AT GENERAL ELECTRIC

For years, GE had focused on developing high-tech products that 'sold themselves'. Unfortunately, the globalization and commodification of technology, combined with rapid advances by

emergent economies, started to impact severely on competitive advantage, differentiation, marketing share and profitability. In 2003 the CEO, Jack Immelt, concluded that it was time to move marketing from a 'staff' to a 'line' role with specific revenue-generating responsibilities. In essence, this meant switching from the traditional product focus to a customer orientation. Suddenly, it was up to marketing to identify and respond to consumer needs, wants and demands – and to do so
profitably.

The initial step was to reinvigorate the marketing team by increasing numbers from 2500 to over 5000. The functional boundaries of the marketing department dissolved as roles changed. CMO roles were created at each SBU and at corporate level. Replacing the traditional job roles, four new categories were introduced: instigators, who were tasked to think strategically and challenge the status quo; innovators, who were to use market insights to come with new ideas; integrators, to break down barriers and bring the various organizational functions together; and implementers, to deliver. Individuals were given specific responsibility for transforming the organization in accordance with their role category. Additionally, a new marketing framework was created comprising three key themes: principles; people; process, and eight key disciplines: strategy and innovation; branding and communications; sales force effectiveness; 'New World' skills; market knowledge; segmentation and targeting; value creation and pricing; commercial aviation. The framework was critical, acting as a rigorous structure for strategic and operational decision-making. To ensure relevance, an annual marketing maturity evaluation process was introduced to enable key players to focus on existing gaps, or shortcomings, and to identify what actions
to take.

GE has become increasingly conscious of the need to treat their customers differently to their competitors, creating technological and service level solutions in response to rapidly changing consumer demands. The focus on marketing *outcomes* has transformed company culture and marketing is now seen as a key strategic activity. The recognition and rewards programme ensures that the development of outstanding performers is a priority.
Customer-centricity prevails. In numerous markets, the company has a growing market share and a healthy year-on-year growth in sales and profits. GE remains one of the global giants, thanks not least in part to reinventing marketing.

1. Discuss how important you think the additional resources (financial and human) might be to the success of GE's marketing. Could the same results have been achieved without the additional investment?

2. Why do you think the new marketing framework was more successful than the traditional models of organizing marketing? Identify the critical success factors.

3. What are the main challenges GE faces and how might the company go about protecting itself against rapidly changing global markets?

# SUMMARY

An organization's ability to strengthen the level and scope of its professionalism lies clearly with its skill and dedication to assimilating learning. Organizations that are unwilling or unable to recognize the lessons inherent in their own experience or that of others will never be the leading-edge companies of tomorrow. In contrast, those that have responded appropriately to the need for organizational revision as result of more integrated and interactive processes have secured, or are on the way to securing, enhanced value through organizational capability and operational capacity.

The essential feature of marketing organization and control is that it 'closes the loop' and connects marketing plans to marketing actions. Ultimately, therefore, the way we manage marketing is the major determinant of commercial success or failure.

The structure of the organization can impede the enhancement of value seriously, and therefore also the development of customer relationships. For example, traditional vertical organizations with a hierarchical structure and functional orientation often favour individual functions at the expense of the whole business and the customer. Cross-functional marketing, as advocated by a relationship marketing approach, focuses instead on the processes that create and deliver customer value, drawing together multi-disciplinary teams which marshal resources to achieve customer-based objectives. An organizational culture imbued with collaborative and empowering practices and a marketing orientation will promote the kind of innovation and inspiration required for such relationship building.

The ongoing search to find the 'right' structure stems from the ever-changing nature of the business environment. Demand patterns alter, new technology emerges, new legislation is introduced, there is an economic crisis and so on. However, experimentation with the different types of structure has shown that, in certain circumstances, some types are going to be more successful than others. For example, the joint, rather than separate, supervision of sales and marketing tends to make it easier to ensure a sensible co-ordination between planning and doing. However, what is most crucial to any organizational structure or culture is leadership – founded in and fighting for the creation and delivery of superior customer value.

# FURTHER READING

Chapters 12–14 in:

McDonald, M. and Wilson, H. (2011) *Marketing Plans: How to Prepare Them; How to Use Them*, Chichester: Wiley

# REFERENCES

Comstock, B., Gulati, R. and Liguori, S. (2010) Unleashing the Power of Marketing, *Harvard Business Review*, (October): 90–98.

Iglesias, J., Sauquet, A. and Montaña, J. (2011) The Role of Corporate Culture in Relationship Marketing, *European Journal of Marketing*, Vol. 45 (4): 631–650.

Verhoef, P.C. and Leeflang, P.S.H. (2009) Understanding the Marketing Department's Influence Within the Firm, *Journal of Marketing*, Vol. 73 (March): 14–37.

# CHAPTER 24
# MARKETING ETHICS

IN THIS CHAPTER WE STUDY:

- how marketing is adapting to the postmodern consumer
- the dismissal of the 'defenceless' consumer
- concerns fuelling the ethical debate on marketing
- the social dimension of marketing activity
- the doctrines of 'caveat emptor' and 'caveat venditor'
- the consumerist road to better marketing
- opportunities afforded by consumerism

# MARKETING IN THE POSTMODERN ERA

Our book would not be complete without a section on ethics. In today's tumultuous times, the way in which businesses conduct themselves with respect to accepted conventions on issues such as human rights and social responsibility, environmental and ecological stewardship and global capitalism has a resounding effect on their presence, and indeed, future in the marketplace. So, what *is* happening, and what *should* happen in marketing's sphere of influence?

As the debate continues, let us consider a few points in respect to marketing's role from an ethical perspective. The old model of marketing *is* changing and *is* responding, albeit imperfectly, to the challenges posed by the postmodern consumer. No one could argue with the notion that society changes over time, and that commerce is affected by (and, of course, affects) such changes. But those who remain in an outdated paradigm gradually disappear. Responsive organizations adapt to the subtle changes taking place about them, and this is reflected in best practice. This best practice is manifested in evolving managerial systems and these state-of-the-art developments are indeed reflected in the research agendas and curricula of the world's top business schools.

Another fundamental point is that best practice is no longer about doing things *to* consumers. The interactionist school has grown in strength on the observation that successful and profitable relationships today have to be dyadic. Best practice today already separates the processing of information about products from the products themselves, as well as encouraging collaborative, co-creative relationships between organizations and consumers.

Through educational resources and marketing guides such as this, some authors are trying to help organizations relate to the postmodern consumer. Of course, it is impossibly difficult to understand a consumer who goes into a retail store on a Saturday, buys on the Internet at home on Sunday, uses a smartphone on Monday, a Blackberry on Tuesday (possibly from more than one country), interactive TV on Wednesday, social media networks on Thursday, and goes to the cinema on Friday, in the meantime reading the *Sun* newspaper, the *Financial Times* and a trade journal. How is a company to go about understanding such a person's profile and preferences, and to adapt its marketing to maximize the value to both supplier and receiver? But marketing processes, such as market segmentation and strategic marketing planning *are* being adapted to take into account such complexity. Leading-edge companies *are* attempting to understand and respond to the atomistic nature of society, as are leading academics.

# IS MARKETING UNETHICAL?

In recent years, dissatisfaction has been expressed by increasingly large numbers of people at the structure of a society that seems to have consumption as both its means and its end. Capitalism presents an unacceptable face, some believe, inasmuch as it promotes the growth of an acquisitive and materialistic society, over-consumption and (if unchecked) financial ruin.

In the late 1960s and early 1970s there was a growing consciousness of the problems that the age of mass consumption brought with it, and a new awareness of alternatives that might be possible, indeed necessary, became apparent. This movement quickly found its chroniclers: books such as Charles Reich's *The Greening of America*, Alvin Toffler's *Future Shock* and Theodore Roszak's *The Making of a Counter Culture* appeared on bookshelves throughout the world. The message articulated in these and other testaments of the movement was basically a simple one: that people could no longer be thought of as 'consumers', as some aggregate variable in the grand design of market planning. They were individuals intent on doing their own bidding.

The ethical pioneers remained for some time on the margins; the corporate world was slow to embrace the ethical ideologies and axioms. Progress was driven primarily by social enterprises established by consumer communities with specific interests. As Mayo (2007) observes, the United Kingdom's first ethical unit trust, for example, was launched in 1984, several decades after the advent of ethical concerns about rampant consumerism and over-consumption. Criticism continued throughout the 1980s and 1990s (in the United Kingdom, particularly as a critique of Thatcherism and New Labour), at which point it became more generally accepted as directly relevant to modern business. Of particular note was Alan Durning's (1992) book, *How Much is Enough?* which criticized the rapid rise of per capita consumption in the developed world, harming the environment while leaving consumers feeling unfulfilled. By the 1990s companies began to see the potential of ethical consumerism and Fair Trade foodstuffs started to appear on supermarket shelves. This trend has continued throughout the twenty-first century up to the present day.

As one of the more visible manifestations of unbridled capitalism and corporate gain, marketing has been singled out for special attention. It has been critiqued widely as playing on the vulnerable, persuading them, by insidious means, to believe they *must* have whatever is marketed to them or their lives are somehow incomplete. This argument is based upon the notion of the consumer as defenceless and gullible. Such a view of marketing tends to exaggerate the influence the marketer can bring to bear. It presupposes extremely limited consumer perceptions and intelligence, and extremely skilled, persuasive marketers.

This last point deserves close examination. Marketing may well be able to persuade people that they want a product, but that process should not be confused with creating a need. The sceptic might respond to this view by claiming, for example, that, 'Nobody wanted television before it was invented; now it is a highly competitive market. That market must have been created.' This argument confuses needs and wants. Clearly, nobody wanted television before it was invented, but there has always been a need for home entertainment. Previously, that need had been met by a piano, a book, parlour games, or something of that kind. Now technology has made available a further means of satisfying the basic need for domestic entertainment – television. Many consumers find that television better satisfies their need for home entertainment than did the piano.

Any argument that depends on a view of the defenceless consumer must be rejected by a scrupulous marketer (indeed, it could be argued that the rise of ethical consumption is, in itself, a manifestation of consumer sovereignty). The consumer is still sovereign as long as he or she is free to make choices – either choices between competing products, or the choice not to buy at all. Indeed, it could be argued that by extending the range of choices that consumers have available to them, marketing is enhancing consumer sovereignty rather than eroding it. We have witnessed consumer power in action with the inexorable rise of e-commerce, driving retailers with poor value propositions off the High Street and entire sectors into cut-throat price competition. It should be noted, too, that while promotional activity may persuade an individual to buy a product or service once, promotion is unlikely to be the persuasive factor in subsequent purchases; although promotion may sell a disappointing product the first time round, it cannot do so on future occasions.

Commercial activities of all kinds, including marketing, have evolved in the light of societal changes. Corporate social responsibility (CSR) is now a mainstream activity, and expected by consumers. As Harrison et al. (2007) observe, consumers' ethical concerns do not mean that they ignore the basic price/quality assessment, but indicate that some additional criteria are brought into play in the decision-making process. Organizations must respond appropriately if they are to survive and flourish, and marketing has a key role to play. It is necessary, therefore, to look closely at the kinds of roles that marketing assumes, and the social and economic systems supporting them.

# ETHICAL CONCERNS

Several specific issues have formed the focus of the debate on the ethics of marketing. The main issues to be discussed include marketing's contribution to materialism; rising consumer expectations as a result of marketing pressure;

and the use of advertising to mislead or distort. Let us look at some of the arguments involved in these discussions.

Marketing, it has been suggested, helps to feed, and in turn feeds on, the materialistic and acquisitive urges of society. Implicit in such criticism is the value judgement that materialism and acquisitiveness are, in themselves, undesirable. Whether or not one agrees with this view, there would seem to be a case here for marketing to answer. The prosecution in this case would argue that marketing contributes to a general raising of the level of consumer expectations. These expectations are more than simple aspirations: they represent on the part of the consumer a desire to acquire a specific set of gratifications through the purchase of goods and services. The desire for these gratifications is fuelled by marketing's insistent messages. Further, if the individual lacks the financial resources with which to fulfil these expectations, then this inevitably adds to a greater awareness of differences in society, and to dissatisfaction and unrest among those in this situation.

The counter-argument that can be used here is that marketing itself does not contribute to rising expectations, and thus to differences in society; it merely makes people aware of, and better informed about, the differences that already exist in society. Indeed, the advocates of the cause of marketing could well claim that, in this respect, its effects are beneficial, since it supports, even hastens, pressures for redistribution. The defence in this case could also usefully point out that materialism is not a recent phenomenon, correlated with the advent of mass marketing.

Much of the criticism levelled at marketing is in fact directed at one aspect of it: advertising. Advertising practitioners themselves are fully conscious of these criticisms, which tend to centre around a few core themes:

- Advertising makes misleading claims about the product or service advertised.
- By implication or association it offers misleading promises of other benefits which purchase and use of the product will bring.
- It uses hidden, dangerously powerful techniques of persuasion.
- By encouraging undesirable attitudes it has adverse social effects.
- It contributes to human unhappiness by promoting the unattainable.
- It works by the exploitation of human inadequacy.
- It wastes skills and talents which could be better employed in other jobs.

Supporters of advertising would point to the fact that advertising in all its forms is heavily controlled in most Western societies, either by self-imposed regulatory codes and bodies, or legislation. As intimated, also, it cannot trigger repeat purchases if initial purchase/consumption is judged unsatisfactory.

The debate about the ethics of marketing often confuses marketing institutions with the people who work in them. Clearly, there are dishonest business people who engage in activities that are detrimental to their fellow citizens. These activities include dubious trade practices, misleading advertising, unsafe products and various unethical practices that are harmful to consumers. However, it seems a grave error to criticize marketing institutions because of the practices of a small number of unethical marketers. It is clear, for example, that there are advertisers who engage in deceptive practices designed to mislead and possibly defraud consumers. Nevertheless, the institution of advertising can be used not only to inform consumers about potentially beneficial new products, such as new, energy-saving technologies, but also to promote non-profit community services, such as theatres and orchestras. This argument can, of course, be applied to all marketing activities.

# MARKETING AND SOCIETY

Any critical appraisal of marketing as an activity must take place within the context of the social and economic systems in which it is practised. The late Wroe Alderson, a leading marketing scholar, suggested the concept of marketing ecology as a useful approach to interpreting marketing's wider role. By this, he meant the study of the continual adaptation of marketing systems to their environments; his suggestion was that the marketing systems in existence at any one time are simply reflections of the contemporary value system dominant in society. In systems technology, this approach would involve seeing marketing as an 'organized' behavioural system that sustains itself by drawing on the resources of the environment and survives only by adapting to changes in that environment. The environment represents not only the immediate surroundings of our customers and suppliers but also the wider phenomena that are embodied in technological, ideological, moral and social dimensions.

More recently, Peter Singer's (1997) advocacy of a less consumption-oriented, simpler life has gained a following. Adopting a consequentialist approach, in which conduct is linked clearly to the outcomes of actions, Singer blames extravagant and conspicuous consumption as a driver of human dissatisfaction and environmental destruction. For Singer, this is a lose-lose game, the solution to which is to live more frugally and be content with less. Allied to this is the 'virtue ethics' approach, in which consumers are encouraged to think very carefully about what they *should* do when faced with a choice of ethical/less ethical products. Virtue ethics is built upon the utilitarian philosophy, famously advocated by Jeremy Bentham and John Stuart Mill, that the 'correct' course of action is that which maximizes utility for the whole community. While few would disagree with the sentiment, the classic ethical dilemma for consumers is epitomized by very practical daily choices: battery hen or free-range organic eggs; RSPCA Freedom Food or sow stall pork? Numerous studies reveal a gap between what consumers say and what they do (in other words, between behavioural intentions and actual behaviour) (see Auger and Devinney, 2007; Carrington et al., 2010; Luchs et al., 2010; White et al., 2012).

While change may not be as rapid or all-encompassing as predicted (or hoped) by ethical pioneers, over the last 50 years or so there has been a marked change in societal norms. There is undoubtedly a radically different moral and ideological climate in society at large compared to the latter decades of the twentieth century. The basic purpose of business activities today has come to be questioned, and not only by those committed to alternative systems of exchange.

As has already been discussed briefly, marketing has been caught up in the broader issue of CSR. Although there is a wide range of opinion about the meaning of 'social responsibility', the implication is always that the organization must look beyond the profit motive. Although unlikely to abandon the profit motive as the primary focus of their attention, company executives are now increasingly engaging in CSR activities as a salient criterion of success. The positive acknowledgement of the imperative of CSR is likely to result in an increase in marketing as an agent of social change. We have already seen the adoption of a marketing approach by government agencies in attempts to gain participation in local planning decisions, care for the countryside, discouraging the smoking of cigarettes and so on.

# CAVEAT EMPTOR

In a perfectly competitive marketplace, all the products or services offered by an organization would meet the needs of its customers and consumers at the requisite level of profits. This is plainly not the case, and some consumers complain loudly about the way businesses operate. What conclusions are to be drawn from this? Are the major companies not based soundly on a marketing philosophy? Or are the strident voices not representative of the wishes of the vast majority of customers?

Consumerism focuses our attention on the problem. Is marketing failing to do its job well, or are a small collection of agitators making something out of nothing? The truth in most cases is probably to be found in the 80/20 rule: 80 per cent of the problem is poor marketing, and 20 per cent is populist agitation.

Traditionally, it has been argued that a bad product will sell only once. Its customers will reject it after unsatisfactory performance, and any organization that persists in offering such products or services cannot survive for long. Consumerists argue increasingly that a passive approach of this kind amounts to shutting the stable door after the horse has bolted. They usually want to see it made illegal for such products or services to be offered on the market in the first place. Most countries have passed a significant amount of legislation in support of this position. Up to the end of the nineteenth century the doctrine of 'caveat emptor' or 'let the purchaser beware' was widely accepted, although customers and consumers had always enjoyed a certain amount of protection as a result of regulations imposed on traders. However, since the end of the nineteenth century, the responsibility for the quality of the product or service sold has fallen more and more on the shoulders of the vendor.

# CAVEAT VENDITOR

Within the European Union (EU), at the time of writing, customer groups have succeeded in obtaining massive legislative support. As an illustration of legislation that supports customers' rights, we can perhaps take the concept of 'implied terms of sale'. In 1973, a statutory responsibility was laid on a supplier of goods in the United Kingdom to ensure that any goods were indeed good for the purpose for which they were promoted and sold. This reversed the dictum 'caveat emptor' to 'caveat venditor', or 'let the seller beware'. Although many business people resisted this trend, it is difficult to see why they should feel that a change of this kind damaged their interests. No marketer, surely, would doubt that trust was an important element in his or her relationship with a customer. That customer groups, or politicians, with or without populist agitation, had to lobby to have laws passed to secure this sort of relationship with suppliers is an indictment of marketing activities throughout Europe and beyond.

The marketing of children's toys and accessories provides an example of how customers, consumers and company objectives can all be satisfied by careful business practice. Successful toy companies and retailers are those that inform consumers about their products. In recent years, Mattel, Heelarious, Tesco and BHS have been targeted by irate parents and consumer lobby groups: Mattel for producing 'sexist' Barbie dolls, Heelarious for high-heeled baby shoes (meant as a joke . . . that largely misfired), Tesco for selling pole dancing kits and BHS for padded bras for girls. In relation to Tesco and BHS, once the offending products were withdrawn, the media (particularly in the online sphere) were full of comment along the lines of who *ever* thought *that* was a good idea? Just how it was possible to make such serious misjudgements?

# CONSUMERISM'S BETTER WAY TO MARKETING

Consumerism is pro-marketing; it wants the marketing approach to business implemented in a sincere rather than a cynical spirit. The cynical implementation that consumerists claim has been all too widely practised is no better than high-pressure salesmanship or misleading puffery. The sincere implementation of the marketing approach entails respect for each individual customer. Indeed, the consumerist argues eloquently that the sort of relationship found between a manufacturer and a customer in, say, a capital-goods market, should be created in consumer markets. And, in so far as that is both economically feasible and what the consumer really wants, marketers must surely want it also.

Broadly, consumerists argue that recognition of the following consumer rights would ensure that a more satisfactory relationship would be built up between organization and customer: the right to be informed, the right to be protected and the right to ensure quality of life. These are highlighted in Figure 24.1.

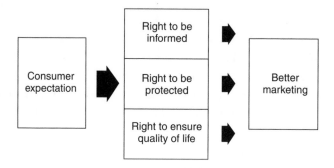

Figure 24.1 Consumerism's way to better marketing

*The right to be informed* of the facts involved in any buyer–seller relationship is clearly a fundamental right. Some of the key aspects, which have already been subject to legislation or regulation in Europe, include the full cost of credit/loans taken up, often known as 'truth-in-lending'; the true cost of an item, under the slogan 'unit pricing'; the basic constituent elements of products, known as 'ingredient informative labelling'; the freshness of foods, discussed generally as 'open-dating'; and 'truth-in-advertising'.

The case against producers is that they either mislead through exaggerated claims or fail to tell the whole truth about their products or services. Consumerists believe that individuals have the right to know these truths. Again, who can doubt that this demand, if sincerely felt, should be met? Who would be unwilling to tell an industrial purchaser the answer to basic questions about any merchandise offered for sale? What other information would customers like?

*The right to be protected* is also a major plank in the consumerist platform. All too often now, consumerists argue, consumers' trust in organizations is abused. Safety standards (which are monitored by government agencies) and the quality of medicines (which are subject to statutory controls) are exceptions that all businesses could learn from. It is certainly the case that the trend within the EU is for many more product fields to be affected by legislative controls. The consumerists' argument that manufacturers should assume liability for any malfunctioning of products offered in the marketplace would appear to have overwhelmed the opposition. In most cases, however, good marketing will go well beyond the minimum standards required – and will not be slow to tell the customer that it does so.

Concerns about the security, privacy and confidentiality of information is another major issue. E-commerce has led to all sorts of worries about how personal information will be used, and who will have access to it. Increases in the incidence of identity theft, hacking and fraud justify such concerns. Data protection legislation is meant to protect consumers, but two major barriers exist: inability to identify the fraudsters (obviously, they use proxies online) and, even if identified, the impossibility of working across jurisdictions minimizes the threat of being caught and prosecuted. Obviously, companies spend vast amounts of money trying to protect consumer data (though it is surprising just how much is *not* encrypted and how much is sold, quite legally, to third parties), but despite their best efforts, data theft and identify fraud continues to rise rapidly.

*The right to ensure quality of life* is perhaps the most difficult demand for the marketing activity to satisfy. Nonetheless, if a meaningful segment of the market needs to perceive the products it purchases as furthering the quality of life, then that is a need that should be respected. The non-biodegradability of packaging, for example, has been shown on occasion to offend substantial numbers of customers. If a sufficiently large group of these customers is prepared to meet an organization's research and development costs, along with the costs involved in changing to a preferred alternative, then good marketing should lead the organization to work with these customers towards a change in its methods of packaging.

It should be emphasized that none of these rights is unfamiliar to marketers of industrial or consumer products. They have become accustomed to responding to similar demands. What is different now is that the process of marketing is no longer done on the initiative of the marketer in a framework of caveat emptor; on the contrary, it is the vendor who, increasingly, must 'be aware'.

Consumerism will affect marketing by bringing into being a more informative approach to all forms of marketing communication. It must, and will, give rise to a greater integrity in the advertising and promotional puffery of the profession, without, one hopes, making life too dull, too much like a company share-issue prospectus. It will give rise to a greater concern among all levels of business management with the long-term social implications of the materialistic bias of Western society. Does the continual emphasis on immediate material expectations bear some responsibility for the level of delinquency in Western society? What are the implications for tomorrow of our present pattern of usage of raw materials or pollution of the environment?

The consumerist argues that in present-day Europe we can certainly afford to trade-off some of today's advantages in favour of the longer-term interests of society.

# CONSUMERISM AS AN OPPORTUNITY

The social emphasis of consumerism, particularly its demands for an enhanced quality of life, is no threat to profitable enterprise. In considering this point, organizations might find it helpful to draw an analogy with changing attitudes to social factors at work. From the mid-nineteenth century, manufacturers were compelled by law to ensure that unsafe machinery was fitted with guards and considerable cost was, of course, incurred in carrying this out. Within the office, modern times have seen a concern to obtain ergonomically designed office furniture and equipment – again, at some expense. It may well be that, in the long term, fewer accidents and a happier workforce will help improve an organization's overall profitability. Even if this does not happen, however, the organization should bear in mind that society expects the cost of health and safety at work to be included in the price of a product or service. Consumerism, like safety at work, presents an opportunity to adjust its approach in accordance with changing social standards. As an articulate expression of customer needs, consumerism demands a marketing response.

Consumerism calls out for the reformulation and development of products and services to meet the requirements both of short-term satisfaction and longer-term benefits. A closer look must be taken at the system of marketing values that asserts that immediate consumer satisfaction and longer-term consumer welfare may be opposing goals for an organization's marketing activity. It is now necessary – and good marketing practice – to promote products that provide consumers with both short- and long-term satisfaction.

In consumer-goods markets, for example, marketing specialists have devoted most of their efforts to promoting desirable and pleasing products, and they have tended to ignore the long-term disadvantages to society that often accompany such products. Consumerism has reminded us vociferously of these disadvantages and, in a very real sense, has given us the opportunity to be better citizens. For example, it is possible now to design and sell a motor car that is considerably safer than in the past. Consumerism, in other words, opens up market opportunities that the astute marketing-based organization will wish to take up. Other examples that can be cited are phosphate-free detergents, lead-free petrol, degradable plastics containers for a host of products, synthetic tobaccos, new nutrient-based breakfast cereals and low-polluting manufacturing systems.

The articulate customer movement known as consumerism is here to stay as a force acting on organizations in their marketplace. If used respectfully, it can provide a significant further input of information in the process of matching the resources of the organization with the needs of its customers.

## SUMMARY

Traditionally, marketing was thought by many to be just another word for 'selling' or, at best, an activity that was appropriate for fast moving consumer goods, but not for the world of industrial products or the growing services sector. The world has changed; attitudes, cultural and societal norms (particularly in the developed world) have shifted, and there is now a greater recognition of the fundamental importance of ethics to corporate success. Marketing has a key role to play. It is, as we have seen, much more than simply 'giving customers what they want'. Marketers require a clear understanding of the place of marketing in the broader societal context, the interconnectedness of ethics and consumerism, as well as the more traditional business of optimizing asset value and driving differentiation in an increasingly competitive world. We conclude that consumerism offers nothing but opportunities to the organization that puts the interests of the customer at the centre of a sustainable business philosophy. Marketing is a prime candidate for carrying the torch!

## FURTHER READING

Harrison, R., Newholm, T. and Shaw, D. (eds.) (2007) *The Ethical Consumer*, Chichester: Sage.

A compilation of chapters from leading authors in the field containing a theoretical framework, exploration of ethical consumption and insights on ethical consumer behaviour.

Arnold, C. (2009) *Ethical Marketing and the New Consumer*, Chichester: Wiley. Written by a marketing consultant, this overview of marketing, ethics and the 'new consumer' includes numerous examples from 'real world' marketing.

# REFERENCES

Auger, P. and Devinney, T.M. (2007) Do What Consumers Say Matter? The Misalignment of Preferences with Unconstrained Ethical Intentions, *Journal of Business Ethics*, Vol. 76 (4): 361–383.

Carrington, M. J., Benjamin A., Neville, B.A and Whitwell, G.J. (2010) Why Ethical Consumers Don't Walk Their Talk: Towards a Framework for Understanding the Gap Between the Ethical Purchase Intentions and Actual Buying Behaviour of Ethically Minded Consumers, *Journal of Business Ethics*, Vol. 97 (1): 139–158.

Durning, A. (1992) *How Much is Enough? The Consumer Society and the Future of the Earth*, London, Earthscan.

Harrison, R., Newholm, T. and Shaw, D. (2007) *The Ethical Consumer*, London, Sage.

Luchs, M. G., Walker Naylor, R., Irwin, J.R. and Raghunathan, R. (2010) The Sustainability Liability: Potential Negative Effects of Ethicality on Product Preference, *Journal of Marketing*, Vol. 74 (September): 18–31.

Mayo, E. (2007) Foreword in Harrison, R., Newholm, T. and Shaw, D. (eds) (2007) *The Ethical Consumer*, London: Sage.

McDonald, M. and Wilson, H. (2002) *The New Marketing: Transforming the Corporate Future*, Butterworth-Heinemann: Oxford.

Reich, Charles A. (1970) *The Greening of America*, Random House, New York.

Roszack, T. (1969) *The Making of a Counter Culture: Reflections on the Technocratic Society and its Youthful Opposition*, Anchor Books, New York.

Singer, P. (1997) *How are We to Live? Ethics in the Age of Self-Interest*. Oxford, Oxford Press.

Toffler, A. (1970) *Future Shock*, Bodley Head, London.

White, K., MacDonnell, R. and Ellard, J.H. (2012) Belief in a Just World: Consumer Intentions and Behaviours Toward Ethical Products, *Journal of Marketing*, Vol. 76 (January): 103–118.

# CONCLUSION

## THE MARKETING CONCEPT

As we have demonstrated throughout this book, the creation of value is intrinsic to marketing and essential for organizations wishing to engage with their target markets. Marketing is a process for understanding markets, for quantifying the present and future value required by the different groups of customers within these markets, for communicating this to all other functions with responsibility for delivering this value and for measuring the value actually delivered. For marketing to be effective, all other functions should be 'market driven'.

In 1776, when Adam Smith stated that consumption was the sole end and purpose of production, he was in fact describing what is now known as the *marketing concept*. The marketing concept implies that all the activities of an organization are driven by a desire to satisfy customer needs. Indeed, the central idea of marketing is of a matching process between a company's capabilities and customer wants in order to achieve the objectives of, and create value for, both parties.

The concept of value can be seen to encompass both the value delivered to the customer by the supplying organization (the 'package' of benefits) and value received by the supplying organization from the customer (the return on investment). This return on investment, in its broadest sense, includes the actual business profit generated by the customer relationship and the wider customer insight gained from it. Clearly, the revenue-producing capacity of the organization depends on the accuracy with which it is able to define and meet customer needs.

### DEFINING A MARKET ORIENTATION

Companies that 'live and breathe' the marketing concept are said to be market led, or having a *market orientation*. While the exact definition of 'market orientation', and whether it is something distinct from or synonymous with a 'marketing orientation', remains the subject of debate, a market-orientated business can be seen to possess the following characteristics:

- concern for customers;
- interest in the business environment;
- a focus on competitors;

- a curiosity about the future;

- an entrepreneurial spirit; and

- a zeal for action.

To be consistent with modern writers, in this book we employ the term 'market orientation' to encompass the organizational attributes that together comprise the features of a market, marketing or customer-focused enterprise. The number of closely related terms that can be collated under the umbrella of 'market orientation' indicates the multi-dimensional nature of the concept, rather than any serious disagreement about the fundamentals of its meaning.

This multi-dimensional quality of market orientation can be illustrated by reference to the ways in which different writers have gone about explaining and exploring the concept. For some, market orientation is essentially a *philosophy*, representing a body of thought that can be applied to an organization or used to underpin the way in which a business is conceptualized or run. Others view market orientation as an aspect of organizational *culture*, where attention is focused on the values, attitudes and beliefs held collectively by an organization's members. Still others conceive the concept as a *process*: a series of actions or activities that constitutes the heart of what it means to be market orientated.

Given this diversity of perception, one way of moving towards a better understanding of market orientation is to identify common themes within the various usages of the term. What becomes strikingly apparent from such an exercise is the emphasis each approach places on the interaction between an organization and its external environment and the myriad of relationships this interaction generates. Thus, while the substance of a market orientation may vary from one observer to another, the object of a market orientation remains the same. Market orientation, therefore, embodies:

> The ability and willingness of an organization to take account of external factors which will affect the possibility of it developing profitable exchanges (however profit is defined by the organization), both now and in the future, and the ability and willingness of the organization to take action as a result of these factors to strengthen important relationships.

This definition of market orientation acknowledges the constraints placed on organizations by internal factors (their 'ability and willingness' and their need for certain outcomes or 'profit') and emphasizes the key activity of effective marketing organizations: understanding and acting on the dynamic of the markets in which they operate, concentrating on critical relationships – namely, the relationships with their customers.

Market-orientated organizations will therefore be interested in the acquisition of intelligence about customers, competitors, market trends and opportunities, and, of course, existing and potential relationships. More important, they will also be interested in the response this intelligence suggests and the actions it prompts.

## ENGENDERING A MARKET ORIENTATION

Instilling a market orientation into an organization is a difficult job. It is easy to accept that long-term survival depends on creating and keeping customers, whether they are paying customers or otherwise, but it is quite another matter to introduce this philosophy into managerial processes. This is because people are subject to a large number of influences and pressures in their work, which will tend to counter the pursuit of marketing principles.

Other orientations that can exist side by side with marketing include production, design, technology, finance, sales and social. These are not 'wrong', and are all needed at certain times to a greater or lesser extent. If, for example, an organization has profitability problems, it will be important that a financial orientation should emerge as a priority to enable the short-term survival of the business. Alternatively, an organization that relies on product innovation and development for its success in the marketplace should encourage a technology orientation within its ranks.

The problem with these various types of orientation is achieving the right balance between them to match the environmental conditions within which the organization operates. Successful organizations are good at matching, not only in terms of the four 'P's, but also in terms of the ways in which they set priorities for themselves. In good times, marketing tends to be forgotten and other priorities dominate, but in bad times marketing becomes the way forward, but by that point it is often perceived as a threat to the other traditional values already embedded in the organization. The point is that, as with other disciplines, marketing needs to exist in an organization. Whether or not it stems from a formal marketing department is irrelevant.

# THE MARKETING FUNCTION

In addition to understanding the marketing concept, it is also necessary to be clear about the difference between the marketing concept (often referred to as 'market orientation') and the marketing function, which is concerned with the management of the *marketing mix*. The management of the marketing mix involves using various tools and techniques in order to implement the marketing concept.

## MANAGING THE MARKETING MIX

The marketing mix is the name given to the main demand-influencing variables available to the organization. The classic description of the marketing mix, although something of a simplification, is as the four 'P's:

1. *Product*: What type and range of product or service should we provide?
2. *Price*: What price should be set for each product or service?
3. *Promotion*: How do we best communicate with our target customers and persuade them to buy our offer? and
4. *Place*: What channels of distribution and what levels of service are appropriate?

This original marketing mix is commonly extended to include additional 'P's, such as Physical evidence (customer service), People and Process. This is said to be particularly applicable to service industries, where service delivery cannot be disentangled from the 'product' being sold and simultaneously consumed.

When developing policies for the various elements of the marketing mix, it is important to be comprehensive, but also to identify those areas that are significant in the markets in which an organization operates. Thus, some organizations use an expanded marketing mix for managerial and planning purposes. This can involve isolating sales plans, processes, people or customer service for special attention. Whatever the case, the key task of the marketing manager is to ensure that the marketing mix is internally consistent and offers superior customer value.

## ACHIEVING CORPORATE OBJECTIVES

What causes business success in the long run, by which we mean a continuous growth in earnings per share and in the capital value of the shares, has been shown by research to depend on four ingredients:

1. An excellent core product or service and all the associated research and development.
2. First-rate, world-class, state-of-the-art operations, where marketing contributes to defining operational efficiency in customer satisfaction terms.
3. A culture that encourages and produces an infrastructure conducive to creativity and entrepreneurialism.
4. Proficient marketing departments, staffed by qualified professionals (not failures from other functions).

Given these ingredients and, above all else, a corporate culture that is not dominated (because of its history) by production, operations or financial orientation, all the evidence shows that marketing as a function makes a contribution to the achievement of corporate objectives. Its principal role is to spell out the several value propositions demanded by different customer groups, so that everyone in the organization knows what their responsibility is in creating and delivering this value.

The creation of winning (suitable, superior and sustainable) value propositions demands a synthesis of knowledge and expertise. An in-depth understanding of customer needs and preferences, and of organizational strengths and weaknesses, is the bedrock of saleable products and services. To be successful, offers must also represent a mutually beneficial arrangement, whereby both parties obtain an acceptable gain for their respective investment.

The regular and ongoing monitoring of marketing planning and performance is therefore necessary to check whether the creation and delivery of value is 'hitting the mark' and doing so cost effectively. Is meaningful information being gathered and employed to optimal effect? Are markets being segmented in such a way that the 'right' customers are targeted? Are resource levels and allocations appropriate and sufficient? Is management providing the inspiration and leadership required to ensure that the whole organization is pulling in the same (correct), direction? These are just some of the questions that organizations need constantly to ask themselves in order to remain valid and viable businesses.

## SECURING CUSTOMER CENTRICITY

A primary concern of the marketing task within a business is to seek to innovate through product and market development, and to strive to enhance competitive performance. Opportunities for productivity improvement tend to be self-limiting in the sense that costs can only be cut so far, and price and product mix adjustments can only be made with limited frequency. On the other hand, the opportunities for innovation and improved competitiveness are limited only by imagination and creativity.

In both cases, it is only by placing the customer at the centre of the business that success can be achieved. Innovation that is not based on the satisfaction of a customer need, either existing or latent, will not succeed – the world is littered with 'better mousetraps'. Similarly, the search for competitive advantage will only be successful if based on a strategy of meeting customer needs more effectively than competitors can. This concept of *differential advantage* lies at the heart of strategic marketing. It could even be argued that the primary task of marketing management is to achieve and maintain maximum positive differentiation over and above the competition in the eyes of customers.

CONCLUSION

Ultimately, therefore, the role of marketing in the organization is, first, to ensure that the orientation of the business is towards the customer, and second, to seek to marshal the resources of the business in such a way as to be perceived by the market as providing benefits superior to those available elsewhere.

There are thus two aspects to marketing. One is about corporate value and culture and the other about strategy and execution. It is important to recognize that to have a marketing orientation and to achieve competitive advantage it is not necessary to have a marketing department, or even a single marketing executive. What is essential is that every move the organization makes is guided by the principles of marketing, and that a customer orientation pervades the organization.

Many books and articles have appeared which have sought to explain the factors that determine business success. Put very simply, those companies where customer satisfaction is an article of faith rather than a convenient slogan will tend to succeed. The surprising thing is that it has taken so long for such a simple concept to gain widespread acceptance!

# MARKETING IN TRANSITION

For many years, marketing was considered to be just another word for 'selling'. As the weight of this book will testify, marketing today is clearly about much, much more. The growth in understanding and appreciation of marketing's role in business has led to the greater realization of its current and future potential. The case for marketing being a major contributor to organizational performance no longer needs to be made. What remains a challenge is the application of marketing principles within a marketplace of unprecedented character and momentum.

## MOVING FROM TRANSACTIONS TO RELATIONSHIPS

In the past, it was more often the case that organizations were structured and managed on the basis of optimizing their own operations, with little regard for the way in which they interfaced with suppliers and, indeed, customers. The business model was essentially 'transactional', meaning that products and services were bought and sold 'at arm's length' and that there was little enthusiasm for the concept of long-term, inter-allied relationships.

The new competitive paradigm that is now emerging is in stark contrast to the conventional model. It suggests that in the challenging global markets of the twenty-first century, the route to sustainable advantage lies increasingly in managing the complex web of relationships that link together partners in a mutually profitable 'value chain'. These relationships span multiple markets, including customer markets, referral markets, internal markets, recruitment markets, influencer markets and supplier and alliance markets. This relationship-oriented approach extends the marketing concept beyond traditional marketing and embraces the entire supply chain to achieve greater customer value at every level in the chain.

## EMPHASIZING CUSTOMER ACQUISITION AND RETENTION

Unlike the transactional, functionally orientated approach, relationship marketing is a cross-functional process concerned with balancing marketing efforts among key markets. A critical issue within the customer market domain is to ensure that customer retention as well as customer acquisition is emphasized. Recognition of the significant link between customer retention and profitability is leading to new and better strategies for strengthening customer satisfaction and loyalty.

More sophisticated use of channels and media, for example, is helping marketers to develop profitable, *long-term* relationships with customers. Successful channel management highlights the importance of managing channel relationships well, from the minimization of channel conflict and risk to the maximization of channel integrity and relevance. Companies can build customer value by offering customers both a wider range of channels and more personalized treatment through multiple channel integration. At the same time, consumers increasingly expect personalized products and services, so integrated channel delivery is becoming a 'must have' rather than a highly differentiated, sustainable source of competitive advantage. Integrated channel strategy now might include direct sales to the end user via e- and m-commerce, combined with indirect sales through intermediaries, such as distributors or brokers, or collaborative outlets involving competitors. The opportunities for reaching and connecting with specifically targeted customers have never been greater – nor have customer expectations been so high.

Customer relationship management (CRM) developed in response to heightened customer expectations and intensified competition, particularly within the context of global markets. CRM emphasizes the use of information technology in managing customer relationships. Advances in database technology have made it possible to know and segment customers in ever more creative ways. Data warehouses can be used to store and search vast amounts of data. Data mining and modelling techniques can reveal otherwise 'invisible' patterns of customer behaviour, which can be translated into customer-specific marketing strategies. CRM reinforces the view that marketers manage – and businesses win/lose – customer relationships, not customers. With this in mind, it is essential not to assume that an off-the-shelf CRM package will

CONCLUSION

'take care of' customer relationships. Ill-timed, ill-informed communications, generated automatically by e-CRM systems (in other words, spam) can have a devastating effect.

## BALANCING CUSTOMER AND COMMERCIAL INTERESTS

As we have seen already, managing customer relationships effectively is a complex and challenging task. Although firms need to be in tune with their markets, customers and competitors, an excessive focus in external matters can distract from the achievement of the returns required for long-term business survival. For many organizations, these returns are measured as profits in one form or another, while for others they may be the achievement of social, charitable or artistic objectives.

Internal factors obviously affect profitability, or the achievement of other types of objective, and should consequently have an equal influence on the practice of marketing. Thus marketing managers must have an appreciation of such areas as resource availability, cost generation and organizational capability, as well as an in-depth knowledge of customer wants and purchase behaviour. Without the former, it becomes difficult to gauge the attractiveness of different marketing opportunities; and without the latter, the business is unfocused.

## OFFERING BENEFITS, NOT FEATURES

Customers buy products and services because they seek the benefits derived from them, not their inherent features. In this sense, products and services are problem solvers. For example, customers buy aspirin to cure headaches, petrol to get from A to B and drills because they need to make holes. Not every product or service benefit will have equal appeal to all customers, or groups of customers. However, through customer dialogue or market research it is possible to establish which benefits customers perceive as being important.

Marketing services should not call for a different philosophy from that underlying the marketing of physical products. Rather, it calls for an even greater emphasis on availability, particularly given the 'perishability' of the service product. Nevertheless, both service and tangible products are increasingly dependent for their success on the suppliers' ability to enhance their appeal though the 'added value' of customer service. Customer service comprises a host of value-adding activities that provide time and place utilities for the customer.

## BECOMING A BEACON, NOT A BOLT-ON

The stature and position of marketing within organizations is clearly changing. Marketing is increasingly being seen more as a business 'beacon' and less as a business bolt-on. From the days when marketing meant simply advertising the same message to a mass audience about what research and development and production and engineering were doing, it has evolved into a pan-company, collaborative expertise that is capable of interactive and individualized dialogue with customers. Its role is no longer confined merely to winning customers and generating sales but to keeping those customers and developing enduring, mutually beneficial relationships with them.

As stated earlier, marketing is essentially a matching process between an organization's capabilities and the wants of customers. By an organization's capabilities, we mean the unique set of resources and management skills that a particular firm has, which are not necessarily capable of taking advantage of *all* market opportunities as effectively, and hence as competitively, as other firms. This matching challenge is compounded further by the context in which the organization operates or 'the marketing environment', which is both complex and ever-changing. It is crucial, therefore, that an organization is able to identify market needs and exploit internal competencies and the marketing environment in order to satisfy those needs. In short, the marketing process is fundamental to commercial success.

# INDEX

Note: Page references to figures are indicated by an '*f*'; to tables by a '*t*'.